ROADSIDE HISTORY OF

# MONTANA

DON SPRITZER

MOUNTAIN PRESS PUBLISHING COMPANY

MISSOULA, MONTANA

1999

Cover painting "Buffalo and Elk on the Upper Missouri" by Karl Bodmer. Courtesy Joslyn Art Museum, Omaha, Nebraska; gift of the Enron Art Foundation


Photos not otherwise credited are by the author.

Maps by William L. Nelson

**Library of Congress Cataloging-in-Publication Data**

Spritzer, Donald E., 1946–
   Roadside history of Montana / Don Spritzer.
      p.    cm. — (Roadside history series)
   Includes bibliographical references (p.  ) and index.
   ISBN 0-87842-395-8 (alk. paper). —
   1. Montana—History, Local.   2. Historic sites—Montana—
Guidebooks.   3. Montana—Guidebooks.   4. Automobile travel—
Montana—Guidebooks.   I. Title.   II. Series.
F731.S67   1999
978.6—dc21                                   99-14330
                                               CIP

Mountain Press Publishing Company
P.O. Box 2399 • Missoula, MT 59806
406-728-1900 • 800-234-5308

*To all Montana's travelers—past, present, and future*

# CONTENTS

About the Cover Art    *viii*

Preface and Acknowledgments    *ix*

Montana Chronology    *xi*

Montana License Plates    *xv*

Introduction
    Montana: A State of Extremes    *1*

1. **The Northern Corridor**    *13*
    US 2 and Montana 327: Fort Union—Wolf Point    *20*
    Montana 16: Culbertson—Plentywood    *24*
    Montana 5 and Montana 13: Westby—Wolf Point    *26*
    US 2: Wolf Point—Malta    *29*
    US 191: Malta—Missouri River    *36*
    Montana 66: US 191—Fort Belknap Agency    *38*
    US 2: Malta—Havre    *40*
    US 87: Havre—Fort Benton    *49*
    US 2: Havre—Shelby    *57*
    I-15: Sweetgrass—Power    *63*
    US 2: Shelby—Browning    *72*
    US 89: Browning—Fairfield    *77*

II. **The Crown of the Continent**    *81*
    US 2: East Glacier Park—West Glacier    *88*
    North Fork Road: West Glacier—Kintla Lake    *96*
    Going-to-the-Sun Road: West Glacier—St. Mary    *100*
    US 89 and Montana 49: St. Mary—East Glacier Park    *114*
    US 89 and Montana 17: St. Mary—Canadian Border    *117*

III. **The Logging Frontier**    *129*
    I-90: Lookout Pass—Missoula    *134*
    Montana 37 and US 2: Eureka—Troy    *151*
    US 93: Eureka—Somers    *155*

US 2: Columbia Falls—Kalispell   *163*

Montana 35 and US 93: Somers—Missoula   *164*

Montana 200 and Montana 28: Ravalli—Heron; Plains—
  Hot Springs   *171*

Montana 200 and Montana 83: Missoula—Bigfork   *174*

US 12: Lolo—Lolo Pass   *180*

US 93 and the Eastside Highway: Missoula—Lost Trail Pass   *182*

**IV. The Mining Frontier**   *195*

I-90: Bearmouth—Butte   *200*

Montana 1: Anaconda—Drummond   *217*

I-15: Monida—I-90   *224*

Montana 43: Chief Joseph Pass—Divide   *229*

Montana 41: Dillon—Twin Bridges   *232*

Montana 287: Twin Bridges—Ennis   *234*

US 287: Hebgen Lake—Lewis and Clark Caverns   *240*

I-90 and Montana 2: Three Forks—Butte   *244*

I-15: Butte—Helena   *245*

US 287: Helena—I-90   *252*

US 12: Helena—Garrison   *254*

I-15 and US 287: Helena—Augusta   *258*

Montana 200: Rogers Pass—Ovando   *264*

**V. The Central Valleys**   *267*

Montana 200: Simms—Great Falls   *273*

I-15: Great Falls—Cascade   *281*

Montana 22 and US 89: Great Falls—Ringling   *282*

Montana 200 and US 87: Raynesford—Lewistown   *288*

US 191: Lewistown—Fred Robinson Bridge   *295*

Montana 200: Lewistown—Circle   *299*

US 12: Melstone—Harlowton   *307*

US 191: Harlowton—Moore   *313*

US 12: Harlowton—US 89   *315*

I-90: Three Forks—Bozeman   *317*

US 191: Bozeman—West Yellowstone   *326*

**VI. The Yellowstone Basin**   *331*

US 89: Gardiner—Wilsall   *337*

I-90: Livingston—Laurel   *344*

Montana 78 and US 212: Columbus—Cooke City   *349*

US 212 and Montana 72: Red Lodge—Laurel     *353*

I-90: Laurel—Wyoming Border     *356*

I-94: Billings—Miles City     *367*

US 212: Crow Agency—Alzada     *375*

Montana 39 and US 12: Lame Deer—Sumatra     *380*

US 12 and Montana 7: Miles City—Ekalaka     *383*

I-94: Miles City—Wibaux     *386*

Montana 16 and Montana 200: Glendive—Fairview     *395*

**Selected Bibliography**     *399*

**Index**     *412*

# ABOUT THE COVER ART

In the summer of 1833 Swiss artist Karl Bodmer, accompanied by his patron Maximillian, Prince of Weid-Neuweid, left on a scientific expedition up the Missouri River aboard a small bateau. They traveled to Fort McKenzie, near the mouth of the Marias River in the heart of Blackfeet country. Bodmer was probably the first European artist to capture some of Montana's scenic grandeur. On their way back down the Missouri that September, the party encountered large herds of bison and other wildlife. Bodmer painted this scene, entitled "Buffalo and Elk on the Upper Missouri," somewhere below the mouth of the Judith River. The watercolor is reproduced here courtesy of the Joslyn Art Museum, Omaha, Nebraska (gift of the Enron Art Foundation).

# PREFACE AND ACKNOWLEDGMENTS

Researching and writing this book has been a wonderful adventure. Other states, I am sure, have histories as rich and as colorful as Montana's. But after traveling every highway and road covered in this book, I am convinced that very few states have people who understand and appreciate their past and their heritage as deeply as Montanans do. It can be seen everywhere—from the scores of historical signs and markers that line our highways, to the historical museums staffed by dedicated volunteers in virtually every community, to the local and county history books carefully compiled by dozens of eager authors.

This book has a solid foundation. It is built upon the hard work of all of those historians, both amateur and professional, who have painstakingly recorded Montana's past. The book can be used as a history text or a roadside guide for touring the state's many historic sites. Yet it is neither a "definitive" history of the state nor a guidebook in the strictest sense of the word. Not every single town or site of interest will be mentioned here. I had to be selective. I often chose the stories on these pages more for their human interest than because of their so-called historical significance. The book, accompanied by a good highway map, should enable one to find all the sites mentioned in the text. At least you shouldn't get lost any more often than I did! And I hope that the book will serve as an inviting gateway to Montana history that will lead you to explore further, through both reading and travel.

In writing this book, I had the help of many more people than can be listed here. Yet some folks went out of their way in providing special help, and they deserve recognition. Wally Long, Dave Walter, Audra Browman, Claire Rhein, Dale Johnson, and Mike Ober each read portions of the text and helped me eliminate some potentially embarrassing factual errors. I take full responsibility for any mistakes that remain.

In virtually every town that my wife, Kathy, and I visited we enjoyed the eager assistance of librarians, museum professionals, and volunteers. Many helped me to unearth difficult-to-find books, photographs, and other research material. Those who were particularly helpful included Myra Gohl, Wayne Raymond, Dan Gard, Paulette Parpart, Dick Fichtler, and JoAnn Hoven in Missoula; Dennis Richards and Chris Mullan at the University of Montana; Lory Morrow and Rebecca Kohl at the Montana Historical Society in Helena; Beth Dunagan and Dierdre Shaw at the Glacier National Park Library and Archives; Natalie Priebe in Whitefish; Greta Chapman in Libby; Lynn Redfield and Rita Kraus in Kalispell; Ethel Montgomery in Polson; JoAnn Woodgerd in Hamilton; Shirley Evans in Philipsburg; Candi Whitworth in Dillon; Jerry Hansen in Anaconda; Joanne Erdall in Virginia City; Lee Silliman in Deer Lodge; Roy Millegan in Whitehall; Terry Gilham in Browning; Buster Ruetten in Cutbank; Dean Hellinger in Shelby; Ruth Fladstal and Margorie Matheson in Conrad; Betty Frederickson in Chester; Valerie Hickman at MSU Northern in Havre; Stacy Garwood in Glasgow; Edgar Richardson in Scobey; Alan Olsen in Roundup; Debra Giron in White Sulphur Springs; Cindy Kittredge and Judy Ellinghausen in Great Falls; Lou Ann Westlake in Bozeman; Elaine Peterson at Montana State University; Gloria Keller and George Brenner in Lewistown; Mary Ellen Crosmer in Stanford; Louise Cross in Glendive; Ruth Franks and Jesse Bennet in Terry; Kristi Baukol and Warren McGee in Livingston; Jim Curry and Brooke Boston in Billings; Warren White in Ekalaka; and Ardyce Jensen in Red Lodge.

Special thanks also to my editors at Mountain Press, Dan Greer and Gwen McKenna, and to Dave Pauli and Gene and Lillian Fairman for the use of computers. Finally, thank you to my wife and travel companion, Kathy. Without her able assistance and patience, this book would not have been written.

# MONTANA CHRONOLOGY

1803    Louisiana Territory purchased from France

1805    Lewis and Clark Corps of Discovery cross Montana

1806    Lewis and Clark return trip; Lewis explores Marias, Clark floats down Yellowstone River

1807    Manuel Lisa erects first trading post in Montana near mouth of the Bighorn River

1809    David Thompson builds Saleesh House near present Thompson Falls

1829    American Fur Company establishes Fort Union near mouth of the Yellowstone River

1832    American Fur Company establishes Fort McKenzie near mouth of the Marias River

1833    Prince Maximilian of Weid and artist Karl Bodmer float up the Missouri River

1841    Pierre Jean De Smet establishes St. Mary's Mission near present-day Stevensville

1847    American Fur Company establishes Fort Benton

1850    John Owen erects trading post at site of St. Mary's Mission

1853    Governor John Stevens surveys Montana for railroad routes

1855    Hellgate Treaty creates Flathead Indian Reservation

1859    First steamboat reaches Fort Benton

Raynolds expedition explores much of Yellowstone Basin

1862    John Mullan completes military road between Walla Walla, Washington, and Fort Benton

Gold discovered on Grasshopper Creek (Bannack)

1863    Gold discovered on Alder Gulch (Virginia City)

1864    Montana Territory created

Gold rush to Last Chance Gulch (Helena)

Vigilantes lynch Henry Plummer

First newspaper (*Montana Post*) published in Montana

1867 John Bozeman killed on upper Yellowstone River

Forts Shaw and Ellis constructed

1869 Territorial prison established in Deer Lodge

1870 Soldiers destroy Blackfeet village on Marias River in Baker Massacre

1876 Combined Sioux and Cheyenne military victory at Little Bighorn

1877 Nez Perce trek through Montana, fight battle at Big Hole, surrender near Bear's Paw Mountains

Forts Keogh, Custer, and Missoula constructed

1879 Fort Assinniboine built near Havre

1880 Marcus Daly purchases Anaconda mine

Utah Northern Railroad enters Montana from the south

1883 Ceremony near Gold Creek marks completion of Northern Pacific Railroad across Montana

1884 Constitutional convention meets in Helena; Congress refuses statehood for Montana

1885 Montana Stock Growers' Association formed

1886–87 Harsh plains winter nearly destroys Montana's range-cattle industry

1887 Great Northern Railroad begins building across northern Montana

1888 Sweet Grass Hills Treaty creates northern Montana's Indian reservations

1889 Montana joins the union as the forty-first state

1891 Charlo's band of Salish forced to leave Bitterroot Valley

1893 Legislature establishes and chooses sites for Montana's universities and colleges

Nationwide silver panic leads to widespread mine shutdowns

1894 Helena chosen over Anaconda as state capital

1896 Populist candidates sweep Montana elections

1898 Anaconda Company purchases Bonner lumber mill

| 1899 | Standard Oil officials take over Butte mines, create Amalgamated Copper Company |
| | William A. Clark bribes legislators in attempt to win U.S. Senate seat |
| 1903 | Amalgamated Copper shuts down Montana operations to force governor and legislature to do its bidding |
| 1906 | Copper baron F. A. Heinze sells his Montana holdings |
| 1907 | Republic Coal Company begins mining near Roundup |
| | Huntley Irrigation Project completed on the Yellowstone River |
| 1909 | Milwaukee Road rail line completed across Montana |
| 1910 | Glacier National Park established |
| | Massive forest fire sweeps through Idaho and western Montana |
| 1912 | Montana Power Company established |
| | Joseph M. Dixon of Montana manages Theodore Roosevelt's "Bull Moose" presidential campaign |
| 1913 | Montana Highway Commission created |
| 1914 | Montana begins issuing vehicle license plates |
| | Montana women gain the right to vote |
| 1916 | Jeannette Rankin becomes first woman elected to Congress |
| 1917 | Industrial Workers of the World agitator Frank Little lynched in Butte |
| | Speculator Mine fire kills 168 men in Butte |
| 1918 | Wave of wartime anti-German hysteria sweeps Montana |
| 1919 | Severe drought marks beginning of agricultural depression; thousands of homesteaders begin leaving Montana |
| 1922 | Drillers strike oil at Kevin-Sunburst Field |
| 1923 | Dempsey–Gibbons heavyweight title fight in Shelby |
| 1924 | Montana's Senator Thomas Walsh helps expose Teapot Dome Scandal |
| 1933 | Construction begins on Fort Peck Dam |
| 1935 | Legislature creates Montana Highway Patrol |
| | Earthquakes jolt Helena |
| 1936 | Beartooth Highway completed |
| 1938 | Milwaukee Road passenger train wreck near Terry kills forty-seven |

| 1941 | First state park established at Lewis and Clark Caverns |
| 1942 | Future Malmstrom Air Force Base established at Great Falls |
| 1943 | Smith Mine disaster at Bearcreek kills seventy-four coal miners |
| 1945 | Montana's first Hutterites arrive from Canada |
| 1951 | Oil boom begins in eastern Montana |
| 1952 | American Legion posts begin placing white crosses at highway accident sites |
| 1955 | Anaconda Company begins open-pit mining in Butte |
| 1959 | Madison Canyon slide kills twenty-eight |
| 1962 | Governor Donald Nutter killed in airplane crash |
| 1963 | Montana's Minuteman missile sites declared operational |
| 1964 | Congress passes Wilderness Act |
| 1970 | Vietnam War and Kent State tragedy lead to student strike at University of Montana |
| 1971 | Montana voters reject a sales-tax measure, elect delegates to Constitutional Convention |
| 1972 | Constitutional Convention meets and drafts a new state constitution, which voters then adopt |
| 1975 | Legislature enacts nation's highest coal severance tax |
| 1977 | Atlantic Richfield Corporation purchases Anaconda Company |
| 1980 | ARCO shuts down smelters in Anaconda and Great Falls |
| 1983 | ARCO suspends copper mining in Butte |
| 1986 | Voters defeat measure to eliminate property taxes |
| 1988 | Large fires sweep through Montana forests; much of Yellowstone National Park blackened |
| 1989 | Montanans celebrate their state's 100th birthday |
| 1996 | "Freemen" surrender near Jordan after long FBI siege<br>Federal agents capture suspected "Unabomber" near Lincoln |

# MONTANA LICENSE PLATES

Montana began registering and taxing motor vehicles in 1913. The tax ranged between five and twenty dollars, depending on the vehicle's horsepower. The state used the money to build, maintain, and improve public highways. A registrar of motor vehicles assigned each vehicle a number in the sequential order that registrations were received. A few counties issued metal plates with the numbers, but most motorists attached their number to a board or piece of leather, which they then hung on the vehicle.

The state began issuing license plates in 1914. In 1925 the legislature appointed Montana's prison warden to manufacture and distribute the plates. For several years, beginning in 1939, the words "prison made" could be found stamped on the bottom of each plate.

*Montana's evolving license plate.* —Plates courtesy Wayne Raymond

# MONTANA LICENSE PLATES

| Plate Number | County | County Seat | Plate Number | County | County Seat |
|---|---|---|---|---|---|
| 1 | Silver Bow | Butte | 29 | Rosebud | Forsyth |
| 2 | Cascade | Great Falls | 30 | Deer Lodge | Anaconda |
| 3 | Yellowstone | Billings | 31 | Teton | Choteau |
| 4 | Missoula | Missoula | 32 | Stillwater | Columbus |
| 5 | Lewis and Clark | Helena | 33 | Treasure | Hysham |
| 6 | Gallatin | Bozeman | 34 | Sheridan | Plentywood |
| 7 | Flathead | Kalispell | 35 | Sanders | Thompson Falls |
| 8 | Fergus | Lewistown | 36 | Judith Basin | Stanford |
| 9 | Powder River | Broadus | 37 | Daniels | Scobey |
| 10 | Carbon | Red Lodge | 38 | Glacier | Cutbank |
| 11 | Phillips | Malta | 39 | Fallon | Baker |
| 12 | Hill | Havre | 40 | Sweet Grass | Big Timber |
| 13 | Ravalli | Hamilton | 41 | McCone | Circle |
| 14 | Custer | Miles City | 42 | Carter | Ekalaka |
| 15 | Lake | Polson | 43 | Broadwater | Townsend |
| 16 | Dawson | Glendive | 44 | Wheatland | Harlowton |
| 17 | Roosevelt | Wolf Point | 45 | Prairie | Terry |
| 18 | Beaverhead | Dillon | 46 | Granite | Philipsburg |
| 19 | Chouteau | Fort Benton | 47 | Meagher | White Sulphur Springs |
| 20 | Valley | Glasgow | 48 | Liberty | Chester |
| 21 | Toole | Shelby | 49 | Park City | Livingston |
| 22 | Big Horn | Hardin | 50 | Garfield | Jordan |
| 23 | Musselshell | Roundup | 51 | Jefferson | Boulder |
| 24 | Blaine | Chinook | 52 | Wibaux | Wibaux |
| 25 | Madison | Virginia City | 53 | Golden Valley | Ryegate |
| 26 | Pondera | Conrad | 54 | Mineral | Superior |
| 27 | Richland | Sidney | 55 | Petroleum | Winnett |
| 28 | Powell | Deer Lodge | 56 | Lincoln | Libby |

The numbers that currently designate each county on Montana's plates were assigned during the early 1930s. In theory they were based on the population of the counties in 1930, with the most populated counties receiving the lowest numbers. But political clout led some counties to receive much lower numbers than they deserved. For example, Powder River County, ranked forty-sixth in population, got number nine!

The state outline map that graces today's plates first appeared in 1933. A bison skull logo showed up in 1938. During the 1950s, plates carried the words "Treasure State." Plates began bearing the slogan "Big Sky Country" in 1967.

To help alleviate a wartime metal shortage, Montana's 1944 plates were made of a fiberboard material. The plates did not hold up well, and farm animals even ate some of them.

In 1976 Montana issued a red, white, and blue plate to celebrate the nation's bicentennial. The plate far outlasted the celebration, as vehicle owners attached stickers to it each year through 1991 rather than purchase a new plate. Beginning in 1987, drivers had the option of purchasing a special plate commemorating the centennial of Montana's statehood. In 1991 a colorful new plate appeared along with a number of special-issue license plates for each of the state's colleges and universities.

# MONTANA:
## A STATE OF EXTREMES

*There is little or nothing moderate about the story of Montana. It has ricocheted violently down the corridor of possibilities.*

—K. Ross Toole, *Montana: An Uncommon Land*

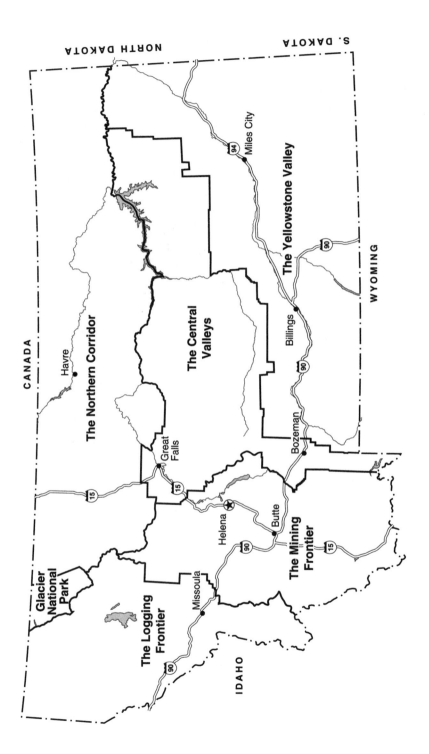

As it straddles the Continental Divide and stretches eastward into the northern Great Plains, Montana presents a landscape as varied as it is vast. From the lofty peaks of Glacier National Park to the rolling prairies of the northeast to the rugged badlands overlooking Glendive and Terry, America's fourth largest state has inspired expressions filled with superlatives. John Steinbeck called it "a great splash of grandeur." John Gunther, in his best-selling 1940s travelogue *Inside USA*, marveled at Montana's "overwhelming sense of power, spaciousness, incurable vitality, wealth and youth."

Even the state's weather bounces between extremes. The lowest recorded temperature in the lower forty-eight states was seventy below zero, which occured atop Montana's Rogers Pass. In eastern Montana, summertime temperatures of 110 degrees are not uncommon. Native tribes, including the Salish and Kutenai in the mountains and the Crow, Gros Ventre, and Blackfeet on the plains, survived only by respecting and adjusting to Mother Nature's extremes. The late-arriving whites took longer to learn their lesson. Freezing mountain blizzards frequently blocked the paths of early explorers and mountain men. A single harsh winter in 1886–87 nearly wiped out Montana's huge open-range cattle herds. Later, prolonged drought forced hundreds of once optimistic dryland farmers to abandon their prairie homesteads as howling gales blew their rich topsoil into North Dakota.

## EXPLORERS AND EXPLOITERS

From the time they worked up the Missouri into present-day Montana late in April of 1805, the men of the Lewis and Clark Corps of Discovery knew that they were encountering a land totally different from anything they were used to. Meriwether Lewis recorded, "We can scarcely cast our eyes in any direction without perceiving deer, elk, buffaloe or antelopes." On their first day in Montana, the explorers experienced the first of many violent clashes with ferocious grizzly bears. Strong prairie head winds frequently impeded their progress, and on at least one occasion the cold air caused water to freeze to their oars as they rowed.

But these men, Montana's first tourists, also marveled at the breathtaking landscape. From the spectacular White Cliffs and thundering Great Falls of the Missouri River to the formidable barrier of the Rocky Mountains, Lewis and Clark described them all in colorful detail. The party traveled more miles and spent more time in what is now Montana than in any other state. On their return trip, the expedition split into two groups so that Lewis could explore up the Marias River and Clark could float down the Yellowstone. Lewis and Clark gave the nation the first reliable map and the first written description of Montana. Generations of Montanans have venerated them as their state's first true heroes.

Close on the heels of Lewis and Clark came the fur traders. Some came in groups, employed by companies based in St. Louis and Canada. Others were independent and worked alone. The traders trekked through every mountain pass and trapped beaver in nearly every stream in Montana. They established a series of short-lived posts on the Missouri and Yellowstone. And they brought to Montana's Native American tribes the twin scourges of liquor and smallpox.

The fur-trade era brought virtually no permanent settlement into Montana. Fort Benton on the upper Missouri was the only post to survive. Yet, as they hauled bales of beaver pelts and buffalo robes east, the fur traders, particularly those working for John Jacob Astor's big American Fur Company conglomerate, established an important precedent. In the words of historian Clark Spence, "It was the first example of eastern corporate capital boldly and without scruple exploiting western resources—a theme that would persist in Montana whether in furs, railroads, or mining."

*Detail of Charles M. Russell mural: "Lewis and Clark Meeting the Flathead Indians at Ross' Hole."* —Montana Historical Society, Helena

# GOLD

Although there is debate over just who found the first gold in Montana and when that event took place, there is no doubt that the first important gold discovery occurred in July 1862, on Grasshopper Creek, a tiny tributary of the Beaverhead River. The following May prospectors made a richer find to the east on Alder Gulch. A year later Abraham Lincoln signed the bill creating Montana Territory.

Montana's placer-mining boom came later than those in other western states such as California, Nevada, and Colorado. Many of the first prospectors spilled into the territory after those other diggings had been played out. Others came from back East via the Missouri River corridor, traversing John Mullan's military road running from Fort Benton to Walla Walla or braving John Bozeman's trail, which cut north from the Oregon Trail at Fort Laramie. Many miners, like the fur traders before them, were a restless breed. They quickly moved from camp to camp and left once they failed to find their bonanza.

But the gold camps also lured storekeepers, saloon keepers, harlots, ranchers, and farmers. Many of those who came to "mine the miners" amassed fortunes much greater than those who spent their time scouring streambeds or digging into hillsides. They also brought permanent communities, a semblance of law and order, and a territorial government.

Montana's first so-called towns were little more than odd mixtures of tents, log cabins, and shacks scattered over an area pockmarked by the gold-hungry miners. One visitor to early Bannack remarked, "If there is such a place as hell, this must be the back door to it." In many camps the miners resorted to powerful hydraulic hoses to get at the gold. Eventually huge dredges destroyed what was left of the streambeds as they unearthed the last remaining gold and left landscapes resembling war zones. Most of Montana's several hundred mining camps disappeared as fast as they sprang up. A few, led by Helena and Butte, grew and diversified.

Montana's mining boom and birth as a territory took place as the Civil War raged in the East. The extreme animosity and hatred spurred by that conflict and its aftermath spilled into Montana and fueled its first political battles. Many of the territory's miners were sons of the confederacy and staunch democrats. That party enjoyed heavy majorities in the first legislative bodies. When Washington sent unionist republican governors and judges to administer the new territory, the result was noisy contention and political gridlock. Not until 1870, when moderate, capable Benjamin Potts took over as governor, did the fighting begin to die down.

By the late 1860s most of Montana's easily mined placer gold was gone. There was no doubt that greater wealth remained buried deep underground, but mining and smelting it required the sort of heavy equipment that could be brought in only by a railroad. Throughout the ensuing decade, a nationwide depression coupled with warfare between the U.S. Army and Montana's Plains Indians kept the eagerly awaited railroads from building through the territory.

## CONQUEST

As hordes of gold seekers and other settlers spilled across their hunting grounds, it was inevitable that Montana's Native American tribes would fight to hold on to what rightfully belonged to them. The fighting skills of the Blackfeet, Crow, Gros Ventre, Assiniboine, Sioux, and Cheyenne had been honed by decades of intertribal warfare. They were among the finest horse soldiers in the world. Isolated clashes between whites and natives, including Indian ambushes of white travelers, led settlers to demand military protection. Between 1866 and 1892, the U.S. Army established a dozen forts in Montana and adopted a policy of hemming in the Indians on reservations. Vitriolic local newspapermen kept matters stirred up with their combination of racism and paranoia. Typical was an 1865 editorial in Virginia City's *Montana Post*, which declared, "It is because we of the mountains know what an Indian is and feel what he does, that we hate him and desire his death."

Eventually some of the nation's final and best remembered battles between white soldiers and Native Americans took place on Montana's plains during the 1870s. In January 1870 soldiers commanded by Major Eugene M. Baker attacked a camp of Piegan Blackfeet on the Marias River. They killed 173 people, burned the village, and forced the survivors to fend for themselves in the forty-below winter. Easterners condemned the so-called Baker Massacre; most Montana newspapers lauded the action.

In June 1876 a force of Sioux and Northern Cheyenne clashed with soldiers seeking to push them back onto their reservations. The Indian victory at the Little Bighorn proved to be relatively inconsequential. By the middle of the following year, soldiers under the command of Colonel Nelson A. Miles, based at Fort Keogh near present-day Miles City, had managed to defeat most of the Cheyenne and Sioux.

It was also Miles who forced the surrender of the Nez Perce near the Bear's Paw Mountains in late 1877. Members of that tribe had waged a heroic and nearly successful struggle against soldiers who had pursued them from their home in northern Idaho across much of Montana. By the decade's end most of Montana's native tribes were confined to ever-shrinking reservations where they were repeatedly swindled by corrupt government agents.

## RAILROADS, MINING, AND CATTLE

The early 1880s brought the Northern Pacific Railroad—the first of three transcontinental lines to cross the breadth of Montana. A decade later James J. Hill ran his Great Northern up the Missouri and Milk River Valleys, and in 1908 the Chicago, Milwaukee, St. Paul, & Pacific ("Milwaukee Road") built its tracks through central Montana.

The railroads brought in the heavy mining and milling equipment that launched Montana's second, longer-lived mining boom. They also opened up outside markets for the cattle and sheep of eastern Montana and the wood products of western Montana. In short, they enhanced the flow of Montana's riches to distant markets and swelled the bankrolls of outside investors.

Montana's open-range-cattle era followed a boom-and-bust pattern that was to be repeated in other Montana industries. Following the wholesale slaughter of the last of the vast plains bison herds in the early 1880s, millions of acres of rich natural grasses beckoned to speculators. Cattlemen, backed by eastern U.S. and British investors, took advantage of lax federal laws to claim huge acreages. They herded in thousands of cattle, eventually overstocking the range.

The bubble burst with the devastating winter of 1886–87. Most of the speculators sold the remnants of their herds at bargain prices. A few stockmen hung on and established a more sensible, longer-lasting cattle and sheep industry based on smaller herds, cultivated hay, and fenced ranches.

Gold, silver, and copper all played important roles in Montana's hard-rock mining era. By the mid-1880s, Montana had emerged as the nation's second leading producer of silver. Silver mining towns such as Granite, Wickes, Elkhorn, and Neihart sprang up throughout the territory's mountain regions. The mines ran full blast as big federal purchases of silver artificially bolstered prices and eastern U.S. and European investors cashed in on the boom.

Then in 1893 Congress voted to stop buying silver. In the ensuing panic, mines throughout the state shut down, idling hundreds of workers. Montanans eagerly joined the Populist Party crusade of William Jennings Bryan, which advocated the unlimited coinage of silver. The Populists, with their platform calling for government ownership of railroads and sweeping agrarian reform, also appealed to disgruntled farmers in eastern Montana.

## THE ANACONDA COPPER COMPANY

As important as silver became to Montana's economy, it was copper that came to dominate much of went on in the state for an entire century, beginning in 1880. In that year Marcus Daly, backed by investors from California, purchased Butte's Anaconda silver mine. As his miners burrowed deep into the hill overlooking Butte, it became apparent that the copper deposits were much richer than the silver veins.

Within five years Daly had erected the world's largest smelter at the new town of Anaconda, west of Butte. The Butte mines were producing millions of dollars in profits for Daly and a handful of other investors, including Daly's chief rival, William Andrews Clark.

Montana's "war of the copper kings" and the corruption of the state's political system that these battles left in their wake has become the stuff of legend. A group of historians, led by Joseph Kinsey Howard and K. Ross Toole, has documented—albeit with some exaggeration of the facts—how Montana's copper barons, along with a few eastern financiers, came to dominate the state's political and economic life as they exploited its natural resources.

Since the demise of the state's copper industry in the early 1980s, other historians have pointed out that Montana's situation was not much different from what had occurred in virtually every other western state. Throughout the West a handful of industrialists, ranging from mining barons and railroad magnates to grain merchants, controlled state legislatures and beat back labor unions with iron-fisted efficiency.

Still, Montana may well have been the western state most heavily dominated by an exploitive corporation. Few, if any, states witnessed the open purchase of voters that took place as Daly and Clark sought to secure the election of Montana's state capital in their rival cities of Anaconda and Helena. Later, in his efforts to secure a seat in the U.S. Senate, Clark openly bribed members of the state legislature, allegedly declaring, "I never bought a man who wasn't for sale."

The degradation of Montana's politics bottomed out in 1903. By then executives from Standard Oil controlled the Anaconda Company. In their fight with upstart rival F. Augustus Heinze, they shut down their entire Montana operation to force the governor to call a special session of the legislature. Because the shutdown threw thousands of copper and coal miners and lumbermen out of work, the governor had no real choice. The legislature quickly passed a company-drafted fair-trials bill that ended Heinze's control of the judges in Butte.

After that the Anaconda Company's methods grew somewhat more subdued, but it continued to dominate affairs in Helena. Whenever the state legislature met, the company's lobbyists operated from "watering holes" in several local hotels, where the amenities flowed freely. In the late 1940s one company lobbyist boasted, "Give me a case of Scotch, a case of gin, one blonde, and one brunette, and I can take any liberal."

Montanans did not always passively accept the Anaconda Company's heavy-handed practices. Butte became one of the most strongly unionized towns in America. Prolonged, sometimes violent strikes disrupted company operations. The radical Industrial Workers of the World (IWW) found a foothold among the company's lumber workers in western Montana. And on election days voters repeatedly sent to Washington progressives who denounced corporate domination. Liberals of various stripes, including Thomas Walsh, Burton K. Wheeler, James E. Murray, Mike Mansfield, and Lee Metcalf capably represented the state in the U.S. Senate.

The legacy of the Anaconda Company partially explains why Montanans during the 1970s narrowly adopted a progressive new state constitution and passed some of the nation's strongest environmental-protection laws. And to make sure that at least some of the wealth from eastern Montana's vast coalfields remained in the state, the legislature passed a coal severance tax so high that it led out-of-state industrialists to refer to Montanans in less than flattering terms.

## HOMESTEAD BOOM AND BUST

At the same time that the battles between the Anaconda Company and its enemies were molding Montana's industrial and political life, people on the prairies of eastern Montana were experiencing their own extremes of prosperity and despair. During the first two decades of the twentieth century, thousands flocked into the region to take up dryland farming. More liberalized homestead laws, along with unprecedented propaganda campaigns by the state's three big railroads and local chambers of commerce, lured in hordes of young people, all eager to make their fortune from a tar-paper shack perched on 320 acres.

Heavy rainfall and high wheat prices, bolstered by demand during the First World War, brought prosperity at first. Between 1900 and 1920 Montana's farm acreage leaped more than 2,300 percent. Then, beginning in 1919, the inevitable cyclical dry spell hit. By 1925 about two-thirds of the estimated 80,000 people who had taken up homesteads during the boom years packed up and left. During that same period, 214 banks—half of the state's total—failed.

During their brief stay Montana's prairie farmers had helped transform the state's political culture. Many joined the radical Nonpartisan League and later the Montana Farmers Union. They passed laws providing direct primaries, women's suffrage, and workers' compensation. In 1916 they

*Breaking soil east of Antelope, Sheridan County.* —JoAnn Hoven private collection

helped to pass a statewide prohibition law and sent Jeannette Rankin to Washington as the nation's first woman elected to Congress.

When drought and depression struck Montana again during the 1930s, even more people left. New Deal relief projects, highlighted by the massive Fort Peck Dam on the Missouri, helped ease the strain for some families. But when the Second World War created the big armaments and shipbuilding industry on the West Coast, many more job seekers abandoned the state.

## MODERN UNCERTAINTIES

Since the end of the war, Montanans have witnessed their share of economic peaks and valleys. Oil discoveries in the Williston Basin briefly brought prosperity to the state's easternmost counties. In the southeast the strip-mining of coal created more jobs, but the demand for coal quickly leveled off.

During the 1980s Montana weathered its worst depression since the 1930s. When the Anaconda Company sold its holdings to the Atlantic Richfield Corporation (ARCO) in 1977, many grew optimistic about the future of the declining copper industry. But within three years ARCO shut down the aging smelters in Anaconda and Great Falls. In 1983 it suspended mining, and Butte's massive Berkeley Pit began to fill with toxic water. At the same time a drought, combined with an embargo on grain shipments to the Soviet Union, hit Montana's wheat farmers. And reduced demand for wood products, coupled with overlogging on private lands, caused sawmills in western Montana to shut down. Statewide, per-capita income dipped to below 80 percent of the national average.

In a sense, Montana in the 1980s was simply experiencing its share of hardship and dislocation as America continued the difficult transition from an industry-based economy to the age of information. Indeed, even during the lean 1980s some areas in western Montana continued to gain population.

During the next decade, that growth skyrocketed as people with computers and modems found they could live just about anywhere they wanted and still communicate with their employers. As crime, pollution, traffic, and malaise plagued the nation's urban areas, many sought sanctuary in the mountains of Montana. As Montana writer William Kittredge mused, "They come bearing money, buy up prime real estate and decorate the hills with trophy houses."

As America's new refugees flood into western Montana, many longtime residents fear that the newcomers are bringing with them the very conditions they had hoped to leave behind. Ugly strip highways lined with homogenous convenience stores and franchise restaurants now greet visitors in nearly every town in the region. Montana's latest boom has threatened this once pristine region with yet another unexpected "extreme"—overdevelopment.

# The Northern Corridor

*The Missouri was first of all a highway, and it is as a highway that it has captured the imagination of mankind—a perilous trail leading from Mississippi swamps to the snow peaks of the Rockies.*

—Stanley Vestal, *The Missouri*

13

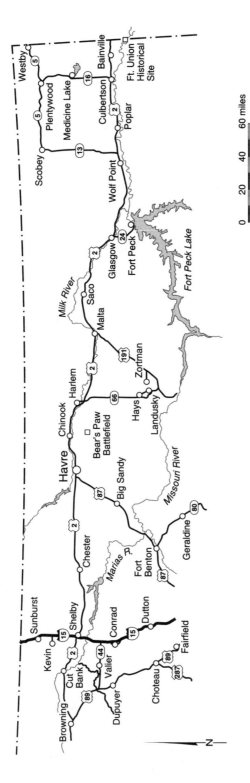

MONTANA

N

0   20   40   60 miles

Westby

Plentywood

5

5

Scobey

Medicine Lake

13

Culbertson

16

Bainville

Ft. Union
Historical
Site

Poplar

2

Wolf Point

Glasgow

24

Fort Peck

Fort Peck Lake

Milk River

Saco

Malta

191

Zortman

2

Harlem

Chinook

Hays

66

Landusky

Bear's Paw
Battlefield

Missouri River

Havre

Big Sandy

87

Chester

2

Geraldine

80

Marias R.

Fort
Benton

87

Sunburst

Shelby

Conrad

Dutton

15

15

Kevin

2

Cut
Bank

44

Valier

89

Fairfield

Browning

89

Dupuyer

Choteau

287

Winding its way eastward across the northern prairies of the future state of Montana, the Missouri River did, indeed, offer a perfect highway for the first white explorers and traders to enter the region. It provided them with a relatively safe, direct route from the Dakota plains to the foot of the Rocky Mountains.

For the original inhabitants of Montana's northern plains, the Missouri was more barrier than highway. The roaming bands of Sioux, Assiniboine, Gros Ventre, Cree, and Blackfeet were poor navigators at best. The horse was their preferred mode of transportation as they followed vast bison herds across lush prairie grasslands. Yet the great river offered them a reliable source of water and timber, so they gravitated to it.

## RIVER COMMERCE

Somewhat surprisingly, when the members of the Lewis and Clark expedition made their way up the Missouri River in the spring of 1805, they did not encounter any of these "locals." Instead, Meriwether Lewis marveled at the vast landscape, "The country on both sides of the Missouri continues to be open level fertile and beautiful as far as the eye can reach which from some eminences is not short of 30 miles." And the wildlife seemed unlimited. Along with deer, elk, and antelope, they observed packs

*Montana's upper Missouri River.*

of wolves and "immense quantities of buffalo" that Lewis further described as "extremely gentile."

Not so extremely gentile were the many grizzly bears the party tangled with. On the day they crossed into what is now Montana, a wounded grizzly chased Lewis some eighty yards before he was able to recharge his gun and kill it. Lewis commented, "It is astonishing to see the wounds they will bear before they can be put to death." Several days later party members fired ten musket balls into a 600-pound grizzly, who still managed to swim onto a sandbar where he finally succumbed.

Ferocious grizzlies did not impede the progress of the expedition nearly as much as the stiff prairie wind that frequently forced them off the river and, on one occasion, nearly destroyed their large pirogue boat. It was late May before the party crossed into present Chouteau County, where they gazed at the spectacular White Cliffs that so impress modern floaters on the wild stretch of the Missouri River below Fort Benton. The Missouri River "highway" continued to provide the Lewis and Clark party unimpeded passage through Montana until the river's Great Falls forced them to portage their boats and goods above the barrier. Only Meriwether Lewis and a smaller party navigated the Missouri when the expedition recrossed Montana on its way back east in 1806. The downstream trip was much faster, as the party paused only long enough to slaughter excessive numbers of wild animals—the first of many such depredations by white hunters and settlers that ultimately eliminated the food supply of the Plains Indians.

During the next seven decades, the Missouri River served as Montana's chief avenue of commerce. On the heels of Lewis and Clark, fur traders plied the river in watercraft ranging from dugout canoes and rawhide bullboats to elaborate wooden Mackinaws and keelboats. The keelboat was a craft up to seventy feet long, propelled either by crewmen working poles or by a long line, or cordelle, fastened to a high mast and pulled along by up to forty men struggling on the shore. Beginning in the early 1830s, these boats carried trade goods upstream from the American Fur Company's base post at Fort Union, near the mouth of the Yellowstone, to Fort Piegan, and later from Fort McKenzie, near the mouth of the Marias. From these posts they transported the bales of beaver pelts and buffalo robes to a lucrative American market.

In July 1833 German nobleman Maximilian of Weid-Neuweid, along with twenty-three-year-old Swiss artist Karl Bodmer, ascended Montana's Missouri River aboard the keelboat *Flora*. Bodmer's sketches and paintings of the spectacular Missouri River country gave the outside world one of its first glimpses of Montana's scenic grandeur.

Trade in buffalo robes was flourishing in the summer of 1859 when the *Chippewa* became the first steamboat to reach the Missouri's head of navigation near Fort Benton. Over the next five years only a handful of steamboats managed to make it that far. They carried passengers eager to reach Montana's newly discovered goldfields.

Eventually smaller "mountain boats"—stern-wheelers riding high on the water to avoid the treacherous snags and sandbars—were arriving regularly at Fort Benton. Historian Hiram M. Chittenden described the impression they made:

> In the midst of this virgin wilderness a noble steamboat appears, its handsome form standing high above the water in fine outline against the verdure of the shore; its lofty chimneys pouring forth clouds of smoke in an atmosphere unused to such intrusion, and its progress against the impetuous current exhibiting an extraordinary display of power. Altogether it formed one of the most notable scenes ever witnessed upon the waters of America.

Although steamboats may have been romantic in appearance, travel aboard them could be anything but comfortable. For the price of seventy-five dollars for deck passage, a traveler could expect to endure howling prairie gales, hailstorms, possible Indian attacks, hunger if no game could be found, and the ever-present danger of fires, boiler explosions, and snags. The boats frequently had to tie up at wood yards to refuel, and often they ran aground on sandbars, causing further delays.

Yet even with such hazards, the Missouri River corridor proved to be the quickest, safest route into Montana Territory. Merchants in Fort Benton amassed fortunes shipping passengers and freight aboard steamboats. Riverboats dominated the upper Missouri trade into the 1880s and the arrival of the railroads.

## RAILROADS AND HOMESTEADERS

When "the Empire Builder," James J. Hill, decided to press his railroad line into Montana, he chose a route that ran just north of the Missouri River before moving up the wide Milk River valley as far as present-day Havre. Here the line cut south toward Fort Benton.

In 1853 the transcontinental railroad survey expedition, led by General Isaac I. Stevens, explored the Milk River valley and pronounced it an excellent corridor to the Rockies across Montana. Between 1862 and 1867 eight wagon trains carried emigrants from the upper Midwest along this Milk River route and south to Montana Territory's goldfields. Tough Yankee frontiersman James Liberty Fisk escorted four of these parties along what came to be known as the Minnesota-Montana Road.

*Dormitory cars for construction crews along the Great Northern route, circa 1887.*
—Liberty County Museum, Chester

In 1878 shipping merchant James J. Hill acquired a bankrupt railroad that he built into the successful St. Paul, Minneapolis & Manitoba. A visit to Montana convinced him that the territory had sufficient mineral and agricultural wealth to support another transcontinental line.

It took Hill until early 1887 to secure permission from Congress to extend his rails across land still claimed by the Blackfeet Indians. The tracklayers entered Montana on June 13. The workforce consisted of more than 9,000 men and some 6,600 horses. Most were involved in grading the roadbed. They moved at a pace of up to seven miles a day. Observing this massive task, Mark Twain's associate Charles Dudley Warner wrote, "Those who saw this army of men and teams stretching over the prairie and casting up this continental highway think they behold one of the most striking achievements of civilization."

The tracklayers followed close on the heels of the graders, placing the ties and hammering down the seventy-five-pound rails with machinelike precision. By September 6 they had reached Havre; by the end of the month, they had passed Fort Benton. When they finally reached Helena in November, Hill's single crew had laid 643 continuous miles of track in just seven and a half months. No railroad had ever been built so rapidly.

In 1890 Hill rechristened his railroad the Great Northern. In October the line began laying rails due west from Havre to the Rockies and on to the Pacific Coast. By 1893 passenger trains of the Great Northern were making regular runs from St. Paul to Seattle in just seventy-two hours. In Montana the railroad and the country it occupied came to be popularly known as the Hi-line. The northern corridor had shifted from the Missouri River onto rolling hills and prairies occupied by steel rails.

With the completion of his transcontinental line, James J. Hill set out to fill the prairie it crossed with people. Prior to the turn of the century, northern Montana was populated largely by cattle on an open range. In 1908 the Great Northern began a vast promotion and colonization program. Hill's agents visited county fairs throughout the East and Midwest, and special exhibition cars toured the nation displaying grain and vegetable crops grown in Montana. Brochures flooded the country touting the Milk River valley as "a poor man's paradise where land was plentiful and a fortune could be made with little effort."

The unprecedented promotion scheme of the Great Northern and Montana's other big railroads bore fruit. Thousands of eager young families loaded their belongings into special boxcars and invested their life savings in 320-acre prairie homesteads. For a modest fee, local land locators hauled them to their remote sections where they erected single-room, tar-paper shacks and began breaking ground. Virtually overnight millions of Montana acres were dotted with farms.

*Members of the Ghekiere family pose on their homestead north of Conrad, Montana, circa 1913.* —Conrad Public Library

For more than a decade Mother Nature cooperated. Unusually heavy rainfall produced huge wheat harvests until 1917. Then the inevitable cyclical drought hit with a vengeance. Plagued by blowing dust, low crop prices, and hordes of insects, the once optimistic settlers left in droves. Of the nearly 80,000 people who had moved into eastern Montana between 1909 and 1918, 60,000 were gone by 1922. The descendants of those who were tough enough and smart enough to weather the bad times populate Montana's Hi-line today.

By the 1920s many refugees from northern Montana's prairies could leave in their Model T Fords over the newly completed US Highway 2. The new road paralleled the route of the Great Northern and was among the first highway corridors across Montana. In a 1921 travel guide a Montana highway official described the route as a good dirt road, but asked motorists for their "patience and forbearance regarding road conditions."

Today US 2 is much improved, but it remains two lanes for its entire length across Montana. It is the chief route for our historical tour of the Hi-line.

## US 2 and Montana 327
# Fort Union—Wolf Point
**80 miles**

### FORT UNION

The site of Fort Union lies a few yards east of Montana in North Dakota, but as the American Fur Company's most important trading post on the Missouri River, it drew its wealth from the rivers and prairies of present-day Montana. Kenneth McKenzie, the autocratic manager of the company's fur trade on the Missouri, supervised construction of the post in 1829. They built it on a high north bank about five miles upstream from the confluence of the Yellowstone. The location was ideal to attract trade from prairie Sioux, Crow, Assiniboine, and even a few Blackfeet.

During McKenzie's reign, Fort Union shipped hundreds of beaver pelts down the Missouri. Declaring "Liquor I must have or quit," McKenzie brought in a still. In the summer of 1837 the steamboat *St. Peters* brought smallpox germs upriver to Fort Union. Smallpox devastated the native tribes of the plains. The 1837 epidemic wiped out an estimated four-fifths of the Assiniboine and Blackfeet.

For twenty-two years, beginning in 1839, Major Alexander Culbertson, with his able Blackfeet wife, Natawistacha, managed American Fur Company affairs from Fort Union. During the Culbertson era, the post dealt mainly in buffalo robes brought in from a number of posts up the Missouri. One early visitor described the post's history as "a continuous series of conspiracies, family feuds, sieges, pitched battles, drunken brawls and cold blooded murders."

As Sioux hostilities increased on the northern plains, Fort Union became an army garrison shortly before soldiers dismantled it in 1867. Today a reconstructed Fort Union proudly sits at the site of the original post. The National Park Service operates this nearly exact replica of the original establishment. It can be reached via a fourteen-mile good gravel road (Montana 327) running southeast from Bainville.

## BAINVILLE

The tiny hamlet of Bainville once boomed as an important railroad junction. From here a branch of the Great Northern ran north toward Plentywood and Scobey. Its roundhouse served as the base for half a dozen freight and passenger trains.

During prohibition, Bainville contained at least seven saloons, innocently labeled "pool halls." Nearby stills produced substances that, according to a local scribe, could have been used as rocket fuel in a later era. The drought and depression of the 1930s sharply reduced both the railroad's business and the population of Bainville. A tornado in the early 1930s hastened its decline by destroying the local armory and grain elevator.

## CULBERTSON

The oldest town in northeastern Montana, Culbertson was named after pioneer fur trader Alexander Culbertson. His son Jack established a ranch just west of here in 1879, and the town arose with the arrival of the Great Northern Railway eight years later. Then for the next two decades, until homesteaders began fencing off the open range, Culbertson served as the rail shipping center for thousands of cattle and sheep.

Following the disastrous winter of 1887, which wiped out much of Montana's open-range cattle herds, ranchers in the Culbertson area began cutting hay and harvesting oats for winter feed. The enormous Diamond Ranch southwest of Culbertson was running 15,000 head of cattle by 1906. After bringing their cattle to the Culbertson stockyards, cowboys from the Diamond and other area ranches celebrated by riding their horses into some of the thirteen local bars and shooting holes in the ceilings.

## FORT PECK RESERVATION

Near milepost 639, US 2 crosses Big Muddy Creek, which marks the eastern boundary of the Fort Peck Reservation. Montana's second largest

Indian reservation, Fort Peck occupies most of Roosevelt County and portions of three bordering counties. It is home for two bands of the Assiniboine tribe and the Yanktonai and Sisseton Wahpeton bands of the Sioux Nation.

*Assiniboine* derives from the Chippewa word meaning "stone boilers." The name likely came from tribal members' unique way of cooking by boiling water with heated stones. The Assiniboine tribe was probably an offshoot of the Yanktonai Sioux, separating from this tribe around 1600. By 1800 the Assiniboine tribe had an estimated 28,000 members. They hunted across a vast domain between the Missouri and Saskatchewan Rivers. Three separate smallpox epidemics reduced their numbers to 4,000 by the time they moved to the reservation area in the 1870s. During the winter of 1884, several hundred more Assiniboine starved to death near Wolf Point after the government failed to deliver the promised rations to the reservation.

In 1877 the Fort Peck Indian Agency moved from its namesake fort to its present location on the Poplar River. At about the same time, U.S. soldiers were forcing the Sioux off their traditional plains hunting grounds and confining them to reservations. Soon many of Sitting Bull's Sioux who had participated in the Battle of the Little Bighorn were living near Fort Peck Agency, where tensions continued to run high.

In December 1880 Sioux Chief Gall and his small band set up camp on the south bank of the Missouri just across from the mouth of Poplar River. Government soldiers began reinforcing the infantry and cavalry already stationed on Poplar River. When Gall refused an order to surrender, the troops moved in and captured the camp after a brief skirmish. Gall's cold and starving people were given government rations and transferred to Fort Buford in the Dakota Territory.

The 1888 Sweet Grass Hills Treaty broke up the huge Indian reservation, which had included virtually all of Montana Territory north of the Missouri River between the North Dakota border and the Continental Divide. It established the present boundaries of the Fort Peck Reservation. Within twenty years the government and tribes had concluded an agreement allotting 320 acres to each Indian then on the reservation. The "surplus" lands then were thrown open to white homesteaders. After the land rush, the Fort Peck Reservation Indians managed to hold on to just under half of the reservation's 2.1 million acres.

As has been the case on most western Indian reservations, unemployment rates have been high at Fort Peck. Government attempts to convert the nomadic tribal members to farmers met with mixed results. The discovery of oil in the 1940s near Poplar and the establishment in the 1970s of A & S (Assiniboine and Sioux) Industries, manufacturing military equipment for the government, bolstered the reservation's economy.

## WOLF POINT

When passing steamboaters observed a number of frozen wolves left on the bank of the Missouri by area hunters, they named the place Wolf Point. A subagency for the Fort Peck Reservation moved here in 1879. A town did not arise until thirty-five years later when white homesteaders took up land on the reservation. After the Great Northern established a division point and built a big roundhouse at Wolf Point, the local press boasted: "If Wolf Point is not now the largest town in Sheridan County she is growing so fast that all other contenders will be obscured by her dust. . . ." Less than a decade later, the Great Northern pulled out its division point and Wolf Point's population plummeted.

Wolf Point is the site of Montana's longest running rodeo, the Wolf Point Wild Horse Stampede. Local Assiniboine and Sioux established the event as a day for horse racing and celebration even before Wolf Point was an incorporated town. Then the Chamber of Commerce, led by E. O. Mickel, made the event a rodeo.

Mickel is perhaps better known as the father of Owen Harlen Mickel, also called Monte Montana. The younger Mickel recalled that while growing up in Wolf Point, "I never really wanted to go to school. I wanted to stay home and play cowboy." At school he practiced his roping on the girls

*Monte Montana twirls a rope in front of the territorial centennial train, 1964.* —Montana Historical Society, Helena

as they came out of the privy. The father and son eventually took their trick-riding and roping act on the road, touring first Montana and later the rest of the country. For decades Monte Montana appeared in parades and rodeos and played small roles in a number of classic western films. In 1993 he rode in his fifty-ninth consecutive Tournament of Roses Parade.

## Montana 16
# Culbertson—Plentywood
47 miles

### MEDICINE LAKE WILDLIFE REFUGE

In August 1935 an executive order from President Franklin Roosevelt set aside the Medicine Lake National Wildlife Refuge as a breeding ground for migratory birds. Two years later a contingent of Civilian Conservation Corps (CCC) workers set up camp in the area and began digging ditches, erecting dikes, and generally making the place a better habitat for waterfowl. By 1970 the refuge's resident flock of Canada geese had increased to more than 800 birds.

### PLENTYWOOD

Plentywood, the county seat of Sheridan County, was in many ways a typical boomtown of Montana's homestead era. The surrounding hills once were home for many open-range cattle, but the arrival of the railroad in 1910 and hordes of homesteaders shortly thereafter made Plentywood a prosperous, bustling community. Then, following the First World War boom years, drought and depression hit. Plentywood's reaction to these events made the community unique and earned it national renown: throughout much of the 1920s, Plentywood was the only town in America governed by self-proclaimed communists.

#### Prairie Radicals

With the economic downturn, farmers throughout Sheridan County organized various socialist groups. North Dakota's Nonpartisan League, with its platform of state ownership of grain elevators and big tax relief for farmers, soon spilled over into Montana.

In 1918 Plentywood's socialist groups combined with the Nonpartisan League to form the People's Publishing Company. They founded a local newspaper, the *Producers News*, and brought in veteran Minnesota newspaperman Charles E. Taylor as its editor. Charles "Red Flag" Taylor was at once brilliant, charismatic, spiteful, and eccentric. He was a spellbinding speaker and a highly persuasive writer. A former homesteader, he quickly won the favor of the region's embattled farmers by championing their fight for economic equality. With Taylor at the helm, the *Producers News* soon became the most widely read newspaper in Sheridan County.

Taylor made no secret of his communist beliefs. He called his paper "an instrument of the class struggle" and called Marx and Lenin "prophets of the inevitable revolution." Spurred by the rhetoric in the *Producers News*, disgruntled farmers elected nearly every candidate who ran under their Farmer-Labor ticket during the early 1920s. They sent Taylor to the state senate.

With so-called Reds in charge, Sheridan County attracted radical members of the Industrial Workers of the World (IWW). The county also became a haven for bootleggers, as Taylor's friend, Sheriff Rodney Salisbury, tolerated the region's rampant illegal booze and gambling. Taylor used his newspaper to launch libelous attacks on anyone who dared to disagree with the newly established order.

Still, few of those in Sheridan County who voted the Farmer-Labor ticket held deep communist convictions. Many abandoned the cause once adequate rainfall and abundant crops returned briefly to the region in the mid-1920s. Then on November 30, 1926, two armed, masked men stole more than $100,000 in cash and bonds from the county treasurer's office. The money was never recovered, and many suspected that Taylor and Salisbury had masterminded an inside job. In 1928 record wheat harvests came in, and nearly every local socialist candidate lost his bid for reelection.

Beginning in 1929, drought and depression returned for a prolonged stay in northeastern Montana. "Black blizzards" plagued the Plentywood area, piling dust so high that it buried the fenceposts. At the height of the Great Depression in 1934, health officials reported that 284 children in Sheridan County were suffering from malnutrition. Such conditions seemed ideal for a return of political radicalism, and the communists again won over many voters.

But by now Taylor and the editors of the *Producers News* who succeeded him had lost touch with the local farmers. As the newspaper's rhetoric grew ever more radical, subscriptions continued to decline. Soon the rival *Plentywood Herald* was declaring, "Two is company, three is a crowd, and four is a Communist mass meeting." In March 1937 Taylor's paper published its final issue; its revolution lay dead. The New Deal programs of Franklin D. Roosevelt helped Sheridan County weather the Great Depression. Then, during the 1950s, the first of many oil wells in the area struck it rich. Still, for decades after the demise of Taylor's revolution people frequently called Sheridan Montana's "Red" county.

*Sheridan County dust storm, 1938.* —Sheridan County Museum, Plentywood

# Westby—Wolf Point
122 miles

## OUTLAWS

As you drive across the rolling hills of northeastern Montana drained by Big Muddy Creek and the Poplar River, you are crossing a favorite haunt of some of the state's most notorious turn-of-the-century outlaws. By the late 1880s, with the bison eliminated, northern Montana's lush grasslands attracted both horse ranchers and cattlemen. Numerous cowhands trailed the herds north into Montana, lost their jobs, and turned to rustling. By the early 1890s a state stock inspector labeled Valley County, which then included all of northeast Montana, "the most lawless and crookedest county in the Union and the Big Muddy is the worst part of it."

Henry Juach, better known as Dutch Henry, was the most notorious. He led a gang called the Wild Bunch, which included among its members Tom Reid, James McNab, Bloody Knife, and Kid Trailer. Because the gang members seldom preyed on area homesteaders, the settlers sometimes of-

26

fered them food and shelter. Kid Trailer was an accomplished fiddler, and even when he had a price on his head he could be found playing for dances throughout the region.

## WESTBY

It seems odd that Montana's easternmost community is called Westby, until one learns that the town originally lay in North Dakota. In 1909 Danish immigrants who had settled in the northwestern corner of North Dakota established Westby. The name combines the Danish word for *town* with the word *west* because of its location along North Dakota's western border.

During Westby's formative years, liquor was prohibited in North Dakota but not in Montana, so the local saloons were all located on the Montana side of the border. The "legitimate" businesses remained in North Dakota. When the Soo Line laid its rails into this region, the railroad's owners decided to locate on the Montana side of the line to take advantage of higher freight rates. Westby's businessmen promptly relocated among Montana's saloon keepers, and by 1914 the North Dakota town site lay virtually abandoned.

## SCOBEY

Scobey, the county seat of Daniels County, is located on the old Woody Mountain Trail. The Sioux bands of Chiefs Gall and Sitting Bull frequently used this route to move back and forth along the Canadian border during their final years of resistance to white invaders.

The Great Northern pushed its rail spur to Scobey in 1913. The railroad paid off its crews the day the line reached the new town. Crewmen went to the town's only bar, the Smith and Boyd Saloon, to celebrate. Smith wound up threatening the rowdies with guns to keep them from wrecking his establishment. When Scobey became the seat for newly formed Daniels County in 1920, a frame building formerly known as One-Eyed Molly's house of pleasure was converted into the courthouse. The remodeled building still stands as one of Montana's most colorful courthouses.

Although drought plagued much of Montana throughout the 1920s, the state's northeast corner enjoyed record wheat harvests during the decade's middle years. Until the railroad built west to Opheim, Scobey won renown as the largest primary wheat shipping point in the world. As many as 300 grain-laden wagons at a time could be seen backed up waiting to unload at local grain elevators. The Great Northern dispatched special trains to haul wheat from Scobey during harvest time.

### Prairie Baseball

During these years of plenty, baseball was the most popular sport in the region. A bitter rivalry arose between teams in Scobey and Plentywood. When the latter town hired black pitching ace John Donaldson, Scobey's baseball boosters knew they had to retaliate. Flush with cash from the prosperous wheat harvests, local businessmen raised more than $3,000 and hired a gold-plated team stocked with professional players.

Among the former minor league and big league players who wound up playing on Scobey's baseball diamond were shortstop Swede Risberg and center fielder Happy Felsh. The pair had earned notoriety as members of the then-corrupt Chicago White Sox. During the "Black Sox" scandal of 1919, players took bribes from gamblers for agreeing to throw the World Series. But the baseball boosters of Scobey were uninterested in a player's past as long as he could help them beat the hated Plentywood nine.

Both Risberg and Felsh spent a big portion of their $600 salaries on illicit booze in Scobey's speakeasy, the Dirty Shame Saloon. But the pair was always ready to play by game time. The 1925 Scobey Giants won thirty games and lost only three while touring Montana, Canada, and as far east as Minnesota. Scobey boosters won thousands of dollars in bets from Plentywood fans after two victories over their eastern rivals. The team

*The 1925 Scobey Giants.* —Daniels County Museum, Scobey

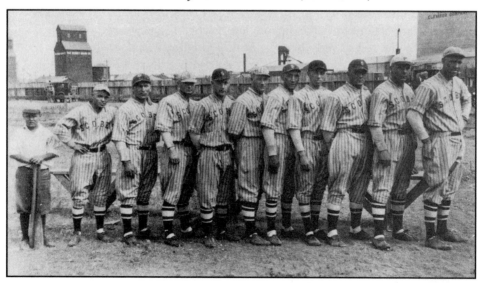

followed no training rules or curfew. In Moose Jaw, Saskatchewan, they left town early after Felsch and Risberg got into a fight with an obnoxious fan and a near-riot ensued.

Risberg, who insisted on pitching in every game he played, quit the team after only one season. After the 1927 season, Scobey's merchant boosters decided that they could no longer afford their high-priced players, abruptly ending the town's era of professional baseball.

US 2

# Wolf Point—Malta

119 miles

## MILK RIVER COUNTRY

For nearly 200 miles from near Nashua to west of Havre, both US 2 and the Burlington Northern Railroad (formerly the Great Northern) parallel the Milk River. The Milk originates near Glacier Park and flows northeast into Alberta before recrossing the border to flow southeast to the Missouri River. Lewis and Clark named the river in May 1805 after observing that its water possessed "a peculiar whiteness, being about the color of a cup of tea with the admixture of a tablespoon of milk." During the 1860s, members of the Fisk and Holmes wagon trains observed up to 10,000 Indians camped near the river as they followed the vast buffalo herds.

For six months a Pony Express route ran along the river until Indian opposition resulted in its abandonment. The forced removal of the native tribes from the region led to an influx of vast cattle herds. The big open-range cattle outfits entered this region after the disastrous 1886–87 winter killed off large portions of their herds in areas south of the Missouri. Once Congress opened up the huge Blackfeet Reservation in 1888, cattlemen simply inserted notices in area newspapers listing their brands and noting roughly the extent of their ranges. The largest of several big outfits was the N Bar N of the Neidringhaus brothers. Headquartered in Canada, the N Bar N ran over 100,000 head of cattle across a huge domain stretching through present Valley, Custer, and Dawson Counties.

Then in 1906 another harsh winter hit, leading Glasgow's *Valley County News* to predict correctly, "The present hard winter will mark the passing of the large cow outfits in Northern Montana." But by then, the first wave of homesteaders was already arriving. Soon they populated the former rangeland and established a string of small towns all along the Milk River stretch of the Great Northern Railway.

## GLASGOW

In 1887 the Great Northern's tracklayers established Siding Number 45 at a wide spot in the Milk River valley. Soon Charles Hall arrived along with his Indian lady companion and a grey horse pulling all of his belongings on a travois. He set up shop in a crude log cabin. Within weeks a tent city complete with five saloons and three restaurants was operating full blast.

The locals did not feel that "Siding 45" was a suitable name for their new town. According to the most popular version of the story, a delegation of station agents from a number of Montana's siding towns visited the Great Northern's offices in St. Paul, where they asked officials to give their towns more suitable names. They finally agreed to have a blindfolded railroad clerk spin a globe and point to random spots. So across the Hi-line today we see Glasgow, Zurich, Coburg, Saco, Savoy, Malta, Harlem, and many other places with exotic international names.

From the beginning Glasgow's progress was linked to the Great Northern Railway. Most of the town's early residents were railroad workers. When workers went on strike against the line in 1894, the populace of Glasgow supported their protest. In 1913 the Fort Peck Reservation opened up to homesteaders, and the railroad brought them in. When drought and low farm prices drove away most of the homesteaders, the land office along with three area banks closed their doors.

The Fort Peck Dam project helped Glasgow weather the 1930s depression. Two decades later another big federal project, the Glasgow Air Base, created hundreds of jobs and brought in several thousand people. Glasgow gained the base project after the local airport had served as a training area for B-17 bomber crews during the Second World War. The new base, constructed in 1955, served as home for jet fighters and B-52 bombers of the Strategic Air Command during the height of the cold war. To secure the project, Glasgow's residents raised much of the money needed to purchase land for the base site. By 1962 the base's population had swollen to more than 7,000. Area merchants came to rely on its $8 million annual payroll.

Then, late in 1964, as part of Pentagon cutbacks, the Air Force announced that it would close the base in four years. Glasgow citizens launched a "save the base" campaign, but their efforts proved futile. The bomber wing shipped out to the western Pacific for temporary duty in the skies over Vietnam. Crews returned to Glasgow just long enough to gather their families and move. In an exodus unseen since the homesteaders pulled out, some 8,000 people left the Glasgow area in just three months. As a result, Valley County lost nearly one-third of its population during the 1960s.

## The County Splitter

Today there are fifty-six counties in Montana. The Hi-line region alone is made up of thirteen counties. When Montana became a state in 1889 it contained sixteen counties. Chouteau and Dawson Counties took in all of northern Montana east of the Rockies. This proliferation of new counties was due in part to the efforts of a longtime Glasgow resident, Dan McKay.

As the homestead boom brought in thousands of new rural residents, many desired to have their seat of government closer to their farms. Progressive-era reformers also pushed to make government more accessible to its constituents. Prior to 1911 it took an act of the state legislature to create a new county. Then the legislature passed the Leighton Act, which enabled citizens to petition their county commission to force a popular election on the question of a new county.

Scottish immigrant and bricklayer Dan McKay recognized an opportunity and became a professional county-buster. An able public speaker and hobnobber, McKay mastered the county creation process. For a fee he took care of the petition filing and vigorously promoted the formation of new counties. Between 1912 and 1923, McKay was the key person behind the establishment of seven new counties on the Hi-line, as well as other counties south of the Missouri River.

In addition to his fee, McKay earned the opportunity to do the brickwork on the new county courthouses. Besides, he enjoyed a good fight. As he once remarked, "If you have never had the thrill of the hardest kind of battle that can be fought without artillery, rifles, and machine guns, you ought to get into a county-splitting fight once." By the end of the twentieth century, reformers seeking to streamline government and reduce taxes were pushing to consolidate some of Montana's smaller counties.

## FORT PECK DAM

If you follow Montana 24 for eighteen miles southeast of Glasgow, you will be driving across one of the world's largest earth-fill dams. The dam is located near the site of the nineteenth-century trading post from which it derives its name.

In 1867 Colonel Campbell Kennedy Peck and his partner, E. H. Durfee, erected a trading post on a narrow shale ledge overlooking the north bank of the Missouri River near an area known as the Big Dry. The place was an ideal landing for steamboats plying the Missouri. From behind a stockade of cottonwood logs, Durfee and Peck ran a successful trading enterprise. They used ice water and booze to lure in area tribesmen. As trade dropped off in the 1870s, the fort became the first headquarters of the Fort Peck Indian Agency for the nearby bands of Assiniboine and Sioux. In 1879, with most of the bison killed off and the Missouri eroding the banks below Fort Peck, the government decided to move the agency to Poplar.

The shale ledge, along with the fort, had long since fallen into the Missouri by October 1932, when Glasgow's mayor and two U.S. Army engineers stood on a point overlooking the area. The engineers pointed out the two high points on opposite sides of the Missouri, between which they were planning to place an earth-fill dam. "My God, man," the mayor responded, "it would cost a million dollars to build a dam across there!" The dam, five times larger than any previous project, wound up costing about 160 times the mayor's estimated amount.

Reputedly intended for flood control, Fort Peck Dam was first and foremost a work-relief project to provide jobs during the worst years of the Great Depression. By 1932 more than 900 farm families in Valley County had received some form of welfare or Red Cross assistance. President Franklin Roosevelt was well aware of the desperate plight of farmers on Montana's northern plains. He pushed for an early start on the Fort Peck project.

In late October 1933 a crew of seventy men, most of whom were former dryland farmers, began clearing brush and cutting timber in the huge area that the reservoir would flood. They worked for fifty cents an hour. For most, it was the first salary they had seen in years. Not everyone welcomed the dam. More than 100 farmers in the reservoir site along the Missouri had to sell out for depression-era prices. Many gave up rich bottomland they had been farming for decades.

By all measures the Fort Peck Dam project was unprecedented in size. Eventually the seventy-man brush-clearing crew swelled to a workforce of more than 10,000. A complex network of railroad trestles led to the dam site. They held the trains that hauled in gravel for the base toes at each end of the dam. Pile drivers pounded away day and night, driving massive steel plates into the ground below the future dam to prevent seepage.

Other workers constructed four gigantic dredges. The seven-foot cutter heads on the dredges could reach up to fifty feet below the Missouri. Here they churned up the clay, which was then piped in a slurry mix to the dam site. Electric pumps sitting on barges moved the slurry through more than twenty miles of twenty-eight-inch pipe. Electricity for dredges and pumps came from the Great Falls area via a 154-volt power line—one of the longest such lines ever strung. In all, 130 million cubic yards of earth traveled to the dam in this fashion.

Beneath the bluffs east of the river, unemployed miners from Butte burrowed deep into the Bearpaw shale. They cut four diversion tunnels, each more than a mile long and twenty-five feet in diameter. In a natural trough

*Railroad trestle leading to the Fort Peck Dam site, 1934.* —Pioneer Museum, Glasgow

*Slurry pipes begin delivering earth-fill for the Fort Peck Dam, 1934.* —Pioneer Museum, Glasgow

east of the dam, crews erected a mile-long concrete spillway equipped with sixteen electrically powered gates. The trough could hold more water than any Missouri River flood on record.

The project was by no means free of disasters. The worst came on September 22, 1938, when a 2,000-foot section of the dam suddenly slid into the reservoir. It destroyed railroad tracks, dredge lines, and equipment, and claimed the lives of at least eight men. Six bodies remain buried somewhere near the dam's east end.

### Fort Peck Shanty Towns

Besides the obvious danger of construction work, the Fort Peck workers and their families endured all variety of hazards and discomfort. Most of them lived in two-room shanties crowded into eighteen makeshift towns near the dam site. Here temperatures ranged from nearly sixty below zero in winter to more then 110 degrees in August. As one resident of Wheeler, the largest of the construction towns, observed:

> Here we are out where there is nothing but thistles, black widow spiders, ticks, rattlesnakes, and heat. We're living in pasteboard boxes and eatin' dirt, with nothing to do when we're not working but guzzle beer and wake up with a headache.

Wheeler was a place reminiscent of the wide-open Montana mining camps of an earlier era. The town's ten all-night saloons served an unlimited supply of beer and red-eye whiskey. Many featured taxi dancers, women who charged a ten-cent glass of beer for each dance. The dancer got to keep half the price of the beer. If she could hold sixty beers, which many could, she made three dollars for a night's work. A short distance from the bars other women offered alternative entertainment in a red-light district known variously as "Happy Hollow" and "the place of horizontal refreshments."

Wheeler and the dam's other construction towns drew national attention. Renowned correspondent Ernie Pyle came here on assignment from the Washington *Daily News*. The newly launched *Life* magazine sent photojournalist Margaret Bourke-White. Bourke-White's pictorial essay in the magazine's premier issue presented what the editors termed "a human document of American frontier life."

Unlike earlier frontier towns, there was very little gunplay in Wheeler. Far more citizens were killed or injured in automobile accidents involving speed and alcohol. Yet amid all the rowdiness, hundreds of families called the Fort Peck construction towns home. Here they managed to build churches and schools and to raise their children, all while putting up with heat, cold, wind, dust, and outdoor plumbing.

By its completion in 1940 an estimated 50,000 workers, mostly Montanans, had contributed to the Fort Peck project. The reservoir behind the massive dam backed up the Missouri for nearly 180 miles and held enough water to cover all of Montana at a depth of two and one-half inches. The project, however, did not bring long-term growth or prosperity to the Glasgow area. Valley County's population in 1950 was about what it had been in 1930.

## SLEEPING BUFFALO

A wood shelter between Saco and Malta houses two boulders known as the Sleeping Buffalo. According to legend, a band of hungry Indians approached the rocks thinking they were buffalo. Nearby, however, they found a herd of real buffalo and were saved from starvation.

The Sleeping Buffalo Hot Springs resort grew up when a wildcat oil driller hit hot artesian water instead. Works Progress Administration (WPA) workers then built swimming plunges. In 1988 a recreation facility called the Buffalo Barn was dedicated when daredevil Robbie Kneivel jumped over it on his motorcycle.

## MALTA

The town of Malta grew up around Siding Number 54 along the Great Northern line. Crews of James J. Hill's St. Paul, Minneapolis & Manitoba Railroad reached this point after having laid eight miles of track in a single day west of modern Saco.

Robert M. Trafton, a recent immigrant from New Brunswick, had noticed the bleaching bones of thousands of buffalo slaughtered by white hunters. Seeing that there was money to be made, Trafton gathered a party of Cree and mixed-blood Indians and set up shop near Siding 54. His makeshift work crews gathered up the bones and deposited them along the railroad right-of-way. Trains then hauled them to fertilizer plants in Minneapolis. Trafton, known as "the bone boss," made up to $18 a ton for these remains of a bygone era.

Once the railroad arrived, cattle and sheep replaced the bison on the lush grasslands surrounding Malta. Soon the Bloom Cattle Company, managed by John Survant, was running 40,000 head of cattle north of the Milk River. To the south, the Coburn Circle C outfit dominated a vast range near the Little Rocky Mountains. And to the southwest, Benjamin Daniel Phillips ran thousands of sheep on an unfenced range controlled from strategically located homestead claims. According to legend, Phillips once got rid of a rival area rancher by kicking down the man's door and informing him, "This bottom isn't big enough for both of us and I'm not leaving."

In Malta, railroad carpenter Martin Nelson put up a stockyard, and the town became a primary livestock shipping point. After months on the open range, cowboys and sheepherders drove their animals here, picked up supplies, and let off steam in the town's bars, gambling houses, and red-light district.

The savage winter of 1906–7 killed thousands of cattle and sheep and led most of the big open-range stockmen to pull out. In August 1908 the Malta *Enterprise* lamented the area's final big cattle roundup:

> This year's [roundup] will mean a complete exodus of the stock owned
> and controlled by the big outfits; for the cowman has at last surrendered
> these great broad and fertile fields to the tiller of the soil.

Throughout most of the first two decades of the twentieth century Malta, like most towns along the Hi-line, bustled with the arrival of thousands of these "tillers of the soil." The boom led Ben Phillips to spearhead the drive to create the county that today bears his name.

The 1920s drought and the following decade's depression impoverished most of the region's farmers. Area businessmen and farmers realized that the only way they could survive would be to put into production thousands of acres of the Milk River basin's irrigable land. This led to the Malta Plan, begun in 1934, whereby "qualified" dryland farmers sold their holdings to the Milk River Resettlement Project. The displaced farm families then received low-interest loans to help them get started on their new irrigated tracts.

The new farms dotted the Milk River valley from Malta to Chinook. The Bureau of Land Management leased the former dryland farms to stockmen for grazing. The Malta Plan was the largest such endeavor in the nation. The Roosevelt administration made it a blueprint for many similar resettlement schemes throughout the impoverished Midwest.

## US 191
# Malta—Missouri River
**81 miles**

### LANDUSKY

US 191 roughly follows a stagecoach route between Malta and the turn-of-the-century mining camps of Zortman and Landusky in the Little Rocky Mountains. Looking at the Little Rockies from the southeast, you can clearly see evidence of the large gold and silver mine begun in 1979 by the Pegasus Gold Corporation. The Pegasus mine is simply the latest of more than 100 years of mining activity in this region.

In August 1884 Powell "Pike" Landusky and two companions discovered placer gold along a small stream they christened Alder Creek. At six feet and 200 pounds, the short-tempered Landusky made his presence felt throughout the Missouri Breaks and the Little Rockies region for decades. Besides prospecting, Landusky made a living as a mule skinner, trapper, woodcutter for riverboats, and cowboy on the big Circle C spread just east of the Little Rockies. He particularly disliked Indians. According to one tale, he was once taken prisoner by a band of eighteen Sioux. He lost his temper and hit one of the Indians on the head with a frying pan. Such belligerence in the face of overwhelming odds convinced his captors that Landusky was a crazed man, so they let him go.

When sober, Landusky had less trouble controlling his temper. He was a responsible father of six children. Landusky and his partners tried to keep their gold discovery in the Little Rockies a secret, but once the word got out a big rush ensued. Most left empty-handed because Landusky controlled the richest claims. Landusky continued to prospect in the region, even though it was still part of the Fort Belknap Indian Reservation. A town bearing his name arose around several quartz gold mines.

*Handful of locals in Landusky, circa 1896.* —Al Lucke Collection, MSU-Northern Archives, Havre

The town of Landusky, like its namesake, acquired a reputation for drunken rowdiness and gunplay. Pike Landusky ruled over the place as postmaster and chief law enforcer. Then, late in December 1894, the three Logan brothers, also known as the Currys, entered a saloon where Landusky was drinking. Local cowboys, the Currys had been feuding with Landusky for months. They caught Landusky, whose heavy overcoat encumbered his defense, and beat him mercilessly before shooting him dead. His alleged murderer, Harvey "Kid" Curry, escaped and gained further notoriety robbing banks and trains.

## VIGILANTE JUSTICE

As US 191 nears the Missouri River, a good gravel road leads east along the river through the Charles M. Russell National Wildlife Refuge. The rugged country in this region on both sides of the river once provided hideouts for bands of men adept at stealing cattle and horses. They stole horses as far away as Wyoming and Canada and resold them in Montana. The horses they rustled in Montana were sold in Canada.

By the mid-1880s area stockmen were determined to rid the territory of this menace. Prominent pioneer rancher Granville Stuart helped organize a secretive band of cowboys led by "Floppin' Bill" Cantrell, an ex–Civil War guerilla. The mysterious group of vigilantes, known as "the Stranglers," rode swiftly and struck suddenly. They allegedly hanged thirty desperadoes in the Missouri River badlands. The ranchers were grateful for the 300 horses the Stranglers returned, and for the marked decline in rustling following the raids. Later, when a woman accused Stuart of hanging innocent men, he simply replied, "Yes, madam, and by God, I done it alone."

**Montana 66**
# US 191—Fort Belknap Agency
**50 miles**

### FORT BELKNAP RESERVATION

Montana 66 runs through the heart of the Fort Belknap Indian Reservation. It is home for members of both the Assiniboine and Gros Ventre tribes. Historically these tribes had been mortal enemies, but they have lived here in relative harmony ever since an 1888 treaty created the reservation. The Gros Ventre have tended to congregate in the area of Hays and Lodgepole, at the southern end of the reservation. Most of the Assiniboine reside closer to the Milk River near Harlem.

Until they acquired the French name *Gros Ventre*, meaning "big bellies," the Algonquian-speaking tribe was known as Ah-ah-nee-nin or "white clay people." They were united with the Arapaho tribe until that group decided to move farther south sometime in the early seventeenth century. The Gros Ventre were among the first Plains Indians to acquire horses. Along with the Blackfeet, they became some of the most skilled bison hunters of Montana's northern prairies.

Both the Gros Ventre and Blackfeet were signatories of the 1855 Stevens Treaty, but shortly after that the two tribes began fighting each other. The Blackfeet ultimately drove the Gros Ventre east to the Milk River country and into an alliance with the Assiniboine.

White traders finished building Fort Belknap in 1873. The post, located south of the Milk River near present Chinook, served as a combination trading establishment and place for area Assiniboines and Gros Ventres to receive their government annuities. By 1878, smallpox, hunger, and alcohol—all plagues of the white invasion—had reduced the Gros Ventre to fewer than a thousand people; the Assiniboine numbered 737. Their plight had not improved ten years later, when the agency moved from Fort Belknap to its current site southwest of Harlem. The reservation retained the name of the old fort.

*Students and teachers at the Fort Belknap Reservation school, circa 1897.*
—Al Lucke Collection, MSU-Northern Archives, Havre

Trade at the new agency attracted a number of white settlers, who established the town of Harlem along the Great Northern line. But the richest area of the reservation lay to the south, in the Little Rocky Mountains. Once whites discovered gold here, they began pressuring the tribes to sell off the mineral-rich portion of their reservation. Negotiators George Bird Grinnell and William Pollock threatened the Indians with suspension of their provision shipments unless they agreed to sell. Grinnell warned them, "Two years from now if you don't make any agreement with the government, you will just have to kill your cattle and then you will have to starve."

Ultimately, tribal leaders relented and agreed to sell the mountainous strip of land for $360,000. This area is still yielding silver and gold. In the late 1960s, the tribes began seeking to regain the Little Rockies, which they called the Island Mountains.

Throughout most of the years they have lived on the reservation, the Gros Ventre and Assiniboine have experienced poverty and hunger. Shortly after the turn of the century, a big irrigation project enabled many to grow wheat, alfalfa, and sugar beets. The same drought that drove so many white homesteaders off the Hi-line plagued Indian farmers as well. In addition, crooked Indian agents stole money and supplies meant for the tribes. Writing from Lodgepole in 1912, a federal farm instructor observed, "The Indians are almost destitute of clothing, bedding and have practically no farming tools to work with and I have saw [sic] all the starvation and misery I care to."

US 2

# Malta—Havre
**88 miles**

## KID CURRY

Near milepost 467, between Malta and Wagner, a historical sign marks the approximate location of Montana's most famous train robbery. On July 3, 1901, a small band of outlaws led by Harvey Logan (better known as Kid Curry) hit the Great Northern's express train. Among those allegedly riding with Curry that day were Robert Leroy Parker (aka Butch Cassidy), Harry Longabaugh (aka the Sundance Kid), and Camilla Hanks (aka Deaf Charlie).

After Curry waved a gun and ordered the engineer to stop the train, they backed it to the siding at Exeter. Here they dynamited the safe, placed $40,000 in currency along with some gold coins into canvas bags, and rode off. The banknotes proved worthless because they were unsigned.

*Alleged members of Kid Curry's gang.* Left to right: *Harry Longabaugh, aka the Sundance Kid; Billy Carver; Ben Kilpatrick; Harvey Logan (Curry); Robert Leroy Parker, aka Butch Cassidy.* —Al Lucke Collection, MSU-Northern Archives, Havre

The sheriff in Glasgow gathered a posse comprising mainly barroom loafers. They managed to steer clear of the Curry gang, but while in Landusky they made an honest attempt to drink up the town's supply of whiskey.

There are several versions of Kid Curry's fate following the Exeter train holdup. Some say he wound up in South America, where he resumed his life of crime. Others claim that he committed suicide after being severely wounded during a train heist in Parachute, Colorado. For decades, old-timers swore they spotted the Kid everywhere from Malta to Big Sandy.

Detective William Pinkerton, who for years tried to catch Curry, said, "He has not one single redeeming feature. He is the only criminal I know of who doesn't have one single good point." But some of the locals felt differently. A number of area ranch hands allegedly had assisted Curry and his gang in eluding the Glasgow posse.

# CHINOOK

Chinook was originally known as Dawes, named after an eastern politician. Later the local newspaper renamed the town Chinook because of the warm winds that melt the winter snows on Montana's prairies. Like most other Hi-line towns, Chinook prospered during the homestead boom. In 1913 area pioneer Lillie Klein Rasmussen wrote that she and her husband could see the lights of fifty-five other homestead shacks from their own place. "We have a Norwegian west of us; English, south; Irish, east; German, here; French, near; and Scotch and Mexican all around." By the time the Rasmussens abandoned their place a decade later, they could no longer see neighbors in any direction.

On the east edge of Chinook stands a 225-foot stack and the remains of a factory that helped the town weather the lean decades of the 1920s and 1930s better than most neighboring communities. In 1924 the Utah-Idaho Sugar Company decided to move its refinery to Chinook after insects infested the sugar beet fields around its facility in Yakima, Washington. More than 100 freight cars moved the factory's equipment from Yakima to Chinook. Farmers in Blaine County agreed to plant 5,000 acres in beets. They

*Utah-Idaho Sugar Company refinery, Chinook.* —Al Lucke Collection, MSU-Northern Archives, Havre

brought in some families of German ancestry from Nebraska, along with Indian workers from the nearby reservations, to help with the harvests.

During its quarter century of operation the Chinook refinery encountered a number of problems. Farmers squabbled with the company over beet prices and an unfair process of weighing their crops. During the Second World War, Mexican nationals, along with some German war prisoners, were brought in to harvest the beets. Guards with loaded rifles stood around the fields. And, for the first time, women worked in the refinery.

High labor costs along with competition from imported sugar led to the plant's shutdown in 1951. But the legacy of Chinook's sugar-refining era lives on. The local high school athletic teams proudly sport the nickname "Sugarbeeters."

## THE RANGE FIRE OF 1991

As you drive US 2 between Chinook and Havre, you pass just north of the scene of one of northern Montana's largest range fires. A late-season thunderstorm touched off a small blaze in the Bear's Paw Mountains in mid-October 1991. Wind gusts up to eighty miles an hour fanned the flames northeast through the dry grassland. By the time the fire stopped just south of Chinook, it had blackened more than 184,000 acres.

In the wake of the fire lay dead livestock, smoldering haystacks, and burned-out barns and homes. But, like many such catastrophes, the Blaine County fire brought out the best in the local residents. Volunteers came in from miles around, first to fight the flames and later to help out those who had lost all their possessions. Chinook resident Debby Gilmore summed up the feelings of many: "I'm still grateful to live in a community that supports each other in the good times and the bad."

## THE BEAR'S PAW BATTLE: FIGHT NO MORE FOREVER

Sixteen miles due south of Chinook on Montana 240 lies the site of the Bear's Paw Battle. Here, on October 5, 1877, following a bloody skirmish and a six-day siege, the Nez Perce Indians surrendered to U.S. Army forces commanded by Col. Nelson A. Miles.

By late September, when the weary Nez Perce reached the northern foothills of the Bear's Paw Range, they had already traveled about 1,800 miles in seventy-five days. Throughout their trek they had to outrace the tireless pursuit of several different contingents of U.S. Army soldiers. The flight from their homeland near the Idaho-Oregon border took them across rugged Lolo Pass, up the Bitterroot River, east into Yellowstone National

Park, and north across the Missouri River toward their ultimate goal—Canada.

The Nez Perce outfought and outmaneuvered the white military forces at every turn. Within forty miles of the Canadian border, their leader, Looking Glass, decided that they were so far ahead of the soldiers they could camp and rest. Unknown to them, 350 soldiers commanded by brash, battle-hardened Col. Miles had been moving relentlessly toward them from Fort Keogh in southeastern Montana.

On September 30, Miles and his cavalry charged into the camp at full gallop. Some 200 Nez Perce reached their horses and fled toward Canada before the soldiers hit. The others backed up to defensive positions atop bluffs overlooking the camp. As the charging soldiers approached, the Indians stood up and opened fire. The soldiers fell back, regrouped, and later charged again. But the Nez Perce held their high-ground positions, and a long siege ensued. Women and children dug caves into the side of the ravine for shelter. The men dug rifle pits.

By now Miles had lost nearly one-fifth of his command. Nez Perce casualties were just as heavy. A stiff wind blew in rain mixed with snow, and the poorly clothed, hungry Nez Perce began suffering from frostbite. During the siege, Looking Glass foolishly stood up and was killed by an enemy sharpshooter. He had been the last surviving Nez Perce military chief. Leadership then fell to Chief Joseph.

Although he was an eloquent speaker and a skilled leader, Chief Joseph was a reluctant warrior. He had argued against retreating from Idaho, but then agreed to serve as camp chief, keeping the tribe's women and children organized throughout the trek. He was not the military genius that the white commanders and later historians and mythmakers depicted him to be.

But now, with his people cold, starving, and facing insurmountable odds, the decision to surrender fell on Joseph's shoulders. In surrendering, Joseph made full use of his gifts for diplomacy and oratory. Historians continue to debate whether or not Joseph actually spoke the words credited to him in his famous surrender speech. Regardless, Joseph's haunting speech came to symbolize the noble but ultimately futile struggle of the Nez Perce and other Native American tribes:

> I am tired of fighting. Our chiefs are killed. . . . It is cold and we have no blankets. The little children are freezing to death. . . . I want to have time to look for my children and see how many of them I can find. Maybe I shall find them among the dead. Hear me, my chiefs. I am tired; my heart is sick and sad. From where the sun now stands I will fight no more forever.

Commanders Miles and Oliver O. Howard promised Joseph that his people would be allowed to return to their Idaho reservation. Instead they were shipped first to Miles' outpost on the Yellowstone, then to Fort Leavenworth, Kansas, and finally to the northwest corner of Indian territory in Oklahoma. Not until 1885 did the remnants of the tribe return to an area in Idaho, closer to their original homeland.

For years, area cowboys and civic groups from Chinook cared for the graves and other landmarks on the Bear's Paw Battle site. A good trail and some excellent interpretive signs mark the battlefield today. The walking tour takes about an hour.

## HAVRE

### *Wide Open Town*

Havre is the largest town in northern Montana. It lies on the Milk River amid some of the state's finest wheat-growing country, and it is the region's chief trade center. Havre is also a town with a past wilder than that of any other Montana city—with the possible exception of Butte.

The area was originally known as Bullhook Bottoms. In 1890 when the Great Northern tracklayers reached here, James J. Hill saw the area had a good water supply and would make an excellent division point and locomotive maintenance center. Hill did not like the name Bullhook Bottoms, however, so local dignitaries renamed it after Le Havre in France. Soon everyone was simply pronouncing the name HAV-er.

A volatile combination of railroaders, cowboys, coal miners, gamblers, prostitutes, and soldiers from nearby Fort Assinniboine gave Havre a reputation as one of the toughest towns west of the Mississippi. In January 1904 a fire wiped out five blocks in the business section. Even though many of the business owners lacked insurance, they rebuilt anyway, running their stores from steam tunnels beneath the city's streets until the more substantial brick structures above ground were completed. Underground Havre had long been home to many businesses operated by the town's sizable Asian population.

Later, in 1904 Hill and a number of his eastern friends paid an unexpected visit to Havre. As the group walked down First Street, they grew increasingly astonished as they observed first a drunk being thrown through the swinging doors of a saloon, then five men fighting with knives in a vacant lot, and finally a man flying through a barroom window just as a cowboy ran out the door shooting. Embarrassed and disgusted, Hill threatened to relocate his roundhouse unless the town reformed. Local leaders promised to get rid of the worst vices. More important, they placed the

Great Northern's dispatchers on the city's payroll so they could warn them every time Hill's railroad car was approaching, giving them time to clean up the place at least temporarily.

Permanent reform in Havre took a bit longer. In 1916 a group of Law and Order League reformers from Chicago toured the American West and pronounced Havre "incomparatively the worst" of all the towns they visited. "It is the sum total of all that is vicious and depraved parading openly without restraint," their report concluded.

The king of Havre's vice was a five-foot-two-inch, cigar-smoking extrovert, Christopher W. "Shorty" Young. Young came to Havre in a boxcar and soon amassed a small fortune as a roulette-wheel operator at a local gambling joint. He used the money to buy out the place's owner. In 1898 he erected a three-story frame building on the west end of town, which he pretentiously named the Montana European Hotel and Grill. It was more popularly known as the Honky Tonk. The building contained a saloon, dance hall, gambling parlor, prizefight arena, and vaudeville theater complete with private viewing boxes. Nearby was a less elaborate structure resembling a modern motel. Here some thirty prostitutes operated from tiny rooms called cribs.

As Havre boomed with the arrival of hundreds of homesteaders and new merchants, Young's establishment made him a rich man. But some of the newcomers brought to Montana a zeal for reform, and one of their favorite causes was prohibition. In December 1918 Montana became a dry state. Two years later prohibition became the law of the nation.

*First Street, Havre, circa 1919.* —Al Lucke Collection, MSU-Northern Archives, Havre

### Prohibition-era Havre

For Shorty Young and the two dozen or so saloon operators in Havre, prohibition simply meant new opportunities. The town's drinking establishments continued to operate despite the efforts of local reformers and state law enforcers. Whenever a raid hit the Honky Tonk, patrons threw their glasses and bottles down a pipe that led to a pile of rocks in the basement, destroying any evidence. Young and his cohorts escaped through Havre's elaborate network of underground passages. Because the saloon owners could afford the best lawyers, most prohibition cases ended in acquittals.

In addition, Young and other Hill County entrepreneurs prospered from the lucrative trade in illegally imported liquor from Canada. Throughout the late nineteenth century, traders from Montana had transported illegal whiskey into Canada. With the onset of prohibition in the United States, the illicit booze reversed its course and began flowing south.

Many impoverished dryland farmers eagerly entered the dangerous but lucrative business of rum-running. Big Hudson, Cadillac, and Oldsmobile cars made daily runs into Canada. Here they picked up all the beer and whiskey they could carry. A full load usually contained fourteen barrels of beer and five cases of whiskey. Such a load earned a profit of about $2,500.

Montana 232 between Havre and the Canadian border runs through the country once frequented by the rumrunners. But as often as not, the bootleggers avoided the roads and cut across open range and farmers' fields. Even with special gears and souped-up engines, the cars with their heavy loads of liquor often bogged down in the mud and snow. At least one borderland farmer turned a nice profit using his team of horses to pull bootleggers' cars up a steep grade.

Shotguns and automatic weapons were standard equipment for the rumrunners, and several died violent deaths. Usually they were shot by rival liquor traders. To end such cutthroat competition, Young and his cohorts formed a secret organization with a stated purpose: "To promote cordial business relations between Montana and the Canadian provinces." This organization, known as the Havre Bunch, made Havre a hub for a network of illegal liquor routes running from Canada into nearly every state in the union. Concealed beneath the streets of Havre were three grain-alcohol distilleries and Shorty Young's big brewery. Not until 1929 were federal agents able to destroy Young's beer plant and begin breaking up the Havre Bunch. They locked up fifty-two businesses in Havre because of bootlegging. Young set fire to his Honky Tonk rather than see it shut down.

The repeal of prohibition in 1933 ended one of the Hi-line's most lucrative industries. When Shorty Young died in 1944, he left a sizable estate to the needy people of Havre. Today visitors can view a small portion of Havre's colorful past with guided tours through a surviving portion of the town's underground passages, with its former business establishments and opium dens.

### Master Retailer

Not everyone who grew rich in Havre came by their fortunes through questionable means. Canadian immigrant Frank A. Buttrey arrived here shortly after the turn of the century. His first general store burned in the town's 1904 fire. But he doggedly rebuilt, and his brick building at the corner of Third Avenue and Second Street became a local landmark.

Aided by an intensely loyal group of employees, Buttrey's store gained a reputation for efficient service. When farmers from a 100-mile radius took the train to Havre to shop, the Buttrey store reimbursed their fares. At the height of the homestead boom, Buttrey's began holding ladies' fashion shows using local women for models. Only women were allowed to purchase tickets. After the first show in 1915, Buttrey noted that the corset demonstration was the most popular event.

During the lean years of the 1920s, Buttrey continued to innovate. He purchased a bus that carried shoppers from nearby Hi-line towns. He installed Montana's first radio station in his store. The station, which began broadcasting in October 1922 featured local news, weather, hog-calling

*Buttrey's department store, Havre, circa 1935.* —Al Lucke Collection, MSU-Northern Archives, Havre

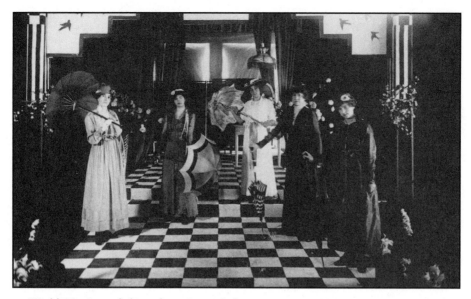

*World War I–era fashion show, Buttrey's department store, Havre.* —Al Lucke Collection, MSU-Northern Archives, Havre

contests, debates, church choirs, and school programs. As a grocer, Buttrey introduced frozen foods and carloads of fresh vegetables to Montana. Buttrey remained a loyal resident of Havre even after his retailing enterprise established stores throughout Montana.

US 87

# Havre—Fort Benton

**75 miles**

### FORT ASSINNIBOINE

Five miles southwest of Havre near milepost 107, you can look east of the highway and see the few remaining buildings of Fort Assinniboine. This military post once contained more than 100 brick buildings. Its reservation took up much of the Bear's Paw Mountains region between the Milk and Missouri Rivers. Following the surrender of the Nez Perce, the U.S. military decided it needed an additional army post in northern Montana Territory. In the spring of 1879 the 18th Infantry Regiment, stationed in Georgia, proceeded overland to Bismarck, North Dakota, where they boarded Missouri River steamboats. They marched the final forty miles north to their new home. Bricks for the barracks, stables, and other build-

*Parade ground at Fort Assinniboine, circa 1889.* —Fred Miller Collection, MSU-Northern Archives, Havre

ings were manufactured on site. The post also had its own steam plant and running water. All the two-story barracks had wide verandas running the length of the buildings.

The African American 10th Cavalry and a young lieutenant, John J. "Blackjack" Pershing, were once stationed here. Among the duties assigned this unit was the forced repatriation of a large band of Cree Indians who were deemed illegal immigrants from Canada.

A rigid castelike system separated officers from enlisted men. Soldiers here saw little action, and boredom often led to heavy drinking and desertions. Many troops from here left for Cuba after the declaration of war against Spain in 1898. Most of the units did not return to Montana, and in 1911 the War Department decided to vacate the post.

The State of Montana purchased 2,000 acres of the reservation for a big agricultural experiment station. Much of the rest of the land later became part of the Rocky Boy's Indian Reservation. Most of the buildings were razed.

### ROCKY BOY'S RESERVATION

South of Fort Assinniboine, US 87 runs along the western edge of Montana's smallest and newest Indian reservation—Rocky Boy's. This 121,000-acre reserve is home for descendants of the Chippewa and Cree Indians who for decades wandered homeless and destitute through much of Montana and southern Canada.

During the 1870s and early 1880s, both the American and Canadian governments signed treaties with most of the Great Plains tribes. A few tribes chose not to take part in these agreements. Among the more prominent were a band of Cree under Chief Big Bear and a group of Chippewa led by their chief, Stone Child, whom the whites called Rocky Boy. In 1885 during the famous Reil Rebellion, Big Bear and some of his Cree followers attacked and killed some white settlers in the Canadian outpost of Frog Lake. After surrendering to Canadian troops, Big Bear received a prison sentence. Eight of his followers were hanged.

Big Bear's son, Imassees (Little Bear), and a small band of Cree escaped to Montana, where they wandered between the Milk River country and the Flathead Reservation. American troops tried repeatedly to force the homeless Cree into Canada, but they quickly slipped back south of the border. At one meeting with the Secretary of the Interior, Imassees declared, "God was taking care of us all right until the white man came and took the responsibility off his hands."

Seeking an ally, Imassees and his people joined the Chippewa of Chief Stone Child, who had migrated into Montana from Minnesota and Wisconsin. Destitute, the two tribes camped on area cattle ranches as well as near slaughterhouses in Butte and Helena, where they scavenged for food. The government attempted to relocate them on the Blackfeet Reservation, but the Blackfeet detested the intruders and they soon parted company.

*Chief Stone Child.*
—MSU-Northern Archives, Havre

As the U.S. Army prepared to abandon the Fort Assinniboine reserve, Chiefs Imassees and Stone Child, aided by prominent Montana whites including Charles M. Russell, Frank Bird Linderman, and Great Falls newspaper editor William Bole, pressed the government to grant this land to the homeless tribes. Many residents of Havre, coveting the reservation for future settlement, loudly protested the notion.

The debate raged for several years before President Woodrow Wilson signed an executive order in 1916 setting aside 56,000 acres of Fort Assinniboine land in the foothills of the Bear's Paw Mountains for the Chippewa and Cree. Eventually the Rocky Boy's Reservation doubled in size. Poverty, overcrowding, and government neglect have plagued the reservation since its creation. Members of the two tribes frequently intermarried, but years on the reservation led many to lose their cultural identity. Recently reservation schools began teaching the children their native languages and customs.

## BIG SANDY

During the early 1880s oxen freighters hauling supplies from Coal Bank Landing on the Missouri River north to Fort Assinniboine found an ideal overnight stop in some lush hayfields amid sandy soil. The small village that arose here soon grew into a big shipping point for area cattle and sheep ranchers.

Big Sandy boomed with the influx of homesteaders beginning around 1910. Each fall hundreds of wagons lined up, laden with wheat, waiting to

*Farmers line up waiting to unload a bumper wheat crop, Big Sandy, 1926.* —Al Lucke Collection, MSU-Northern Archives, Havre

unload at the town's five big grain elevators. Flush with cash, many residents purchased automobiles. For a time Big Sandy boasted that it had more autos per family than any town in Montana. The streets got so crowded that an eight-miles-per-hour speed limit went into effect. During the dry and lean 1920s, things got less crowded after two-thirds of Big Sandy's 1,700 people left.

## LEWIS AND CLARK'S DILEMMA

Near the small community of Loma, the Marias River joins the Missouri. Rowing up the Missouri, the members of the Lewis and Clark expedition reached here on June 2, 1805. At this juncture the Missouri divided into two forks of equal size. The mud-filled stream flowing slowly from the north was the Marias River. To the south the explorers saw clearer, swifter water, which was main stem of the Missouri. Overcome with uncertainty about which fork was the Missouri, they spent the next ten days in the area.

The Indians who had told them about the Missouri's Great Falls had neglected to tell them of this fork. Lewis tentatively concluded that the south fork had to be the Missouri because its clear waters obviously came from mountain snowmelt. Most of the others in the party reached the opposite conclusion because the Marias looked more like the muddy river they had been following. Lewis worried that to make a wrong decision here "would probably so dishearten the party that it might defeat the expedition altogether."

The leaders sent exploration parties up each of the forks. Lewis found the reports of the two groups insufficient to make a decision. The following day he and Clark led separate, larger parties up the two forks. Clark's group had relatively easy going southwest up the Missouri. They observed new snow in the nearby mountains. Up the Marias, Lewis and his men had a more difficult time. Camping on open prairie, they spent a miserable night in the cold rain. The rafts they had built to float back downstream worked so poorly that they abandoned them. They alternated between wading in chest-deep water and struggling across the steep bluffs overlooking the river.

After returning to the division point nearly everyone in the party except Lewis remained convinced that the northern branch was the Missouri's main stem. Lewis named the tributary Marias after his cousin Maria Wood. He and Clark then told the men that they had decided to follow the clear southern fork, and the party moved south.

# FORT BENTON

## *The World's Innermost Port*

Nestled snug against the north bank of the Missouri River, Fort Benton was Montana's first commercial hub. For a quarter of a century beginning in 1860, the town boomed as the head of navigation on the Missouri. It earned renown as the world's innermost port. During that brief time, as historian Hiram M. Chittenden recorded, Fort Benton "saw more romance, tragedy and vigorous life than many a city a hundred times its size and ten times its age."

In 1845 Alexander Culbertson established Fort Lewis on the south side of the Missouri near the rapids, above present-day Fort Benton. Fort Lewis was one of many attempts by the American Fur Company to establish an outpost for trade with the Blackfeet tribes. After the Indians complained of the difficulty of crossing the Missouri to get to the post, Culbertson rebuilt it downstream on the north bank. On Christmas night 1850, he rechristened it Fort Benton in honor of the famous senator from Missouri, Thomas Hart Benton. Today portions of this original fort have been restored in the city park near the riverfront.

For years the remote outpost thrived as a big shipping point for buffalo robes and other furs. By the early 1860s Lt. John Mullan completed work on the 624-mile military road that linked Fort Benton to Walla Walla, Washington, across the Continental Divide on the Columbia. In 1859 the steamboat *Chippewa* ascended the Missouri as far upstream as the mouth of the Marias. From then on, riverboats began hauling goods and passengers up the Missouri to Fort Benton.

As Montana's gold camps boomed during the 1860s, the Missouri proved to be the fastest, safest artery for bringing emigrants into the territory and for transporting gold back east. Dozens of steamboats arrived and tied up at Fort Benton's docks during the brief navigation season that ran from late May to early July. The 2,400-mile trip upstream from St. Louis took nine weeks; the return voyage lasted about two.

As the town on the river blossomed, residents began calling it "the Chicago of the Plains." Certainly Fort Benton possessed Chicago's cosmopolitan flavor. As one contemporary noted:

> In the streets of the town was a throng of varied and picturesque humanity; lumbermen from Minnesota and farmers from many parts of the great valley; Confederate sympathizers from Missouri and Union men from the Western Reserve; miners from the Pacific Coast and fur traders and hunters of the vanishing Northwestern wilderness, Indians of many tribes, desperadoes and lovers of order; miners, traders, clergy-

*Levees on Front Street, Fort Benton, 1879.* —Montana Historical Society, Helena

men, speculators, land seekers, government officials—all the exuberant array of the American frontier.

In addition, early Fort Benton contained sizable populations of Chinese and African Americans. White citizens failed in an attempt to establish a separate school for black children.

With its docks piled high with trade goods of great variety and a steady parade of stagecoaches and freight teams loading and heading to the goldfields, early Fort Benton was a noisy, bustling place. Most of the town's population was transient and male. In later years even the local newspaper described early Fort Benton as "a scalp market, the home of cutthroats and horse thieves." The press referred to the few local women as "our fair but frail citizens." Local men seeking brides sometimes ran advertisements in eastern publications. As late as 1876, an editorial railed against the practice of men bathing in the river at the levee, noting that the bachelors "don't look well with their clothes off, and might be mistaken for catfish."

The owners of the steamboats tying up at Fort Benton, along with those who ran the big freight teams, reaped healthy profits. Mountain boats often cleared $50,000 in a single season. But as Montana's placer goldfields played out, Fort Benton declined in importance. Then, beginning in 1875, Fort Benton experienced a second boom era that made millionaires out of a handful of men whom historian Paul Sharp appropriately labeled "the merchant princes of Benton."

Spurring this new era of prosperity was the arrival of a large contingent of Canada's Northwest Mounted Police just north of the international border. The Mounties came west to end the rampant lawlessness and illegal bartering of liquor to Indians. Fort Benton's merchants were eager to meet the Mounties' demand for provisions.

Pioneer merchant Isaac G. Baker came up the Missouri in 1864 to serve as Pierre Chouteau's chief clerk at Fort Benton. Within a year he and a brother had established their own trading firm. Three years later Thomas C. Power arrived with a stock of goods to sell to gold seekers. He too established a flourishing business. And one year later the Conrad brothers, William, Charles, and John, arrived in Montana as refugees from their ruined family plantation in Virginia. Still in their early twenties, the Conrads began working for Isaac Baker and eventually bought out his company.

Fort Benton's merchant princes engaged in a wide variety of business enterprises, including fur trading, banking, retailing, mining, wagon freighting, and the notorious whiskey trade. Power and Baker even ran their own lines of Missouri River steamboats. For years boats with a large, block letter *P*, for Power, between the smokestacks were a familiar sight on the upper Missouri.

*Stern-wheeler* Helena *at Milk River landing. Note the block letter* P, *the logo of the Power steamboat line.*
—Haynes Foundation Collection, Montana Historical Society, Helena

Under the management of the Conrad brothers, I. G. Baker & Company became the largest mercantile firm in the northwest, with outlets on both sides of the international border. In a single year the company handled up to twenty million pounds of merchandise orders for the U.S. government alone. These merchants made Fort Benton a trade center whose business activities reached from New Orleans to the Arctic Circle.

But Fort Benton's second boom, like its first, proved short-lived. The completion of the Canadian Pacific and Northern Pacific rail lines in the early 1880s left Fort Benton isolated in the middle of the 400-mile gap between two transcontinental railroads. The Missouri River simply could not compete with railroads as a trade artery. Anticipating Fort Benton's emergence as a big railroad center, local merchants built a bridge across the Missouri and erected the luxurious three-story Grand Union Hotel. The two structures stand today as symbols of misplaced optimism.

Once Jim Hill's Great Northern Railway reached Fort Benton in the late 1880s, the town took on an appearance like that of many other communities along Montana's Hi-line. The town became a shipping center first for livestock of the open range, then for the bumper wheat harvests of Chouteau County.

Today Fort Benton is one of Montana's premier tourist attractions. Visitors can relive much of the town's rich past by walking along its restored riverfront. Fort Benton also has two of the state's finest historical museums—the Museum of the Upper Missouri and the Museum of the Northern Great Plains.

US 2
# Havre—Shelby
102 miles

## HOMESTEAD-ERA BOOMTOWNS

Looking at a map of US 2 along the Hi-line, you will see the names of a string of small towns. As you drive between each of the county seats—Shelby, Chester, Havre, and Chinook—at six- to ten-mile intervals, a grain elevator looms on the horizon. Each elevator marks a town that sprang to life along the Great Northern Railway around 1910. Each community owes its existence to the immigration of homesteaders, and each served a hinterland dotted with shacks sitting on 320-acre plots. Besides a grain elevator, each town contained a school, a land locator, several lumberyards, two or three banks, a newspaper bent on promoting growth, and several hundred people with big dreams.

*Threshing wheat, Liberty County, circa 1915.* —Liberty County Museum, Chester

On the highway between Havre and Chester, the towns of Kremlin, Gildford, Hingham, Rudyard, Inverness, and Joplin all grew up on the prairie with high aspirations. In 1910 the Kremlin newspaper, *Chancellor,* boosted the community as "the bustling, booming, growing trade center for hundreds of homesteaders who have filed on 600,000 acres of highly productive loam soil." In Gildford, the *Tribune* boasted, "Gildford is a town that can do nothing but grow and prosper." In 1911 Hingham's *Review* recorded, "This time last year there was no semblance of a town here. Now, we have a thriving town in which over twenty firms are each doing business." And the *Index* called Inverness "a town with many possibilities, situated in the heart of the greatest agricultural land in the state of Montana."

These towns and dozens like them throughout eastern Montana managed to hang on through the drought and depression decades. Each still serves an agrarian hinterland, contains a grain elevator as the economic center of town, and supports a school as the educational and social center. Other homestead-era boomtowns no longer show up on the map. One in Liberty County, called Utopia, lasted only a year.

# CHESTER

Chester outshone all the other small homestead communities between Havre and Shelby. In 1919 it defeated Joplin in an election to become the county seat of Liberty County. Chester's growth stemmed largely from the efforts of two men of divergent backgrounds and interests—Brown B. Weldy and Charles Baker.

By the time the homesteaders began arriving, Chester was already the center of a cattle and sheep empire stretching north to the rich rangeland of the Sweet Grass Hills. When the land rush hit, Fort Benton's *River Press* recorded that Chester was so filled with land seekers that "tents are being provided for temporary shelter." Also filled to overflowing was the Prairie Inn, a ramshackle hostelry owned by Brown B. Weldy. Weldy was also a land locator, merchant, postmaster, justice of the peace, and newspaper editor.

Above all else, Weldy was a booster. As one historian later noted, "B. B. Weldy seemed to be the sort of person that made you think you heard an enthusiastic brass band in the background when he spoke and the urge to fall into step was overwhelming." Weldy promoted many causes, including irrigation projects, women's suffrage, and county splitting. In one of his rare negative moods, he complained, "The people of Chester would rather buy beer than spend money boosting Chester."

Besides Weldy's Prairie Inn, Chester's other landmark building during this era of prosperity was the Chester Trading Company. This general store was already well established in 1908, when Indiana merchant Charles F. Baker and his partner Alex Wright purchased, renovated, and enlarged it. For years Baker had been traveling in covered wagons laden with winter clothing throughout the ranch country along the Canadian border. Known as "the prairie schooner merchant," Baker often spent several days on each cattle or sheep ranch selling his clothing to the families and hired hands.

A sign atop Baker and Wright's store in Chester proclaimed We Sell Everything. That remained the store's motto until it closed in 1980. The Chester Trading Company sold groceries, clothing, hardware, wagons, farm machinery, furniture, lumber, and gasoline. The store was perched on three and one-half acres of land surrounded by a high fence. Ranchers and sheepmen often penned up their animals here as they awaited shipment.

During hard times, Baker and Wright granted customers credit terms that sometimes ran several years. Following the Second World War, the store was no longer the popular community center it once had been, and Baker sold only groceries. Baker was particularly proud of his expensive tiled meat case. He once entered the store unarmed to chase away a

*Chester Trading Company store.* —Liberty County Museum, Chester

burglar. When asked why he had not taken a gun, he replied, "We might a got shootin' back and forth and hit my meat case."

## GALATA

Galata lies nearly abandoned today, but it once was a big Hi-line railroad center. David R. McGinnis, an official with the Great Northern, founded the town here because he liked the site, where a small creek ran down from the Sweet Grass Hills. He built a ten-room hotel and a number of other buildings to house businesses, but the town failed to attract settlers. McGinnis later recalled, "Cowboys, jam-full of life, coming there to ship stock, in their excess of joy of living would playfully shoot the doorknobs off the vacant buildings."

McGinnis doggedly boosted his town in newspapers throughout the Midwest, and eventually the immigrants poured in. Like many Hi-line boomtowns, Galata had large numbers of Scandinavian settlers, who celebrated Norway's independence day each year with a big lutefisk feast.

## SHELBY

### *"The Fight"*

Montana's most famous fight, other than the Battle of the Little Bighorn, took place in the tiny railroad stop of Shelby on July 4, 1923. Flush with cash from recently discovered oil fields and led by an eccentric mayor, Shelby decided to stage a heavyweight boxing match between world champion Jack Dempsey and challenger Tommy Gibbons. It was a clear case of rampant boosterism prevailing over common sense, but the event briefly put Shelby, Montana, in the national limelight.

The community of Shelby Junction arose in the early 1890s at the crossroads of the Great Northern's main line and the Great Falls & Canada Railway—a narrow gauge running north and south.

Early Shelby consisted of tents strung out on a gumbo mudflat. Great Northern official Peter P. Shelby, for whom the town had been named, allegedly remarked, "That mudhole God-forsaken place . . . never will amount to a damn."

But area ranchers and cowboys soon discovered Shelby and its bar where fifty cents bought two shots of whiskey and a decent meal. The town once made statewide news when a group of local celebrants greeted a traveling opera troupe at the train station with a demonstration of reckless gunplay. News reporters denounced the "cowardly, brutal" act, and a judge levied heavy fines on the perpetrators.

The homestead boom and subsequent discovery of oil in the Sweet Grass Hills swelled Shelby's population to just over 1,000. Among those who had acquired some fast, easy money from oil was the town's mayor, James Augustine Johnson. On a cold January night in 1923, Johnson and other businessmen were in a local saloon when the subject of staging a prize fight came up. After downing several bottles of bourbon, the group set their minds on hosting no less than a bout for the world's heavyweight title.

They persuaded Mike Collins, a fight promoter from Minneapolis, to visit their prairie hamlet located hundreds of miles from any large population center. Thinking he could dissuade the Shelby boosters, Collins told them that they would need to raise at least $100,000 and build a 40,000-seat arena. Shouting "We can do it!", Shelby's enthusiasts piled up more than $25,000 in cash onto a table. This converted Collins.

The biggest obstacle to Shelby's scheme proved to be Jack Dempsey's greedy manager, Jack "Doc" Kearns. He insisted that his fighter would need $300,000 in advance. The Shelby boosters paid Kearns a third of the amount at once and agreed to pay off the remainder in two installments before the bout. Bout promoter Loy Molumby boldly predicted that the fight would gross nearly $1.5 million.

Dempsey set up his training camp in Great Falls along the banks of the Missouri. He sparred with local challengers and purchased two purebred bulls at a livestock sale. Tommy Gibbons trained in Shelby, where he and his family lived in a rented house. He had been guaranteed no money for the fight.

*Wooden arena for the July 4, 1923, Dempsey-Gibbons fight dwarfs much of nearby Shelby.* —Marias Museum, Shelby

Meanwhile carpenters worked frantically on the huge arena. A million and a quarter board feet of pine lumber and two boxcars of nails went into the octagonal structure. As their expenses mounted, the promoters negotiated last-minute loans to make the second payment to Dempsey and his manager. This led to rumors that the fight would not take place. The special trains canceled their planned trips, making the eventual fight a financial disaster.

Without the chartered trains, only about 10,000 fans showed up. Many of them had not purchased tickets. At fight time a Great Falls reporter observed, "extending back were the great open spaces, row upon row of pine boards, shining in their newness and pathetic in emptiness."

Finally, in desperation Kearns and the promoters announced that they would let the remainder of the crowd in for ten dollars apiece. Once the fight began, those still unable to pay crashed through the gate.

The fight itself proved nearly as exciting as the circus that had preceded it. Temperatures in the arena hovered in the high nineties, which took a toll on the fighters. Gibbons gamely held on to last the entire fifteen rounds—something no previous challenger to Dempsey had managed to do. At the fight's conclusion, fans began hurling bottles, seat cushions, and other assorted objects into the ring. One correspondent noted that the place wound up looking "like a Belgian village being sacked by the Huns." Adding to the fiasco, a rainstorm turned the roads leading from Shelby into seas of mud, making things miserable for those trying to leave town.

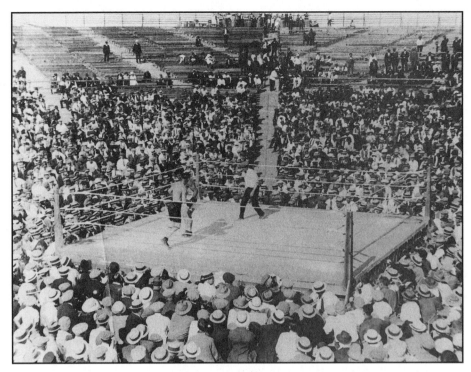

*Jack Dempsey and Tommy Gibbons square off in a less-than-packed Shelby Arena.*
—Marias Museum, Shelby

In the end the only ones who profited from Shelby's day in the sun were Jack Dempsey and his manager. Soon after the bout, banks in Shelby, Great Falls, and Joplin closed their doors—all three failures were attributed to the loans they made to promote the fight. Through it all, Mayor Johnson remained upbeat. He proudly declared, "Well, we saw a fight, didn't we?"

I-15
# Sweetgrass—Power
**96 miles**

## OIL FIELDS

Motorists on I-15 between Shelby and the Canadian border are passing through the heart of one of Montana's oldest and richest oil fields. Prior to the discovery of oil, the region had been a popular hunting ground for the Blackfeet. Later it became prime sheep-raising country.

The Sweet Grass Hills to the east consist of three large buttes made of volcanic rock. Prospectors discovered gold here in 1884, setting off a short-lived rush. All the miners were trespassing on land that still belonged to the Blackfeet. Soldiers occasionally chased the miners off, but they would return as soon as the soldiers left.

The historic Whoop-up Trail from Fort Benton ran north through this region into Canada. Later the North-Western Coal & Navigation Company of Lethbridge, Alberta, built a narrow-gauge rail line to Great Falls. The line, popularly known as "the Turkey Track," carried trains laden with coal from Lethbridge to the smelter in Great Falls.

The rail line was hastily and poorly constructed. Often workers simply set the track down on the flat prairie without bothering to grade. This led to some interesting accidents. Stiff winds sometimes blew trains from the tracks. And if this were not harrowing enough, area cowboys enjoyed riding alongside the engines and shooting over the engineer's head just to watch him duck.

At 4 A.M. on March 14, 1922, veteran wildcat oil driller Gordon Campbell hit a gusher four miles north of Kevin. Campbell had tapped into a pool of oil and gas that ran clear to the Canadian border. Soon hundreds of wooden derricks sprang up throughout a vast region that came to be known as the Kevin-Sunburst Field.

A handful of homesteaders made fortunes selling off their oil-rich holdings. The tiny farm communities of Sunburst and Sweetgrass became oil boomtowns, housing hundreds of oil-field and refinery workers and their families in wooden shacks. New towns such as Oilmont and Kevin sprang up.

Work on the oil rigs was often dangerous. Men died or lost limbs when clothing became tangled in machinery or belts. Fires broke out on the wells and often burned for days. By far the most dangerous and exciting jobs belonged to the "nitro shooters." These brave (or foolhardy) individuals used large amounts of highly explosive nitroglycerine to blast unproductive wells, hoping to free up the oil encased in nearby rocks.

Nitro shooters usually manufactured their own explosives. They put them into large copper cans with cork stoppers and hauled them to the wells in special "shooting cars"—big autos with soft springs and trunks lined with rubber. They poured the nitro into a metal shell and lowered it into the well. Here a homemade time bomb set off the charge. Sometimes the nitro went off before it got to the well. One shooter wagon exploded near Shelby, leaving a hole six feet deep. Only small fragments of the car and driver were found.

*Drillers bring in another gusher on the Kevin-Sunburst Field, 1922.* —Marias Museum, Shelby

By the mid-1980s the Kevin-Sunburst Field had produced more than $200 million worth of oil. By then, most of the wells had been converted into "stripper wells," working to extract the last precious drops from the once rich region. The area's refineries had long since gone out of business, and the oil boomtowns had reverted to their former status as farming and ranching communities.

## THE WHOOP-UP TRAIL

The section of I-15 from Canada south to Dutton passes through country once traversed by hundreds of oxen teams pulling trade wagons from Fort Benton into Canada. Most of the Whoop-up Trail has long since been plowed under, and no modern road follows its corridor. A highway marker at a rest area near milepost 319 commemorates this important nineteenth century travel route.

Among the first whites to use the trail were the whiskey traders. During the late 1860s and early 1870s, these men toted a small amount of trade goods and a large amount of liquor from Fort Benton to the area just north of the Canadian boundary. Here they established more than forty "whiskey posts"—places that consisted of a crude cabin or two. They plied their illicit trade, gaining the last remaining buffalo robes from the Blackfeet in exchange for "whoop-up bug juice."

The ingredients of this evil concoction varied. One recipe called for adding a quart of alcohol to a modest amount of Missouri River water. To add flavor, molasses, black chewing tobacco, red peppers, Jamaican ginger, strychnine, lye, or rattlesnake heads might go into the mix. Taking full advantage of the Indians' weakness for alcohol, free traders such as John J. Healy and his partner Alfred Hamilton made a fortune. As historian Paul Sharp recorded, "The free traders fought each other, resisted the monopoly of the honorable company, and tricked the Indians as they freely violated the laws of both countries in their greed for profits." And they did it with financial backing from Fort Benton's most respected merchants.

Finally, in 1874, as smallpox and alcohol pressed the Blackfeet to the verge of desolation, a contingent of Northwest Mounted Police moved in. They quickly chased off the American traders and destroyed their posts. The collapse of the whiskey trade did little harm to the merchants of Fort Benton. The Mounties needed food and provisions, which the Americans were happy to supply. Soon large trains of wagons pulled by mules and oxen began their slow, tedious runs up the Whoop-up Trail.

A bull train consisting of thirty wagons, each pulled by eight to ten teams of oxen, could carry up to a hundred tons of freight at the rate of fifteen miles a day. The mule skinners and bullwhackers had to be highly skilled to keep the wagons moving northward. Besides manipulating whips and harnesses, they employed a symphony of profanity directed at the animals. One Canadian clergyman marveled, "The fully developed bullwhacker never pauses or stutters when he is once roused to a full display of his power, but launches forth in a torrent of the fanciest expletives." Another visitor noted that he could easily determine the religious background of a mule skinner simply by listening to his swearing.

Construction of the Canadian Pacific rail line in 1883 opened up the region to eastern Canadian merchants. Steamboats and wagons proved unable to compete with the railroads, and traffic on the Whoop-up Trail came to a halt.

*Bull team in downtown Fort Benton.* —Montana Historical Society, Helena

## THE BAKER MASSACRE

South of Shelby near milepost 357, I-15 crosses the Marias River. On July 20, 1806, Meriwether Lewis and three other members of the returning expedition camped about a mile west of here. Exploring the Marias to determine its potential as a trading route, Lewis kept a sharp lookout for the Blackfeet, who he feared would steal their horses.

Nearly sixty-four years after Lewis traveled up the Marias, this stretch of river provided the backdrop for a tragic clash between whites and Native Americans. Throughout the 1860s a growing stream of prospectors and other settlers encroached on the once vast hunting ground of the Blackfeet Nation. In retaliation, small groups of Blackfeet waged guerilla-style warfare against the interlopers—stealing horses, burning homesteads, killing travelers. As alcohol did its work, tribal chiefs lost control of some of the younger warriors.

On the evening of August 17, 1869, renegades from Mountain Chief's Blackfeet band murdered prominent Helena-area rancher Malcolm Clarke. Spurred by sensationalist journalists, Montana's ranchers and miners demanded revenge and implored the U.S. military to put an end to the Blackfeet threat.

Amid the clamor, Gen. Philippe Regis de Trobriand, the commander at Fort Shaw just south of the Missouri, remained cool. "The only Indians within reach are friendly," he reported, "and nothing could be worse than to chastise them for offenses of which they are not guilty." But Gen. Philip Sheridan, in command of the army's Missouri Division (which included Montana Territory) pushed for quick, harsh retaliation. In January 1870, 200 soldiers under the command of Bvt. Col. Eugene M. Baker moved north to Fort Shaw. From Chicago Sheridan issued his orders: "If the lives and property of the citizens of Montana can best be protected by striking Mountain Chief's band of Piegans, I want them struck. Tell Baker to strike them hard!"

As the wind howled and temperatures dipped to thirty below zero, Baker led his men north. On January 23 they reached a Blackfeet encampment on the Big Bend of the Marias. They assembled that night and attacked at dawn. Just before the attack Baker's scout, Joe Kipp, warned the commander that the camp was that of the friendly Chief Heavy Runner, whom Baker had been told not to bother. Baker ordered the attack anyway. Heavy Runner emerged from his tepee, waving a paper that guaranteed his protection. He was among the first to be killed. For nearly an hour, the soldiers rained bullets into the camp. Then they set fire to the tepees.

Of the 173 Piegan Blackfeet killed, most were women and children. Many had been suffering from smallpox. Baker then confiscated the camp's horses and turned the surviving Indians, hungry and poorly clothed, into the freezing countryside to fend for themselves. Meanwhile, Mountain Chief's band, forewarned of Baker's raid, managed to escape.

When Blackfeet agent, Lt. W. A. Pease, delivered an honest assessment of the incident, eastern newspapers and members of Congress were outraged. But in Montana most whites applauded the action. The events on the Marias lent instant infamy to Eugene Baker. Following the bloody affair, Blackfeet raids on Montana settlements dropped markedly, and there were no further skirmishes between the U.S. military and the Blackfeet Nation.

## VALIER

Midway between Shelby and Conrad, Montana 44 runs fifteen miles west to Valier. Valier lies on the north shore of Lake Francis. This reservoir is part of the vast irrigation system that gave birth to the town of Valier. Originally the area was a rich hay meadow and winter grazing range for the

*Belgian immigrants arriving to take up homesteads at the irrigation project near Valier.*
—Conrad Public Library

cattle herds of a large ranch known as the Seven Block. The Conrad brothers of Fort Benton owned this 200,000-acre spread and had begun work on irrigation projects on the ranch before selling out to W. G. Cargill in 1909.

Cargill enlarged the irrigation project the Conrads began. He organized the Valier Land and Water Company and advertised widely to attract settlers. The company even constructed one of the nation's shortest independent rail lines, the Montana Western, which hauled passengers and freight twenty miles between Valier and Conrad.

When Monsignor Victor Day of Helena looked at Valier as a site for a Catholic parish, he realized that church members would need to be imported. He turned to his native Belgium to recruit colonies of settlers. Beginning in 1912, three separate groups of Belgians arrived by train and took up homesteads. Even though the land was irrigated, getting started proved difficult. One Belgian settler recalled picking more than 100 wagonloads of rocks from his new spread.

For two decades beginning in 1912, Valier also supported one of Montana's largest militia units, Company D. The company's commander, Col. James T. Stanford, spearheaded a fund-raising drive for construction of a large armory. The armory featured two big turrets and one of the best dance floors in the state until it burned down in 1929. Nearly every businessman in town served with Company D. The unit saw duty in Butte during a 1914 labor uprising and later along the Mexican border during the Pancho Villa insurrection.

# CONRAD

Sometime in the 1880s veteran frontiersman Joe Kipp told Fort Benton merchant kings William and Charles Conrad about the rich cattle range-land to be found in present Pondera County. By 1886 the Conrads were occupying large sections of land. By the turn of the century their Circle C outfit lay claim to a 200,000-acre domain called the Seven Block.

When in 1890 the narrow-gauge railroad called the Turkey Track punched through this area, the trading post of Pondera grew up along the tracks as a place for area sheep ranchers to load their wool for shipment. Eleven years later, the Great Northern purchased the railroad and converted it to standard-gauge track. The new line ran a mile west of Pondera, so the entire town moved to the tracks and renamed itself Conrad in honor of William G. Conrad. At this time the Conrad brothers also began construction of one of Montana's largest irrigation projects.

The irrigated land, as well as much of the area's unirrigated land, lured in hundreds of settlers during the Hi-line homestead rush. In 1919, as drought and depressed wheat prices began taking their toll on area farmers, Conrad became the county seat for newly formed Pondera County. The town beat out nearby Valier for the honor by employing the catchy jingle, "Oh by gum, by gee; Conrad is the place for me!" Soon, many were feeling that Conrad was *not* the place for them as bankruptcies abounded, and the local flax mill and brick kiln shut down.

Then, in 1927 E. B. Emrick struck the first gusher in what became the Pondera Oil Field. Eventually thirty rigs dotted the area. Crews stayed in tar-paper shacks at a site known as Gallup City. The shacks were usually located wherever the trucks bringing them in got stuck in the mud and dumped them off. Oil man and future Montana governor Hugo Aronson founded the town, which derived its name from his nickname, the Galloping Swede. Gallup City lacked utilities and plumbing, but cash and bootleg liquor flowed freely.

## A Casualty of Peace

Five miles north of Conrad on I-15 is the Ledger exit. A paved road runs for thirty miles east of here. Where the pavement ends, you will see looming above the wheat fields a massive concrete structure covering more than a city block. This huge unfinished edifice with six-foot-thick walls of steel and reinforced concrete is all that remains of a cold war–era boom and bust.

In March 1969 President Richard Nixon announced the decision to begin construction of the Safeguard antimissile system, designed to protect the nation's nuclear missiles. Because north-central Montana was dot-

*Concrete remains of unfinished antiballistic missile complex east of Ledger.*

ted with Minuteman missile silos, the area between Conrad and Shelby was chosen as one of the first Safeguard sites. As the future construction center, Conrad stood to gain up to 9,000 new residents and millions of dollars in federal construction money.

Throughout the early 1970s planning and construction proceeded on schedule at radar installation and missile sites between Conrad and Shelby. Defense Department grants helped ease the impact of Conrad's population boom on schools, roads, and public utilities. In March 1972 the government announced the signing of a $160 million contract with the Peter Kiewit Construction Company. Conrad's future seemed rosy.

On March 30 Conrad's *Independent-Observer* announced on page one that it had received a telegram from Washington stating that the army had chosen to disband the Safeguard missile system. But when readers turned to page sixteen for more details they saw a short note: "April Fool!" Two months later the joke became reality as President Nixon negotiated the Strategic Arms Limitation Treaty with the Soviet Union. Among its provisions was an agreement to abandon work on the Safeguard antiballistic missile (ABM). Now the *Independent-Observer* headline read, "Flash! Blast! Fallout! Residents await the aftermath of the ABM treaty."

The aftermath proved to be the total abandonment of the unfinished missile complex. In its wake were cancelled contracts, idle equipment, thousands of unemployed construction workers set to leave town, and a community embittered by the experience. Merchants who had speculated on the continued boom implored the government for compensation. A newspaper editorial called Conrad "the unwed mother of world peace."

Eventually the federal government agreed to assist in completing roads and schools, which by then were well under construction. Amid the rancor, Conrad's mayor remained calm. When asked how the pullout would affect his town, he correctly predicted, "It will put us back to the prosperous farming community we have been for fifty years. We aren't broke, we're just hurt a little."

## DUTTON

The town of Dutton is another product of the homestead boom. Norwegian-immigrant land locators George and Sam Sollid founded the town in an effort to cash in on the influx of immigrants. George Sollid proved to be a highly effective promoter. He lured hundreds of his fellow Scandinavians with ads in their newspapers. He promised them wealth and a chance to live in a new land amid neighbors who spoke their native language. The result was that 60 percent of the homesteaders settling around Dutton shared a common ethnic heritage. As each family arrived at the depot, George Sollid was there to greet them. For a $25 fee, he located and hauled them to their new farm.

Unlike most of northern Montana's land locators, who were speculators working on commission for the railroads, Sollid was independent and honest, and he stood behind the people he served. He was committed to the growth of Dutton. Even after the drought and exodus came, Sollid resold many abandoned farms and looked after much of the land people left behind.

## US 2
# Shelby—Browning
**58 miles**

## CUT BANK

Situated just east of the Blackfeet Indian Reservation, the town of Cut Bank is near the site of Montana's first hostile clash between whites and Native Americans. On July 21, 1806, after traveling up the Marias River, Meriwether Lewis and three of his men camped on Cut Bank Creek about a mile southwest of the present town. Lewis was exploring the Marias, hoping it extended northward into present Canada so that he could lay claim to the region. The next day the party moved twenty-eight miles up Cut Bank Creek, where Lewis realized that the river emerged from the southwest. Here, at a place Lewis dubbed "Camp Disappointment," the party spent four days.

The explorers then moved southeast to the Two Medicine River, where they encountered a band of eight Piegan Blackfeet. Lewis regarded this tribe as dangerous and had hoped to avoid contact with them. Still, the two groups initially got along well. They camped together near where modern Montana 358 crosses the Two Medicine. The following morning, one of the Indians tried to steal a gun. In the resulting skirmishes, Reuben Fields stabbed one of the Piegans, and Lewis later shot another. The explorers wisely fled the area. These killings left behind a legacy of animosity and distrust toward white American traders and settlers. The Piegans remained hostile for decades.

By the time construction crews for the Great Northern entered this area in 1890, smallpox and the white man's liquor had decimated the Blackfeet, who were by now confined to their present reservation. More than 300 men worked on the railroad bridge across Cut Bank Creek, where the town named for the creek arose. When the bridge was about half built it burned, so crews had to start over.

Cut Bank grew and prospered as a railroad center; it was in the middle of prime cattle and sheep country. Ranchers and their hands frequented

*Oil rig dominates the skyline of 1920s Cut Bank.* —Buster Ruetten private collection

the town's eight saloons, two-story bordello, and Chinese and Japanese restaurants. The first school was in an abandoned saloon. The school doubled as a funeral home.

Several severe winters took their toll on the area cattle herds. By 1912 much of the open range had been fenced off as homesteads. The sheep weathered the winters far better, and the area continued to export thousands of sheep and tons of wool throughout most of the twentieth century.

Ironically, Cut Bank enjoyed its greatest boom during the late 1920s and early 1930s, when most of the rest of the nation was in the depths of the Great Depression. During this period, oil drillers tapped into what proved to be one of Montana's richest oil and natural-gas fields. They hit oil at a relatively shallow level. It was of such high quality that some called it nearly pure gasoline. Soon out-of-state companies began investing in the area. A number of derricks even sprang up inside Cut Bank's city limits. The town's population grew steadily until the oil began running out in the 1970s.

## THE BLACKFEET RESERVATION

From just west of Cut Bank to the boundary of Glacier National Park, US 2 runs through the heart of the Blackfeet Indian Reservation. It is home to descendants of the Piegans, one of three bands of the Blackfeet Nation that once dominated the region east of the Rockies from eastern Saskatchewan to the Missouri River headwaters.

The Blackfeet were known for their hunting prowess, skilled horsemanship, and fighting ability. White anthropologists say that the Blackfeet moved west from their original home north of the Great Lakes sometime in the 1600s. By the time Lewis and Clark moved up the Missouri, the tribe had long since acquired horses and rifles. They were the most feared and respected tribe on Montana's northern plains.

For three decades following Meriwether Lewis's tragic encounter with Piegan hunters, only a few American fur traders ventured into the domain of the Blackfeet. The tribe enjoyed better relations with the British and Canadian traders. They resented the Americans for killing off their animal resources and for trading arms with their enemy tribes.

Eventually the Blackfeet came to value the trade goods the Americans based at Fort Union brought them in exchange for buffalo hides. In 1855 Governor Isaac Stevens negotiated the first of a series of agreements that wound up reducing the Blackfeet domain to their present reservation. Like most of the treaties that followed, the Stevens agreement promised perpetual peace, annual payments, and education in exchange for allowing whites free passage across the tribe's reduced territory.

*Flag raising ceremony, Blackfoot Agency, 1911.* —Browning High School

During the thirty years following the 1855 treaty, the Blackfeet witnessed the slaughter of their bison herds and suffered through epidemics and periods of starvation that sharply reduced their numbers. Reservation Blackfeet grew dependent on the rations delivered sporadically at the government agency. During the starvation winter of 1883–84 those rations did not arrive, and about 600 people died. Then, with James J. Hill eager to press his rails west across tribal lands, the Blackfeet negotiated the 1888 treaty in which they gave up all land east of the Marias River. Tribal members still call this the time "when we sold the Sweet Grass Hills."

Although the federal government hoped to convert the remaining Blackfeet from hunters to farmers and stock breeders, the agents they sent to do the job were bent on one task—to defraud the tribe and government. As historian William Farr recorded, "Year after year, Blackfeet agents and their administrative staffs simply stole, swindled or wasted away the annual tribal income aimed at providing for the Piegan future." And white cattle barons led by William G. Conrad consistently grazed and drove their herds illegally on tribal lands.

*Sherburne Mercantile, Browning.* —Browning High School

Despite such adversity a number of Blackfeet managed to establish profitable cattle and horse ranches. Attempts at irrigation and farming proved less successful. Throughout the twentieth century, economic progress on the reservation has been sporadic. Many Blackfeet moved away from the reservation, lured by steady jobs. With the passage of the 1934 Indian Reorganization Act, the Blackfeet became one of the first tribes to draft a constitution and create a tribal council.

### BROWNING

In 1894 the federal government decided to relocate the Blackfeet Indian Agency to a new site in the Willow Creek Valley. Joseph Kipp established the first trading post here, and others soon joined him. Among the early arrivals were J. H. Sherburne, who migrated from Indian territory (i.e. Oklahoma), where he had been a successful merchant. From his store in Browning, Sherburne purchased meat from the Indians to be shipped out on the Great Northern. He bought Indian horses to sell to area homesteaders, grubstaked miners seeking gold in present-day Glacier Park, and invested in oil wells on the reservation. Sherburne's home served as the town's first school. Today one of Browning's chief attractions is the first-rate Museum of the Plains Indian.

# Browning—Fairfield

US 89 between Browning and Choteau offers a spectacular view of the Rocky Mountain front. The road roughly parallels a portion of one of humankind's longest-used travel routes, the Old North Trail. People have traversed this corridor that skirts the Continental Divide for at least 5,000 years. Long before the first horses arrived in North America, people on foot, with their dogs pulling travois, moved along this important route.

## THE FLOOD

Between Browning and Dupuyer, the highway crosses both the Two Medicine River and Birch Creek. In June 1964 both rivers flooded and brought tragedy to residents living along them. During a thirty-hour period up to sixteen inches of rain fell on the Continental Divide. The rain combined with melting snow turned usually pristine streams into raging torrents.

Two Medicine River left its banks in the valley near where US 89 crosses. A pickup truck laden with seventeen people drove into a hole and was caught in the current. The driver escaped in time, and rescuers saved seven passengers. But nine others, ranging in age from two to eighty-four, drowned.

To the south, a flash flood shot down Birch Creek after the Swift Dam gave way. There was no time to warn residents below, and within minutes twenty people drowned. Elsewhere the floods washed out bridges, tore up miles of highway, drowned livestock, and left 400 reservation residents homeless. Still, damage would have been far worse had it not been for the rescue work carried out by members of the Blackfeet Agency. Indians and non-Indians worked together courageously to save lives.

### DUPUYER

Dupuyer is one of northern Montana's oldest communities. Traders and cattlemen began settling here in the late 1870s. The origin of the town's name is disputed. Some believe the name came from a French word meaning "delouse," so dubbed after a party of trappers came here to remove the lice from their clothing.

Julian Burd established a general store here in a small log building. His first consignment of trade goods consisted of two barrels of whiskey, a caddy of chewing tobacco, and several boxes of cigars. Early Dupuyer was a lively place, as cowboys came here to let off steam. On one occasion the rowdiness in Burd's store and saloon got out of hand. Burd later counted 200 bullet holes in the saloon and 40 more in the store. Another local drinking establishment, known as the Beaverslide, stood along the steep bank of a creek. Unruly customers were simply tossed out the back door, where they found themselves sliding down the slick bank into the creek.

## BYNUM

The Bynum area boomed in the early 1880s, when cattlemen drove their animals onto the rich grasslands. James Gibson established the famous Flying U ranch here as thousands of cattle ran free until the freezing winter of 1886–87. At first cattle from here had to be driven to Billings or Havre for shipment. Once the Great Northern extended its tracks in 1913, the newspaper in Choteau boasted: "Little Chicago was a good name for Bynum a couple months ago, but before summer is over you will hear it spoken of as greater New York." Bynum's population peaked at 225 during the homestead boom.

## CHOTEAU

The first whites to settle in the Choteau area were Jesuit priests led by Adrian Hoecken. In 1859 they founded a mission three miles south of the present town of Choteau. They abandoned it in less than a year because the Blackfeet proved hostile. Sandstone bluffs called the Priest Buttes stand south of town as a reminder of the mission. In the 1940s Methodists erected three crosses on the buttes to commemorate Easter.

For eleven years beginning in 1868, an Indian agency located about three miles north of Choteau served area Blackfeet. The town of Choteau grew up in the center of cattle and sheep country. In 1893 it became the county seat for Teton County. According to Choteau's most famous citizen, novelist A. B. Guthrie Jr., the Teton River and the county derived their name from the French word for a woman's breast. Trappers likely named the river after the nippled buttes that stand out from its shores.

## EGG MOUNTAIN

A gravel road leads west from Choteau for ten miles to a small hill known as Egg Mountain. The mountain gained its name relatively recently. In 1978 a team of fossil hunters led by Shelby native Jack Horner made some of the most significant discoveries in the history of paleontology.

The area of the find is known as the Willow Creek anticline, part of the Two Medicine formation—a thick wedge of shale and sandstone extending all along the eastern edge of the Rocky Mountains of northern Montana. The formation was laid down during the late Cretaceous period, between 72 and 84 million years ago. During that time a huge inland sea covered much of Montana. Along its shores many species of dinosaurs roamed in vast herds, similar to those of the bison who came millions of years later.

Horner entered the area after accidently coming across several bones of juvenile duck-billed dinosaurs at a rock shop in Bynum. Shop owner Marion Brandvold led him to Egg Mountain, where Horner and his fellow dinosaur diggers discovered a treasure trove. They found complete fossilized skeletons of baby dinosaurs along with numerous eggs. More important, they found evidence that dinosaurs were hatched in nests and that the parents cared for their young, bringing them food, much as birds do today.

As Horner later recalled, "In this case, we were fairly sure we had found a creature with an extraordinarily interesting new behavior, completely unknown for dinosaurs: parenting." They named the new species of dinosaur *Maiasaura*, after a Greek work meaning "good mother lizard."

Horner was far from a conventional paleontologist. One colleague labeled him "the Zen master of fossil finding." He flunked out of college seven times before learning that dyslexia was causing many of his academic problems. He spent years taking every course in paleontology he could find, without earning a degree.

Horner and his cohorts eventually found the remains of a large herd of *Maiasaura* and concluded that the animals possessed a social structure of sorts. Because the young grew so fast, the scientists also surmised that the animals were likely warm-blooded. Following the Egg Mountain digs, Jack Horner continued to pursue his fieldwork in sites scattered throughout Montana. The Nature Conservancy purchased Egg Mountain to preserve this area so rich in the remains of Montana's ancient past.

### FAIRFIELD

Fairfield arose as the central community of the Sun River Irrigation District. This homestead-era project eventually brought more than 78,000 acres under irrigation. The Milwaukee Road rail line reached here in 1916, and soon the town contained three grain elevators and a circular bandstand in the middle of Main Street. After World War I, when the agricultural depression hit, Teton County took over Fairfield's unsold lots for delinquent taxes. The town did not begin to recover until the late 1930s.

# THE CROWN OF THE CONTINENT

*To me there is but one step between this and heaven and
I'd like heaven to look like this.*

—Mrs. Ida Goos

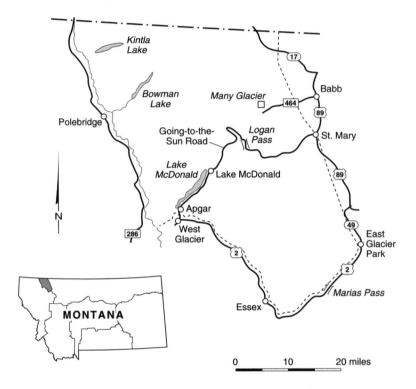

Kintla
Lake

Bowman
Lake

Many Glacier

17

Babb

464

89

Polebridge

Going-to-the-
Sun Road

Logan
Pass

St. Mary

Lake
McDonald

Lake McDonald

89

Apgar

West
Glacier

49

East
Glacier
Park

286

2

2

MONTANA

Marias Pass

Essex

N

0        10        20 miles

The mountains are breathtaking. It matters little whether the motorist approaches Glacier National Park from the south through the West Glacier entrance or from the east via East Glacier or Many Glacier. That first glimpse of the peaks and ridges of the Continental Divide near the U.S.-Canadian border causes one to pause in wonder. Even seasoned travelers who have visited Colorado with its loftier mountains or Switzerland with its better publicized scenery are taken aback by the rugged delicacy of Montana's glacierland. Writing in the 1940s, war correspondent Ernie Pyle marveled:

> I wouldn't trade one square mile of Glacier for all the other parks put together. The vast valleys that you look down into, the unbelievable great peaks . . . rising above you . . . and the tumbling white streams, and the flowers and the silent little lakes around the bend all have an isolation and a calm majesty that to me make Glacier Park more than just a place.

Geologists describe the area in more prosaic terms. To them the mountains are merely huge slabs of sedimentary rock. Around 65 million years ago, this rock broke away from its original home to the west, along the Lewis overthrust fault line, and slid eastward. Material for the rock began accumulating more than a billion years ago in a large shallow sea. Each of the distinctive colors—mostly tan, red, dark green, and light gray—represents a separate deposit of sediment from that ancient sea.

## MOTHER NATURE CARVES A WONDERLAND

All the ridges, hills, and valleys found in the park today have been sculpted into the landscape relatively recently. Sometime between 2 and 3 million years ago, the first of several great ice ages sent huge glaciers down the region's valleys. Many of the glaciers were more than a thousand feet thick. They spilled over the ridges, leaving only the highest peaks in the Rockies visible above them. After the last glaciers melted, about 10,000 years ago, they left behind the jagged ridge tops and mountain lakes that so impress modern visitors.

The few scattered glaciers found in the region today are tiny compared to their ice age predecessors. They are even much smaller than they were a century ago, when pioneer scientists first mapped them. Most geologists feel that the park's modern-day glaciers are not the remnants of the last ice age but formed much more recently.

The last of the great ice age glaciers may not quite have receded when the first people entered these mountains. In 1993 archaeologists began searching the park for artifacts of ancient man. They discovered an obsidian spear dating back 10,000 years and came across evidence of ancient hunters pursuing bighorn sheep and mountain goats at elevations as high as 7,500 feet.

## MAN ENTERS GLACIER

The modern Indian tribe most often associated with the area is the Northern Piegan band of the Blackfeet Nation. Actually, the Blackfeet were mainly bison-hunting plains dwellers who sometimes ventured into the mountains to ambush enemy tribes. But because the eastern half of Glacier Park once lay within the Blackfeet Reservation, whites came to associate the tribe with the park. Early-twentieth-century publicity efforts by the Great Northern Railway reinforced this tie: encouraged by the railroad, Blackfeet dancers entertained tourists as they disembarked from the trains. Later, renowned Montana writer James Willard Schultz assigned Blackfeet names to geographic features in the park. These names were more often the product of Schultz's imagination than of tribal tradition.

In truth, the Salish and Kutenai tribes from west of the Rocky Mountains probably entered the Glacier region much earlier and spent far more time in the area than did the Blackfeet. The Kutenai were skilled mountain hunters. They had unusually well-developed leg muscles from chasing deer, bighorn sheep, and mountain goats through the steep terrain. A branch of the Assiniboine known as the Stoney Indians also frequented the present park. The Kutenai branded this tribe the Cutthroats because of their habit of decapitating their slain enemies.

The same fear of the Blackfeet that kept other native tribes away from many of Glacier's passes also dissuaded white trappers and explorers, including Meriwether Lewis, who gazed from afar on Montana's northernmost Rockies during his return trip in 1806. Until the late nineteenth century, only a few intrepid souls ventured into the forbidding mountains. Most preferred to take safer routes both north and south of the present park.

In the 1850s whites began to enter the area with the express purpose of exploration and mapping. As part of his railway route survey, Isaac Stevens sent engineer A. W. Tinkham from the west and surveyor John Doty from the east in search of the illusive Marias Pass. Each mistook the steeper Cut Bank Pass to the north for Marias and concluded that there were no suitable railroad routes in the area. Captain John Paliser's British Northwest expedition later entered the northern reaches of present Glacier Park. That party also concluded that railroad building here would be extremely difficult. For nearly thirty years afterwards, save for an occasional prospector, the mountains lay largely undisturbed by whites.

The last two decades of the nineteenth century saw a new breed of explorers, mainly scholars and naturalists, come into Glacier. Unlike previous white visitors, who came seeking economic opportunities, these men were drawn solely by Glacier's natural wonders. The most noteworthy of these explorers, Professor Raphael Pumpelly, Dr. Lyman B. Sperry, and George Bird Grinnell, made repeated and extensive visits to the area.

All three found the glaciers themselves to be the chief lure. The men observed, mapped, and climbed on these massive ice fields. Glaciers in the park still bear the names of this trio and stand as monuments to their work.

By the early 1890s James J. Hill had completed his Great Northern transcontinental rail line. The tracks skirted the southern edge of present Glacier Park, crossing the divide at Marias Pass. The railroad brought quick changes to this land of glaciers. Settlers in the area of Belton (present West Glacier) began catering to wealthy visitors arriving on the passenger trains. Railroad publicists spread tales of the glaciers, massive waterfalls, ferocious grizzly bears, and other mysteries of nature, luring more than a few curious thrill seekers into the region.

Glacier's apparent promise of undiscovered deposits of gold and silver in its many unexplored reaches drew more whites. Prospectors illegally entered Blackfeet territory in the mountains east of the divide. Gold-hungry miners rushed in to stake their claims, but once they found that there was no mother lode to be found in this rugged backcountry, they quickly left.

## GLACIER PARK IS BORN

Army lieutenant John T. Van Orsdale was the first person to suggest that Montana's northernmost Continental Divide country should receive special protection. After completing two treks across Cut Bank Pass, he sent a letter in 1883 to Fort Benton's *River Press* that argued, "A great benefit could result to Montana if this section could be set aside as a national park."

By the turn of the century, pioneer naturalists had concurred. In 1891 Grinnell expressed the notion that the government should purchase the mountains around St. Mary Lakes and turn the region into a national park. Several years later, Sperry voiced the same sentiment regarding the Lake McDonald area.

But the idea of government protection for Glacier languished until 1906, when lumber interests began eyeing timber along the shores of Lake McDonald. This motivated some prominent Flathead Valley citizens to urge Congress to ban logging in the region and turn it into a national park.

At the same time, Grinnell was persuading officials of the Great Northern, particularly James J. Hill's son and successor, Louis, to support the idea of a national park. Hill was astute enough to see the potential for bolstering his line's tourist-passenger traffic if these unique mountains could be preserved and developed into a gigantic resort.

Soon, the diverse interests pressing for creation of Glacier National Park persuaded Montana's small congressional delegation to push through the bill that President William Howard Taft signed in 1910. But some of the measure's opponents insisted on adding amendments to protect their special interests—such as mining claims, homesteads, potential railroad routes, and reclamation projects—within the boundaries of the new park. Clearly, national park status did not guarantee preservation.

## NATURE PRESERVE OR PLAYGROUND?

Much of the history of Glacier National Park since its founding can be viewed in terms of the struggle to strike a balance between the two main reasons for its creation—to preserve the pristine natural wonders of the area and to facilitate its enjoyment by as many people as possible. During the first several decades of managing the park, federal officials leaned toward the "enjoyment" side of their mission. They cooperated with the Great Northern as it established its network of resorts, chalets, roads, and trails throughout the park.

Within five short years the Great Northern had completed most of its hotels and chalets. Through its "See America First" campaign, the railroad spent hundreds of thousands of dollars each year to promote its new playground. The line's popular new logo, featuring Rocky the mountain goat, graced every Great Northern freight car and brochure.

The Great Northern's efforts paid off. As American business boomed during the Roaring Twenties, each summer the line packed its passenger cars and its hotels with well-heeled tourists. The new National Park Service eventually came up with enough funding to build bridges, ranger stations, campgrounds, and trails. Because no highways penetrated the region, the typical tour of Glacier consisted of a train ride to Belton or East Glacier, a stay at a luxury hotel, and from several days to several weeks on horseback in the backcountry under the watchful eye of a seasoned guide. Most working-class Americans could not afford the Great Northern's gold-plated tour packages.

Once the 1930s depression hit, the railroad lost much of its wealthy clientele. By then, most visitors arrived in their Model A Fords. Such trips became more inviting once the highway across Marias Pass was completed in 1930 and the Going-to-the-Sun Road slashed through the heart of the park two years later. This new breed of tourist shunned the fancy hotels and chalets in favor of modest campgrounds developed by Civilian Conservation Corps (CCC) work crews. During the Second World War, the Park Hotel Company continued to board up and dismantle its now dilapidated chalets.

Throughout the half century since World War II, most of the important news coming out of Glacier Park has involved the growing influence of the conservation ethic. During the late 1940s, a grassroots effort thwarted an attempt by the Army Corps of Engineers to construct a dam on the North Fork of the Flathead River. The proposed reservoir would have inundated much of the park's west side.

During the early 1960s the park's ambitious "Mission 66" development plan came under heavy fire from environmentalists bent on protecting the area from further man-made "improvements." In 1974 the United Nations designated Glacier one of its World Biosphere Reserves. The park then became a study zone helping to determine the extent to which mankind is altering the planet's natural ecology. The park has come a long way

*First tour buses across Logan Pass on the new Going-to-the-Sun Road, July 1933.*
—Glacier National Park

since the early days, when elk and moose were slaughtered to use their meat as bear bait and extensive horse trails and campgrounds demolished fragile alpine flora.

US 2
# East Glacier Park—West Glacier
**56 miles**

## LOUIS HILL

"The work is so important that I am loath to intrust the development to anybody but myself." Thus announced Louis W. Hill late in 1911, when he declared his semiofficial retirement as president of the Great Northern Railway so as to devote all his time to making the newly created Glacier Park the "playground of the northwest."

The Glacier Park Hotel at East Glacier Park stands today as the most striking landmark to Hill's energy and devotion. Like his father, James J. Hill, Louis Hill recognized the importance of the bottom line. Just prior to launching the five-year flurry of hotel construction and road building, he observed, "Every passenger that goes to the national parks, wherever he may be, represents practically a net earning."

But in other ways Louis Hill stood in contrast to his illustrious father. He was more interested in the public relations end of the business than in the nuts and bolts of building and running the railroad. Sporting a dark red beard and pince-nez glasses, the dapper Hill was a product of America's finest schools. He inherited his father's managerial skills but was much more adept as a public speaker.

Louis Hill supported the move to create Glacier National Park, then went to work to develop it. He personally selected the sites and supervised the construction of the large hotels at East Glacier and Many Glacier and the string of mountain chalets throughout the new park. All were in the Swiss motif as he had specified.

### Glacier Park Hotel

Hill's first big project was the Glacier Park Hotel. The railroad purchased 160 acres of Blackfeet reservation land just east of the park at Midvale. In 1912 crews built a train depot and the place was renamed East Glacier Station. Tourists had to be housed in tents near the depot while Hill's workers labored on the enormous new hotel. Hill brought in two architects from Chicago and directed them to design the building after the large log structure that had housed the forestry display at the 1912 Portland Exposition.

*Glacier Park Hotel nearing completion.* —Glacier National Park

That spring the first of fifty carloads of huge Douglas fir logs began arriving from Washington and Oregon. The largest of these, which formed the support pillars in the lobby, were nearly six feet in diameter and fifty-two feet long. Workers left the bark on the logs as they hoisted them upright to frame the central lounge. To this day uninitiated visitors ask hotel employees if the trees supporting the lobby are "still alive."

The 150 masons and carpenters finished the structure in just over a year. Built at a cost of more than a half million dollars, the hotel included a dining room, plunge pool, hospital, fire station, and music room, complete with modern steam heat and telephones. An annex built a year later gave the place a capacity for 400 guests.

Ever the publicist, Hill staged an elaborate gala to open the new hotel in June 1913. More than 600 veteran employees of the Great Northern attended a banquet that also celebrated James J. Hill's seventy-fifth birthday. The Blackfeet pitched their tepees on the grounds of what they were by now calling "the big tree lodge." Trainloads of excursionists came to witness the tribal ceremonies and dances. The only mishap occurred when old Chief Heavy Breast, dancing into the early hours of the morning, suffered a heart attack and died.

### More Great Northern Projects

For Louis Hill, completion of the big hotel was merely another step in his grand scheme for the park. He supervised construction of the first road on the park's east side. It ran from East Glacier Station to Swiftcurrent Lake, the site of the new Many Glacier Hotel. He initiated a program to build and improve scenic trails so that hikers and horseback riders could penetrate the interior of the new park.

To make wilderness excursions as comfortable as possible, the Great Northern erected tent camps and Swiss-style alpine chalets at strategic points throughout the park. Hill located his chalets with an eye toward their scenic backdrop. As a result construction proved extremely difficult. At the Going-to-the-Sun chalet complex at the upper end of the main St. Mary Lake, logs had to be rafted up the lake and then hoisted up a cliff. The two-story chalet at Gunsight Lake sat in the middle of an avalanche chute; it did not survive its second winter.

Even as he was completing his crash building program, Hill launched a formidable national publicity campaign to bring in visitors. He hired an official park photographer. He accompanied the delegations of Blackfeet, whom he dubbed "the Glacier Park Tribe," as they toured the country in a special train that stopped everywhere from the White House to New Orleans at Mardi Gras. He established a lecture bureau and chartered expense-paid tours for writers and travelogue speakers, who were then expected to help sell the new wonderland.

And in his endeavors, Hill usually enjoyed the cooperation of the park's managers. The Park Service allowed Hill's employees to mine coal, graze livestock, sell liquor, string wires, install hydroelectric plants, and cut all the timber they needed to construct the hotels and chalets—all within the boundaries of the park. As historian Michael Ober observed, "It was a case of an impoverished Interior Department issuing a blank check to a wealthy railroad for the pioneer development of a national park."

For the first fifteen years after their construction, the chalets, along with the big hotels at East Glacier and Many Glacier, prospered. When Louis Hill envisioned his network of visitor facilities in Glacier, he scarcely could have foreseen a not-too-distant future when his railroad would be struggling to jettison the entire operation. The chalets were the first to fall victim to the Great Depression and the automobile boom. The Great Northern closed them down one by one and eventually demolished the log structures at St. Mary, Cut Bank, and Going-to-the-Sun.

The stone chalets at Sperry and Granite Park fared better. In 1954 the Great Northern donated the two chalets to the National Park Service. They continued to take in guests until 1992, when the Park Service closed them because of antiquated sewage disposal systems. Beginning in 1994, a renovation program funded by federal and privately raised dollars began rehabilitating the two buildings. As in days of old, work crews laboring in wilderness isolation received supplies by mule train.

## Marias Pass

Driving over Marias Pass, most motorists do not realize they are crossing the Continental Divide. At just over 5,200 feet, the pass is among the lowest in the entire Rocky Mountain chain. It is also difficult to believe that such an ideal passage with its gentle slopes lay largely unused until the Great Northern laid rails across it in 1891.

Until the Blackfeet moved south from Canada, Marias Pass was a favorite route of the Salish and Kutenai as they trekked east to hunt buffalo. But too many ambushes by the Blackfeet led the western tribes to abandon Marias for safer but more difficult crossings to the north. Fear of the Blackfeet also probably led many of the Indian guides to steer the first white explorers away from Marias. In 1854 both of railroad speculator Isaac Stevens's survey parties managed to miss this most obvious route.

The Indian trail across the pass was mostly overgrown and blocked by fallen timber by the late 1880s, when James Hill's St. Paul, Minneapolis & Manitoba Railroad reached the Havre area, and "the Empire Builder" contemplated his final push west. By 1889 Hill needed to find an easy northern passage across the Rockies so badly that he sent his top surveyor, John F. Stevens, to search for the elusive route in the snows of December.

In assigning Stevens this daunting task, Hill could not have found a more qualified person. By the time the Great Northern hired him in 1889, the powerfully built, thirty-six-year-old Stevens had already survived attack by Indians and near-death by fever in Mexico and had supervised construction of a railroad through 400 miles of swamp and pine forests in Michigan's Upper Peninsula. As Stevens later remarked, "I became tough and hard physically . . . I learned to adapt myself under the most primitive conditions."

When the Great Northern's chief engineer asked Stevens if he had the nerve to enter the mountains in the dead of winter, Stevens recalled: "At that time my middle name was 'nerve.'. . . I at once accepted the invitation." Stevens and a small group set out from Fort Assinniboine. They soon encountered a succession of blizzards. Once they reached the Blackfeet Agency near the foot of the Rockies, they learned that the horses could no longer travel through such deep mountain snow. Stevens then procured the help of a Flathead named Coonsah. The pair constructed crude snowshoes and set off on foot, taking only what food and blankets they could carry on their backs.

Trudging through snow up to four feet deep, they reached an area called False Summit, where Coonsah refused to go farther. Stevens pressed on alone. After several aborted attempts, he walked directly into Marias Pass. He continued west down Bear Creek until he was certain that he was looking into the Pacific watershed. He then struggled back to the summit, where conditions forced him to spend the night. Unable to keep a fire going in the extreme cold, he tramped out a track in the snow and walked back and forth to keep from freezing.

The next morning Stevens found Coonsah nearly frozen to death but managed to get him back to civilization. At the Blackfeet agency, he learned that the temperature had reached nearly forty below zero during his nightlong ordeal atop Marias Summit.

Stevens's "discovery" of Marias Pass cut more than 100 miles from the Great Northern's line to the West Coast and saved the railroad the possible necessity of blasting a tunnel through the Rockies. Stevens worked for James Hill for another fourteen years and later explored the pass through the Cascades that eventually bore his name. A few years afterward, President Theodore Roosevelt assigned Stevens to supervise an even greater engineering challenge—construction of the canal across the Isthmus of Panama.

*John Stevens at the dedication of his statue atop Marias Pass, 1925.*
—Glacier National Park

In 1925 Stevens returned to the scene of his historic stay atop Marias Pass to help dedicate a bronze statue of himself. For years this statue stood atop a promontory overlooking the Great Northern tracks. In 1989 workers moved it to its present location near the highway, after a sculptor repaired thirty-two vandal-inflicted bullet holes.

Today the Stevens statue stands next to the other long-familiar Marias pass monument—a miniature likeness of the Washington Monument. On completion of the Theodore Roosevelt Highway across Marias Pass in 1930, workers erected this sixty-foot-tall monument to the highway's namesake. For years it stood in the middle of the highway, splitting the lanes of traffic and looming as an rude awakening to motorists crossing the pass on foggy nights. Because it posed such a safety hazard, crews finally moved it to its present site, just off the north edge of the highway at the Marias Pass summit.

## MCCARTHYVILLE

Within months of John Stevens's walk across Marias Pass, crews for the Great Northern began surveying and building tote roads in preparation for tracklaying. Cutting the grade proved hazardous work. Wagons sometimes had to be lowered down the steepest inclines using ropes wrapped around trees. It was impossible to bring heavy machinery into more remote areas, so workers removed dirt in large trays sliding along greased poles.

Five miles west of the summit of the pass, the construction camp of McCarthyville became the center of activity. One visitor termed the place "a seething Sodom of wickedness."

Shootings were common. In 1892 melting spring snows revealed nine bodies—the remains of confrontations during the previous winter. One local gambler, "Slippery Bill" Morrison, managed to preserve his winnings by hiding the money inside the railroad spike keg that he used for a stool at the card table. Like most railroad construction camps, McCarthyville was deserted once the line was completed.

## ESSEX

Unlike McCarthyville, the railroad town of Essex has survived as the home for crews of helper engines needed to pull trains across Marias Pass. Because snowfall here averages more than 240 inches each winter, workers are always busy keeping the tracks open. Near the town's rail yard stands the picturesque Isaak Walton Inn. When they built the hotel during the late 1930s to house railroad personnel, investors hoped it would also become a popular lodge for Glacier Park tourists. This plan never materialized, but the place eventually became the center of a growing cross-country skiing business, with trails leading into Glacier and the nearby Great Bear Wilderness Area.

Crews from Essex have frequently been called out to help clear away the wreckage of trains swept down the steep slopes of Marias Pass by avalanches. Several times trains laden with grain have tumbled off the track, and their dumped cargo has produced an instant feeding ground for local bears. In 1929 an avalanche hit the Great Northern's fast-mail express just after the engine and first car pulled into a tunnel. The slide buried six cars and killed a mail clerk, a track walker, and a section foreman. More crewmen would have perished had they not been sitting in the first car playing cards when the disaster struck.

## THE FLOOD OF 1964

For many years the only uncompleted section of US 2 was the stretch across Marias Pass. This situation left the park virtually cut in half and forced the Park Service to maintain a separate subheadquarters and maintenance facility at East Glacier. Until completion of the road in 1930, auto drivers wishing to cross the Continental Divide had to load their vehicles onto a Great Northern flatcar at either East Glacier or Belton and then board a passenger train. The railroad charged five fares to move two people and their vehicle across the divide.

In 1964 area residents got to revisit this era of inconvenience when one of the most devastating floods in Montana history washed out large sections of the highway, leaving them stranded. Record rainfall and melting snow turned streams throughout the park into raging torrents. Washouts left freight trains marooned at Essex. At Nyack, ten miles east of West Glacier, the flooding Flathead River formed a lake that poured rocks and mud onto the highway, forcing an aerial evacuation of residents.

Eventually the fifty people stranded at Essex set up their own shuttle to West Glacier. The operation required seven vehicle transfers—one at each place where the flood had cut the highway. Later, a special bus equipped to travel on both highways and railroad tracks transported the Great Northern crews from Essex back to Whitefish. For weeks following the flood, both the rail line and highway south of Glacier Park remained closed. The Going-to-the-Sun Road through the center of the park became a temporary US 2. It took several summers to repair all the road damage.

## WHITE CROSSES

Approximately fifteen miles southeast of West Glacier, between mileposts 173 and 174, just off the north side of US 2, stands a marker holding nine identical white crosses. This monument of sorts marks the site of the worst traffic accident in Montana history. Early on a Saturday evening in mid-January, 1984, a school bus carrying members of the Whitefish High School wrestling team, together with their coaches and cheerleaders, slammed head-on into an empty fuel tanker truck that had just jackknifed on the icy road. Nine victims died on impact. Some of the wrestlers carried injured peers out the rear emergency exit just before the bus exploded into flames.

The accident was a stark reminder of the hazards braved by thousands of Montana's young people every weekend, as scores of teams set out to travel great distances over treacherous roads. Athletic and other student activity trips of 300 miles or more are a common occurrence in this large, sparsely populated state.

As anyone who has driven Montana's roads knows, the stand of white crosses here is not the only example of such markers. From mountains to plains, these virtually identical crosses appear as silent little reminders for motorists to exercise caution. The crosses began in 1952 as a brainchild of Floyd Eaheart, a member of Missoula's Hellgate American Legion Post. After a tragic Labor Day weekend during which six motorists were killed, members of Missoula's legion secured permission from the Montana Highway Commission to begin placing the white crosses at the scenes of fatal wrecks.

It was not long before every one of Montana's approximately 130 Legion posts was manufacturing and placing crosses along the highways. Although each cross was anchored in a five-gallon bucket of concrete, they were sometimes crushed by snowplows. Two crosses on a curve south of Shelby were demolished when a car smashed through them. Shortly after the accident, three crosses marked the scene. Over the years friends and relatives of accident victims have reacted to the crosses in different ways. Some tore them down; others decorated them with flowers or wreaths.

When the program was in its infancy, legion members faithfully erected new crosses and repainted the old ones. Today many of the crosses have fallen into disrepair, as legion posts have neglected or discontinued the program. The Highway Department has not allowed the crosses to be placed along the interstates. In many areas of the state, Montana's roadside crosses appear headed toward the same destiny as the once common Burma-Shave signs.

# West Glacier—Kintla Lake

## THE RED BENCH FIRE

Compared to the rest of Glacier Park, the west side, bounded by the North Fork of the Flathead River, experiences light visitor use. Traffic is moderate on the unpaved roads that wind along both sides of the river. Motorists nearing Polebridge at the park's northwestern entrance drive through miles of blackened forest—the result of the Red Bench fire.

The lightning-caused blaze ripped through a huge area of the North Fork Valley. Because the fire took place in 1988, it was overshadowed by the more destructive fires in Yellowstone Park that year. Certainly residents of Polebridge did not disregard the fire. Once the flames had jumped the North Fork River on September 7, they shot across the area known as Big Prairie and roared east toward Bowman Lake. More than 1,600 firefighters from as far away as Alaska and Florida waged a frustrating battle.

A caravan of cars and pickups evacuated civilians from Polebridge. As the flames neared town, a crew commander remarked, "We could have the Fifth Army and we wouldn't stop it." Using a tanker truck, firefighters hosed down the historic Mercantile and the saloon next door just before the blaze broke through the bordering woods. The two buildings some-how survived, but twenty-five other structures in the area—along with the old pole bridge across the North Fork—succumbed to the flames. Finally,

*Crews at Polebridge during the September 1988 Red Bench fire.* —Glacier National Park

an early-season storm dumped six inches of snow in the area, dowsing the worst of the flames.

Red Bench proved to be one of the largest fires in Glacier Park's history. Three-quarters of the 37,000 burned acres lay within park boundaries. It also claimed the life of an Idaho firefighter.

Prior to around 1970 park rangers and historians generally judged forest fires harshly. They frequently used words like "holocaust" and "cataclysm" in describing such events. No firefighting method was judged too rash as long as it helped halt the destruction. In 1967 for example, crews employed bulldozers to dig a massive fire line around a park blaze. The mess they made will long outlast the damage caused by the fire. But by the time of the Red Bench fire, management officials regarded forest fires as vital natural occurrences that renewed forests by removing damaged old growth and years of accumulated deadfall, recycling their nutrients into the soil. As long as they posed no great threat to human life or structures, park officials allowed many fires to burn until Mother Nature quelled them. Today's visitors are witnessing the birth of a new forest in the section of the park burned over by the Red Bench fire.

## SKYLAND CAMP

In the fall of 1921 Col. L. R. Gignilliat, the superintendent of Indiana's Culver Military Academy, visited Glacier Park, seeking a suitable location for a summer camp for his school's cadets. He pronounced the park's more developed east side "too tame" and decided to locate his camp along the southwest shore of Bowman Lake. Park officials at that time were still courting private developers to improve Glacier for tourists, so they backed Gignilliat's scheme.

The next year workers erected a mess hall, a chalet, and other buildings at what was dubbed Skyland. Tourists used the facilities whenever the cadets were not there. Conditions were spartan. Only a crude wagon road reached the area. When camp was in session, each cadet was assigned a horse, which he took to even more remote branch camps on the Kintla Lakes. Besides horsemanship, the young campers studied orienteering, wildlife, plant life, and geology.

By 1924 Gignilliat had secured a five-year use contract from the Park Service. He then returned to Culver, leaving his son Fred to manage Skyland. Problems quickly followed. Fred Gignilliat allowed the camp to languish while he took a guide position with the Glacier Park Saddle Horse Company. In 1925 the park superintendent expelled young Gignilliat from the park after he and several fellow guides engaged in a "drunken carousel" at the Waterton Lake Chalet.

*Skyland Camp headquarters on Bowman Lake.* —Glacier National Park

With Fred denied access to the park, his older brother Leigh, along with a companion, Richard Nesbit, took over the camp. Unfortunately, Leigh Gignilliat was no more responsible than his brother. He and Nesbit became infamous visitors to Belton and points south as they shot by in their "high powered Packard roadster." The pair bounced checks and reneged on their obligation to pay the required concession fee to the park. Glacier's superintendent concluded that Skyland had devolved into "a convenient summer camp for the Gignilliat family and their friends."

Heeding warnings from park officials, Colonel Gignilliat sent Culver's Capt. M. W. Armstrong to try to clean up the mess left by his sons. Armstrong opened Skyland Camp as a tourist facility in 1926, but forest fires forced an early closure. The following year, Armstrong tried again to revive the camp, but visiting tourists quickly grew tired of the captain and his harsh military regimen. The camp continued to lose money until 1929, when Gignilliat's contract with the National Park Service expired.

During the next decade the facility remained unused as Gignilliat vainly sought a buyer. In 1940 park officials informed him of their plans to dismantle the camp. That summer, crews razed all the structures except the chalet known as Rainbow Lodge. The enraged colonel blamed the Park Service for the camp's failure because it had never constructed a decent road to Bowman Lake. Until his death, he clung to the hope that his wilderness camp for boys could somehow be restored. Today a campground occupies the site of Skyland Camp. The only reminder of this unique endeavor by the man from Indiana is the Rainbow Lodge, which now serves as the area ranger station.

## BLACK GOLD

For visitors who navigate the stretch of winding dirt road to Lower Kintla Lake and then hike the length of the lake's north shore, it is difficult to imagine that they are approaching the site of Montana's first oil well. The thought of Montana oil usually conjures up images of derricks and pumps standing before a backdrop of desolate prairie country. But there is also oil beneath the mountains of northwestern Montana.

Knowledge of oil seeps in the area was common among the Native Americans and early fur traders. The arrival of the Great Northern Railway stirred renewed interest in the valley of the Flathead River's North Fork. Homesteaders began staking claims. Horse thieves and opium smugglers moved back and forth between the railroad camps and the Canadian border. And hunters began shooting bears whose hides reeked with the odor of kerosene. Soon prospectors found the oil-coated pool where the bears had been wallowing, near Kintla Lakes.

Development of the Kintla Lakes oil resource required big outside capital. In 1900 a group of businessmen formed the Butte Oil Company. To get the necessary equipment into this wilderness, the company cut a crude road from the south end of Lake McDonald to the foot of lower Kintla Lake. Others staked claims along the North Fork from Belton to the Canadian border. One speculator gushed, "My firm conviction is that the Flathead field will prove the most profitable new oil territory opened in twenty years."

Drilling equipment came by rail to Belton. From there it took five teams of horses and twenty men plagued by biting horseflies to haul it to the head of lower Kintla Lake. Here a sawmill cut lumber for the drilling rig. Other supplies reached the area via rafts on the lake or by sleds once the lake froze over. By late November 1891, workers had completed the eighty-foot-tall derrick.

For seven months crews at Kintla drilled through the thick rock until their drill bit snapped off at the 1,000-foot depth, causing a long delay. Meanwhile the other oil boomers failed to develop their claims, and interest in the region rapidly subsided. During the 1902 winter, disaster struck the well. At the 1,400-foot depth, drillers struck not oil, but highly flammable gas. The gas accidently ignited and the ensuing fire leveled the derrick, cabins, and sawmill.

The Butte Oil Company lost its entire $40,000 investment. The company made feeble efforts to restart the operation, but no other well was ever drilled in the region. Shortly after the creation of Glacier National Park, government officials worked to improve the crude road into the oil country, but it remains today one of the roughest auto routes through the park.

During the early 1970s a new generation of oil men began to look anew at the Glacier Park region. They sank wells on the Blackfeet Indian Reservation just east of the park and near the western border in the Kintla Lakes vicinity. Others hoped to search for oil inside the park itself. Park officials, as they had for sixty years, opposed such potential "development." If an oil bonanza lies beneath the ancient rocks of Glacier Park, it is likely to stay there for some time to come.

Going-to-the-Sun Road
# West Glacier—St. Mary
**50 miles**

## A CHALLENGING ROAD

Throughout history people have built roads primarily to make getting from one place to another easier and to shorten the time of travel. The Going-to-the-Sun Road is an exception. It is neither a convenient nor a quick route. Its main reason for being is to enable as many people as possible to enjoy the scenic wonders of Glacier National Park.

Today's critics of the highway feel that it is an ecological disaster. Supporters view it as a marvel of engineering. Both groups are at least partially right. It is also a challenge to motorists. Even experienced mountain drivers can feel their stomachs tighten as they negotiate the steep, narrow passage to the 6,646-foot summit of Logan Pass.

But it can be dangerous to feel too intimidated. In June 1962 a middle-aged couple from Canada fell victim to one of the most bizarre accidents on this or any highway. As her husband drove up the steep ascent, Alice Jean Leckie grew so frightened that she leaped into the backseat and lay face down. Near the Garden Wall a huge rock tore loose, shot across the roadway and flew into the car's left rear door, killing Mrs. Leckie instantly. It took a front-end loader to remove the boulder.

This thrilling route did not spring up overnight. From the time Glacier became a national park, government officials and others envisioned constructing a road across one of its scenic passes. Glacier's first superintendent, William Logan, ran three miles of road through the swamp between Belton and Apgar. A survey in 1914 suggested that Logan Pass provided the most scenic and practical route across the park. By 1924 Logan's original road had been extended along the shore of Lake McDonald as far as Avalanche Creek.

The Park Service then resurveyed the unfinished portion of the proposed road. Before surveyors could even begin working each day, they had to walk several miles and climb more than 2,500 feet. They then hacked through thick brush and tiptoed along the edges of high cliffs.

After the survey, engineering crews worked along the same cliffs. When the field engineer asked his chief for a pay increase for his men because of the dangerous conditions, the boss replied that engineers were trained to work in such places. Later, the chief made an inspection tour. As the field engineer led his boss across the cliffs, he turned around to notice him clinging to the wall with his knees trembling. He walked back and quietly asked the chief, "How about that raise for the boys?" The reply came instantly: "Give them anything you want!"

*Stonemasons work on a retaining wall for the Going-to-the-Sun Road.*
—Glacier National Park

After the surveyors left, it took three full seasons for contractors to complete the westside road to the top of Logan Pass. At its peak, the project required 300 workers. The rugged topography dictated the construction methods. Trains of pack animals hauled in most of the supplies. A good horse or mule could carry three fifty-pound boxes of dynamite.

Dynamite proved to be the most widely used commodity. Cutting through the Garden Wall section required about a pound of explosives for each cubic yard of material removed. Workers dangling from ropes along the cliffs planted the dynamite and powder charges. To prevent sparks, which could set off the volatile powder prematurely, they wore heavy wool socks over their hobnailed boots.

Until the road-cut was wide enough for motor vehicles, horses pulled in sleds loaded with compressors, culverts, and other heavy equipment. Small, track-mounted gas locomotives hauled away cars filled with debris. Eventually steam shovels, Caterpillar tractors, and Model T Ford dump trucks finished the job. A reporter for the *New York Times* witnessed a tractor slip off the edge and tumble 200 feet down the mountain, only to return to the roadway on its own power.

Each spring, snowslides delayed construction. An occasional forest fire forced the men to abandon the project to battle the blaze. Hungry bears were a constant problem. Workers in the field had to hang their lunches high in trees. In the camps, food had to be stored in specially designed buildings mounted on stilts studded with nails. Porcupines, with their unique appetites, gnawed at the tires of construction equipment. And once, a buck deer wandered into a blasting zone, only to receive a last-second reprieve when it became entangled and tore loose the wires leading to the dynamite.

Hard hats were neither required nor in vogue. A few workers wore surplus World War I army helmets, but most chose to work bareheaded among the frequently falling rocks. Still, only one worker died as the result of being struck by a rock. The project's other two casualties, not surprisingly, were the results of falls.

By the 1929 season motorists could reach the top of Logan Pass from the west side, but the road was far from complete. The project east of the divide proved extremely difficult, because it required a 408-foot tunnel through Mount Piegan. Workers could not get heavy equipment to the tunnel site, so they lugged most of the debris out using handcarts. They hand-carried the heavy boxes of dynamite, first down a steep switchback trail and then down a rope ladder dangling over a cliff. A misstep could mean a fall of more than 1,000 feet. Small wonder that a few men upon

*Dedication ceremonies for Going-to-the-Sun Road, July 15, 1933.* —Glacier National Park

reaching the ladder stared at it briefly, turned around, set down the dynamite, and resigned.

On July 15, 1933, the road officially opened to through traffic. Park naturalist George C. Ruhle, who named the highway Going-to-the-Sun, organized an impressive dedication ceremony. Nearly 5,000 people gathered atop Logan Pass and witnessed the Piegan chiefs pass a pipe of peace to the chiefs of their ancient enemies, the Salish and Kutenai.

Almost overnight the road changed the essence of the Glacier Park experience. When the project began in 1925, 40,000 people visited the park; by 1936 the number had reached 210,000. With a brief hiatus during World War II, the numbers climbed steadily until by 1969 more than one million people were touring the park annually. An estimated 95 percent of them confined their time in Glacier to the short drive across Going-to-the-Sun Road. Ruhle complained, "At first this was primarily a walking and horseback-riding park. . . . Now they skim through it in an automobile and they cling to it like a shipwrecked sailor to a raft."

## WEST GLACIER AND LAKE McDONALD

Nearly twenty years before Louis Hill and the Great Northern launched their big push to install visitor accommodations on the east side of Glacier Park, a number of small entrepreneurs established lodging facilities, guide services, and a crude transportation corridor between Belton and the north end of Lake McDonald. Belton, whose name was changed to West Glacier in 1949, began catering to tourists as soon as the Great Northern's tracks reached the place.

In 1893 Edward Dow built a crude log hotel. A year later he replaced it with a two-story frame building. Visitors carried their own luggage from the train station to the hotel. If they arrived at night, they found a sign in the window telling them which rooms were unoccupied. Meanwhile, near the north end of Lake McDonald, homesteader George E. Snyder built another small hotel. To bring visitors to this isolated spot, Snyder purchased a forty-foot steamboat.

Lake McDonald's pioneer tourists had to be a hardy lot. After arriving at the Belton depot, they walked the quarter mile to the Middle Fork of the Flathead River, where a rowboat ferried them across. There they boarded a buckboard and bounced along the rutted road to Snyder's steamboat, moored at the foot of Lake McDonald. Once aboard the boat, the boiler usually made it too hot to stay below decks. Topside passengers had to dodge sparks, which frequently burned holes in clothing. At the head of Lake McDonald they could stay in small cabins or Snyder's hotel and ride saddle horses into the backcountry.

One year before the establishment of Glacier Park, the Great Northern constructed the first of its chalet complexes at Belton. The hotel, a dormitory, and two Swiss-style cabins featured running water, acetylene lights, and central heating.

Meanwhile on Lake McDonald, Snyder had sold his holdings to Kalispell merchant John E. Lewis. In 1913 Lewis began building a massive new hotel on Lake McDonald that he boasted would be "far superior" to the Great Northern's facilities. An architect from Spokane designed the building with an alpine motif. Most of the materials had to be freighted via wagon team to Lake McDonald, where barges carried them to the north end of the lake. Even though they did all the log work by hand, Lewis's large work crew finished the building in just ten months.

The lodge, known to the locals simply as Lewis's, proved a rousing success. Its ornate lobby became a popular local gathering place as area residents flocked to weekend dances, sewing bees, and temperance meetings. An elevator could carry guests from their elegant two-room suites to a rooftop garden overlooking the lake.

The Lewis Hotel drove the Great Northern's chalets in Belton out of business. In 1929 the railroad conspired with the Park Service to force Lewis to sell out. The Park Hotel Company threatened to build a large lodge right next to Lewis's hotel unless he agreed to sell to the government. They reminded Lewis that the Great Northern handled all bookings in the park. Thus pressured by the government-railroad monopoly, Lewis agreed to sell. The Park Service could not afford to buy the hotel, so the Great Northern paid half the purchase price in exchange for a twenty-year lease. Thus the Lewis Hotel became the Lake McDonald Hotel.

### The CCC in Glacier

Besides serving as headquarters for the National Park Service, Belton (West Glacier) was the site of the main base camp for Glacier's Civilian Conservation Corps (CCC). Begun in 1933, the CCC was a noble experiment designed to put unemployed young men to work in the nation's for-

*Civilian Conservation Corps workers stringing telephone cable.* —Glacier National Park

ests and national parks. In Glacier, during the ten-year life of the program, thousands of men served six-month stints.

Coming at a time when the Great Depression had reduced park budgets and the Great Northern was beginning its withdrawal from the park concessions business, this influx of "free" labor proved a godsend to park officials. CCC boys constructed 250 miles of new trails, cleared debris from the newly completed Going-to-the-Sun Road, built bridges and storage sheds, erected fire lookouts, planted fish, fed elk, and performed landscaping chores.

The influx of automobile tourists left the park in dire need of campgrounds. Throughout the park, CCC crews paved parking spaces, installed fire grills and garbage dumps, and built picnic tables, benches, and outhouses. The Avalanche Creek campground, five miles northeast of Lake McDonald, is one of the many facilities improved by CCC workers.

The young men also spent months clearing burned timber left by recent forest fires. Working at a time when a burned-over forest was regarded as an eyesore, the crews felled snags and cut up logs for shipment to points east, where they became lumber or firewood. Even at this early date, some observers criticized such projects because they reduced the forest's ability to restore itself naturally. In partial response, CCC workers left some snags standing for cover and homes for birds.

The most ambitious CCC project in Glacier was the completion of the park's 450-mile system of telephone lines. In 1938 enrollees lugged twenty-eight tons of cable from the Avalanche Creek Campground to Hidden Lake and across Logan Pass. Each man carried forty-five pounds of the steel line at a time. For aesthetic reasons, they had to bury the entire cable. Park officials judged the completed system one of the best in the nation.

Because most enrollees came from cities east of the Mississippi River and were so far from home, desertions were rare. Some of the eastern boys had to put up with local prejudices, especially in the beginning. Before the first crews had even arrived, a Kalispell editor branded them "street slum foreigners." The African Americans enrolled at the Anaconda Creek camp saw a few We Cater to White Trade Only signs posted by merchants in Belton. But as the CCC workers proved their value and businesses supplying the camps enjoyed a sudden surge in earnings, much of the criticism subsided.

The CCC declined in 1942 as the military siphoned off most of the nation's young men to fight in the Second World War. The CCC camp at Belton, however, remained occupied after small crews of conscientious objectors began arriving. The men were sorely needed to fight fires.

## SPERRY GLACIER

Near the Lake McDonald Hotel, a trail climbs due east and winds its way toward Gunsight Pass. A spur leads north to Sperry Glacier. The route is noteworthy because it was one of the first man-made trails in the park. It is the handiwork of Professor Lyman B. Sperry and a group of his students from the University of Minnesota.

In 1893 the Great Northern Railway recruited Sperry to explore the region north of the line's station at Belton in search of glaciers "of sufficient size or of such striking features as to be of interest to the public, and near enough to our line to be made accessible." The following year Sperry visited the area with local game hunter Charlie Howe. Howe spotted the glacier that bears Sperry's name. In 1902 Sperry's Minnesota students worked on the trail without pay for the opportunity to spend a summer in the mountains.

Sperry Glacier was also probably the first park ice field to have a tourist fall into one of its crevasses. In 1906 forest ranger Frank Liebig used his axe to dislodge a woman who had wedged herself in the ice after a thirty-foot fall. At a nearby camp, as Liebig recalled, "Some men and women filled her up all night with hot brandy until she was glorious drunk. . . . The woman never even said thank you for getting her out of the glacier."

## GRANITE PARK AND TROUT LAKE

### A Night of Terror

Near the sharp switchback known as the Loop on Going-to-the-Sun Road, the trail leading to the Granite Park Chalet intersects with the highway. Trout Lake, which is reached by a steep trail running from near the northwest end of Lake McDonald, and Granite Park were the sites of separate tragedies in a single night. In the early morning hours of Sunday, August 13, 1967, at these two remote locations separated from each other by ten miles of mountainous terrain, grizzly bears attacked and killed two young women. Both victims were nineteen-year-old summer employees of the Glacier Park Hotel Company. Their deaths were the first bear-related fatalities since the park's founding fifty-seven years earlier.

The grizzly bear has long been one of the most admired and feared carnivores in North America. The huge animals were once common throughout the mountains and plains of the American West. But by the time Glacier Park was established, white hunters had long since chased the grizzlies to a few remote outposts in the Rocky Mountains near the Canadian border.

Generally, when a grizzly smells or hears a human, it moves quickly in the opposite direction. During the years of horse tours in Glacier Park, there were very few encounters with grizzlies. The pack trains were large, and a person mounted on a horse presented a formidable foe. Decades of relative peace had led park officials and visitors alike to grow complacent. Rangers did not enforce regulations against feeding the bears.

Following the Second World War, thousands of new visitors began taking advantage of modern, lighter camping equipment. As they trekked into the bears' wilderness domain, encounters with grizzlies increased dramatically. Still, by 1967 no one had yet died in Glacier from a bear attack. So when Roy Ducat and Julie Helgeson hiked to Granite Park Chalet on August 12, neither worried much about grizzlies. All that summer the major attraction at the chalet had been a pair of grizzlies that fed each evening on garbage. When Ducat and Helgeson camped downhill near the chalet, they did not realize they were near the pathway of feeding bears.

Late that night Ducat staggered into another camp dazed and bleeding. He told the shocked campers that a bear had dragged Helgeson down the hill. At the chalet, three physicians who were among the guests treated Ducat's wounds. They delayed searching for Helgeson until a helicopter brought in an armed ranger.

*Park rangers load the carcass of an alleged killer grizzly into a helicopter.*
—Glacier National Park

Following a trail of blood, the search party found Helgeson, barely alive some three hours after the attack. They managed to carry her up to the chalet before she died from her massive wounds. After escorting fifty-nine frightened people out of the area, rangers shot and killed three bears as they fed in the chalet garbage dump. The rangers found no conclusive evidence that any of the trio had killed Helgeson.

There was no doubt, however, about the identity of the bear that attacked five young hikers at Trout Lake that same August night. All summer a scrawny, brown female grizzly had been terrorizing campers and fishermen on the lakeshore. It displayed none of the usual fear of humans. Park officials seemed oblivious to repeated complaints. After the bear tore up the camp of two young boys from Columbia Falls, the official park report coldly concluded, "No action taken. Backcountry incident." By August, park rangers were so busy fighting forest fires that they had no time to investigate problem bears.

On the fatal weekend, five young park employees hiked the steep trail to Trout Lake. They had just begun cooking their evening meal when the emaciated grizzly charged into their camp, chased them away, and ate their food. Terrified, they moved their sleeping bags near the lakeshore and built a large fire.

Around 4:30 A.M. one of the campers, Paul Dunn, awoke to see the huge bear standing over him. He leaped up and dashed to a tree, cutting his legs as he climbed to the top. Three of the other four young people managed to scurry to safety. But Michele Koons became wedged in her bag when the bear bit down onto the zipper. Perched helplessly in the trees, Koons's four companions heard her screams.

At dawn the four shocked survivors rushed to the ranger station at Lake McDonald. Accompanied by two of the hikers, seasonal park ranger Leonard Landa hastened to Trout Lake. A trail of sleeping-bag feathers and blood led them to Koons's remains. Landa and fellow ranger Bert Gildart later returned to the area. They found and shot the grizzly near Arrow Lake.

Following the incidents, the Park Service fell under heavy criticism. Much of it was justified. After 1967 a flood of new bear regulations went into effect. Dumps at campgrounds and lodges were bear-proofed. At all trailheads rangers posted instructions for safe procedures in bear county. Rangers removed nuisance bears and closed trails at the first sign of bear trouble. But the well-intentioned new rules could not avert all bear attacks. A few have been fatal. Glacier is a wilderness where risks to visitors can be considerably greater than in a zoo or animal park where bars keep animals and people safely separated.

*Without a Trace*

More than forty years before the fatal grizzly mauling of Julie Helgesen, the Granite Park Chalet played a role in another mysterious tragedy. Early on the morning of August 24, 1924, Joseph Whitehead, an engineer from Chicago, and his younger brother William, a student at the Massachusetts Institute of Technology, set off from Granite Park on a twenty-mile hike to the Lewis Hotel on Lake McDonald. They were never seen nor heard from again.

The Whitehead brothers were not like those foolhardy adventurers who occasionally got lost or suffered falls in Glacier's mountains. They were intelligent and cautious. Before they disappeared, their well-planned two-week sojourn in the park had proceeded without a hitch. In their final letter to their mother in Chicago they wrote, "Don't worry, . . . we won't go into any danger."

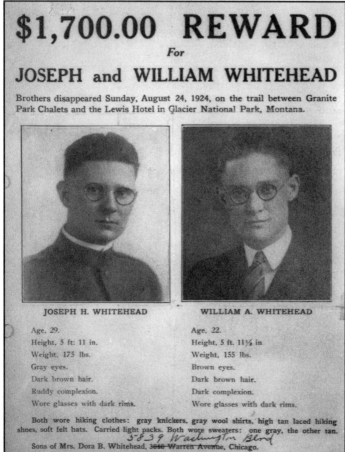

*Reward poster for the missing Whitehead brothers.* —Glacier National Park

On September 1, after the young men failed to return to Chicago on schedule, their mother reported them missing to park officials. A prolonged manhunt, involving seven search parties, systematically covered the park and found nothing. Their persistent mother, Dora, persuaded National Park Service officials to keep searching. Even President Calvin Coolidge wired Glacier officials, instructing them to spare no expense in their efforts.

Eventually, many feared that the brothers had fallen victim to foul play. Dora Whitehead posted a $500 reward. Louis Hill added $1,000 to the fund. The money loosed a flood of false leads. Late in September, members of a horse party reported that they had met two young men around noon on August 24 hiking along Logan Creek about ten miles from the Lewis Hotel and only a few miles from the road to Lake McDonald. In November the FBI took over the case. After a long investigation, one agent speculated that the boys had drowned while fishing in McDonald Creek.

The following summer Dora Whitehead and her daughter visited Glacier and retraced her sons' final route. They failed to uncover anything new. The next year, FBI Director J. Edgar Hoover closed the Whitehead case. An agent from the Butte office concluded that the only way the disappearance could ever be solved would be by "accident, pure and simple."

Such an accident has never happened. The most popular theory is that the Whiteheads walked down the trail from where the horse party saw them to somewhere along the road northeast of the Lewis Hotel. Here someone in an automobile abducted them for unknown reasons. They were carrying less than $100 between them. The Whitehead case remains today much as the Park Service described it in 1924: a "most perplexing and inexplicable mystery."

## THE HAYSTACK CREEK FUNNEL

### Avalanche

Five miles northwest of the summit of Logan Pass, travelers are thrilled by the scenic Weeping Wall. Near here, at a place known as the Haystack Creek funnel, a saga played out in late May 1953 that was at once a tragedy and a miracle.

Each spring, beginning around mid-March, crews venture up the snow-covered Going-to-the-Sun Road to wage battle with Mother Nature. Their goal is to remove the winter's snowpack, which can drift up to seventy feet deep on Logan Pass. As the region's merchants came to depend on the tourists streaming through Glacier Park, pressure mounted to get the road cleared at the earliest date possible. Occasionally a plow has slipped off the edge. The threat of snowslides looms constantly.

On the morning of May 26, 1953, four experienced road clearers began working their rotary plow near the Weeping Wall. A blizzard had left nearly twenty inches of new snow in the area. The plow kept bogging down at the spot of a recent slide. After watching the struggling plow, foreman George "Blackie" Beaton decided that dynamite would provide the quickest way to get rid of the problem snow. Supervisor Jean Sullivan brought in the explosives, and they sent Fred Klein back to Sullivan's pickup to fetch the blasting caps. When Sullivan asked Beaton if he thought it would be safe to set off the charge, the foreman replied, "Hell, she won't come down. We'll blow it and be out of here in half an hour."

The words had scarcely left Beaton's mouth when the slide hit. It was what experienced mountaineers call a "sneaker slide." It made only a soft swishing sound as it shot through the avalanche chute, so the four men on the roadway received no warning. Bill Whitford, sitting in the cab of the plow, could not even begin to jump clear in time. Sullivan leaped down into the road-cut made by the plow so the slide would not sweep him down the mountainside. The last thing he saw before being buried was the plow going off the edge.

Around noon Ray Price, a crew foreman who had been working above the Weeping Wall, walked down the road to check on the lower plowing operation. He came upon a confusing scene. He saw Sullivan's pickup parked just below a field of undisturbed snow. Deciding that the men probably had taken the plow back for repairs, Price proceeded down the road. Finally, after he encountered workers of the afternoon shift walking up the hill and they told him they had not seen the other crew, he realized what had happened. He radioed for help.

As a fog bank rolled across the area, frantic searchers began digging into the snow. They soon uncovered Fred Klein, alive but badly injured. A few minutes later they found Bill Whitford's crushed body. Hours of frustration then followed.

Among the searchers was Jean Sullivan's close friend Dimon Apgar. Apgar calmly surveyed the area and began sinking holes into the snow above the roadbed. He correctly reasoned that his friend would have dived into the cut for protection. It took him several hours and two dozen holes before he finally uncovered Sullivan's head. The 59-year-old road worker had been buried under seven and a half feet of snow for nearly eight hours by the time rescuers freed him. They rushed him to a road camp and placed jugs of hot coffee wrapped in towels next to him. Within a half hour Sullivan was alert. He recalled that after being buried, "The snow was heavy. I wasn't cold or afraid for myself; I knew they would dig me out."

It took searchers aided by a bloodhound until three o'clock the following morning to find Blackie Beaton's body. Within four days, Sullivan was

*Workers frantically search for road crewmen buried in May 1953 avalanche.* —Glacier National Park

out of the hospital and back on his job clearing the highway. Going-to-the-Sun Road did not open until June 24 that year—the latest date in the road's history.

The disaster at Weeping Wall led road crews to proceed more cautiously. Watchmen and plow operators began wearing radio headsets for early warnings. They carried signaling devices for quicker recovery from burials. Still, there have been several other close calls—especially near the Haystack Creek funnel.

## ST. MARY LAKES

### Hugh Monroe

The beautiful St. Mary Lakes region was the favorite stomping ground of Hugh Monroe, possibly the first white resident of Glacier Park. A native of Quebec, Monroe came to the plains east of Glacier's mountains in 1814 as a teenage employee of the Hudson's Bay Company. The company had sent him to live among the Piegan Blackfeet, hoping he could learn their language and act as an interpreter during trade negotiations.

Young Monroe gained the favor of Lone Walker, a Piegan chief, after he demonstrated his prowess as a hunter and fighter. Monroe's bravery earned him the Blackfeet name Rising Wolf. He married one of Lone Walker's daughters, Ap-ah-ki. The couple had ten children and lived together until her death in 1874.

During his sojourns in the mountains, Monroe frequently stayed along Lower St. Mary Lake. It was during one of these stays, sometime in the 1840s, that he held a christening ceremony on the lower lake. He and a group of Indian friends erected a cross of logs and named the lake St. Mary. For years thereafter, Monroe and his large family hunted and trapped around the lake.

During the Sioux Indian Wars of 1876–1877, two of Monroe's grandsons served as scouts, first for George Armstrong Custer and then for Nelson Miles. Later, one of these grandsons, Billy Jackson, guided George Bird Grinnell on a monthlong exploration trek through the mountains of the future Glacier Park. Grinnell named Mount Jackson in his honor.

By the end of the nineteenth century, the aged Monroe was growing destitute as the bison and other game animals he hunted for a living disappeared. He depended on friends and relatives for support. He lived his final years in a tent next to his son's log cabin at East Glacier.

**US 89 and Montana 49**
# St. Mary—East Glacier Park
**33 miles**

## RED BUSES

Even on short trips on the roads through and around Glacier Park, you are likely to encounter at least one of the bright red buses. Usually they are filled with excited visitors, eagerly listening to the commentary of a driver well-versed in the park's geology, ecology, and history.

The tour buses have been fixtures in Glacier Park for as long as the roads they travel across. From the time he began building the Great Northern's string of hotels and chalets around the park, Louis Hill recognized the necessity of linking them with roads and trails. Construction crews had no sooner finished the new roads when the horse-drawn coaches of the Brewster Brothers Transportation Company began hauling tourists.

*Tour buses leaving the East Glacier depot, circa 1914.* —Glacier National Park

Later, Montana native Rowe Emery formed the Glacier Park Transportation Company and began running motor vehicles up and down the new roads. The horse coaches soon disappeared. Emery then established the first authorized motor-transportation utility in any national park. The White Motor Company of Cleveland custom-designed the twelve-passenger buses. At the rear of each was a drop-down endgate for carrying luggage. During the first year, 1914, the big dips in Glacier's crude roads kept tearing off these rear-end racks.

Recalling that formative year, the bus line's first manager noted that "there were no garage buildings of any kind. We parked this equipment under the trees and used packing cases for our parts room. Oil and gasoline were kept in barrels on skids where we could fill buses and trucks."

The first year of business went relatively smoothly for the new buses. The company advertised "a very delightful ride of four and one half to five hours" from Midvale (East Glacier) to Many Glacier. In 1915 the ride became less than delightful. Constant rainstorms throughout the summer produced perpetual delays. Passengers reached their destinations late, tired, irritable, caked with mud, and wishing they had never heard of Montana's mountain paradise. Milk River Flats, just south of St. Mary, turned to a sea of gumbo. Here former teamster Jack Galbraith turned a tidy profit. He hooked his horses to each stuck bus, sat on the fender, and combined horse power with bus power to pull the vehicle across the abyss.

The Park Service eventually received funds needed to improve the road along Glacier's east side. By the time Emery sold his company in 1927, the buses were covering both sides of the park. Until the road crossed Marias Pass in 1930, the company relied on the Great Northern to haul their buses, drivers, and passengers to Belton. From here they would complete their grand tour. At decade's end there were more than sixty of the red buses—along with sixteen large touring cars—carting visitors to accommodations in Glacier Park. They also travelled to the newly opened Prince of Wales Hotel in Canada's adjoining Waterton Park.

Today's buses still sport the same basic design, which the company feels is ideal for their specified purpose—sightseeing in Glacier Park. The custom-built bodies still ride atop chassis built by the White Motor Company.

## TWO MEDICINE

Just over six miles north of East Glacier, drivers may enter the park along the lakes known as Two Medicine. They nestle against Rising Wolf Peak, named in honor of Hugh Monroe. Here the Great Northern began

*President Franklin D. Roosevelt waves his hat during a 1934 excursion in the park.*
—Glacier National Park

construction of one of its first chalet groups in 1911. Most of the material for the large dormitory and dining hall came from timber cut around the lakes. Park rangers demolished and burned most of the buildings in 1956, long after the Great Northern had abandoned them as money losers. Today a log store is all that remains of the complex.

On a pleasant August evening in 1934, one of the chalets at Two Medicine became the center of the nation's attention. It was here that President Franklin D. Roosevelt delivered one of his famous, inspirational "fireside chats," broadcast to homes throughout the land. Roosevelt described to his listeners the grandeur of Glacier Park. The speech was the concluding event of a daylong presidential excursion of the park.

After the president's party arrived at Two Medicine, several singing groups of CCC boys serenaded them, and Blackfeet Indian dancers entertained. The Blackfeet inducted President and Mrs. Roosevelt into the tribe, giving him the name Lone Chief. Mrs. Roosevelt received the title Medicine Pipe Woman.

US 89 and Montana 17

# St. Mary—Canadian Border

30 miles

## ALTYN

The road linking US 89 at Babb to the tourist complex at Many Glacier skirts the north shore of Lake Sherburne. During the decade preceding the establishment of Glacier Park, the area experienced a typical Western mining boom, followed closely by a typical Western oil rush. Had either event produced a find of lasting duration, the history of this region's mountains might have been much different.

The rush of miners into the Swiftcurrent Valley literally started out with a bang. On the morning of April 15, 1898, a volley of shots rang out, and soon hundreds of prospectors in wagons, on horses, and on foot stampeded into the "ceded strip" of land recently purchased from the Blackfeet tribe. The small town of Altyn sprang up near the western end of the present reservoir. Most of the mineral claims were along the slopes and valleys of rivers feeding into the Swiftcurrent.

The most ambitious claim was a lead mine on Cracker Lake. The mine never produced an ounce of commercial ore, but that did not stop investors from pouring in enough money to sink a 1,300-foot shaft into the mountain. They used a block and tackle to haul an eight-ton concentrator

*Mining operation in the Many Glacier area, circa 1908.* —Glacier National Park

up the steep bed of Canyon Creek. Once the mine proved worthless, Altyn began to die.

Just as the hard-rock claims fell into disuse, another wave of optimists began staking claims along the Swiftcurrent River. The object of their interest this time was oil. In 1901 Sam Somes, the owner of the Altyn Hotel, set off a charge of dynamite in his copper mine. On inspecting his work, he noticed oil seeping through the rock. He began drilling and struck oil at the 500-foot depth. Legend has it that Somes, in an effort to raise capital, carried oil from his well into Great Falls banks and poured it onto the desks of potential investors.

By 1906 a dozen wells lined the valley. Five of them were pumping Montana's first oil in amounts that paid off. A newspaper in Butte predicted that the field would soon be "second to none in the world." Then water began penetrating and polluting the wells. Investors lost interest and the field shut down. Today the remains of the abandoned wells lie beneath the waters of Lake Sherburne.

## MANY GLACIER

Had he searched the entire northern Rocky Mountains, Louis Hill probably never could have found a better location for the Great Northern's second largest hotel than the northeast corner of Swiftcurrent Lake. Here visitors can gaze at some of the most spectacular peaks in all of Glacier Park. Excellent hiking trails lead in all directions from the hotel called Many Glacier.

Unlike the hotel at East Glacier, Many Glacier was built mostly from materials native to the area. Local stone went into the foundation and the huge fireplace gracing the lobby. The company erected a sawmill near the lake and cut more than 2 million board feet of timber for the new building. Crews floated logs down the area's lakes to the construction site. Even most of the furniture was made from native wood.

The hotel, built in 1915, had 240 rooms, making it the largest in Montana at the time. Like most other Great Northern buildings in the park, the design was Swiss and featured overhanging roofs and balconies. The decor was an odd mix. The lobby featured a striking circular staircase. Near the center stood a tall stone fountain surrounded by a pool filled with trout. Overhead hung dozens of oriental lanterns. Bison skulls and the skins of area animals decorated the balcony area. A set of totem poles was brought in for good measure. The dining hall featured canvases of picture writing done by Blackfeet Indians. These were later replaced by banners representing the cantons of Switzerland.

The building was largely self-sufficient, with its own water supply and power plant. The hydroelectric facility located near Swiftcurrent Falls was so noisy that operators had to use an insulated phone booth to communicate with the outside world. A firehouse bell alerted them whenever the phone rang.

College-age people recruited nationwide have served hotel guests ever since its first seasons. During most of those years, waitresses and bellmen have dressed like Swiss peasants. Each year during the 1920s, Many Glacier's manager, A. J. Binder, deliberately hired several "bad apples" just so he could fire them early in the season as an example to the other workers.

For years following the hotel's completion, park officials urged the Great Northern to clean up Many Glacier's idle sawmill and unsightly lumber piles. In 1925 Park Service Director Stephen Mather, accompanied by his daughter, visited Many Glacier. After he saw the mill still standing, Mather rounded up a workforce and set more than a dozen charges of dynamite. He then invited hotel guests to step outside and watch the show. He personally lit the first fuse, over the protests of hotel manager Binder. The explosion blew out the entire east side of the mill building. When asked

*Many Glacier Hotel, 1932.* —Glacier National Park

about his motive, Mather simply replied, "I'm celebrating my daughter's birthday."

In 1936 a cataclysm of a different sort struck Many Glacier. In late August strong winds caused a fire on Heavens Peak west of the Garden Wall to leap the Continental Divide near Granite Park. It raced down the Swiftcurrent Valley directly toward the Many Glacier Hotel. The wall of flame leveled a campground, a ranger station, and dozens of cabins in its path.

At the hotel, every available vehicle was drafted to evacuate guests. Tour guide Will McLaughlin recalled, "People were running back and forth in near panic. We started down the road leaving the scene that looked like the end of the world."

But the Many Glacier Hotel miraculously escaped the fire. Hotel employees and others stood on the roof and balconies. With brooms, hoses, and buckets of water they managed to douse all the embers as they hit the building. When they were not throwing water on the fire, they were throwing it on one another. It took them hours to dry out around the lobby fireplace.

By the time of the 1936 Heavens Peak Fire, Great Northern officials had soured on their unprofitable hotels in Glacier. After the fire had passed, the manager of Many Glacier telegraphed company headquarters in St. Paul announcing triumphantly, "We have saved the hotel!" He received a single-word response: "Why?"

## THE FATHER OF GLACIER PARK

Each year hundreds of hikers ascend the five-mile-long trail leading from the Many Glacier Hotel to Grinnell Glacier. The mass of ice remains a popular attraction, even though it has shrunk tremendously since the time, more than a century ago, when George Bird Grinnell braved its crevasse-filled surface.

Grinnell first visited Montana's northern Rockies in August 1885. As he stepped off the stage at Fort Benton, he was greeted by James Willard Schultz, the man whose writings had lured him into the area. Schultz lived among the Blackfeet, married a Piegan woman, and wrote extensively about his experiences. He had submitted an article to Grinnell's *Forest and Stream* magazine that described a hunting and fishing trip in the Rockies just south of the Canadian border. The article so fascinated Grinnell that he left his home in New York at once to see the region for himself.

By the time he began exploring the future Glacier Park, Grinnell was no stranger to wild country. He had grown up fishing and hunting with the sons of naturalist John James Audubon along the shores of the Hudson River. He tried working in his father's stock-brokerage firm, but his real love lay in the natural sciences. In 1874 he accompanied Custer's 7th Cavalry in a reconnaissance of the Black Hills. After witnessing the slaughter of bison and other Western big-game animals, Grinnell became a lifelong conservationist.

During his 1885 excursion with Schultz, Grinnell shot a mountain sheep, and named the mountain on which he killed it "singleshot." The party then went to the river that Grinnell named Swiftcurrent after learning that its Blackfeet name meant "swift flowing river." As they proceeded up the valley, Grinnell spotted a "superb glacier." Fighting wind, rain, and snow crusted so hard that it cut their feet, Grinnell and his half-Indian guide approached the huge ice field.

The miserable weather ultimately forced the party to retreat but, two years later Grinnell returned to explore the glacier. His party struggled up a trail so narrow that its rock ledges shredded the packs on their mules. Moving on foot, they reached the upper end of the lake just below the glacier, where the rock walls seemed to block passage. Using channels carved

*George Bird Grinnell strikes a pose atop his glacier.*
—Glacier National Park

by old waterfalls, they scrambled to the glacier itself. Grinnell estimated its thickness at 700 feet. Near the glacier's edge they spotted a bighorn ram, which Grinnell shot.

Grinnell returned to these mountains periodically for nearly four more decades. He continued to name the area's natural features, including Mount Jackson, Gunsight Pass, Mount Reynolds, Mount Allen, and Mount Stimson. Between trips he wrote long articles about his adventures. He launched a campaign to make the area a national park. In a 1901 article in the popular *Century* magazine, Grinnell's words brought Glacier to the nation's attention:

> Far away in northwestern Montana, hidden from view by clustering mountain peaks, lies an unmapped corner—the Crown of the Conti-

nent. . . . No words can describe the grandeur and majesty of these mountains, and even photographs seem hopelessly to dwarf and belittle the most impressive peaks.

Later Grinnell began bringing his wife, Elizabeth, into his mountain paradise. Although she suffered from a fear of heights so acute that she frequently became ill during their excursions, she hid the fact so well that Grinnell never knew it.

After viewing the damage done by the area's short-lived mining and oil booms, Grinnell grew more determined to turn it into a national park. He spurred the Audubon Society and the Boone and Crockett Club—two organizations that he had helped to found—to press Congress to pass the bill creating Glacier National Park. In the end it was Grinnell, not Louis Hill and the Great Northern Railway, who was the chief force behind the legislation that created Glacier National Park.

Once Grinnell's playground became the nation's, his visits to the area grew less frequent. Whenever he visited Glacier, he complained about the crowds. He lamented being "pushed off the trail every few minutes by the multitude." But while the aged Grinnell was grousing about the rush of tourists, he realized that had the region not received national park designation it would have been "cut bare of timber, dotted with irrigation reservoirs, the game killed off, the country burned over." In 1926 President Calvin Coolidge, upon presenting Grinnell with the Theodore Roosevelt Medal for Conservation, recognized his crowning achievement: "The Glacier National Park is peculiarly your monument."

## THE WORLD'S LARGEST DUDE RANCH

The road running east from Babb leads five miles to Duck Lake. Here the Glacier Park Saddle Horse Company grazed, bred, branded, broke, and shod thousands of horses during the company's heyday between the two world wars. Throughout this era the most popular method of viewing Glacier Park was from the back of a horse. A single outfitter catered to the needs of up to 10,000 visitors each year. The eastern press called Glacier the "world's largest dude ranch."

Even before Glacier became a national park, area ranchers and homesteaders began offering horse tours into the backcountry. Eventually the Park Service found the many small operators difficult to deal with, so officials encouraged consolidation. By 1915 the company, organized by Kalispell attorney W. N. Noffsinger and his son George, had won the contract as Glacier's sole horse concessionaire. The company ran horse tours from every hotel and chalet around the edge of the park. As the Park Service constructed and improved trails, the tours became more elaborate. Each season more than a thousand horses could be found throughout the park. Visitors could take guided excursions lasting anywhere from a day to a full month.

High in the mountains, the company established tent camps at places such as Red Eagle Lake, Waterton Lake, Goathaunt, and Fifty Mountain. Here weary riders could rest in silk tents with wood floors furnished with wash basins, iron beds, and soft mattresses. As an embellishment, the Great Northern mounted railroad locomotive bells atop four passes along the most popular horse trails. Tourists enjoyed bell-ringing ceremonies to celebrate crossing the Continental Divide.

Looking after some 100 novice equestrians riding along steep, winding mountain trails was never easy. But dozens of mounted guides called "dude wranglers" proved up to the task. Glacier's wranglers were a restless breed.

*Author Mary Roberts Rinehart visits Blackfeet at their Glacier Park tepee camp.*
—Glacier National Park

Among the finest were young Blackfeet from the reservation, because they knew Glacier's mountain trails better than anyone. The guides dressed themselves and their horses in colorful western costumes. Tourists loved the "movie cowboy" look.

Among the largest and most popular guided tours through Glacier were the annual excursions of the Howard Eaton party. Eaton ran a dude ranch in Wyoming. Each summer he gathered 150 or so cohorts, and they raided Glacier Park en masse. Their treks lasted several weeks. Members camped in individual tents and enjoyed meals served by a gourmet chef. Artist Charlie Russell and renowned mystery writer Mary Roberts Rinehart were among the celebrities who toured the park with Eaton each year.

Although the Eaton tour was among the most luxurious of all the horse treks across the park, it was not for the fainthearted. Rinehart told harrowing tales of stampeding horses; of leading their mounts down precipitous, shale-covered trails; riding for hours in rain through deep mud; and of braving plunge baths in mountain lakes. Rinehart wrote that crossing the park on horseback was "a triumph of endurance rather than of courage."

The growing popularity of the automobile, coupled with the completion of highways around and through Glacier Park, finally killed the horse-excursion business. In 1942, after the entire park virtually shut down for the duration of the Second World War, the Glacier Park Saddle Horse Company closed up shop.

### CHIEF MOUNTAIN

The stretch of Montana 17 that leads from Glacier Park into Canada's Waterton Park is referred to as the Chief Mountain International Highway. Its name derives from the most striking landmark along the route, a huge block of limestone that broke off from the Lewis overthrust to rise in stunning isolation at the western edge of Montana's northern prairie. Early white mapmakers labeled the mountain the King, but it was known as Chief Mountain by the time young Henry L. Stimson made the first recorded ascent to its summit in 1892. Stimson learned that others had been there before him when he found a decomposed bison skull at the top. Stimson later achieved renown as the United States secretary of war and secretary of state, serving on the cabinets of three different presidents.

## REMOTE OUTPOSTS

For years the Glacier-Waterton area stood as the only unsurveyed section of the U.S.-Canadian international boundary. In 1861 British surveyors marked the boundary from the park's western border to the summit of the Continental Divide. Not until 1874 did a similar group survey the border east of the divide. Their job became more difficult after a grizzly attacked their string of pack animals.

Once Glacier became a national park, its first rangers patrolled this isolated border region. Their duties ranged from fighting forest fires to arresting poachers, smugglers, and timber thieves. They also had orders to kill "undesirable predators" such as wolves, coyotes, and mountain lions. Once prohibition became the law of the land, their chores expanded to include interdicting whiskey runners.

Appointed by Glacier's rotund first superintendent, William R. Logan, this first crew of rangers were rugged veterans of the Forest Service. They were used to the type of patrol duty that meant spending months in crude, isolated mountain cabins in the dead of winter. The brushes with death and feats of courage and endurance of Glacier's early rangers is the stuff of legend.

When Albert Reynolds became one of the park's first rangers, he was well into his sixties. By then his backcountry skills had earned him the nickname Death-on-the-Trail. Reynolds disliked horses, so he made his rounds on foot. He regularly hiked seventeen miles just to pick up his mail. Even in blizzards and subzero weather, he covered at least fifteen miles a day moving between the camps of one-room log cabins.

In December 1912 Reynolds slipped on the ice of Waterton Lake and sustained a concussion. Later he trekked ten miles as the temperature reached forty below. By the time he reached a cabin, he had frozen both of his heels. Seeking help, he braved a final seventeen-mile hike to the cabin of his friend "Kootenai" Brown. Here he lay in agony for a week before dying. Shortly before his death, he wrote, "For years my home has been in the mountains. I love them and everything in them." Today, Reynolds Peak near Hidden Lake stands as an appropriate monument.

## COSLEY LAKE

Cosley Lake, near the headwaters of the Belly River, is another park landmark named after one of that first corps of rangers. In the Belly River valley, Joe Cosley carved a name for himself as a miner, trapper, park ranger, and poacher. He had learned fancy riding and shooting at an early age. Sporting long hair and a Buffalo Bill-style goatee, he blew most of the money he made trapping on expensive clothes and riding equipment. Even during his brief stint as a ranger, Cosley trapped park animals illegally on the side. Following the outbreak of the First World War, he joined the Canadian Mounted Rifles. While serving in France, he reportedly killed more than sixty enemy soldiers.

*Joe Cosley, park ranger turned poacher.* —Glacier National Park

After the war, Cosley returned to his favorite borderland mountain haunts, where he resumed shooting and trapping animals. He managed to elude arrest until 1929, when ranger Joseph Heimes cornered him at a winter camp. Heimes found the place filled with beaver and muskrat hides. During their tense march to the Belly River ranger station, Cosley tried to bolt several times, only to be tackled by the determined Heimes.

At Kalispell the park commissioner found Cosley guilty of poaching. After friends paid his fine, Cosley hitched a ride to Logan Creek, put on snowshoes, and rushed thirty miles overland back to his cabin. Park rangers, meanwhile, drove back to near the Canadian border, where they hiked toward Cosley's cabin from the east to confiscate his worldly goods. By the time they reached the cabin, it had been cleaned out. All tracks had been erased. As far as anyone knew, Joe Cosley never returned to the Glacier-Waterton area.

Several generations of rangers patrolled Glacier's border country alone, often on foot. Today, radios, airplanes, and other modern equipment make the rangers' work somewhat less demanding. But this rugged wilderness in Montana's northern Rockies still poses a challenge and promises adventure to all who enter.

# THE LOGGING FRONTIER

*Nature was in a kind and very thoughtful mind when she created Western Montana. She reserved for it much that was beautiful in her generosity, and in her thoughtfulness so arranged all that it should be capable of the highest development by man.*

—W. H. Smead

93 Eureka

37

93

2 Troy
Libby

Whitefish 40
Columbia
Falls
286
2

Kalispell

82 Bigfork

Noxon

*Clark Fork River*

200

*Flathead
Lake*

93

35 Swan Lake

28

Hot
Springs

*Flathead R.*

Polson

Ronan 83

Thompson
Falls
*Lookout
Pass*
Saltese
Plains
De Borgia
200

93

National Bison Range

St. Regis

Superior

St. Ignatius

90

Alberton

Seeley
Lake

93

*Blackfoot R.*

Missoula

Bonner

200

12

Lolo

90

*Lolo Pass*

93

Stevensville

*Bitterroot River*

MONTANA

Hamilton

Darby

93 Sula

0          20          40          60 miles

When he wrote the above words in 1905, W. H. Smead, a speculator in real estate, was hoping to cash in on the opening of the Flathead Indian Reservation to white settlers. Yet, knowingly or not, he captured much of the essence of that section of Montana lying between the Continental Divide and the crest of the Bitterroot Range separating Montana from Idaho. This area of about 12,000 square miles was, indeed, a place of rare beauty and potential wealth crying out to developers. Trappers, merchants, prospectors, homesteading farmers, and lumbermen all entered the region seeking a portion of its riches. And over the years, many have observed with alarm the damage that some of these exploiters did to the region's irreplaceable natural beauty.

## CARVED IN STONE

The jagged peaks, lush forests, pristine lakes, and broad valleys of western Montana are the result of forces that began more than 60 million years ago. Ancient rocks from somewhere in eastern Idaho gradually moved upward and eastward to form Montana's Rocky Mountains. The most striking feature of the northern Rockies landscape is the Rocky Mountain Trench. This huge valley runs south from Canada's Yukon and contains Montana's Flathead River and Flathead Lake.

The region's major east-west valley, the Clark Fork, was scoured to its present level by a series of cataclysmic events during the ice ages. As the great glaciers moved south from Canada and filled the valley, an ice dam formed near present Pend Oreille Lake in Idaho. The dam impounded the Clark Fork River to form Glacial Lake Missoula, about the size of Lake Ontario. As temperatures warmed, the ice dam eventually burst. The lake drained in a matter of hours. In what may well have been the greatest flash flood in the history of the planet, a 1,000-foot wall of water shot down the Columbia Gorge at forty-five miles per hour. The flood released a volume of water greater than the combined flows of every stream in the world. Geologists estimate that Glacial Lake Missoula filled and drained violently at least forty times during the two great ice ages. Today evidence of this lake can be seen clearly in the shoreline marks along hills surrounding Missoula.

## THE VALLEYS AWAKEN

The Bitterroot Valley has long been a popular trade route. Near the upper Bitterroot at Ross' Hole, Lewis and Clark crossed the Great Divide from Idaho and first encountered the Salish (or as the whites preferred to call them, Flathead) Indians. Although the Salish claimed most of western

Montana as their domain, they centered in the Bitterroot Valley. Here, some forty years after Lewis and Clark passed, missionaries established Montana's first white settlement. And it was from here that white duplicity forced the Salish to leave several decades later.

Western Montana's valleys remained hardly populated by whites into the Civil War era. Once gold was discovered in places east of the Continental Divide, fortune seekers traversed the crude military road engineered by John Mullan through the valleys of the Clark Fork and St. Regis Rivers. The settlement of Hellgate arose west of present-day Missoula. By the time the rails of the Northern Pacific reached Missoula in the early 1880s, the town was already becoming the metropolis of western Montana.

To the north, settlement by whites came even later. The harsh winters, rugged terrain, and hostile Piegan Blackfeet just across the divide discouraged all but the most venturesome from entering the upper Flathead and Kootenai Valleys. Along the loop of the Kootenai River in the extreme northwest corner of Montana, two distinct bands of the Kutenai Indians ruled over their remote domains. Members of the lower band were fishermen who seldom left the valley. The upper Kutenai often ventured from their home on the Tobacco Plains, south of present Eureka, to hunt bison east of the divide. Like their Salish neighbors, the Kutenai were peace-loving people who lost their homeland to invading whites.

When James J. Hill's Great Northern Railway pushed across Marias Pass in 1891, Kalispell was born. It became the region's commercial center. The rails brought in settlers and enabled a few enterprising souls to begin exploiting some of the richest forests in North America.

## A TIMBER BOOM

The boost that the railroads gave the lumber industry throughout western Montana was twofold. First, the Northern Pacific, the Great Northern, and the late-arriving Milwaukee railroads all needed wood for their own ties, bridges, and trestles. Second, the rail lines eased transport of the lumber, opening up nationwide markets for Montana's forest products. From the closing decades of the nineteenth century through the late decades of the twentieth, the lumber industry, for better or worse, dominated the economic and social life of the entire region.

Today, motorists driving to Darby, St. Regis, and Eureka cannot miss the evidence of timber harvesting. Aging clear-cuts disrupt the blanket of dark green along many ridges. Smoke-belching diesel trucks still haul piles of logs from the woods. Nearly every town has its sawmill, even though many now lie idle.

The industry grew from shallow roots. In 1845 at St. Mary's Mission, Father Anthony Ravalli constructed a crude water-powered saw using four wagon wheels welded together. A fifth wagon wheel, flattened and toothed, served as the blade. Later, other small mills arose near the territory's first mining camps.

By the 1880s the huge copper operation of the Anaconda Company in Butte had developed a voracious appetite for mine timbers and wood fuel for smelters. Entrepreneurs in Missoula were eager to meet their needs as well as the demands of the railroads. Within a short time loggers had cut away all the easily accessible stands of timber near the large rivers. As rival firms grabbed for more remote trees, tempers flared. In Cramer Gulch near Hell Gate Canyon, woodsmen could get into a fistfight over possession of a single log.

By the end of the century the Anaconda Company had also taken advantage of the timber boom. The mining giant bought out a major lumber firm and subsequently became the state's largest lumber producer. But there was room for others. Julius Neils built large mills in Libby and Troy that rivaled the Anaconda Company's output. The Great Northern Railway's Somers Lumber Company mill on Flathead Lake floated their cut logs down the Swan River. From the Bitterroot River to the Kootenai, scores of

*Logging by rail, McCoy Gulch south of Darby.* —Bitterroot Valley Historical Society, Hamilton

smaller mills were turning out boards, ties, planks, posts, and poles. But once Montana's lumber trade tied itself to national and world markets, it fell subject to cyclical booms and busts. Local crises ranging from floods and fires to labor strife also plagued the industry.

The twentieth century witnessed a revolution in the way logs were brought from the forests. For decades, the big lumber firms operated large camps in the woods where rugged Scandinavian and French Canadian axmen would fell trees and haul them in horse-drawn sleds to dumping points on the riverbanks. Each spring, great log drives would clog the rivers. Later, steam-powered skidders and makeshift railroads replaced man- and horsepower. These were in turn displaced by Caterpillar tractors and diesel trucks.

The lifestyle of the lumberman also changed. Early loggers were usually single men who lived in the woods until payday, when they would flood into town to do their drinking, womanizing, and fighting. Today's workers may commute up to 100 miles to and from the woods each day. Most have families and are active in their communities. As one modern logger lamented, "When they fight now its because they don't like each other. . . . It used to be just for fun."

Today in the seven counties of western Montana, dozens of lumber mills still employ hundreds of workers. But it was not the lumber industry that stimulated the unprecedented economic and population growth the region experienced during the 1990s. As University of Montana economist Thomas Power noted, the economy of western Montana was expanding "because this is an attractive place to live, work and do business."

**I-90**
# Lookout Pass—Missoula
**104 miles**

## MULLAN'S MILITARY ROAD

The route of I-90 from Coeur d'Alene, Idaho, to Deer Lodge parallels a historic route known as the Mullan Road. The roadway actually stretched 640 miles from Walla Walla, Washington, to Fort Benton. The Mineral County Museum in Superior treats the road and its builder, army lieutenant John Mullan, as a topic of special interest. The museum hosts an annual John Mullan Day.

Although short in stature, John Mullan possessed the grit and determination that led to a distinguished military career. Upon his graduation

*Lt. John Mullan.*
—Mansfield Library Archives,
University of Montana, Missoula

from the U.S. Military Academy, Mullan was assigned to the Northwest Survey Expedition under Maj. Isaac I. Stevens. The Stevens survey was looking for potential routes for a transcontinental railroad.

Young Mullan so impressed Stevens that he entrusted him with command of a small party of men who spent the winter and spring of 1854 stationed in the Bitterroot Valley, exploring mountain passes. Mullan cemented friendly ties with members of the Salish tribe. One of them showed him the low pass across the Continental Divide between present Garrison and Helena, which today bears Mullan's name. In seeking the best route across the more challenging Bitterroot Range, Mullan explored along the lower Clark Fork River. Spring floods plagued his travels. This led him mistakenly to conclude that the far more arduous route up the St. Regis River and across Sohon's Pass (just south of Lookout Pass) would be the best one for the military road that was taking shape in his mind.

During a lengthy sojourn back east, Mullan helped Stevens lobby Congress for the funds needed to build a wagon road from Walla Walla to Fort Benton. In the spring of 1859, Mullan organized a crew of more than 100 soldiers and 90 civilian workers to begin construction of the twenty-five-foot-wide road. The most challenging section proved to be the thick forests of present northern Idaho and western Montana. Throughout the hot summer, Mullan and his men hacked their way through a complex network of trees, fallen timber, steep ridges, gullies, and ravines. "Justice cannot be done to the industry and fortitude of the men while mastering this wilderness," Mullan later wrote. Mullan had hoped to reach the Clark Fork River before winter, but early snowfall forced the party to halt in the canyon of the St. Regis, where they set up Cantonment Jordan. In a crude shelter, Mullan compiled his field notes while his men repaired equipment. Much of their livestock froze to death. With the arrival of spring, the party purchased replacement horses from the Bitterroot Salish, and construction resumed.

As the crews cut the road near the north bank of the Clark Fork, they encountered a six-mile-wide spur of rock that Mullan dubbed "the big mountain." For six weeks they blasted and cut their way along the edge of the rugged bank. One premature detonation put out a worker's eye. Once past this obstacle, the remaining route to present-day Missoula proved easier. Here Mullan received word that a detachment of soldiers had reached Fort Benton by steamboat. They awaited completion of Mullan's route so that they could proceed overland to Walla Walla.

Mullan and his work crew hastened up the Clark Fork and Little Blackfoot Valleys, across Mullan Pass, and on to Fort Benton, which he reached on August 1. They did more surveying than actual road building. By then Mullan's main goal was to prove the practicality of his route. He turned his wagons over to the commander of the soldiers, who proceeded westward on the new road. With Mullan and a small crew clearing away obstacles ahead of the soldiers, the trek to Walla Walla took just 57 days.

Having demonstrated his road's usefulness, Mullan set out the following spring to improve it. He spent the entire summer cutting a new road and building numerous bridges in the rugged forests from present-day Coeur d'Alene to the Clark Fork River.

It was well into November by the time Mullan and his men reached the junction of the Clark Fork and Big Blackfoot Rivers. They erected winter quarters consisting of four cabins and began building a large bridge across the Blackfoot. They spent most of their time huddled around fires weathering one of the coldest winters in the memory of the native tribes. In January one of Mullan's civilian employees set out on foot carrying mail to Salt Lake City, but soon his moccasins froze to his feet. Rescuers hauled him back to Mullan's camp, where the doctor amputated both the man's legs. After surviving this traumatic winter, Mullan proceeded to Fort Benton, where he dismissed his work crew.

Although the initials *MR* on marker poles along the way denoted a military road, the route soon became known as Mullan Road. It proved unimportant as a military highway, but within four years of its completion thousands of prospectors and emigrants had used the route. They frequently had to make their own repairs on the road, because the government failed to maintain it. The strangest outfit to use the road was a pack train consisting of seven camels carrying freight to Montana miners. The mere sight of these beasts stampeded horses. Near Blackfoot City a prospector shot one of the grazing camels, mistaking it for a moose.

In 1883 Mullan returned to the region of his early exploits to participate in the ceremony marking the completion of the Northern Pacific's transcontinental railroad. Recalling his labors, he remarked, "If there was any conviction firmly lodged in my mind, it was the conviction that the day was coming when a line of Pullman sleepers would cross down through Hell Gate Canyon."

## THE INFERNO OF 1910

Today, travelers moving up and down Lookout Pass through the narrow defile of the St. Regis River encounter a veritable sea of green. The lush pine, spruce, and fir forests reveal few reminders of the holocaust that blackened this entire region on both sides of the Bitterroot Divide. A lot of healing has taken place since that momentous forty-eight-hour period in late August 1910.

The preceding winter had brought adequate snowfall. Then Mother Nature turned off the faucet. Expected spring rains failed to arrive. By early July lightning had torched thousands of fires in northern Idaho and western Montana. Rangers of the then-infant U.S. Forest Service recruited firefighters anywhere they could find them. Loggers, miners, and even derelicts from the skid rows of Butte and Spokane were all marched into the woods to man fire lines. With pay at twenty-five cents an hour, their efforts were often less than enthusiastic.

Still, this ragtag army managed to hold some 3,000 fires in check. By mid-August it appeared as though the region might make it through the fire season with losses lower than expected. Then, on August 20, in the words of the regional forest boss, "all hell broke loose." Elers Koch, supervisor of Montana's Lolo National Forest, recalled the turn of events:

> For two days the wind blew a gale from the southwest. . . . Little fires picked up into big ones. Fire lines which had been held for days melted away under the fierce blast. The sky turned a ghastly yellow, and at four o'clock it was black dark ahead of the advancing flames.

*Small portion of the aftermath of the 1910 firestorm, Lolo National Forest.*
—USDA Forest Service, Northern Region

Hundreds of small fires merged into one gigantic wall of flame. At wind speeds up to seventy miles an hour, the firestorm charged northeast from Idaho's Clearwater Forest into the Coeur d'Alene Forest and across the Bitterroot Divide into Montana. The wind uprooted large trees and hurled them into the air. Fire crews stood helpless and then grew desperate to escape. Old-timers later recalled crazed men flinging themselves into the flames. In all, seventy-eight firefighters and seven civilians perished, most of them on the Idaho side. A crew of eighteen burned to death near a cabin on Big Creek off the St. Joe River. Another eight men suffocated in the Bullion Mine near the Montana-Idaho line.

But many survived, thanks to the quick thinking of their leaders. Ed Pulaski ordered his crew of more than forty men to lie down inside a mine tunnel on Idaho's Placer Creek. The men emerged badly burned but alive. On the Northern Pacific line in Montana, firefighters ran toward a railroad tunnel. Convinced the draft would suck the fire through the tunnel, an astute crew member warned them, "If you want to get roasted quick that's a good place to do it." They returned to their camp, built a backfire, and weathered the firestorm.

As the flames shot down the St. Regis ravine, bridges and ties of the newly completed Milwaukee Road line were swept away. Rails buckled in the heat. A refugee train reached Taft and loaded most of the citizens. Determined rangers sought to save the Forest Service station there, but they got little help from the townspeople. Many had tried to drink up Taft's liquor supply before the fire hit, so they were in no condition to assist.

Farther down the line the blaze made quick work of the false-fronted wooden buildings in the hamlets of Haugan and DeBorgia. At Haugan, residents found refuge in a pit they shared with terrified deer and bears. Again, the local hotel remained filled with men downing as much whiskey as possible.

The small mining town of Saltese also lay in the path of the blaze and seemed doomed. A makeshift crew of railroad workers and forest rangers strung out a fire line and poured water on every rooftop, saving the town. A reporter from Missoula recorded, "At the moment the fire hit, there was a roar as of a thousand cyclones and there was the awful realization of the force of the onrushing destroyer."

As the fire swept north into the lower Clark Fork Valley, it leveled a railroad station and the sawmill at Trout Creek. On Swamp Creek near Noxon, the blaze trapped a large crew of firefighters on a steep ridge. Panic-stricken, four of the men tried to outrun the flames. They did not make it. The rest of the crew burrowed into the ground and survived.

Finally, in the early morning hours of August 22, the wind shifted, and rain began to fall. It took more than a week for the rain to douse all the fires. The blowup left more than 3 million acres of forest blackened. The fire had covered an area the size of Connecticut. Many refugees who flooded into Missoula and Spokane had escaped with only the clothes on their backs.

Far to the east, the fire produced a phenomenon known as "the five dark days." When the plume of smoke hit Buffalo, New York, streetlights were turned on at noon for visibility.

The most lasting legacy of the 1910 fire was the philosophy it instigated among forest managers. Forty years later forester William Greeley summarized, "Congress and the Forest Service now realized that fire protection was the number one job of the Forest Service." The result was teams of smoke jumpers, bulldozed fire lines, and a network of trails to facilitate access to potential burns.

Only in recent years did foresters begin having second thoughts about this policy. Prior to 1910, lightning-caused fires would burn up to half a million acres in Montana each year. As part of a natural process, the mosaic they created prevented larger fires from breaking out. Fire suppression has created vast areas of old, diseased, and dying trees ripe for another holocaust. But now, seekers of solitude have built their homes in those trees. A fire manager for Montana's Lolo National Forest concluded, "The clock is ticking. The right lightning strike at the right time in the right weather and there will be disaster."

## TAFT

### *The Wickedest City in America*

Five miles east of the summit of Lookout Pass an exit on I-90 designates the Taft area. The freeway literally lies on top of the site of one of the wildest construction camps in the annals of railroad building. Named after U.S. president William Howard Taft, the town arose in 1907 as the center of operation for crews working on the Milwaukee Road's 8,771-foot-long train tunnel through the Bitterroot Divide at St. Paul Pass.

At the height of construction, some 2,000 men labored day and night clearing the rail route through the mountain at a rate of about six feet a day. Many of the unskilled immigrants spoke no English. They had been shipped west in cattle cars, courtesy of labor contractors in New York. A depression that year pushed wages down to a dollar a day. The "coyote men" who engaged in the dangerous business of packing gunpowder in the cold, wet tunnel earned more—about $2.50 a day.

*Taft during its heyday.* —Mansfield Library Archives, University of Montana, Missoula

After work the men converged in Taft, where the proprietors of twenty-seven saloons and several gambling halls, along with at least 200 prostitutes (known locally as "canaries"), eagerly waited to separate them from their money. Edith May Schuller, one of the few married women living in Taft, recalled that "murders, fights, and shootings spelled the normal, for the day when nothing of the sort occurred was indeed rare."

Taft's isolated location in rugged mountains eighty miles from the nearest sheriff encouraged the lawlessness. Reportedly after one spring snowmelt, more than a dozen bodies were found in nearby ravines or behind the drinking establishments. Horror stories of the debauchery in Taft led the Missoula Ministerial Association to petition county officials to revoke the liquor licenses of all the saloons. "Our county is becoming notorious from New York to Seattle," the petition noted. Indeed, the Chicago *Tribune* labeled Taft "the wickedest city in America, a plague spot of vice."

But neither the church leaders of Missoula nor a fire that wiped out the business district were able to tame Taft. During the fire, saloon patrons simply lugged the piano and cases of champagne to the streets, where their reveries continued. The embers had not yet cooled before the saloon owners began rebuilding.

Then in January 1909 the Milwaukee's tunnel "holed through," and the workers drifted to other jobs. Most of what was left of Taft burned during the 1910 forest fire. The hotel with its elegant mahogany bar survived as a popular roadside attraction until the freeway arrived in 1962. With the abandonment of the Milwaukee Road line in the late 1970s, the St. Paul Pass tunnel was boarded up and ownership shifted to the U.S. Forest Service. Both the tunnel and the rail route across the Bitterroot Divide are still regarded as engineering marvels.

## CEDAR CREEK

One mile east of Superior, I-90 crosses Cedar Creek, a small tributary of the Clark Fork River. During the early 1870s, hundreds of people flooded the upper reaches of this stream. It was the biggest gold rush ever witnessed in western Montana.

In 1870 French Canadian prospectors Louis Barrette and Adolph Lozeau discovered a rich placer area on Cedar Creek. They christened it Louisville Bar. They vowed to keep their discovery a secret, but Lozeau told some of his drinking partners. This touched off the rush. Missoula merchant Frank Worden observed, "It is not often we like to say anything about stampedes, but we are now having one of the wildest ones we ever saw."

Ultimately several thousand people, mostly white and Chinese men, flocked to the tiny gulch and staked more than 2,700 claims. The original discoverers made their fortune by selling overpriced food and whiskey to the gold seekers and ferrying them across the Clark Fork. In fact, most of those who got rich from the rush were merchants. A census in the summer of 1870 showed the two wealthiest men on the gulch to be a restaurant owner and a wholesale liquor dealer.

Unlike most placer gold rushes that ended after only a year or less, the Cedar Creek boom lasted nearly five years. When the gold played out on one section of the creek, prospectors simply relocated upstream. The result was a succession of boomtowns—Louisville, Forest City, Mayville—each located farther up the creek. Most were like Louisville, which one observer described as "a city with streets 20 feet wide, and cabins, shanties and shelters perched on every spot, and men as densely thronged as in a bivouac." Ultimately more than 10,000 people came and left the region.

By late 1874, the excitement was over. People abandoned the final boomtown of Mayville in such a hurry that the bakery, saloon, and pool hall stood fully furnished for years. Even the billiard balls lay in place on the tables. Estimates of the gold extracted from Cedar Creek range from $4 to $10 million. Of more lasting duration were the scars left on the streambed after the miners used hydraulic hoses to get at deeper ore.

A later mineral boom on Iron Mountain north of Superior lasted even longer. Throughout most of the 1890s, a tramway with huge buckets on steel cables carried ore to a mill in Superior.

### ALBERTON

The community of Alberton arose and existed solely as a result of the Milwaukee Road rail line. Named after a president of the line, Albert J. Earling, Alberton flourished for years as a major division point. After the railroad left western Montana in 1980, the depot became a senior citizen's center and a Milwaukee caboose became a museum. The town continued to celebrate Railroad Days each July in memory of its departed industry.

Alberton's most memorable and tragic episode was also railroad related, but it took place long after the Milwaukee had pulled out. At 4 A.M. on April 11, 1996, five tanker cars on an eastbound freight train jumped the tracks a mile west of town. A cloud of deadly chlorine gas spewed from one of the ruptured tankers. It left motorists on I-90 temporarily blinded and gasping for breath. As one trucker later recalled, "You feel like your lungs are on fire."

In Alberton, sirens aroused people from their sleep, and they were quickly evacuated to Missoula. The effects of the toxic fumes hospitalized more than 100 people. One person, a transient aboard the train, died from breathing the gas. For the next seventeen days, the residents of Alberton lived in motels in Missoula as crews cleaned up the mess in their town.

## COUNCIL GROVE

It is often necessary for drivers to leave the beaten path to get a close-up look at historical landmarks. If you exit the freeway at Frenchtown and proceed north toward Missoula on Mullan Road, you will encounter a number of significant places. Several miles east of Frenchtown stands a box-like brick structure known as Primrose Substation. It is the best-preserved transformer house remaining from the era when the Milwaukee Road ran electric locomotives from Harlowton, Montana, to Avery, Idaho.

By turning south onto a short dirt road near milepost 5, motorists reach Council Grove, the site of one of Montana's most important treaty councils between whites and Native Americans. With its meadows and clumps of tall trees near the banks of the Clark Fork River, the place today looks much like it did in 1855. In the mid-July heat of that year, more than 1,200 members of three tribes parleyed with a band of twenty-two whites led by Washington territorial governor Isaac Stevens.

*Chief Charlo.*
—Mansfield Library Archives, University of Montana, Missoula

The Indians sat on their blankets as their leaders—Victor of the Salish (or Flathead), Alexander of the Pend d'Oreille (or Kalispel), and Michel of the Kutenai—listened to Stevens try to persuade them to give up most of their land and move onto a common reservation. It took eight days of hard bargaining before the matter was settled. The final Hellgate Treaty was a vague, makeshift document that left one very important matter—the final location of Victor's Salish—up in the air. Victor refused to move his people north to the Jocko Valley favored by the other two chiefs. So finally, Article 11 of the treaty allowed the Salish to retain their Bitterroot Valley south of Lolo Creek until the area "shall be carefully surveyed and examined." No whites would be allowed to settle there until the survey was complete. If the survey determined the Bitterroot to be better suited for the tribe, part of the area would be set aside as a reservation for them.

The Pend d'Oreille and Kutenai moved to the reservation in the Jocko Valley (now known as the Flathead Reservation). Here their welfare was left largely in the hands of Jesuit missionaries, after the government reneged on promises to supply them with schools, instructors, farming tools, and cash.

Meanwhile, in the Bitterroot Valley Victor and his people resided in peace for fifteen years, even though whites continued to move in. Following Victor's death in 1870, his only son, Slem-hi-key (Little Claw of the Grizzly Bear), christened Charlo, became chief. Pressured by petitions from white settlers, President Ulysses S. Grant agreed to force the Indians onto the Jocko reservation. In August 1872 his agent, Gen. James A. Garfield, came to arrange a treaty. The Salish resisted. They argued that because seventeen years had elapsed since the government had promised to survey their land, this constituted tacit approval of their remaining in the Bitterroot.

After Garfield promised houses and cash allotments, two subchiefs, Arlee and Adolf, put their marks on the articles of agreement. Charlo refused to sign. Yet when the published version of the treaty appeared, Charlo's mark mysteriously appeared at the bottom. Garfield later rationalized the forgery, stating that once the removal began, Charlo would join his other chiefs to keep his tribe intact.

Following this bit of skulduggery Garfield returned to Washington, where he was eventually elected president. Charlo remained in his Bitterroot home, embittered and mistrustful of all whites. As more homesteaders flocked into the valley, Charlo's people sank into poverty.

Finally in 1891, with his people now near starvation, Charlo announced, "I will go. . . . My young men are becoming bad; they have no place to hunt. My women are hungry. For their sake I will go. . . . I do not believe your promises." On October 17 the Salish folded their tents, assembled on the main street of Stevensville, and rode single file down the Bitterroot Valley. Some of the whites lining the street wept as they bid farewell to longtime friends. Charlo refused to cast a backward glance.

## HELLGATE

Four miles west of downtown Missoula, on Mullan Road, there is a convenience store called Hellgate Trading Post. It sits near the site of the first white settlement in the Missoula area. Among those accompanying Isaac Stevens during his 1853 railroad survey of western Montana was young Christopher P. Higgins. After resigning from the army in 1860, Higgins went to Walla Walla, Washington, where he entered the trading business with his friend Francis L. Worden. Higgins talked Worden into taking a pack train of merchandise, along with a heavy steel safe, across the Bitterroot Divide on the new Mullan Road.

They set up shop in a tent near where the Bitterroot River joins the Clark Fork—a strategic place to pick up traffic moving in all directions. They named the place Hell Gate Ronde after the canyon on the east end of present Missoula. The canyon, in turn, derived its name from early French Canadian trappers who called the area *Porte d'Enfer*, or Gates of Hell, because the Blackfeet frequently ambushed travelers here.

The settlement of Hellgate also became a dangerous place. It seldom had more than twenty residents, but in its four-year existence nine people met violent deaths here. In the dead of winter in 1864, a band of vigilantes rode in from Virginia City and lynched saloon keeper Cyrus Skinner and three others whom they suspected of evil deeds. Later that year, two card players shot at each other simultaneously during an argument over two and a half dollars. One gambler died instantly; the other bullet killed the bartender. Journalist Arthur Stone later wrote of Hellgate, "Its people were strong and healthy. Those who died, died quickly and without the preliminary of being sick."

## MISSOULA

### University Town

After Higgins and Worden moved their store from Hellgate to a site next to the flour mill they had erected near Rattlesnake Creek, Hellgate was abandoned, and Missoula was born. It is not surprising that Missoula evolved into the most important trade center in western Montana. It sits at the hub of five great river valleys—those of the the Jocko and Big Blackfoot Rivers to the north, the lower Clark Fork, the upper Clark Fork, and the

Bitterroot, which flows north into the Clark Fork roughly at the upper-lower division point.

The town of Missoula grew quickly. A military post established in the mid-1870s assured protection from Indian threats. Timber-rich forests assured a solid industrial base. But it was the decision by the Montana legislature in 1893 to locate the state university in Missoula that gave the town character and made it more than just a crossroads trade center.

Missoula has long been one of Montana's most politically and culturally diverse communities. In response to a contest by the local newspaper in 1993, one entrant wrote, "You're so Missoula if you wash your pickup before driving it to the symphony." Montanans sometimes decry the town's "radical" bent and compare it to other university towns such as Ann Arbor, Michigan; Madison, Wisconsin; and Berkeley, California. But Missoula's protests have generally been tamer than ones in those places.

Missoula's first big street demonstration had more to do with the lumber industry than the university. On a September evening in 1909, a nine-

*Jeannette Rankin.*
—Mansfield Library Archives,
University of Montana, Missoula

teen-year-old woman, six months pregnant, stepped off the train in Missoula. Elizabeth Gurley Flynn had come to help her husband organize the area's lumber-camp workers and migrant farm laborers. The Flynns belonged to the radical Industrial Workers of the World (IWW).

The couple staged rallies on downtown street corners, hoping to sway disgruntled workers to join their cause. At first the demonstrations were peaceful. Then a group of soldiers from Fort Missoula accused Mrs. Flynn of attacking them. Police had to intervene to protect Flynn from the soldiers. The incident goaded Missoula's city fathers to order enforcement of the town's law prohibiting street speaking. Arrests and jailings followed. Union newspapers in Butte and Spokane decried this infringement of free speech. They urged "every free born American . . . to go to Missoula and help the workers there win out." Scores of people heeded the call. They no sooner disembarked from the Northern Pacific trains when they proceeded to a street corner and were arrested and jailed.

Stubborn police and city officials failed to realize that they were furthering a plan orchestrated by Flynn. As the jails overflowed and meals for the prisoners depleted the city's coffers, Missoula's leaders began having second thoughts. When police tried to free the prisoners, they refused to leave. One man, who had left jail briefly to visit his wife, demanded to be let back in. The guard on duty told him, "You're out. Now stay out!" to the laughter of the crowd.

Faced with no other choice, the city fathers relented. The union regained its right to demonstrate. Missoula was the proving ground for this tactic of civil disobedience. IWW speakers employed the same methods, with less success, in towns throughout the Northwest. Elizabeth Gurley Flynn went on to become the president of the Communist Party of the United States. She died in Moscow in 1964.

### Woman of Peace

Another Montana woman, also from Missoula, made a far more lasting impact on her state and nation. The oldest of seven children, Jeannette Rankin was a quiet, timid girl while growing up on her father's ranch on Grant Creek north of Missoula. After graduating from the University of Montana, she worked briefly as a teacher. A stint at the University of Washington in Seattle in 1909, where she worked with prominent suffragette Minnie J. Reynolds, hardened Rankin into an activist for women's equality.

She embarked on a national speaking campaign on behalf of the suffrage cause. Rankin's work helped sway Montana to grant women the right to vote long before it happened nationwide. In fact, when she was elected to the U.S. House of Representatives in 1916, most women still were not allowed to vote. As the first woman ever to serve in either house of the United States Congress, Jeannette Rankin drew nationwide attention. Her vote against American entry into the First World War produced widespread press commentary, even though several dozen other Congressmen voted the same way.

The war and its aftermath wedded Rankin to the antiwar cause. Ever the fierce independent, she chose to live in a one-room house in Georgia without electricity or running water. From there she organized the Georgia Peace Society. Testifying before a congressional committee in 1934, Rankin declared, "You can no more win a war than you can win an earthquake."

Rankin's outspoken views aroused the ire of patriotic groups in Georgia. Some called her a communist. In Montana, however, she was still popular enough to win election to Congress in 1940, after her advertising branded her Democratic opponent a communist. But as the nation inched toward involvement in another world war, Rankin's pacifist leanings fell into disfavor. Then she unleashed a firestorm of anger by voting against America's declaration of war against Japan following the attack on Pearl Harbor. After casting the sole vote in Congress against war, she could only sigh, "I have nothing left now except my integrity."

The vote destroyed Rankin's political career, but throughout the long remainder of her life, she stood as an outspoken advocate of world peace. As the war in Vietnam raged, Rankin, then in her late eighties, emerged at the forefront of the antiwar movement. In January 1968 she marched in Washington with a group of 5,000 women who called themselves the Jeannette Rankin Brigade. During her final years, she seemed happy to be working for peace with what one biographer termed "an oddball combination of hippies, feminists, pacifists, antiwar students and various radicals."

To this day, opinion about Jeannette Rankin and all that she symbolized remains very much divided in Montana. Some honor her memory; others curse her name. But Rankin statues grace prominent places in both Montana's capitol building and the Statuary Hall in Washington D.C.

### University of Montana: Independent Minds

In speaking at the dedication of the Missoula University in 1895, Montana pioneer Wilbur Fisk Sanders urged the pursuit of learning for its own sake and concluded, "Hold not up to these pupils hopes of money or office . . . their high service is to save the world from shame and thrall." From a modest start, with fifty students and four teachers in an old Missoula public school building, the university has weathered more than 100 years of tight budgets, underpaid faculty, and students seeking to "save the world from shame and thrall."

From the beginning Missoula took pride in its university. City fathers had lobbied (bribed) legislators with five gallons of whiskey, a case of beer, a case of wine, and 350 cigars to win the university for the town. City founders C. P. Higgins and E. L. Bonner donated land nestled against the base of Mount Sentinel for the campus.

As the university grew, students and teachers asserted their independence. Missoulians and outsiders watched their demonstrations with curiosity—sometimes in support, sometimes in anger. The removal of popular university president Edwin Craighead in 1915 touched off the first organized protest. After Craighead rubbed a Missoula banker the wrong way, the state board of education decided to fire him. Protest meetings and a petition by the students failed to alter the course of events.

During the First World War university president Edward O. Sisson, schooled in Germany, advocated tolerance at a time when few were in a tolerant mood. After Sisson scheduled a socialist to speak at a student forum, many demanded closure of the forum. Shortly after the war, economics professor Louis Levine challenged Montana's economic giant, the Anaconda Copper Company, by publishing a study of the Montana's unfair system of mine taxation. This led the university chancellor to suspend Levine from his teaching post. The flap drew national attention. Outcry from students and alumni led to Levine's reinstatement.

Several years later, another storm arose after professor Sidney Cox allowed a campus literary magazine to publish the phrase "son-of-a-bitch." Again the Anaconda Company was scandalized. Company newspapers demanded an investigation of the university for "moral turpitude." Cox soon left Missoula for a professorship at Dartmouth, and things calmed down again.

During the 1950s intolerance made life uncomfortable for many at the university. Montana's American Legion complained that teachers at Montana's universities in Missoula and Bozeman were associated with subversive organizations. Montana University professor and renowned social critic Leslie Fiedler drew particular wrath for his barbed commentaries.

Throughout the 1960s, the advance guard of the postwar baby boom flocked into Missoula, swelling enrollment and making their presence felt. Civil-rights demonstrators marched from campus to the courthouse lawn. Students demanded more voice in university governance, so president Robert Pantzer appointed them to key committees. But by far the greatest cause of campus strife was America's involvement in the war in Vietnam. As early as 1962, the student newspaper, the *Kaimin*, was raging, "Our country has been wrong too righteously too often and seldom more so than in southeast Asia where it is waging a non-constitutional war."

*University of Montana rally protesting the Kent State slayings, May 1970.* —Mansfield Library Archives, University of Montana, Missoula

Protests came to a head early in May 1970 after President Richard Nixon sent American troops into Cambodia. On May 4, Ohio National Guard troops killed four students on the campus of Kent State University. The following day, Montana joined hundreds of other universities in loud outcry. Some 2,000 students rallied on the campus oval. More than one-third of students and faculty began a weeklong boycott of classes.

The following day, a small group of students occupied the old men's gym, site of the offices for ROTC military training. After President Pantzer agreed to suspend ROTC for the week as a small step to avert violence, the student group abandoned their sit-in. They continued to demand an end to military training on the campus, and it was agreed to put the issue to a vote among students and faculty.

The chaotic week ended when about forty young men burned their draft cards during a candlelight vigil. A week later, students and teachers voted overwhelmingly to retain the ROTC program on campus. In the end both President Pantzer and the students received praise for keeping the protests free of violence. Many other campuses had not been so lucky.

Still, there were those who denounced the university's teachers and students for their boisterous behavior. Student striker Charles Briggs perhaps best summed up the significance of the protests when he observed, "I find it difficult to believe human beings attending a university can attend classes and largely ignore what occurs in the world at large."

# Eureka—Troy

## KOOTENAI COMMERCE

The highways running between Eureka and Troy parallel the Kootenai River as it loops into Montana from Canada. For much of this length, the Kootenai is no longer a river. Its waters form Lake Koocanusa, backed up behind the massive Libby Dam which was completed in the mid-1970s.

Before white settlers arrived in the area, generations of Kutenai Indians plied this river in their unique, slender boats with long projections at each end. Flotillas of up to 300 boats were a common sight as the various tribal bands visited one another.

Steamboats arrived on the Kootenai relatively late. Unlike on other rivers, where railroads meant the demise of riverboat traffic, in the Kootenai country the arrival of the Great Northern in the early 1890s gave river travel its first real impetus. The railroad reached Libby just as the rich North Star Mine began operating in British Columbia on the upper Kootenai. The nearest smelters lay far to the south at Great Falls, Montana, and Everett, Washington. Seeing the opportunity, former Texas cattleman B. Walter Jones and partner Harry Depew launched the *Annerly*. Passengers slept on the deck and cooked meals on a coal stove in the middle of the boat. For most of the next decade, this small stern-wheeler and its larger successors hauled ore and passengers between the Canadian mines and the port of Jennings, east of Libby.

The treacherous waters of the Kootenai claimed a number of steamboat casualties. The most spectacular wreck occurred when two stern-wheelers, *Gwendoline* and *Ruth*, entered the canyon above Jennings. A log lodged in the *Ruth*'s wheel, sending it crashing out of control against rocks on the shore. As the *Gwendoline* charged down the river behind it, the wreckage of the *Ruth* blocked the narrow channel. The collision tore off most of the starboard side of the *Gwendoline*. The Kootenai steamboat era ended in 1898, when the rails finally reached the Canadian mines.

*Kootenai River steamboat at Libby.* —Lincoln County Library, Libby

Shortly after the steamboats disappeared from the Kootenai, the final phase of the river's commerce began, with big log drives downstream, first to Canada's Kootenay Lake and later to the Weyerhaeuser Mill at Bonners Ferry, Idaho. Each spring "river pigs" armed with long poles prodded the logs to their destination. About a decade after they began, the Kootenai log drives ended when the Montana legislature ruled that timber cut in Montana could no longer be milled outside the state.

## EUREKA

### *Lumber Strike*

Eureka lies near the northwest corner of Montana, nestled between a ridge of mountains and the Tobacco River. It is hard to believe that this peaceful little town, with its historic park at one end and sawmill at the other, was the point of origin for one of the nation's most widespread and bitter lumber strikes.

During the early decades of the twentieth century, loggers and mill workers in Montana had reasons to feel disgruntled. The pay was not enough to support a family. The men risked injuries from misdirected axes and saws, trees falling in the wrong direction, and huge log loads toppling from sleds. They lived in camps in the woods where up to forty men slept in uninsulated bunkhouses on straw mattresses infested with lice. District Forester F. A. Silcox once wrote his superiors that the lumber workers were being "treated not quite as good as workhorses."

Because most loggers were unskilled, the craft unions did not bother recruiting them. But the radical Industrial Workers of the World, or Wobblies, took more interest in their plight. Recruiters for the IWW understood well the alienation these men felt. IWW rhetoric of class warfare and economic revolution found fertile ground in the woods of western Montana.

In March 1917, IWW delegates met in Spokane and announced plans for a series of strikes throughout the region. Within weeks 100 employees of the Eureka Lumber Company had walked off the job. After striking workers kept others away from the rivers, where logs awaited the spring drive, the entire mill shut down. A panicked press reported that several hundred Wobblies had set up a "jungle camp" near Fortine, south of Eureka, where they were threatening violence.

Company officials wired the governor for military assistance. In asking for federal troops, Governor Samuel Stewart took advantage of wartime hysteria, declaring that "several Germans and many other foreigners" were among the strikers. Soon forty soldiers patrolled the streets of Eureka while another eighty-five guarded the Great Northern Railway property. This intimidating display of strength had its effect. By the end of the month, most strikers had returned to work.

Although the IWW effort in Eureka failed, it touched off strikes throughout the region. In Libby, Columbia Falls, and Whitefish, strikers were met by angry citizen committees and law enforcement officers. The Kalispell city council passed a sedition ordinance, making it a crime to advocate disrespect for any local law. As the strikes spread to the big Anaconda Company mill in Bonner, manager Kenneth Ross blamed the turmoil on "German sympathizers and the spies of Germany."

But most strikers had no special interest in the war. They hoped only to gain an eight-hour work day, higher wages, and improved working conditions. Charges against them of treason and violence usually proved baseless. By September, when the strikes collapsed, more than 100 Wobbly leaders had been charged with various acts of sabotage and sedition.

To his credit, Anaconda Lumber Company manager Kenneth Ross recognized that the strikes stemmed from real needs among the loggers. He convened a meeting of the Montana Lumber Manufacturers' Association in Missoula and persuaded the headstrong mill operators to begin making improvements. Soon lumberjacks were sleeping on beds with real springs.

## LIBBY AND TROY

The imposing mountains, deep ravines, and dense forests along the southern loop of the Kootenai River kept settlers away for decades after whites first explored the region. The area became known as the Montana Wilds. Potential visitors were further discouraged after Kutenai Indians ambushed and killed three members of the first party of prospectors to discover gold on Libby Creek in the mid-1860s.

The placer mines along Libby Creek were just beginning to boom when the Great Northern Railway reached this area in 1891. Owners of Libby's business district relocated their buildings to be near the rails. Building material was close at hand. Early residents carried lanterns at night to keep from falling over the stumps of the trees felled to build their houses.

Early Libby was so isolated that even the prostitutes who usually swarmed into such boomtowns failed to show up. But the town still had its share of wildness. When one Henry Van Wyck felt threatened by a man called French Charley, he retaliated by blowing off Charley's head with a shotgun. Van Wyck pleaded self-defense, was acquitted, and later became a prominent justice of the peace.

With the railroad came the equipment needed for hard-rock mining in the surrounding hills. The Snowshoe Mine in the rugged Cabinet Mountains near Libby produced more than a million dollars in lead, silver, and gold.

Downstream from Libby, the town of Troy grew up as a Great Northern division point. Soon, as one settler recalled, "fifteen saloons gaily lit were filled to the doors with wild men and wild women yelling, singing, dancing, and cursing with glasses lifted high." During the construction days, Troy had such a reputation for lawlessness that whenever trains rolled through the town the car doors were kept locked to avert holdups.

The great forest fire of 1910 threatened to wipe out the entire town. Men used a railroad company hose to soak the buildings in the business district. A locomotive was kept steamed up and ready to evacuate everyone. Only a shift in the wind saved Troy from a fiery demise.

The 1910 fires were still raging when Minnesota lumber magnate Julius Neils arrived in Libby. He bought up huge tracts of burned and unburned forests in the area at salvage rates. He also purchased Libby's Dawson Lumber Company mill and reorganized it as the Libby Lumber Company. Neils and his sons built this mill into the mainstay of Libby's economy. It changed hands several times in the late twentieth century before being purchased by the Stimson Lumber Company.

# Eureka—Somers

## WHITEFISH

### *The Big Mountain*

In terms of hype and overdevelopment, Montana's ski areas cannot measure up to places in Colorado, Vermont, or California. But the quality of skiing here compares favorably to those places. Of the state's four large destination ski resorts, one—Whitefish's Big Mountain—stands as a monument to the spirit of community dedication and hard work.

Like so many towns in Montana, Whitefish arose as a result of a decision made by the manager of a railroad. Ten years after completing his Great Northern line, James J. Hill decided, in the name of speed and efficiency, to relocate the transcontinental route away from Kalispell and through the Whitefish Lake area. The few settlers here scurried to place a town next to the tracks, even though one of them pointed out that the place was "a heavily wooded, swampy marsh, full of green frogs, lizards, and other creeping things." They cleared away the thick trees. A workforce of local hoboes and transients, known as "Weary Willies," removed the stumps. The railroad and nearby lumber mills gave Whitefish a solid economic base.

In the 1930s, local residents began skiing down the slopes of the Big Mountain, north of town. A small group formed the Hell-roaring Ski Club. Led by Whitefish High School science teacher Lloyd "Mully" Muldoon, members of the club walked up the mountain and skied down on crude, heavy skis with iron bindings forged by a local blacksmith. Their bamboo ski poles were frequently employed as splints after skiers broke their legs. Muldoon recalled carrying children into their houses with broken legs and nearly being attacked by irate parents. In 1939 Muldoon staged Montana's first high school ski meet on the Big Mountain. Following the Second World War, local promoters began thinking seriously about developing skiing as a major industry. They invited Great Falls ski enthusiasts George Prentice and Ed Schenck to study the mountain. Schenck later wrote, "When we finally struggled to the top, we found breath-taking, vast, open snowfields where you can ski in any direction . . . and sunshine—all the things a skier dreams about."

Schenck and Prentice agreed to stake $20,000 of their own money in the venture. The Whitefish Chamber of Commerce raised the rest of the needed cash by selling stock. Throughout much of 1947 Schenck, Prentice,

*Ski entrepreneurs Ed Schenck* (left) *and George Prentice stand on the Big Mountain.* —The Big Mountain, Whitefish

and an army of volunteers performed most of the work, so payrolls were modest. Still, residents often had to be cajoled into purchasing more stock just to keep the struggling enterprise afloat.

Late in the December evening, before the new area was scheduled to open, workers installed the lift motor and attached the T-bars to the cable, using a flashlight to read the instructions. A crowd gathered the following morning. The motor sputtered and the first skiers took off. To the horror of Prentice and Schenck, the lift sent riders ten feet into the air and spun them in circles. They realized too late that the lift's retracting spring they'd just wound up had already been wound at the factory. Most of the skiers had never ridden a T-bar, so they thought this was how it was supposed to work. The crowd cheered as Prentice and Schenck struggled to keep from laughing.

The citizens of Whitefish continued to nurture their fledgling enterprise. Townspeople worked on weekends to widen the road to the small lodge. Local restaurants provided meals for the crews. During the first season, a lift support broke and volunteers lugged the repair timbers up the hill through waist-deep snow. Floodlights borrowed from the local theater enabled them to work through the night. In spite of such mishaps, by 1949 the people of Whitefish felt ready to stage a major ski event—the National Downhill, Slalom and Combined Races. Townspeople boarded the racers in their homes for free.

Eventually the enterprise began to show a profit. More tows were added, runs cleared, and lodges built. Today the mountain can accommodate up to 6,000 skiers a day on a greater area of skiable terrain than Aspen's. Tommy Moe, America's 1994 Olympic downhill gold medal winner, grew up in Whitefish and learned to ski at Big Mountain. When asked how all this happened, Schenck and Prentice often told people: "It's easy. All you have to do is find a town like Whitefish."

### DEMERSVILLE

Settlement in the country north of Flathead Lake preceded the arrival of the Great Northern Railway, but not by much. Many settlers came in from the south. They detrained Northern Pacific cars in Ravalli and moved up crude overland roads beside the lake. It was not long before entrepreneurs converted Flathead Lake from a transportation barrier to a thoroughfare.

In 1883 a large sailboat, the *Swan*, began carrying passengers and freight from Dooley's Landing near present-day Polson to points several miles up the Flathead River north of the lake. Calm water on the lake and the river's current made these trips a weeklong ordeal, but once the boat changed owners it gained a new steam engine and a new name, the *U.S. Grant*. Soon other steamboats, with names like *Pocahontas, Dora, Mary Ann, Crescent*, and *Tom Carter*, competed in hauling passengers and freight on the north-south lake route. The gem of Flathead Lake was the *State of Montana*, a stern-wheeler measuring 150 by 26 feet. The boat boasted a bar and eighteen luxurious staterooms.

Some of these steamboats fell victim to storms, ice on the lake, boiler explosions, and fires caused by sparks. Once the Great Northern Railway reached the upper Flathead, the boat business plummeted. The southern half of Flathead Lake witnessed a brief revival of steamboat traffic in 1910, when the Flathead Indian Reservation was opened up to white settlement.

At the height of the Flathead Lake steamboat era, French Canadian merchant Telesphore J. "Jake" Demers recognized an opportunity. He built a general-merchandise store at Gregg's Landing, the head of navigation on the Flathead River north of the lake. He immodestly changed the name of the place to Demersville. Fully loaded boats began arriving daily. Most of

*Demersville street scene, 1891.* —Thain White Collection, Flathead County Library, Kalispell

the freight deposited at the docks consisted of construction materials for the advancing rails of the Great Northern.

Because Demersville had the region's only bank, railroad workers flocked in to cash their checks and blow their money. The town sold more than seventy saloon licenses. A single policeman tried to keep order. One reporter noted, "Robberies in these resorts were so common as to attract little attention, while rare was the morning that did not reveal a more bloody tragedy."

The town's justice of the peace, Charley "Old Shep" Shepherd, once fined a dead man for having a concealed weapon. After finding a twenty-dollar gold piece along with a revolver in the dead man's pocket, the judge announced the fine, grabbed the gold, and walked away.

In 1891 a fire wiped out an entire business block in Demersville. One saloon proprietor sat astride the roof of his establishment as a bucket brigade passed water up to him to wet down his building. Generous quantities of bottled beer also went up the side of the building to keep up the courage of the firemen. More beer than water ended up being poured on the roof, but the building did not catch fire.

Later that same year, the Great Northern chose to run its line through the new town of Kalispell, just to the north. A few optimists in Demersville predicted that the Northern Pacific would build a branch up the shore of Flathead Lake to their town, but most residents began relocating to Kalispell. By the end of 1891, Demersville lay nearly vacant.

## KALISPELL

### *The Town the Conrads Built*

By the time Charles E. Conrad and his wife, Alicia, visited the Flathead Valley in 1890, he was already a wealthy man. Charles and his brother, William, had built a freighting and mercantile empire from their base in Fort Benton. They bought and sold all types of goods, established banks, and invested in cattle ranches. The Conrads had planned to move to Spokane, but after viewing the majestic Flathead country they changed their minds.

Still craving new business ventures, Conrad went to St. Paul, Minnesota, to visit his old friend James J. Hill. Hill agreed to locate a division point for his Great Northern Railway wherever Conrad chose to buy land. Conrad persuaded several Flathead Valley settlers to sell land to him, named the place Kalispell, and began platting a town site.

*Charles E. Conrad.*
—Conrad Mansion, Kalispell

On the last day of December 1891, the Great Northern's first locomotive arrived. Citizens of Kalispell staged a big celebration. Flags, bunting, and four large arches trimmed with evergreen saluted Hill and his railroad. Mary Kimmerly, the first white female resident of the Flathead Valley, and pioneer rancher Nicholas Moon drove a silver spike as the band played "Yankee Doodle." The crowd then dined on barbecued oxen, lit bonfires, and danced at a grand ball. The eccentric Moon stayed in Kalispell just long enough to visit the local red-light district, then packed up his belongings and moved to Canada where, he said, he could get some peace and quiet.

From the beginning, however, the Great Northern experienced problems on its route through the Kalispell area. The curves and steep grade on the line west of town finally led officials to reroute through Whitefish. People in Kalispell were furious. The local newspaper called James J. Hill a tyrant. Citizens hanged his effigy close to the place where the arches had proclaimed his virtues just a decade earlier.

Some feared that Kalispell would go the way of Demersville. Charles Conrad had been dead for two years when the Great Northern abandoned

*Alicia Conrad.*
—Conrad Mansion, Kalispell

Kalispell in 1904, but by then he had helped give the town a solid economic base. The Conrad National Bank had grown into the largest such establishment in northwestern Montana. By the turn of the century, some forty sawmills were cutting lumber and ties in the woods around Kalispell.

A large population of Chinese residents gave Kalispell a cosmopolitan flavor. Many lived in underground dens below their business establishments. They invited all the town's residents to help them celebrate the Chinese New Year with food and fireworks. Still, the bigoted local press berated them and accused them of smuggling opium from Canada.

For years after Charles Conrad's death, the elaborate Norman-style mansion he and Alicia had erected served as Kalispell's main social center. The renowned Spokane architect Kirtland Cutter designed the house which sat on seventy-two wooded acres. Cutter traveled east to pick out the oak trees for the paneling. The rock came from a formation near Essex that Cutter had spotted from the train. Tiffany's in New York furnished the stained glass.

On Christmas Day 1895, the year the house was finished, the Conrads invited to their home Kalispell residents who otherwise would have spent their holiday alone or in boarding houses. The hosts served their guests sumptuous food near a huge candlelit tree, and Santa left gifts for every-

*The Conrads' Norman-style home.* —Conrad Mansion, Kalispell

one. A week later, everyone in town attended a grand New Year's ball at the Conrad mansion.

Alicia Conrad continued to host parties and balls until her death in 1923. The most memorable event took place one Halloween after a fire had burned a huge hole through the mansion's roof. Mrs. Conrad simply incorporated the fire damage into the party decor, decorated the place with Spanish moss, artificial bats, and lifelike volcanoes, and called it Dante's Inferno.

Following Alicia's death, other family members occupied the mansion until the mid-1960s, when it fell vacant. Local children called it "the haunted house." Finally, in 1975 Conrad's youngest daughter, Alicia Campbell, donated it to the city of Kalispell and restoration work began. Today visitors enjoy guided tours of this historic landmark, located six blocks east of Kalispell's Main Street, at the corner of Fourth and Woodland.

## SOMERS

### Lumber Company Town

The tiny community of Somers sits on the north shore of Flathead Lake. By the end of the nineteenth century, James J. Hill's Great Northern Railway was looking for a permanent source of lumber and railroad ties. Hill convinced his friend, veteran Minnesota lumberman John O'Brien, that the forested region between Kalispell and Flathead Lake held potential as a site for a big sawmill.

O'Brien purchased 350 acres from Tom McGovern, who had homesteaded on the lake's north shore, and began erecting the mill. O'Brien recruited many loggers and mill workers from Stillwater, Minnesota, and the Great Northern hauled them west at a reduced fare.

When the O'Brien lumber complex opened in 1901, it included plants for manufacturing and treating ties and producing finished lumber. O'Brien agreed to supply 600,000 three-cornered ties to the Great Northern each year for the next twenty years. Most workers earned twenty cents an hour; sawyers made six dollars a day. Many lived in company-built houses, shopped in a company store, and paid the company a dollar a month for the services of a doctor.

The company also erected a ten-foot-high fence around the town, possibly to help keep out union organizers. Despite the fence, the Industrial Workers of the World found a foothold at the Somers mill. By 1910 three strikes had shut down the plant, but finally the union managed to improve wages and working conditions.

For many years, up until 1931, logs reached the mill via river drives from as far away as Swan Lake. Once the drives emptied into Flathead

162

Lake, large rudder booms captured the logs, and tugboats pulled the entire mass across the lake to the Somers mill. Later, trucks displaced the river and lake drives. In 1948 the Great Northern closed down the Somers operation because of the diminishing supply of timber on company land.

US 2
# Columbia Falls—Kalispell
### 14 miles

### COLUMBIA FALLS

James A. Talbott arrived in the Columbia Falls area from Butte, just as the Great Northern was pushing its line through Marias Pass. Talbott and fellow speculators banked on the likelihood that the railroad would make the place a division point. In 1891 they bought up land, built a big hotel, and chartered a bank. They also managed to drive real estate prices so high that James J. Hill chose to locate his rail center in Kalispell.

Undaunted, Talbott decided to develop some coal deposits on the North Fork of the Flathead, float coal down the river on flatboats, and sell it to the railroad. Finding this process a bit slow, Talbott launched the steamboat *Oakes* on the upper Flathead. The boat's maiden voyage proved to be her last. Upstream from present Coram at a place called Red Lick Rapids, the engine failed and the boat drifted down the raging river. It eventually took on so much water that it capsized. The men on board barely escaped the icy water. They then endured a long, cold hike back to civilization. Later entrepreneurs salvaged the boat's winch, which was used for years afterward to pull stumps.

Talbott's other business ventures proved more profitable, and he erected an elaborate three-story mansion, Shellrock Manor. Following Talbott's death, his son-in-law turned the house into a motion-picture studio. In 1921 the studio turned out *Where Rivers Rise*, the first movie ever made in Montana. The film, about a logging feud among tough lumberjacks, proved a bust, and the studio folded. Twenty years later Shellrock Manor burned to the ground.

Columbia Falls had fewer than 700 residents until after the Second World War. Then the lumber industry revived, and the 564-foot-high Hungry Horse Dam was built. With cheap electricity available, the Anaconda Company brought in its large aluminum reduction plant and the population tripled.

163

# Somers—Missoula

## YELLOW BAY

### Flathead Cherries

Highways run along both the east and west shores of Flathead Lake. The drive along the west shore is faster, but the more scenic route is Montana 35 along the east shore. About midway down the lake on the east side, just inside the Flathead Indian Reservation, lies Yellow Bay. This is the site of the University of Montana's Biological Research Station. Professor Morton J. Elrod established the station in log farm buildings at Bigfork in 1899. Thirteen years later he moved the station to Yellow Bay. It was one of the first freshwater laboratories in the nation.

The Yellow Bay area is also the site of the first of many cherry orchards to line the east shore of Flathead Lake. Oscar Moen planted cherry and apple trees here in the early 1920s. Later each of the six Robbin brothers from Kalispell bought land here and began growing cherries on a larger scale. To clear away the thick forests and stumps they used dynamite and a Model A Ford engine hooked to a drum and steel cable.

The trees demanded constant care, so the brothers built cabins on the land. When the first cherry crops came in they hired area high school students to do the picking for two cents a pound. The Robbins then built a warehouse and packing plant near the highway. Motorists were eager to stop and buy cherries for ten cents a pound. Soon other orchards and fruit stands sprouted up along the shore. Before long, Flathead cherries were being shipped as far away as St. Paul, Minnesota.

Through the years, Flathead cherry growers have had to fight a constant battle with blossom-killing frosts, late spring rains that cause the fruit to split, and fruit flies. In 1936 a killer winter wiped out nearly every tree on the lake. A similar freeze in February 1989 killed more than 90 percent of the Flathead's cherry trees. Each time, stoic owners of the small orchards lining the lake began replanting. Historian R. C. Robbin termed the enterprise begun by his ancestors "largely a labor of love rather than a profitable venture."

## THE FLATHEAD RESERVATION

From Yellow Bay south to Evaro, seven miles north of I-90, motorists on Montana 35 and US 93 are on the Flathead Indian Reservation. Established by the Hellgate Treaty of 1855 for the Salish (or Flathead), Pend d'Oreille (or Kalispel), and Kutenai tribes, much of the reservation became eligible for white settlement thirty-two years later, when the Dawes Act passed. It took Congress another seventeen years to authorize the survey of the reservation and to begin making allotments. Prospective white homesteaders registered for a drawing in which 3,000 people gained the opportunity to make a down payment on a homestead. Among the first winners was a bachelor machinist for the Great Northern who said he was searching for a lady partner who could shoot ducks and milk cows.

After a second drawing failed to exhaust the supply of available land, the reservation was thrown open to the public with squatter's rights applying. During the 1910 homestead rush, Polson filled with excited land seekers. An extremely hot and dry summer caused many of the would-be farmers to sell out for whatever price they could get. Others simply abandoned their land. But some stayed on. Soon the Flathead Irrigation Project brought them needed water. The Montana Power Company completed Kerr Dam in the late 1930s, enabling electric pumps downstream from Polson to send water through an elaborate system of canals and reservoirs throughout the southern part of the reservation.

## POLSON

Generations of Salish Indians called the southern end of Flathead Lake *pied e'lai,* or "foot of the lake." In 1880 Harry Lambert built a log general store here, and people referred to the settlement as Lambert's Landing. It was nearly two more decades before the place gained a post office and changed its name to Polson.

David Polson and his Nez Perce wife had begun ranching northwest of Lambert's Landing in 1870. Polson was an accomplished fiddler, much in demand at local dances and Indian powwows. He died shortly after his namesake town was founded.

*Flathead Lake steamboat* S. S. Klondike *approaches the port of Polson.*
—Flathead Historical Museum, Polson

The town of Polson did not began to boom until the opening of the Flathead Reservation to white homesteaders in 1910. The Flathead Irrigation Project and nearby Kerr Dam bolstered the local economy. During the Great Depression, when most of Montana was losing people, Polson actually doubled its population. Many dryland farmers who had gone broke in eastern Montana came into this region hoping to start over. In 1954 Polson became the site of Montana's first plywood mill.

## RONAN

The community of Ronan derives its name from Maj. Peter Ronan. Ronan spent sixteen years as the government agent on the Flathead Indian Reservation. Some of his predecessors had proven to be swindlers who overbilled the government for supplies that they then failed to deliver to the Indians. Ronan served the tribes with honesty and compassion until his death in 1892.

The town of Ronan has experienced a number of traumas. In August 1912, a fire broke out in an automobile garage during a windstorm. By the time firemen got their chemical engine charged, half the town was ablaze. When the smoke cleared, most of the business district and the flour mill lay in ashes.

*1912 fire blackens much of downtown Ronan.* —Flathead Historical Museum, Polson

### Gangsters

At noon on June 18, 1929, two masked men entered the Ronan State Bank, waved pistols around, and stole $3,000. One dazed bank employee grabbed a pistol and chased the getaway car, firing into the air. A robber shot back, striking him in the arm. The robbers sped north, where they switched cars and drove back through Ronan undetected before proceeding south. The local press correctly surmised that the robbery was "without doubt the work of an expert gang."

Over the course of the summer the seven gang members—all men in their 20s—robbed businesses and individuals from St. Ignatius to Wolf Creek. They made their getaways in stolen sleek, high-powered Hudson and Studebaker touring cars.

The press fed eager readers every detail of the crime spree. The Montana Bankers' Association offered a big reward to anyone who could produce "any dead bank robbers." Sheriffs from Helena and Great Falls ambushed four of the gang in a shack on the Missouri River. Two managed to escape during the barrage of gunfire. Late in August, lawmen armed with sawed-off shotguns and rifles captured two more robbers holed up in a cabin near Helena. Floyd Grote, identified as one of the leaders of the gang, was never caught.

Two men eventually confessed to the robbery in Ronan. Tom Martin, the other gang leader, was convicted and sentenced to fifty years in the state prison for robbing the Great Northern Depot in Helena. Bobby Kelly, the mysterious "woman in white" who often accompanied the robbers during their crimes, was later found murdered in a Helena brothel.

## FORT CONNAH

A highway sign six miles north of St. Ignatius marks the nearby remains of Fort Connah, the last trading post of Britain's Hudson's Bay Company to be built south of the U.S.-Canadian boundary. American officials in Oregon had warned the company that a post here would violate international agreements, but in 1847 they built it anyway. From here Angus McDonald, his son Duncan, and other post custodians conducted trade with area tribesmen until 1871.

The elder McDonald, a veteran mountain man, carried a full set of Shakespeare's works with him in his travels. He married the sister of a Nez Perce chief. At one powwow on the reservation, he painted his upper body bright red, donned an eagle-feather warbonnet, and matched skills with the best of the Indians in their games.

## The Mission at St. Ignatius

The oldest town on the Flathead Reservation, St. Ignatius predates the reservation itself. In 1854 Jesuit Father Adrian Hoecken moved his mission from eastern Washington to be closer to the Indians that the missionaries were trying to reach. The site at the foot of the Mission Mountains had long been a popular rendezvous place for area tribes. Here the missionaries erected a log cabin and a chapel. Soon more than 1,000 Indians had set up their tepees nearby.

Ten years later, four Sisters of Providence arrived from Montreal and opened a girls' boarding school and hospital. Besides the regular subjects, the sisters taught cooking, sewing, gardening, laundry, and dairy work. Because the early reservation Indian agents hoarded federal money, the nuns traveled through Montana's mining camps begging for funds among the many Irish Catholic prospectors.

In 1875 the Jesuits brought in a printing press from Europe. They taught the Indian boys how to set type, and soon they were printing Bible stories in their own language. Later a group of Ursuline nuns arrived and estab-

*1850s drawing of the St. Ignatius Mission complex.* —Mansfield Library Archives, University of Montana, Missoula

lished a kindergarten for the reservation's homeless orphans. By the early 1890s, the schools at St. Ignatius were educating 320 Indian children. Then, a child who "believed there would be no classes if there were no school-building" set a fire that destroyed both the school and dormitory. Although the education effort had survived the fire, a total cutoff of federal aid in 1901 dealt a crippling blow to the work of the Jesuits and nuns. From then on enrollment dropped and the schools struggled.

The beautiful brick church that stands on the mission site today was completed in the winter of 1894. Fifty-eight murals painted by Jesuit Brother Joseph Carignano grace the interior of the church. Carignano worked as a cook and handyman at the mission. A self-taught artist, he could work on his paintings only between his regular chores. He was known as a quick painter. His frescoes, depicting biblical scenes and the life of St. Ignatius Loyola, took only fourteen months to complete. Carignano helped decorate several other churches in the Pacific Northwest including Missoula's St. Francis Xavier Church.

## THE NATIONAL BISON RANGE

The National Bison Range covers a section of the Mission Valley southeast of St. Ignatius. Visitors can reach it from a road that cuts north from Montana 200 near Dixon. Here up to 500 bison—along with deer, big-horn sheep, antelope, and elk—roam on a protected preserve.

By the mid-1880s white hunters and settlers had all but exterminated the 60 million bison that had blanketed the Great Plains. The animals remained in only a few tiny pockets. One of these was the Mission Valley on the Flathead Reservation. Accounts differ as to how they got here.

According to one popular version, Sam Walking Coyote, a young Pend d'Oreille living among the Salish, had been hunting with the Blackfeet in the Milk River country sometime during the early 1870s. While here he married a Blackfeet, but because he already had a wife back home on the Flathead Reservation, he now was living in defiance of tribal rules against polygamy. Some of his Blackfeet friends suggested that he take several bison across the mountains to the Flathead country as a peace offering. He trained six of the animals to follow his horse and herded them into the Mission Valley. As Walking Coyote resumed living among the Salish his bison multiplied. In 1884 he decided to sell them to reservation ranchers Michel Pablo and Charles Allard. Walking Coyote took his $3,000 cash payment to Missoula. After several days of wild celebration, he was found murdered beneath the Higgins Street Bridge, his money gone.

In the Flathead tribal tradition, it was a man named Latati who brought the bison onto the reservation. When young Latati's father died, his mother married Walking Coyote, who sold the bison to the two ranchers unbeknownst to his new family.

By the time Charles Allard died in 1896, the Pablo-Allard herd had grown to more than 300 animals. Pablo held on to his share of the herd, but Allard's heirs sold theirs. In 1907, as the government prepared to open the reservation to white homesteaders, Pablo sold his 600 bison to Canadian buyers. They made plans to haul them north of the border by rail. But first, the headstrong animals had to be rounded up and loaded into the reinforced stock cars waiting at the railhead in Ravalli.

Pablo built corrals, hired twenty-five of the reservation's best cowboys, and the roundup began. The task proved more of a challenge than expected. As one of the cowboys later recalled:

> The buffalo is nothin at all like a cow-critter. A buffalo ain't afraid of nothin and don't stick with the herd like a cow will. And strong—a big bull could toss a horse and rider fifty feet! Weren't no good to argue!

Pablo finally built a large winged corral near the Flathead River. The corral enabled drivers to funnel the animals into reinforced crates, load them onto wagons, and haul them to the Ravalli railhead.

Every step in the process was hazardous. Two old bulls, whom the cowboys named Corbett and Sullivan after two leading boxers of the age, proved extremely surly. The wranglers finally managed to get them into the rail-

*Specially constructed wagons remove bison from the Flathead Reservation.* —Flathead Historical Museum, Polson

road cars and breathed a sigh of relief. Then Corbett broke through the side of the car and trotted off. In the end, it took five years to get the herd safely into Canada.

About the time that the Pablo roundup was getting under way, William T. Hornaday and members of the American Bison Society began planning a preserve for the animals somewhere on the Flathead Reservation. President Theodore Roosevelt signed the enabling bill in 1908, and the society raised the needed funds to purchase the nucleus herd of forty bison. Most of these came from Kalispell's Conrad family, who had bought them from Allard a decade earlier. The refuge at Moiese was the first area in Montana established specifically to preserve a single species.

Montana 200 and Montana 28

# Ravalli—Heron; Plains—Hot Springs
### 130 miles

Montana 200 follows the Jocko River west to its junction with the Lower Clark Fork near Paradise, and then parallels the larger river along the Cabinet Gorge to the Idaho line. The lower Clark Fork country has frequently been referred to as western Montana's "banana belt." Early newspapers attributed its consistently high temperatures to a Pacific chinook warmed by a "Japanese current." The broad, circular valley west of Paradise became known as Horse Plains because both Native Americans and early fur traders drove their horses here to winter in the mild climate.

## WEEKSVILLE
Northern Pacific Railroad crews pressing west up the Clark Fork in 1882 consisted of nearly 3,000 Chinese laborers and about half as many whites. Newspaper reporters referred to the head of construction as "the front." A series of temporary, bustling work-camp towns followed the front as it moved. One of the rowdiest of these was Weeksville, located about ten miles west of Plains.

Stories of the outlawry in Weeksville differ somewhat in their particulars. All of them tell of at least four desperados with the colorful names Dick the Diver, Ohio Dan, Nick the Barber, and Billy the Kid (presumably not the same Billy of Arizona renown). All four met their demise at the hands of enraged citizens during the winter of 1882–83.

Railroad workers descended on Weeksville each evening to do their carousing. They frequently fell prey to outlaws who would steal their money and sometimes dump their unconscious bodies into the Clark Fork River.

Finally a group of fed-up locals decided to rid the place of its worst offenders. Dick the Diver was seen as one of the ringleaders. On December 5, 1882, a mob dragged him out of a saloon. Pleading for mercy, Dick raised such a fuss that someone shot him in the back before his lynching. A similar mob then captured Billy the Kid after he had bragged about robbing construction workers. He fought free of his captors, ran to the river, and jumped in. A volley of shots followed him, and his body disappeared.

Nick the Barber and Ohio Dan tried to rob a construction train near the Thompson River. Alert crewmen thwarted the attempt. One of the pair took a bullet in the foot and was using crutches when a posse captured them. Just west of Weeksville, as a reporter from Idaho recorded, "the two wretches were led to separate trees and swung into eternity." For years a pair of crutches marked the grave site near the railroad right-of-way.

## Hot Springs

### Magic Waters
Before the arrival of the whites, generations of Native Americans had pitched their tepees on Camas Prairie, about twenty miles northeast of present-day Plains. Here they would soak in the "big medicine" mud pools and drink the healing waters. As settlers began populating the route of the Northern Pacific through present Sanders County, local newspapers told

*Bathers relax at the Camas Prairie Hot Springs.* —Mansfield Library
Archives, University of Montana, Missoula

of the "remarkable hot springs . . . which have effected surprising cures in rheumatic and kidney diseases."

Once the Flathead Reservation opened to homesteaders, the number of campers around the springs grew. They erected wooden bathtubs inside rooms with canvas roofs. Modest bathers pinned handkerchiefs over the holes in the side of the tent to assure privacy. As the bathers demanded less rustic facilities, they raised money to make improvements.

Stories abounded about the amazing curative powers of the waters. In the 1950s, the local newspaper at Hot Springs used the slogan "Limp In . . . Hop Out!" on its masthead. Over the years the bathhouse has been managed both privately and by the U.S. Department of Indian Affairs. In 1941, when a new structure was dedicated, the famous Indian athlete Jim Thorpe showed up as the honored guest. By the 1970s the bathhouse had begun to lose money. The structure fell into disrepair and closed permanently in 1985.

## THOMPSON FALLS

Thompson Falls sprang up as a railroad stop and the jumping-off point for some 10,000 gold seekers rushing into northern Idaho during the winter of 1883. At first, officials of the Northern Pacific favored making nearby Belknap the chief rail center for the lower Clark Fork Valley. When they refused to allow passenger trains to stop at Thompson Falls, boosters piled logs onto the tracks, forcing a stopover. While the railroad crews removed the logs, the locals boarded the trains and tried to persuade travelers to stay longer and even settle here.

### *The Great Geographer*

It is most appropriate that a town in Montana is named after David Thompson. The exploits of this British fur trader, explorer, surveyor, and mapmaker rival those of even Lewis and Clark. Thompson and his party were the first known white men to explore the lower Clark Fork and Kootenai Rivers, view Flathead Lake, and travel the entire length of the Columbia River.

At age fourteen, Thompson became an apprentice for the Hudson's Bay Company. He spent the next ten years exploring and mapping rivers in west-central Canada. When Hudson's Bay officials refused to allow him to indulge in the exploring and mapping he craved, he jumped to the rival North West Company.

After several thwarted attempts to cross the Continental Divide, Thompson, accompanied by a party of traders that included his half-Chippewa wife and baby, reached the headwaters region of the Columbia. Here they established Kootenay House and spent a hungry winter besieged by hostile

Blackfeet. The following spring Thompson led a party of five men down the Kootenai River into present Montana.

A devout Anglican, Thompson forbade the use of alcohol in any of his transactions. Once, the company insisted that he take two kegs of liquor across the divide. He had the kegs tied to the wildest horse in the pack string. The horse proceeded to bang the kegs against rocks and soon relieved itself of the load. No more alcohol went west with Thompson's crews.

In 1809 Thompson established two more outposts for trade—Kullyspel House on Lake Pend Oreille and Saleesh House near the mouth of Ashley Creek, just east of present Thompson Falls. Saleesh House was a crude structure of small poles, with mud and grass chinked into the open spaces. Here Thompson spent the winter, enjoying the region's mild climate while he surveyed the surrounding countryside.

After his return east, Thompson's company instructed him to explore, map, and claim the area from the lower Columbia River to the Pacific Ocean. The journey proved trying from the beginning. Freezing December temperatures, marauding Blackfeet, and desertions plagued Thompson's party. It took them nearly eight months to cross the Divide and to float the Columbia to its mouth. Here they found that Americans had already established the trading post of Astoria. Thompson fell under harsh criticism for losing this "race for empire." Yet in the process he had managed to survey and map the entire length of the Columbia.

Thompson returned to Ontario, where he constructed a map of western North America that was so accurate it served as a standard reference for seventy-five years. After raising thirteen children, he died in poverty and was buried in an unmarked grave. Decades passed before he gained deserved recognition as one of the world's greatest practical geographers.

Montana 200 and Montana 83
# Missoula—Bigfork
129 miles

## BONNER

### The Big Mill
Motorists driving through Bonner on Montana 200 just north of its junction with I-90 are flanked on one side by the huge, blocky structure housing one of Montana's largest sawmills. On the opposite side of the road are the neat houses erected decades ago by the Anaconda Company to serve as homes for families of the workers at their sawmill. The highway

*Anaconda Company sawmill in Bonner.* —Bitterroot Valley Historical Society, Hamilton

then winds east up the Blackfoot River, which for many years was the main conveyor of logs for the Bonner mill.

In 1882 Hiram Farr sold the future town site of Bonner to the lumber magnates of Missoula. The alleged price was $100 and a cow. The community of Bonner grew up around the sawmill. The conglomerates that have owned the mill have dominated the town's social and economic life. For years residents bought their groceries and other provisions from the Anaconda Company store, and mill employees had their store bills deducted from their paychecks. Workers not residing in company houses usually stayed in a large "bachelor quarters" or the elegant Margaret Hotel—both owned by the company.

Bonner's namesake, Edward L. Bonner, and his business partner, Richard A. Eddy, were pioneer merchants who founded the famous Missoula Mercantile Company. By the time the Northern Pacific ran its rails into western Montana, young Andrew B. Hammond had begun to replace Bonner as the company's driving force. Hammond and Eddy recognized a rare business opportunity and agreed to meet the railroad's need for wood. A month after the railroad contract was signed, 300 men were in the forests cutting trees for bridge timbers, ties, and pilings.

A year later, Eddy and Hammond joined Butte mining magnate Marcus Daly and the Northern Pacific to form the Montana Improvement Company. This conglomerate signed a twenty-year "sweetheart" contract with the railroad. It would supply the line with all its wood products for the 925 miles between Miles City and Walla Walla, Washington. In return, the railroad agreed to haul the company's lumber for half the going rate.

Montana Improvement also gained control of timber rights throughout the Northern Pacific's huge land grant. Company lumberjacks cut trees indiscriminately along the railroad right-of-way on both railroad and government lands. This led the U.S. Interior Department to sue the company for stealing trees from public land. Because the area in question had never been surveyed, the suits dragged on for years before the company prevailed. Meanwhile, Eddy and Hammond built a dam to hold logs near the mouth of the Blackfoot River and built a sawmill nearby.

The Bonner mill reportedly was the largest between Wisconsin and the Pacific Coast. Besides supplying the railroad, it produced thousands of feet of mine timbers for the copper mines in Butte. In 1898 Marcus Daly's Anaconda Copper Company purchased the Bonner mill, along with vast timber holdings up the Blackfoot River. Soon nearly half the mill's output was going to the mines in Butte or to the smelters in Great Falls and Anaconda.

During the ensuing decades Anaconda's lumber department survived a variety of crises. The Industrial Workers of the World tried and failed to unionize lumberjacks and mill workers during the First World War. In January 1919 the entire mill burned to the ground. It was up and running again by September. William A. Clark, Daly's chief rival for economic supremacy in Butte, erected his own sawmill just west of Bonner at Milltown. The innovative Western Lumber Company mill had a steam-driven power plant and a large boom to keep its logs from floating downstream. Following Clark's death in the mid-1920s, the Anaconda Company purchased the mill and soon closed it down.

By 1972 the Anaconda Company was losing money on its overseas copper mining operations. To raise capital, it sold its Bonner mill to Champion International Corporation. By mid-decade Champion's Bonner plywood plant was among the largest in North America, producing 250 million feet annually.

## LOG DRIVES

Montana 200 east along the Blackfoot Canyon, then north on Montana 83 toward Seeley Lake, retraces the route of some of Montana's most spectacular log drives. During the early years of the sawmill at Bonner, lumberjacks felled the trees lining the banks of the Blackfoot River and floated the logs to the mill. Once these stands of pine and larch disappeared, the job grew more difficult. Large horse-drawn wagons and sleds hauled the logs to the riverbank, where they would await the spring flood to carry them downstream. Occasionally the logs would jam. One such pileup in 1888 backed logs up the Blackfoot for more than two miles.

In 1906 the Anaconda Company purchased a large stand of timber at the south end of Seeley Lake. Company manager Kenneth Ross decided

*Logjam clogs the Blackfoot River near Bonner.* —Mansfield Library
Archives, University of Montana, Missoula

that the logs could be floated down the tiny Clearwater River to the Blackfoot. He ordered crews to build three dams on the Clearwater to hold the logs back. That spring, as the logs filled the first artificial pool, crews dynamited the dam. The ensuing flash flood carried the logs to the next dams, which were blown out in succession. As the explosions reverberated through the valley, the logs shot down the river and into Salmon Lake. Here a boom pulled by a hand-turned winch moved them to the outlet and down the river again. Throughout the thirty days of the drive, crewmen known as "river pigs" prodded the logs downstream. The men were soaked and exhausted by the time they reached Bonner.

Eventually steel rails reached the Anaconda Company's remote logging camps and the Blackfoot River drives came to a halt. As historian John Toole noted, "Of all the dangerous enterprises in the old west, none was so dramatic, colorful, or exciting as 'bringing in the drive.'"

## THE SWAN VALLEY

The sparsely populated Swan Valley lies between two spectacular wilderness mountain ranges—the Missions to the west and the Swan Range to the east. During the early decades of the twentieth century, the Somers Lumber Company floated millions of feet of logs the length of Swan Lake and down the Swan River to their mill on Flathead Lake. To assist their efforts, lumbermen hauled a steam locomotive by barge across Flathead Lake and by movable rails up to Swan Lake. In winter the engine pulled loads of logs across frozen Swan Lake.

## THE BOB MARSHALL WILDERNESS AREA

Although logging has long been a mainstay of the Seeley-Swan region's economy, tourism plays a role at least as important. Each year hunters, fishermen, hikers, and adventure seekers flock to this valley, the western gateway to Montana's largest wilderness complex—the Bob Marshall. Highways surround it, but no roads penetrate the rugged mountains of this region, which is larger than the state of Delaware.

The Bob Marshall Wilderness preserves the memory of one of the most fascinating characters ever to hike a backcountry trail. In many ways, Robert Marshall seemed an unlikely candidate to have his name enshrined in the rugged mountains of Montana. He grew up in New York City, the son of a wealthy attorney. But Bob's father, Louis, also loved the wildlands. From the family's summer home in the Adirondacks, young Bob and his brother climbed every peak in that mountain range. He later recalled:

*Bob Marshall.*
—Mansfield Library Archives, University of Montana, Missoula

> As a boy I spent many hours in the heart of New York City, dreaming of
> Lewis and Clark and their glorious exploration into an unbroken wil-
> derness which embraced three quarters of a continent.

Because of a heart condition, Bob Marshall probably shouldn't have done physically strenuous work; because of his family's fortune, he really needn't have worked at all. But his love of the outdoors led him to a career with the U.S. Forest Service. For three years, beginning in June 1925, Marshall was stationed at the forest experiment station in Missoula.

As a scientist, the eccentric Marshall was mediocre. Only in Montana's outdoors did he feel at home. His marathon hikes were legendary among local Forest Service workers. The men often made wagers on how long his treks would take. Marshall's attire consisted of blue jeans, a blue work shirt, wool socks, and a pair of sneakers. He taxed his frail heart to the limit. By the time he was thirty-six he had logged 200 wilderness day hikes of more than thirty miles each.

Following his stint in Missoula, Marshall pursued graduate study at Johns Hopkins University. Here he wrote his most widely read work, "The Problem of the Wilderness." Admirers called it "the Magna Carta of the wilderness movement." Marshall defined wilderness as an area with nei-ther permanent human inhabitants nor mechanical conveyances. He called for an organization of people to fight for "the freedom of wilderness."

Marshall then began working to make his wilderness goals reality. He and a handful of like-minded individuals formed the Wilderness Society, which soon grew in size and influence. Years after Marshall's death the society drafted and secured passage of the nation's first wilderness protec-tion bill.

Despite his reputation as a maverick and a socialist, Marshall worked hard and rose in the ranks of the Forest Service. In 1937 he secured an appointment as chief of the Division of Recreation and Lands. This posi-tion enabled him to convert threatened wild areas into protected wilder-ness. In only two years he single-handedly added more than 5.4 million acres to America's loosely structured wilderness system. And he continued his marathon hikes. Although he managed to survive a shipwreck in the arctic, an attack by a grizzly bear, and getting lost in the rugged Lolo Pass country, his heart finally gave out. He was thirty-eight at the time of his death. Two years later, 950,000 acres in western Montana were set aside in his name.

Passage of the Wilderness Bill in 1964 solidified the status of the Bob Marshall area. For decades before it enjoyed wilderness protection, the re-gion had been a favorite haunt of outfitters and would-be adventurers. Many of their camps contained luxuries such as beds, carpeted floors, and meals served on china. Outfitters stored their equipment in large caches deep inside the wilderness. Pressure from the Forest Service eventually forced guides to reduce the amount of stored material and the size of their excursion parties.

Far more threatening to the Bob Marshall and Montana's other wilderness areas have been the forces of exploitation and development. Loggers and miners have often opposed "locking up" these remote regions. During the early 1980s a Denver firm, searching for oil and gas reserves, proposed setting off explosives for 200 miles along the edge of the Bob Marshall. Preservationists demonstrated and wrote letters, blocking the "bombing of the Bob," but the battle over the status of Montana's unspoiled country goes on. To Bob Marshall and his successors, it has always seemed arbitrary to place an economic value on wild country. When asked once how many acres of wilderness America needed, Marshall replied, "How many Brahms symphonies do we really need?"

## US 12
# Lolo—Lolo Pass
**33 miles**

### TRAVELERS REST

The Lewis and Clark expedition entered western Montana through the back door. Early in September 1805 they trekked north up the Salmon River, across the mountains near Lost Trail Pass, and down the East Fork of the Bitterroot River. Upon reaching the upper Bitterroot, in a valley known today as Ross' Hole, they obtained horses from the Salish Indians camped there. Then the explorers rode north down the Bitterroot for three days through steady rainfall to the mouth of Lolo Creek.

Here, near the present community of Lolo, Lewis recorded: "The weather appearing settled and fair I determined to halt the next day, rest our horses and take some celestial observations. We called this creek Travellers Rest."

After their brief rest, the party moved west up Lolo Creek and across the Bitterroot Divide. US 12 across Lolo Pass roughly traces their route. They followed the trail used by the Nez Perce in their hunting expeditions from their Idaho homeland to Montana's plains. Unknown to Lewis and Clark, this was one of the most rugged passes in the entire Bitterroot Range. Snow and fallen timber blocked the route. Pack animals rolled down the steep mountainsides. The game, so abundant to them on the plains, disappeared. They killed and ate some of their horses.

The snow arrived early on Lolo Pass and stayed late. When Lewis and Clark returned the following spring, they waited until mid-June before they even attempted to recross the divide. Even then, ten-foot drifts forced them to retreat and wait another week. Just after crossing back into present-day Montana, they stopped long enough to bathe in the waters of Lolo Hot Springs. Even though the return trek across Lolo Pass proved less difficult than their first crossing, they were grateful to be back at Travelers Rest. They camped for three more days.

On July 3 Lewis and Clark parted company, taking separate routes. Lewis and the smaller group proceeded down the Bitterroot and made a perilous crossing of the raging Clark Fork, where Lewis fell from a raft and nearly drowned. They proceeded up Hell Gate Canyon and the Blackfoot River toward the Missouri. Clark and his group moved south. US 93 follows their route up the west side of the Bitterroot to the point where they cut east across Gibbon's Pass.

## THE LOLO TRAIL AND FORT FIZZLE

Lewis and Clark were the first of many white explorers to discover the hazards lying in wait on the path across Lolo Pass. When John Mullan surveyed the area for a possible rail route, he found it the "most difficult of all examined." In 1866 another group of army surveyors and engineers hoped to build a wagon road across the pass to the goldfields of northern Idaho. They hacked through dense timber and plowed through six-foot snowdrifts in June. Finally, the crew settled for a crude trail. Today's US 12 closely follows this Lolo Trail.

Eleven years after its construction, the Lolo Trail was part of the route the Nez Perce Indians took as they fled from their northern Idaho homeland. The docile Nez Perce appeared to be the least likely tribe to become involved in what turned out to be one of the bloodiest, most shameful episodes in the history of white–Native American relations. They were respected among early traders as honest, peaceful breeders of fine horses.

Then greedy prospectors and homesteaders trespassed and settled on their land. The usual series of broken treaties shrank their reservation until, by 1877, General Oliver O. Howard was trying to force them onto a tiny piece of land along Idaho's Clearwater River. Just when it appeared that the tribe's leaders were willing to move, young Nez Perce warriors killed four white settlers. This touched off a series of battles during which the Nez Perce chiefs repeatedly outfought the blundering Howard.

Generations of schoolchildren have been taught that Chief Joseph was a brilliant strategist who outfoxed white soldiers in a running battle across

Montana. In reality, Joseph was a diplomat and camp chief who, according to Nez Perce survivors, did no leading on the battlefield. Joseph's gift was oratory, and he tried eloquently to talk the other chiefs out of moving into Montana. Failing this, Joseph had no choice but to join his fellow tribesmen as they sought refuge either among Montana's Crow tribe or in Canada.

By the time the Nez Perce crossed Lolo Pass, Howard had already failed several times to bring this "war" to a conclusion. To cover up his ineptitude, he created the "Joseph myth." Howard and his defenders simply could not fathom that a group of Indians could fend off trained white soldiers unless they were being led by a military genius. Joseph was assigned that role.

As he dallied, reluctant to plunge across treacherous Lolo Trail, Howard sent a message to Captain Charles Rawn. Rawn commanded a small garrison at an unfinished fort in Missoula. Howard urged him to delay the Nez Perce escape through Lolo Canyon until he arrived in pursuit. Upon learning of the approaching Nez Perce, many settlers in the Bitterroot Valley panicked. They feared that Chief Charlo's disgruntled Salish would join the hostile tribe from the west and a bloodbath would ensue. Some settlers cowered in hastily built barricades dubbed "Fort Run" and "Fort Skeddadle."

Others volunteered to assist Rawn's troops. They built breastworks and dug rifle pits in a narrow part of Lolo Canyon flanked on the north by ridges so steep that the local press smugly declared, "a goat could not pass, much less an entire tribe of Indians." Then, on the morning of July 28, Rawn and his men stared in amazement as the Nez Perce paraded across the "impassable" ridge north of their barricade, just out of rifle range. As they rode by, some of the warriors were joking and laughing. The place was forever dubbed "Fort Fizzle."

To the relief of the Bitterroot residents, the Nez Perce quickly moved up their valley without incident. Charlo and his Salish remained neutral. Today an interpretive display and picnic area adorn the site of Fort Fizzle. It is located near milepost 28, about four and a half miles west of Lolo.

## US 93 and the Eastside Highway
# Missoula—Lost Trail Pass
### 97 miles

## THE BITTERROOT VALLEY

The Bitterroot River, Valley, and Mountains receive their name from the small, rosette-shape bitterroot plant, which in May forms a small pink or white blossom. Because it was one of the first edible plants to appear each spring, the Salish sought its nourishing roots. A sackful of cleaned bitterroots was once considered a fair trade for a horse. In 1895 Montana's legislature made it the official state flower.

In 1854 John Mullan speculated that the Bitterroot Valley would soon be "one villaged valley, teeming with life, and bustle and business." Today, Mullan's prediction continues to be realized. During the first half of the 1990s, population here grew at a rate nearly five times the national average.

## STEVENSVILLE

Stevensville deserves the title "cradle of Montana civilization." It is the home of St. Mary's Mission and the pioneer trading post Fort Owen. The mission stands as a memorial to the determination of the Salish Indians to learn of a strange and powerful new religion. According to the most popular tale, sometime after 1815 a band of Iroquois wandered into Salish territory and told them of a unique band of men wearing black gowns who could talk to the Great Spirit. They decided to travel to the "large village by the big water" (St. Louis), where they could find the "blackrobes." Three times the Salish sent delegations east. Each failed to bring back the blackrobes.

Finally, in 1839 two Iroquois named Young Ignace LaMousse and Peter Gaucher reached Council Bluffs, where they found Belgian-born Jesuit priest Pierre-Jean De Smet. De Smet's first stay in present Montana was brief, but he promised to return.

On September 24, 1841, De Smet, with two young priests and three lay brothers, reached the Bitterroot Valley after a journey of five months. Near present Stevensville, they cut down two trees and erected a cross. They built the first church out of cottonwood logs held together by wooden pegs. De Smet named both the mission and the mountain to the west St. Mary's. The following spring, the priests (called blackrobes) taught the Salish how to grow vegetables.

Four years later a young Italian Jesuit, Father Anthony Ravalli, came to the mission. Ravalli was a true Renaissance man, knowledgeable in medicine, literature, and the natural sciences. He brought with him two millstones, which became the workings for Montana's first flour mill. He also set up a still that extracted "medicinal" alcohol from native camas roots.

At first the Salish worked willingly at the mission, sowing and harvesting vegetables and operating the flour mill. But the blackrobes tried to discourage their customary bison-hunting expeditions and forbade their practice of polygamy. Ultimately many rebelled, and the mission closed in 1850.

*Father Anthony Ravalli.*
—Mansfield Library Archives,
University of Montana, Missoula

Father Ravalli remained and tended to the spiritual and medical needs of Indians and whites throughout western Montana. In 1866 he reopened St. Mary's Mission and erected a new church and a hospital. At the time of his death in 1884, Ravalli was one of the region's most highly esteemed residents. Today the Bitterroot Valley's Ravalli County bears his name. After Chief Charlo's band of Salish were forced to leave their valley homeland, St. Mary's ceased operating as a mission. The church in Stevensville remains a prominent historic site.

### FORT OWEN

When the Jesuit fathers decided to sell their property at St. Mary's Mission in 1850, they found an eager buyer in John Owen. Born in Pennsylvania, Owen had traveled west as a civilian supplier for a military detachment at Fort Hall, Idaho. In Montana's first real estate transaction, he purchased the mission and erected a log trading post surrounded by a wooden stockade. Later, more substantial adobe walls replaced the palisades.

The heavyset Owen had a sedate manner, but he was a hard worker. With the able assistance of his common-law Shoshoni wife Nancy, he planted grain, put in an orchard, erected a gristmill, and began breeding livestock. Cash was a rare commodity at Fort Owen. Most transactions were through barter. John Owen served as banker and credit manager.

Jesuit priest Lawrence Palladino noted Owen's honesty: "He was esteemed and trusted by the Indians as well as by the whites. His word was always good." Owen's rapport with the Salish led to a brief term as the Flathead Indian agent. He grew impatient with the federal government's inability to send the tribes supplies they needed.

When Isaac Stevens's railroad survey and later the Mullan Road construction crews arrived, trade at Fort Owen boomed. Owen was known throughout the region for his hospitality. He enjoyed serving his guests iced lemonade and stronger liquid potables. But by the mid-1860s Hellgate, strategically located on the main east-west corridor, had become the chief trade center.

When his wife died in 1868, Owen never recovered from the loss. His social drinking became problem drinking, and his financial problems piled up. After being judged insane, Owen was finally sent to Philadelphia to spend his last years with relatives.

Following its sale at public auction, Fort Owen fell into disrepair. During the 1950s, archaeologists unearthed hundreds of artifacts from the fort and its grounds. Today the partially restored fort, just northwest of Stevensville, is open to summertime visitors.

## THE BIG DITCH

Between Florence and Hamilton, motorists along the Bitterroot Valley may take the Eastside Highway east of the river. The route runs past the Lee Metcalf Wildlife Refuge and through the towns of Stevensville and Corvallis. It also runs near a huge canal that parallels the Bitterroot River. Known as the Big Ditch, this canal is a reminder of one of the wildest land promotion schemes in Montana history.

Around the turn of the century, valley orchardist Samuel Dinsmore hatched a plan to plant hundreds of small apple orchards on irrigated land east of the Bitterroot River. Other local entrepreneurs jumped on the idea as a quick way to make money by buying land cheap, bringing water to it, and selling it at a tidy profit. They persuaded Chicago financier W. I. Moody to put up the money to get started, and the Bitterroot Valley Irrigation Company was in business.

The company constructed a dam between Hamilton and Darby on Lake Como. From there a twenty-four-foot-wide canal carried water east to the Bitterroot, where it was siphoned beneath the river and forced up onto the sunny benchlands of the east shore. Here the massive ditch carried the water for seventy-five miles down the valley.

Six huge steam shovels dug the canal. They crept along rails laid inside the ditch. People traveled for miles to watch the iron monsters gobble up

*Steam shovel mishap on the Big Ditch.* —Bitterroot Valley Historical Society, Hamilton

great bites of earth. Crews mounted wooden flumes on trestles to carry water across the ravines. One day a shovel began making its way across one of these trestles when the structure collapsed and the machine tumbled into the gulch. Workers dismantled the shovel and loaded the pieces into a huge wagon. It took fifteen teams of horses to pull each piece back up the hill.

Even before the Big Ditch was completed, the selling job began. Using the pitch "five acres and easy street for life," promoters looked east for buyers. Particularly, they wanted to attract academians from university communities in the Midwest.

They laid out the community of University Heights near Darby. The town's chief planner was a young architect popular among Chicago's socialites. Frank Lloyd Wright designed a central clubhouse and a dozen cabins. A critic dubbed it "serfs cottages paying homage to the manor house." Wright then moved to a pine-covered ridge north of Stevensville, where he platted the town of Bitter Root. The only building he ever built here was the Bitter Root Inn, which became headquarters for the irrigation company.

*Bitter Root Inn, designed by Frank Lloyd Wright.* —Bitterroot Valley Historical Society, Hamilton

By 1910 several hundred men were busy clearing land and planting thousands of acres of McIntosh apple trees. The promotion worked. Potential buyers came to Missoula by rail at company expense. Here chauffeurs driving big red Locomobiles hauled them from the depot to the Bitter Root Inn, where they dined on Montana steaks and were served free drinks.

Many of the out-of-state buyers built houses on their land, but most chose not to live in the valley. From the start poor weather, tree diseases, and competition from fruit growers in Washington plagued the Bitterroot apple industry. Within a few years, the speculative bubble burst. The Chicago bank that held a $2 million mortgage against the Bitterroot Irrigation Company foreclosed, and the company went bankrupt. A few people had gotten rich; others had lost their life's savings.

Most orchardists turned to raising livestock, vegetables, or wheat. The Big Ditch continued to bring water to the eastside benchlands. The Bitter Root Inn burned in 1924.

## HAMILTON

### Marcus Daly and His Horses

As it nears Hamilton, the Eastside Highway skirts the old Bitterroot Stock Farm. On this property stands the refurbished mansion of Marcus Daly.

To call Marcus Daly a Montana legend would be an understatement. As a teenager Daly immigrated from Ireland. He came west, learned the mining trade, and made connections. After he settled in Butte, Daly used his ties with wealthy investors to establish the Anaconda Copper Company. The company grew to dominate Montana's economy for more than half a century. It made Daly a rich man.

Sometime during his travels Daly visited the Bitterroot Valley. He fell in love with the area and vowed to make his home here. In August 1888 the newspaper in Corvallis recorded: "Marcus Daly of Anaconda is making preparations to establish a horse ranch in the valley." Eventually, Daly acquired more than 15,000 acres just east of the Bitterroot River. He established an agricultural enterprise that rivaled his Anaconda mining empire in size and complexity.

The Daly ranches had at least nine separate units. They threshed more than 70,000 bushels of oats each year and cut 500 tons of hay a day during mowing season. More than 300 miles of ditches irrigated the fields. By the turn of the century, the ranches were running more than 5,000 head of beef cattle, 500 hogs, and 1,000 milk cows. To handle the milk, Daly built the region's first creamery and hired dairymen from Wisconsin to run it.

*Copper king and founder of Hamilton, Marcus Daly.*
—World Museum of Mining, Butte

Thousands of fruit trees and shade trees from around the world graced the property. Daly brought in an expert from Denmark to handle the nursery. The ranch grew massive amounts of celery, which Daly sold to the railroad.

The mansion did not reach its final form until Mrs. Daly had it rebuilt shortly after her husband's death. It boasted twenty-five bedrooms, fifteen baths, and five marble fireplaces carved in Italy. The grounds featured an artificial lake planted with trout.

The Daly ranches employed hundreds of people. To house them, in 1890 Daly founded the town of Hamilton (named after one of his foremen). He established a sawmill there that was soon cutting timbers for the Butte mines from logs floated down tributaries of the Bitterroot.

But central to the entire operation were the horses. No one is sure when and why Marcus Daly acquired an interest in horse racing. Working against the advice of experts, he was determined to demonstrate that horses raised in a cold climate at high elevation would display superior endurance.

Daly spared no expense to prove his point. He hired Butte's finest mining engineer to design the barns and stables and to lay out the three race-tracks. The covered track had its own heating plant. The red-painted stables could house up to 300 horses. Sick and injured animals were treated in a horse hospital complete with operating room and Turkish bath. Daly's horses traveled in steam-heated railcars and slept in quarters with hot and cold running water. Daly once quipped, "I could put the horses in the house and move out to the barn and I would still get the best of the deal."

Daly's trotters and thoroughbreds won races. Sporting copper and green colors, they would first race on tracks in Montana, away from the prying eyes of eastern scouts. They then went to the East Coast, where they often raked in big purses and bet winnings for their proud owner. The horses had such Montana names as Ravalli, Bitter Root, and Missoula, but Daly's favorite and finest thoroughbred bore the New York name of Tammany.

After Tammany finished first in eight out of fourteen races, winning more than $100,000, Daly agreed in 1893 to pit his horse in a match race against New Jersey's finest thoroughbred, Lamplighter. More than 50,000 people watched as Tammany came from behind to win by four lengths and set track record. On the train ride home, Tammany developed pneumonia and nearly died. Daly's vet managed to nurse him to health by feeding him champagne and port ale. Later Daly had a brick stable known as Tammany Castle built for his horse. Freshly cut flowers were brought to the carpeted stall each day.

After Marcus Daly died in 1900, all his horses were sent to Madison Square Garden and auctioned off. Bloodlines from the sale led to four winners of the Kentucky Derby.

### Spotted Fever

Follow Fourth Street south from downtown Hamilton and you will soon reach the Rocky Mountain Laboratories. This research facility arose as the result of the fight against a disease once believed to be exclusive to the Bitterroot Valley.

In the spring of 1873, two homesteaders died from a strange and horrible malady. Each spring the disease claimed a few more victims, many of them children. There were no known cases outside the Bitterroot Valley. The first symptoms were headache, fever, and joint pains. Then a rash caused the skin to turn dark and mottled. The Indians called it "blue disease." Others called it spotted fever. Death usually came within two weeks.

By the turn of the century, the state and federal governments were concerned enough to send physicians and scientists to the Bitterroot Valley. In 1902 Minnesota doctor Louis B. Wilson ran autopsies on six of the victims. He found wood-tick bites present in every case and a malarial-type parasite present in each victim's blood.

Wilson left the area before he could link the disease to ticks, but later researchers grew to accept this hypothesis. The locals had their own theories. Some blamed decaying pine needles or the sawdust at abandoned lumber camps. The tick theory tended to frighten away prospective settlers, so real estate dealers questioned its validity.

The U.S. Public Health Service sent in Charles W. Stiles. He held medical degrees from the finest schools in Europe. Yet once in the Bitterroot, Stiles was perfectly willing to bow to the wishes of worried realtors. He wrote his superiors that "in justice to property interests of the valley and peace of mind of the inhabitants," they should quickly publish the results of his work, which "absolutely and totally" failed to prove that ticks caused the disease. The land speculators were happy; Montana's health officials were unimpressed.

Then, Howard T. Ricketts arrived in Missoula from Chicago. He set up a laboratory in a tent on the lawn of the Northern Pacific Hospital. Working mostly alone and funded only by small grants, Ricketts demonstrated that the disease could be transmitted among guinea pigs by the bite of a certain wood tick. Later he recruited students from Bozeman's Montana State College. They experimented with ways to control tick populations. Several students caught spotted fever and died.

By 1908 Ricketts was ready to start working on a preventative serum, but the Montana legislature delayed in providing needed funding, so he left the state. Two years later, while experimenting with typhus fever in Mexico, Ricketts, at age thirty-nine, died of that disease. That same spring, spotted fever claimed fourteen more victims in the Bitterroot.

Rather than continuing Ricketts's research on a vaccine, federal health officials tried tick eradication. They dipped livestock in an arsenic fluid. They trapped, shot, and poisoned rodents. By 1917 the U.S. Public Health Service confidently declared that they had spotted fever under control.

But people continued contracting the disease. In 1921 the brother and sister-in-law of Montana governor Joseph M. Dixon died after being bitten by ticks at a picnic. The governor launched a statewide campaign to eliminate the disease. Federal doctors set up a laboratory in an abandoned schoolhouse south of Hamilton. A sign on the door warned, Enter at Your Own Risk! Finally, Dr. Roscoe Roy Spencer and others produced a serum from the bodies of dormant ticks. Gradually residents agreed to be inoculated, and cases of spotted fever dropped markedly.

In 1928 the state of Montana erected the Rocky Mountain Laboratory complex in Hamilton. Six years later the federal government purchased the facility. Scientists here produced spotted-fever vaccine for shipment throughout the world. They still conduct extensive research on other insect-borne and viral diseases.

*Original site of Rocky Mountain Laboratories.* —Bitterroot Valley Historical Society, Hamilton

## *The Great Log Haul*

Darby, Montana, is nestled in the shadow of the Bitterroot Mountains, about twenty miles south of Hamilton. In the spring of 1988 the town became the focal point for one of the most unique protest demonstrations ever to take place in Montana or anywhere else. "The Great Northwest Log Haul" involved hundreds of fully loaded log trucks and covered more than 250 miles of US 93. The issues in question were many—jobs, wildlife, land use, resource conservation. Montanans had been squaring off over these matters for decades.

During the 1960s Americans experienced a great environmental awakening. It took many forms. In western Montana it focused on practices of the U.S. Forest Service and private timber companies that many longtime residents found shocking. In a series of hard-hitting articles, the *Missoulian*'s environmental reporter Dale Burk called the U.S. Forest Service to task for sanctioning timber clear-cutting in the Bitterroot drainage.

Himself the son of a Montana logger, Burk quoted seasoned lumbermen and longtime Forest Service personnel. All expressed concern over a perceived shift in forest management methods in the Bitterroot during the 1960s. Area ranchers complained that the clear-cuts had destroyed their watershed by causing excessive spring runoff, which silted their irrigation ditches.

Photos of denuded landscapes crossed with bulldozer trenches accompanied Burk's articles. Many compared the practice to strip-mining. In

*1960s clear-cut in the Bitterroot National Forest.* —USDA Forest Service, Northern Region

1970 a study committee comprising University of Montana foresters released a long indictment of logging in the Bitterroot Forest. The report,
along with widespread public condemnation of the unsightly clear-cuts,
led to reforms in the Bitterroot. Elsewhere, things did not change as much.

Some twenty years after Burk's exposure of the "clear-cut crisis," another *Missoulian* environmental reporter, Richard Manning, cast his inves-
tigative eye toward Montana's two largest timber companies. During the
1980s, Champion International Corporation and the Plum Creek Timber
Company owned about 1.7 million acres of forest land in western Montana. Their scattered holdings added up to an area larger than Delaware.
Manning revealed that both companies were logging their land at a pace
that would quickly strip them of all marketable timber.

Nationally, the 1980s were a heyday for hostile corporate takeovers.
Firms like Champion and Plum Creek had undervalued assets (i.e., trees)
that made them tempting targets. So both companies, according to Manning, decided to log off their land. After viewing the results, Manning
concluded—like Dale Burk before him—"This is forestry at its harshest,
not really forestry at all, but more a form of strip mining."

When the large timber companies flooded the market with logs and
lumber, prices dropped. Pressure from preservationists, sportsmen, and others sometimes led state and national foresters to "lock up" public land
preventing logging. All this wreaked havoc on small mills and independent loggers. Those who managed to stay in business grew very frustrated.
They blamed environmentalists for tying up timber sales with long legal
protests that cost them their jobs. Wilderness advocates countered that
most job losses in the lumber industry were the result of automation.

Reflecting the feelings of many, Bruce Vincent, the owner of a small,
family-run, contract logging operation in Libby, observed, "I've seen a way
of life going down the drain. Many have left the area looking for work.
They were born here, lived here all their lives. They belong here." Vincent
became the chief organizer of the Great Northwest Log Haul.

On May 13, 1988, twenty diesels pulling loads of logs rumbled out of
Eureka. All along US 93, more big rigs joined the convoy. In the end, more
than 300 log trucks pulled into Darby and delivered their loads to the
Darby Lumber Company—one of many small Montana mills short of
timber. The demonstration was peaceful, but it sent a powerful message.

Western Montana's convoy drew national attention. Yet after the diesel
smoke had cleared, the same conflicts and frustrations remained. Mills
continued to close, hurting the small towns dependent on them for jobs.
Champion International sold its big mills in Montana. Plum Creek, dubbed
by one Congressman "the Darth Vader of the timber industry," promised

to become a better steward of the land. And the "wilderness versus work" arguments continued in the legislative halls, courtrooms, classrooms, barrooms, and living rooms of Montana.

## ROSS' HOLE

Just before US 93 begins its climb up Lost Trail Pass into Idaho, it runs through the broad valley of the Bitterroot River's East Fork. The area is known as Ross' Hole. For three decades after Lewis and Clark passed down the Bitterroot, the valley served as a thoroughfare for fur trappers. The list of mountain men who came through here reads like a who's who of the era—Jedediah Smith, Tom Fitzpatrick, Joe Meek, Kit Carson, and dozens of others. But Alexander Ross is the one who left his name. Prior to leading the 1824 expedition, Ross had spent many years as a trader in the Pacific Northwest. He was a rigid Calvinist with little patience for anyone not conforming to his high ideals.

Ross was preparing to give up fur trading and head east when he received an appointment to lead a trapping brigade into Idaho's Snake River country. Among the 137 members of the expedition were Americans, Canadians, and Indians from various tribes. Many were women or children. Of this mixed crew, Ross later complained, "A more discordant, headstrong, ill-designing set of rascals God never permitted together in the fur trade."

On March 12 the party reached the headwaters of the Bitterroot. They found themselves surrounded by mountains covered with snow at least eight feet deep. Ross named the spot the Valley of Troubles. Determined to break through their snowy entrapment, the men began plowing out a route using the horses. As each animal plunged into the drifts, Ross observed, "nothing was to be seen of our eighty horses but a string of heads and ears above the snow." They progressed only a few hundred yards each day. Overnight, blizzards filled their plowed trail with snow. The exhausted trappers grew angry. At one point Ross had to force a man to remain in the camp at gunpoint.

Finally, in mid-April the party crossed over into the Big Hole Basin. Ross recalled the harrowing final day:

> Children calling out with hunger, men with thirst, women affrighted, dogs howling, a scream here and a scream there; yet amidst all this bustle, anxiety, and confusion, we pressed forward safely across after fifteen hours exertion.

Once they reached the Snake River, the brigade secured more than 5,000 beaver skins. Despite this success, Ross's superior, Governor George Simpson, relieved him of his command. He labeled Ross an empty-headed man "full of bombast and marvelous nonsense."

# The Mining Frontier

*I am going to stay here one year more and see what I can do in that time. If I can't make anything in that time I shall come home. . . . It is a hard life at best, full of self denial and hardship. . . . Yet there is some constant excitement. Everyone expects to make a fortune any minute.*

—Cornelius Hedges

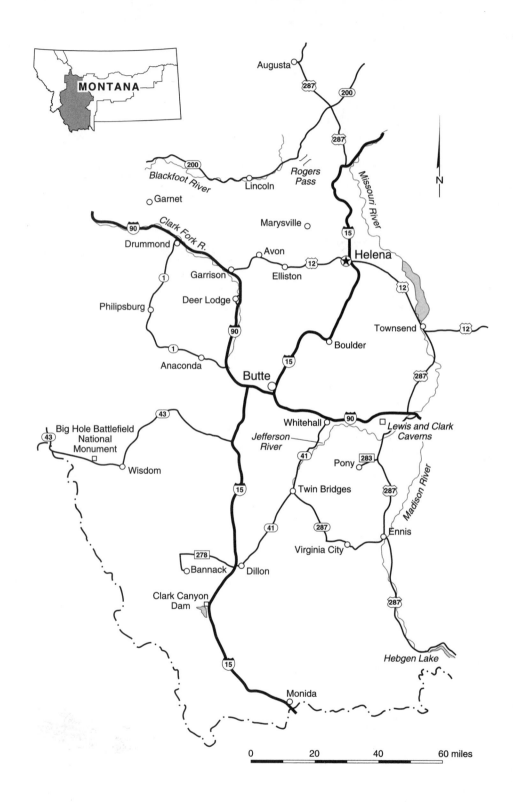

MONTANA

Augusta

287 200

287

Blackfoot River   Rogers
Lincoln   Pass

Garnet

200

Marysville

15

90   Clark Fork R.
Drummond

Avon

12   Helena

Garrison   Elliston

1

Deer Lodge

Philipsburg

12

Townsend   12

90

Boulder

1   15

Anaconda   287

Butte

43   Whitehall   90   Lewis and Clark
Caverns

Big Hole Battlefield   Jefferson
43   National   River   41
Monument   Pony   283

287

Wisdom

15   Twin Bridges

287

41   Ennis

287   Virginia City

278

Bannack   Dillon

Clark Canyon
Dam

287

15   Hebgen Lake

Monida

0        20        40        60 miles

Cornelius Hedges wrote the above from the diggings at Helena's Last Chance Gulch in 1865. He could just as easily have been residing on Alder Gulch, Grasshopper Creek, or any of several dozen other small streams rich in placer gold and crawling with restless men seeking quick fortunes. The Montana mining boom of the mid-1860s transformed, virtually overnight, a rugged, desolate region into a civilized (or at least semicivilized) territory.

Montana's placer gold rush and later, longer lasting hard-rock silver and copper booms, stretched along the southern two-thirds of the state's Continental Divide. The region is bounded on the east by the upper Missouri River and its headwaters—the Madison, Jefferson, Beaverhead, and Big Hole Rivers—and on the west by the upper Clark Fork River and its tributaries—the Blackfoot River, Flint Creek, and Silver Bow Creek.

In 1805 members of the Lewis and Clark expedition traversed the entire length of this section of Montana from north to south. Underground wealth was the last thing on their minds as they struggled up the Missouri River. Their chief concerns were securing enough wild game to feed themselves and finding native tribes willing to trade with them for the horses they needed to cross the mountains.

After navigating as far as their boats would go up the Jefferson and the Beaverhead, they negotiated with Sacajawea's people, the Shoshoni. They secured enough horses to carry them through Lemhi Pass. On their return trip the following year, Clark and most of the party explored the Big Hole Basin while Lewis led a band of men up the Blackfoot River to the upper Missouri.

Then, for almost sixty years, these rich mountains and valleys reverted to their ancient status as a common hunting ground and crossroads for most of the region's Native American tribes. During this period they were joined by parties of mountain men seeking the fine pelts of the beaver, otter, and mink. In 1859 John Mullan punched his military road up the Deer Lodge Valley, crossed the Great Divide at the pass that bears his name, and surveyed the route eastward through the Prickly Pear Valley near present Helena and on to Fort Benton.

## PRECIOUS METALS

Credit for Montana's first gold discovery is usually given to the freelance prospector-trader Francois Finlay, also known as Benetsee. In 1850, on a tributary of the upper Clark Fork called Gold Creek, he found traces of gold. Yet neither Finlay's discovery nor James and Granville Stuart's similar find in the same area eight years later touched off Montana's boom.

197

*Hydraulic placer-mining operation near Bannack.* —Beaverhead County Museum Archives, Dillon

The real rush waited until 1862 for the discovery of rich gold deposits on Grasshopper Creek, a small tributary of the Beaverhead River. Soon hordes of rootless prospectors were scouring the creeks along Montana's Continental Divide. The big strikes came in rapid succession—Alder Gulch, Last Chance Gulch, Confederate Gulch, Bear Gulch. By the time Montana's placer-mining era ended, nearly 500 such gulches had yielded gold. Most were, in the words of Montana writer Dan Cushman, "poor man's bonanzas." Only a handful of men grew rich digging and panning the riverbeds.

Most of the wealth wound up in the hands of those wise enough to realize that supplying the day-to-day needs of the miners was far more lucrative than scouring the streambeds. The mansions that eventually sprang up in Helena and Butte were the property of freighters, ranchers, merchants, and bankers like William Andrews Clark, Charles Broadwater, and Conrad Kohrs. Likewise, most of the towns that endured were trade centers such as Deer Lodge, Helena, Dillon, and Townsend. Bannack, Nevada City, Elkhorn, and scores of other places that depended solely on the supply of precious metals disappeared as soon as their gulches and mines played out. Yet even though these camps wound up as ghost towns, they served Montana well. The mining rush led to the formation of Montana Territory in 1864 and to statehood twenty-five years later.

Eventually, in the early 1880s railroads tapped into this vein of mineral wealth. The Utah & Northern arrived from Salt Lake, and the Northern Pacific ran its transcontinental line to Helena and down the Deer Lodge Valley. The railroads made it much easier to haul the ore from the territory's burgeoning hard-rock mines and to bring in the heavy equipment needed for milling the ore near the mine sites.

Once the placer streams played out, prospectors combed the hills in search of the elusive "mother lode." The result was a bonanza of gold and silver mines begetting boomtowns such as Garnet, Marysville, Granite, and Butte. Throughout the 1880s and early 1890s, silver rivaled gold in importance, and Montana led the nation in its production.

## THE COPPER ECONOMY

Ultimately another, less precious metal, copper, came to dominate Montana's mining industry. For an entire century, beginning in the early 1880s, the seemingly endless supply of copper-laden ore from Butte's "richest hill on earth" produced jobs for many, unparalleled fortunes for a few, unprecedented political corruption, and a poisoned landscape whose cleanup promises to last well into the twenty-first century.

The monumental battles among Butte's copper barons, and between the miners' unions and the monolith that was the Anaconda Company, dominated Montana's politics and economy. It also made for great theater. Writing in 1923, University of Montana professor Arthur Fisher called the contest between Anaconda and would-be reformers "the leading sporting event in Montana. Davids go forth to the blare of trumpets to battle with Goliath. And their whitening bones strew the wayside like the skulls of the bison which once roamed Montana's plains."

This all ended in the early 1980s. Montana's copper industry had been in a decade-long decline. The Atlantic Richfield Company, which owned the Anaconda Company's Montana properties, shut down the decaying smelter in Anaconda and the open-pit mining operation in Butte. Thousands lost their jobs. But by then the region's economy had diversified. Agriculture, tourism, and lesser industries all played a role. By decade's end, even mining was showing signs of rejuvenation.

A historic excursion through Montana's Continental Divide country reveals a region whose past has been dominated by mining. But the place has other stories to tell as well.

*Anaconda Company miner using a Leynor-type drill.*
—World Museum of Mining, Butte

## I-90
# Bearmouth—Butte
**88 miles**

### BEARMOUTH

### *Train Robbers*

Bearmouth, near the junction of Bear Gulch and the Clark Fork River was once a popular stop—first for the stagecoaches along the Mullan Road, and later for the passenger trains of the Northern Pacific. The area, with its steep timbered hillsides, was also the scene of three armed train robberies during a span of less than three years.

*Damaged Northern Pacific mail car following May 1905 robbery near Bearmouth.* —U.S. Bureau of Land Management, Missoula

In October 1902 a lone robber, wearing a mask made from a grain sack and armed with a .30-.30 rifle and two Colt revolvers, stopped the train. Engineer Dan O'Neal made a grab for the robber's rifle. The move cost O'Neal his life. The bandit escaped and was never apprehended.

Less than two years later, two heavily armed masked men halted a train. Five sticks of dynamite failed to blow open the railroad safe. A second, larger charge not only opened the safe, but blew apart the mail car. A detective for the railroad tracked down and apprehended one of the robbers in Spokane. His partner was captured in North Dakota.

During the third robbery, in May 1905, a bandit again dynamited the train's safe. As he bent over to pick up the loot, a daring railroad worker struck him across the head with a piece of wood. Following this robbery, the Missoula press understated, "Bearmouth appears to be an unlucky place for the North Coast Limited."

## BEAR CREEK

To reach the Bear Creek Road, take the I-90 exit at Bearmouth and drive five and a half miles east. From there, a steep dirt road leads eleven miles north to Garnet ghost town.

Bear Creek was one of Montana's last placer streams to be discovered. It was also one of the richest. Within two short years, beginning in 1865, some 5,000 miners took more than five tons of gold, worth over a million dollars, from tiny Bear Creek and its numerous tributaries.

Miners cut tunnels fifty feet deep to reach the richest ore, which lay near bedrock. Some men assumed a permanent crouch or bear-like gait from working in the tunnels, which were only five feet high. Because of this slouch and their habit of engaging in brawls in the camp's seventeen saloons, the men came to be known as "Beartown tough."

The wagon road up Bear Creek was among the steepest in the territory. Miners had torn up the creek bed so severely that they forced the road to climb the canyon wall. Wagons frequently slid down the steep banks, taking their teams with them. On one occasion a wagon loaded with a corpse bound for burial at Deer Lodge lost its load at night. The body was never found.

Fortune seekers returned to this area during the 1930s depression. They used floating dredges to chew up the streambed in an effort to extract the final remnants of gold.

## GARNET GHOST TOWN

Near the headwaters of Bear Creek, nestled nearly atop the Garnet Mountains, is the gold-mining camp of Garnet. It is accessible via a steep road up Bear Creek or an easier road running south from Montana 200. Garnet is one of Montana's best-preserved ghost towns.

The first big gold deposit discovered in the area became the Nancy Hanks Mine, named after Abe Lincoln's mother. By the mid-1890s, a dozen other mines were operating in the area. Gold ore from here was so rich that it could be hauled down by wagon to Bearmouth, then loaded onto railroad cars and taken to Anaconda or Great Falls for smelting, and still yield a healthy profit. Hauling ore from the 6,000-foot ridge proved a real challenge. Sometimes the brakes of the heavily loaded wagons would give out. Whenever this happened, all the driver could do was pray that the horses could outrace the runaway wagon to the bottom before they met a stagecoach coming up the hill.

The town itself was a makeshift affair. Crude cabins lacking foundations were strewn up and down the mountainside. There were no city blocks and few named streets. Most of the mines were within walking distance from town, and they operated throughout the harsh winter months.

Garnet lacked much of the rowdy nightlife and violence of Montana's more colorful mining camps. The local jail served mainly to sober up drunks. Most miners lived here with their families and were loyal union members. Garnet's Union Hall was the main social center, where everything from

*Mussigbrod Mine and mill in Garnet.* —U.S. Bureau of Land Management, Missoula

dances to church services took place. Garnet had no baseball team, but it once organized a football squad. During an early practice session the ball went flat. No one could figure out how to inflate it again, so the team disbanded.

By 1905 most of the rich gold veins were running thin, and people gradually left. During the 1930s, with the rise in gold prices, Garnet enjoyed a brief revival, but by mid-century it was deserted. Vandals, arsonists, and souvenir hunters ravaged the area. Around 1970 a group of dedicated volunteers began efforts to safeguard and preserve Garnet. To-day about forty of the original structures still stand.

## THE FINAL SPIKE

If you look south of I-90 at milepost 171 between Gold Creek and Garrison, you should catch a glimpse of a crude white sign. It marks the approximate place where the last railroad spike was driven to complete the Northern Pacific transcontinental line on September 8, 1883. The rest stop off the eastbound lane just west of this location has a nice interpretive display commemorating the event.

The final-spike ceremony marked the culmination of a long process that began during the mid-1850s, when U.S. Army surveyors explored the area for feasible rail routes. In 1864 Congress chartered the Northern Pacific Railroad Company. It gave the company the largest land grant in American history—60 million acres, an area equal to that of the six New England states.

Because of the land grant, Congress refused to underwrite construction costs. The banking house of Jay Cooke and Company became the Northern Pacific's sole financial agent. In 1873 Cooke's company collapsed, leaving the line destitute. For four years, construction stalled at Bismarck, North Dakota, as the Northern Pacific perched on the brink of bankruptcy. Finally, in 1879, under dynamic company president Frederick Billings, work resumed. Near the west end of the line, in the Columbia River basin, German-born rail magnate Henry Villard already owned several railroads. To avert competition, Villard lured in enough investors to purchase control of the Northern Pacific.

Once Villard took over, construction accelerated. Throughout 1882 and early 1883, crews comprising mostly Chinese workers pushed across eastern and western Montana. As the route entered central Montana, engineers decided to sink tunnels through both Bozeman and Mullan Passes. On July 2, 1882, a cave-in at the Mullan Tunnel west of Helena wiped out five months' work. Villard had crews construct a series of switchbacks across the pass to be used until the tunnel was completed.

Meanwhile, builders from the west were encountering their own set of problems. Spring storms led to landslides and washouts along the lower Clark Fork right-of-way. It took carpenters six months to build two huge wooden trestles. As the line neared completion, unexpectedly high construction costs were creating serious financial headaches for Henry Villard.

The two work crews finally joined up near Gold Creek in August 1883. In deciding to stage an expensive last-spike ceremony, Villard had two purposes in mind. He wished to celebrate his greatest personal triumph, and he needed to win over his German and British financial backers before they received the news of the railroad's red ink.

Villard spent nearly a quarter of a million dollars on the gala event. Special trains hauled the dignitaries west from St. Paul, Minnesota. At the site of the ceremony, near the mouth of Gold Creek, workers had erected a wooden pavilion with seating for a thousand guests. Flags, bunting, and pine boughs decorated the outside.

The ceremony, scheduled to begin at 10:00 A.M., did not get under way until midafternoon. While crossing the makeshift switchbacks on Mullan Pass, one of the coaches loaded with British aristocrats detached from its train and collided with an oncoming locomotive. The occupants barely escaped injury. Most of the two to three thousand Montanans who gath-

*People awaiting arrival of trains for the Northern Pacific's last-spike ceremony.*
—Haynes Foundation Collection, Montana Historical Society, Helena

ered at Gold Creek expected that the railroad would feed them a big meal. The dignitaries, however, dined aboard their railcars, and no food was offered to the assembled masses. So they were fairly irritated by the time the bands began playing.

The collective mood did not improve as the speakers faced what was now only a small group of Europeans in the pavilion. Then the featured orator, former Secretary of State William Evarts, delivered a long, monotonous diatribe. Between each speech the crowd chanted to hear from the main celebrity present—former President and Civil War hero Ulysses S. Grant. Finally Grant made a few casual remarks.

By the time the final spike was driven it was too dark for the photographers to record the event. The crowd milling around the workers was so thick that only a few could see what was happening. Once the deed was done, one observer recorded, "The band played, the cannon banged, the locomotives tooted and whistled, and the multitude cheered." Villard and his guests, happy and well-fed, reboarded their trains and headed for more celebrations on the West Coast. The Montanans rode home, their stomachs still rumbling.

The new rail line left Henry Villard with a $14 million cost overrun, and he soon resigned as Northern Pacific president. But the union of the rails left Montana Territory much less isolated. As an Oregon journalist noted, "The transcontinental railroad has annihilated time and space. . . . "

## DEER LODGE

The Deer Lodge Valley is a fifty-mile-long, high meadow bounded by lofty mountains. Many native tribes passed through here and hunted the deer who fed on the lush grasses.

The valley seemed ideal for raising beef cattle when John Grant, the son of a Hudson's Bay Company trader, arrived here in 1859. At the western end of the valley, near the confluence of the Little Blackfoot and Clark Fork Rivers, Grant erected the region's first cabin. A sign placed by the Society of Montana Pioneers marks the site on the eastbound ramp leading from Garrison Junction onto I-90. From here, Grant purchased and fattened up trail-worn stock from travelers headed to Oregon. He found a big market for his Montana beef in the new gold camps springing up throughout the region.

By 1862 Grant had moved his ranch headquarters east to the vicinity of present-day Deer Lodge. He built a fine two-story house. Within four years Grant decided to sell out. He found an eager buyer in Conrad Kohrs.

*Grant-Kohrs ranch house with electrified Milwaukee Road track in foreground.*
—Powell County Museum and Arts Foundation, Deer Lodge

Kohrs had run away from home in his native Denmark at age eleven. Years later he came to Montana, hoping to strike it rich in the goldfields of Bannack. He soon realized that he could make more money supplying beef to the prospectors. Shortly after he purchased the Grant ranch, Kohrs returned east briefly to court and marry Augusta Krus. For the next fifty-two years the couple presided over an ever-growing cattle empire.

Even though Kohrs eventually grazed cattle in Canada, eastern Montana, and four other states, he kept his main ranch in the Deer Lodge Valley. So when the blizzards of 1886–87 wiped out most of eastern Montana's open-range cattle herds, Kohrs still had a base from which to rebuild. At Deer Lodge he began breeding some of the West's finest Herefords and shorthorns.

In 1918 Kohrs and his partner, John Bielenberg, sold the Deer Lodge ranch. For more than a decade it languished in caretaker status. Then as the Great Depression ravaged Montana, Kohrs's grandson, Conrad Kohrs Warren, took over the ranch. For nearly four decades Warren operated a successful, albeit much smaller, livestock operation. Then in 1972 Warren sold the historic ranch to the National Park Service.

A Park Service restoration effort rejuvenated the ranch house and surrounding buildings. Today visitors can view the Kohrs house, which with its elegant Victorian furniture looks much like the home from which Conrad and Augusta Kohrs presided over one of the West's greatest cattle operations.

### The Prison

By 1869, when the territorial legislature voted to locate the penitentiary here, Deer Lodge was already a bustling trade center. Inadequate funding plagued the prison from the beginning. To save money, lawmakers voted to erect only a small wing of the proposed facility. The structure contained fourteen cells. It was so poorly built that the local press commented, "It will require about as many guards as it would to herd the same number of prisoners on the prairie."

The combined monthly salaries of the warden and three guards was $440. The governor once fired a warden because he had purchased two dollars worth of toothbrushes for the prisoners. In 1877 a second tier of cells was placed on top of the original wing. Fifteen years later the prison had the capacity to house 140 inmates. But by then 198 men called the place home.

Beginning in 1893, warden Frank Conley presided over a massive expansion and construction program at the prison. He relied primarily on convict labor. A thick concrete-and-stone wall replaced the board fence. Prison crews also worked on other state government buildings and built

*Old Montana State Prison tower. Note damage from bazooka shot during 1959 riot.* —Powell County Museum and Arts Foundation, Deer Lodge

nearly 500 miles of roads. Conley felt that hard work was the best form of rehabilitation. "Here in the freedom of the mountains," he declared, "the petty criminal develops brain and brawn."

Conley managed to survive an escape attempt during which an inmate stabbed him several times. But he couldn't successfully dodge charges that he had skimmed off thousands of state dollars for personal use. Governor Joseph Dixon fired him in 1921.

For the next four decades the prison deteriorated. During the 1930s jobless men convicted of petty crimes swelled the population far beyond the facility's capacity. Then, bowing to pressure from labor unions, the state legislature ended convict labor and the sale of prison-manufactured goods. Forced idleness caused pressure to build inside the decaying facility.

By the 1950s the prison was a disgrace to the state. Governors habitually appointed inexperienced partisan hacks to the wardenship. Two rural sheriffs, a road engineer, a cattle rancher, a salesman, and a railroad conductor took turns running the place. After a minor riot in 1957, the governor reluctantly promised reform and hired an experienced warden. When the future warden, Floyd Powell, visited the prison, he pronounced it "a hell-hole. . . the worst I'd ever seen."

On April 16, 1959, two hardened criminals—Jerry Myles and Lee Smart Jr.—led a dozen other prisoners in an escape attempt. They overpowered the guards, killed a deputy warden, and held the warden hostage. Warden Powell escaped execution only after the inmate' sent to do the deed had second thoughts and allowed him to leave. National Guard troops surrounded the prison and a tense standoff ensued. Finally the soldiers and police fired a bazooka at the guard tower where the ringleaders reputedly were. Behind a screen of tear gas, they stormed the prison and rescued the hostages. As the end approached, Myles shot Smart in the head and then turned the rifle on himself.

The 1959 disturbance was not a riot over prison conditions, as deplorable as they were. Still, the botched escape attempt focused attention on the decaying facility. Initial public reaction was negative. In 1960 voters rejected a proposal to build a new prison. The legislature then cut the prison's budget and Powell resigned in disgust.

Finally, in the early 1970s funding was approved for a new prison. In 1979 the last inmate left the old prison on the main street of Deer Lodge. Later the city converted it into a museum. Now hundreds of visitors each year see firsthand the place that a 1931 legislative committee labeled "a disgrace to civilization."

## THE BIG CLEANUP

Motorists driving from Missoula to Butte on I-90 are traveling through the nation's largest Superfund cleanup area. It is actually four separate cleanup sites, all stemming from a single cause—pollution from the production of copper.

During the late nineteenth century, Butte's first smelters were located near the mines and, especially during the winter, toxic fumes formed a thick, sickening pall over the city. Some mines did not even bother using a smelter. They simply laid the copper sulphide ore among logs in huge piles and ignited them, a process known as heap roasting. The piles smoldered for weeks and released clouds of smoke and poisonous particles. The smoke was so thick that citizens literally groped their way around town. All the vegetation in Butte died, and people suffered from burning eyes, nosebleeds, gagging throats, and frequently deadly pulmonary disease.

Eventually Butte passed an antismoke ordinance. But after smelter owners threatened to shut down if the city tried to enforce it, the city backed down. Meanwhile, copper baron William Andrews Clark was declaring, "I must say that the ladies are very fond of this smoky city . . . because there is just enough arsenic there to give them a beautiful complexion."

Once Marcus Daly erected his copper smelter in Anaconda in 1894, Butte's air cleared up considerably. But Deer Lodge Valley farmers complained of crop failures and livestock dying from the poisons emitted by the smelter. The Anaconda Company erected a huge smokestack in an attempt to disperse the smoke. The farmers complained that the big stack simply threw the deadly arsenic over a wider area, and they sued Anaconda. The case went to the U.S. Supreme Court before the company finally prevailed.

Besides poisoning the air, the Butte mines and smelters sent toxic waste down Silver Bow Creek and the Clark Fork River. In 1891 the U.S. Fish Commission announced that, after netting the Clark Fork thoroughly in the Deer Lodge area, they "did not find any fish whatever." In 1918 Anaconda built two dams and settling ponds on Silver Bow Creek near Warm Springs. But even a third, larger dam and treatment facility erected in the 1950s failed to eliminate periodic fish kills in the Clark Fork.

In 1977 the Atlantic Richfield Company (ARCO) purchased the Montana copper operations of the Anaconda Company. Even ARCO spokespeople themselves later admitted that it was one of the most ill-advised corporate decisions in American history. Within a few years ARCO had shut down Butte's open-pit mine and Anaconda's smelter. At about this same time, the federal government was launching its Superfund pollution cleanup program. Soon the mess caused by Montana's copper industry became a colossal cleanup site, and Atlantic Richfield was stuck with the bill.

The Environmental Protection Agency rated the area among the worst in the nation—even more toxic than New York's infamous Love Canal. After mining ceased in 1983, Butte's main copper mine, known as the Berkeley Pit, filled with poisoned water. In 1995 several hundred snow geese were found dead in the new lake. Downstream, the reservoir at Milltown, east of Missoula, was so full of copper waste that drinking water became tainted. The cleanup was projected to cost hundreds of millions of dollars and to last for decades.

# FAIRMONT HOT SPRINGS

## Melee

An exit off the I-90 midway between Butte and Anaconda leads to Fairmont Hot Springs. Formerly called Gregson Springs, the place was the site in 1912 of an epic battle. The miners' union from Butte and the Anaconda smelter workers made the mistake of staging their annual picnic at the same place on the same day. Several thousand quarts of beer and a tug-of-war between the rival unions produced an eruption. After the Anaconda men lost the tug-of-war, someone threw a punch; someone else hurled a bottle; and the war was on.

After a valiant struggle the outnumbered smeltermen retreated to nearby hills. A railroad baggage car carried the wounded to hospitals in Butte and Anaconda. The next day the Butte press reported, "The afternoon sun was hidden from sight by the clouds of flying bottles."

# BUTTE

## The Richest Hill on Earth

Butte, Montana, is a city with a past so rich that one could easily produce a "Streetside History of Butte" just as thick as this volume. Butte has always possessed a uniqueness that once led someone to describe it "the world's only island completely surrounded by land." While most of Montana's mining camps disappeared after promising beginnings, Butte defied the odds. It boomed, flourished, and dominated Montana's economic and political life for at least three-quarters of a century.

The town had a shaky beginning. In 1864 prospectors found promising placer deposits on a shimmering tributary of the Clark Fork that they christened Silver Bow Creek. Gold here did not come close to matching that found in Montana's richer camps. By decade's end only a handful of people remained in the area.

Some prospectors found the quartz outcrops on nearby Butte Hill much more interesting than the gold in the stream below, as quartz is often an indication of gold or silver ore. The complex silver ore proved difficult to process, so the early mines went broke. Then, in the mid-1870s William L. Farlin erected the area's first stamp mill to process the ore, and he turned a nice profit. Others soon followed, and Butte boomed as a silver camp.

As Butte's silver rush was getting under way, the first of Montana's famous triumvirate of "copper kings" arrived. William Andrews Clark was an aloof little man with a penetrating gaze and a knack for making money. By the time he visited Butte, he was already growing rich as a freighter, merchant, and banker. He bought several silver claims. A crash course in

*View of Butte from Dublin Gulch, circa 1904.* —World Museum of Mining, Butte

mineralogy completed Clark's transition from merchant to miner. In 1879 he directed the construction of Butte's first copper smelter.

### The War of the Copper Kings

The man who more than anyone else launched Butte's copper era, Marcus Daly, began working silver claims in Butte for partners in Salt Lake City. Later he bought a share of a modest silver claim, the Anaconda, and persuaded three wealthy Californians to join him in forming the Anaconda Mining Company. At the 300-foot level the silver played out, but Daly received reports of rich copper deposits. An experienced practical miner, Daly himself went down into the mine, looked around, and declared to his foreman, "Mike, we've got it." They had struck the largest deposit of copper sulphide ever found.

Daly's discovery in 1881 launched Butte's transition from a silver camp to a copper camp. Within five years Butte had surpassed Leadville, Colorado, as America's leading metal-mining center. With its economy based largely on copper, the town survived the 1893 crash in silver prices that killed many of Montana's other mining towns. By century's end, more than 47,000 people—including a rich mix of Irish, Cornish, Finnish, Italian, Slavic, and dozens of other nationalities, crowded into Butte and the surrounding area. It became the richest, rowdiest, toughest, and ugliest town in the Rocky Mountains.

And presiding over it all were the warring copper barons. Marcus Daly's generous, open demeanor stood in stark contrast to that of his chief rival, William Andrews Clark. As the Clark-Daly feud ran its course, it led to graft and corruption in Montana and its legislature. Each combatant managed to win a few rounds. Daly thwarted Clark's bid to gain a seat in the U.S. Senate. Clark supported Helena in its selection over Daly's town, Anaconda, as Montana's capital.

The battle did not end until Daly sold his Anaconda holdings to the Amalgamated Copper trust, led by Standard Oil financiers. By then Butte's third copper king had risen to prominence. Writer Joseph Kinsey Howard accurately described Fritz Augustus Heinze as "the most adept pirate in the history of American capitalist privateering." The well-educated son of wealthy New York parents, he arrived in Butte at age nineteen. He possessed, in the words of historian Michael Malone, "the torso of a Yale halfback" and large blue eyes. The women of Butte took to young Fritz Heinze

*Maverick copper baron Fritz Augustus Heinze.* —World Museum of Mining, Butte

right away. His nightly drinking, gambling, and carousing in Butte's red-light district became legendary.

Heinze was also a serious student of mining. He learned the details of the complex ore veins beneath Butte Hill. Once he acquired his own mines, he used this knowledge and Montana's "apex law" to good advantage. Simply stated, the apex law said that whoever owned the land where an ore vein surfaced could follow that vein, even when it faulted and ran into a mine claimed by someone else. Soon Heinze had workers in his Rarus Mine raiding the ore body of Amalgamated's Michael Davitt Mine.

The Amalgamated Copper trust repeatedly sued Heinze, but because the young upstart controlled the judges of Butte, he prevailed in the courtroom. Beneath Butte, the battle over ore took a serious turn when the rival miners used dynamite, smoke pots, powdered lime, steam, and high-pressure hoses for weapons. Two men were killed and dozens of others injured in this underground warfare.

After Heinze's judges threatened their very ability to operate in Montana, the Standard Oil magnates shut down their entire Montana operation. Thousands of Montanans, from lumber workers in western Montana to the copper miners of Butte to the coal miners in central Montana, were thrown out of work in October 1903.

Heinze in turn depicted himself as the champion of the little man against the copper behemoth. His eloquent oratory won over the Butte citizenry, but in the end Amalgamated blackmailed Montana's legislature, forcing lawmakers to pass a "fair trials" bill. This enabled Amalgamated to disqualify Heinze's judges. Checkmated, Heinze sold his holdings to Amalgamated. He returned to New York, where he lost most of his fortune on Wall Street. After years of hard living, he died in November of 1914 of cirrhosis of the liver.

With Fritz Heinze gone, the Amalgamated Copper trust tightened its stranglehold on the economy of Montana and the lives of thousands of miners in Butte. Still, the mines prospered, and for decades Butte enjoyed an unrivaled reputation for boisterous behavior. The mines operated twenty-four hours a day, so the saloons stayed open around the clock to accommodate miners as they got off their shifts. After work nearly every miner headed to his favorite watering hole to enjoy a "one-bit" shot of whiskey. A dime purchased a "Shawn O'Farrell"—an ounce of whiskey with a beer chaser. Most bars also served free meals of smoked meats, cold cuts, and imported cheeses.

On East Galena Street, Butte's line of brothels rivaled those of San Francisco's infamous Barbary Coast. Most prominent was the Casino—a combination saloon, dancehall, prize-fight arena, theater, and bordello. More than 100 women worked here, and its doors never closed.

Yet Butte was also a place for families. Churches flourished, and each summer children flocked to nearby Columbia Gardens Amusement Park to enjoy the roller coaster, carousel, and other rides. Young couples danced in the large pavilion.

By 1890 half the population was foreign-born. The Irish predominated. St. Patrick's Day was (and still is) the town's biggest holiday. The worst outbreak of ethnic violence occurred on July 4, 1894, after two saloons foolishly displayed the shields of the anti-Catholic American Protective Association. Angry Irishmen set off half a box of dynamite in front of one of the establishments. In the ensuing riot, half the paving stones on west Broadway were torn up and used for ammunition. Firemen were called in to hose down the crowd. Instead, the Irish fire crews turned their hoses on the offending saloons and gutted them.

Below Butte, life was even more dangerous. The huge gallows frames—some still visible on Butte's skyline today—lowered "chippy" cages crowded with miners at extremely high speeds until they reached their work site, sometimes 2,000 feet below. Here they often sweated in 100-degree-plus heat using hammers, shovels, dynamite, and air drills. Inexperienced, farm-born immigrants operating dangerous mining equipment created an extremely

*Miners at the Diamond Shaft, Butte, circa 1914.* —World Museum of Mining, Butte

hazardous workplace. Injuries were so frequent that local drugstores sometimes put crutches on sale. In June 1917 in the Speculator Mine, a miner's carbide lamp ignited the frayed insulation of an electrical cable. The fire quickly spread throughout the shaft, and 168 men died.

Miners fortunate enough to avoid such mishaps faced an even deadlier foe. Inside the mines drills filled the air with silica dust, which clogged the workers' lungs. Eventually hundreds succumbed to silicosis, tuberculosis, and pneumonia.

Often the miners' unions in Butte were too weak to force the Anaconda Company and others to improve mine safety. During the nineteenth century, Butte's unions flourished as they took advantage of the rivalries among the local copper kings. Then the Amalgamated trust consolidated its power, and the miners union split between a procompany faction and a radical wing spurred by the Industrial Workers of the World (IWW).

Hostility between these groups reached a head in the summer of 1914 when bloody riots broke out in the streets. A series of dynamite charges destroyed the local union hall. Each side blamed the other for the sabotage. As fighting continued, National Guard troops came in to restore order. The Anaconda Company declared an open shop, refusing to recognize any union—a situation that lasted for twenty years.

Despite such setbacks the union spirit remained strong in Butte. Workers from musicians and bartenders to schoolteachers became strong union members. In 1946 family members of striking miners ransacked the homes of people who had dared to cross the picket lines.

### The Lady of the Rockies

Near the top of the east ridge of the Continental Divide overlooking Butte stands a stark white statue of the Virgin Mary. Placed on the mountain in 1985, the ninety-foot monument is more than just a religious icon. It symbolizes the fortitude and perseverance of the people in the town below. Indeed, at the time of the statue's erection Butte needed a boost. In 1983 the Atlantic Richfield Company curtailed mining in the huge Berkeley Pit. For the first time in more than a century, copper was not being mined in Butte.

The "Lady of the Rockies" statue was the brainchild of longtime Anaconda Company worker Bob O'Bill. He vowed that if his wife recovered from a serious illness, he would place a statue of the Madonna on the high ridge east of Butte. O'Bill and a small group of dedicated workers and financial backers never wavered from their goal. Cynics derided the project as a colossal waste of time and money. Some wags suggested that a more fitting statue would be a bowling pin or a beer bottle.

Welder Leroy Lee, who constructed the statue, had no experience as a sculptor. He worked without blueprints, using only a small model as a guide. Fittingly, structural metal for the project came from Butte's old underground copper mines.

To hoist the six sections of statue onto the mountain, backers secured the use of a National Guard helicopter. The December 1985 airlift tested both the strength of the helicopter and the mettle of its crew members. Tragedy nearly hit when the arms section began swinging out of control. The helicopter shot down the ridge to make an emergency landing. When the final section eased into place, people below began celebrating. They held a victory parade downtown in freezing weather.

By the time of the statue's completion, spirits in Butte were uplifted for other reasons as well. The town was beginning to diversify its economy. A small-business incubator was established. Missoula businessman Dennis Washington reopened some of the old ARCO mines. Plans were well under way to construct the nation's first high-altitude sports training facility, complete with a speed-skating rink. As one worker declared, "The statue symbolizes that the people here can accomplish anything if they really want to."

Montana 1
# Anaconda—Drummond
57 miles

## ANACONDA

### *The Smelter City*

Visible for miles along I-90 between Deer Lodge and Butte, the now-dormant smokestack near the base of the Pintler Range stands as a constant reminder of the copper-smelting industry that once dominated this region. After investigating many potential locations for a smelter, Marcus Daly and his partners settled on a ranching area on Warm Springs Creek, twenty-six miles northwest of Butte. In June 1883, while camped at the future site, Marcus Daly spotted a dead cow. "Do you see that cow?" Daly asked the rancher. "Main Street will run north and south in a direct line from where we stand, right through that cow."

Within two months the new town had 1,500 residents. Most lived in tents. One early resident described Anaconda's first Independence Day:

> Having nothing else to do but drink, nearly the entire population began
> to tank up early and kept at it all day. Fearing a wholesale shooting

*1928 aerial view of Anaconda's Washoe Smelter and stack.* —Anaconda–
Deer Lodge County Historical Society, Anaconda

scrape, the few men who kept sober went around collecting the guns of those who were drunk.

With the completion of the smelter, Anaconda took on an air of permanence. Anchoring the downtown area was Marcus Daly's showcase hotel. The four-story brick structure featured cathedral-glass windows and marble fireplaces. On the floor of the barroom was a large mosaic portrait of Daly's favorite racehorse, Tammany. For years anyone caught standing on the horse's image had to buy drinks for the house.

Daly hoped that his hotel, completed in 1888, would soon house state legislators as they convened in what he believed would be Montana's new capital city. In November 1894 voters went to the polls to choose between Daly's smelter city and Helena for the permanent site of Montana's capital. Daly's chief rival, William Andrews Clark, backed Helena's bid, and the ensuing fight was one of the liveliest, most corrupt electoral contests Montanans had ever witnessed.

Many disliked both cities. Helena, the temporary capital, was already entrenched in power and wealth. Anaconda was a "company" town owned largely by one man—Marcus Daly. Yet everyone enjoyed the free drinks, cigars, and five-dollar bills dispensed by both sides in the weeks leading up to the election. In the end all of Daly's money could not buy enough voters. Helena prevailed by nearly 2,000 votes.

After Anaconda lost the capital fight, Daly seemed to lose interest in his new town. He built a mansion in Hamilton and devoted more time to his racehorses. The huge copper output from Butte's mines insured that Anaconda and its smelter would continue to prosper. Within three years of the town's founding, a new, larger smelter—the Lower Works—went up a mile east of the original smelter. Because the railroads began charging such high rates to haul ore from Butte, Daly built his own railroad. It was one of the first to be powered by electric locomotives.

By the late 1890s the Lower Works could no longer handle the volume of ore coming from Butte's mines. Daly made plans to build an even larger smelter across the valley from the original plants. More than 1,000 carloads of brick and 20 million board feet of lumber went into the new Washoe Smelter.

Eventually the gigantic plant was treating 15,000 tons of ore a day. It was also spewing out vast amounts of sulphurous smoke and arsenic. Hoping to mitigate the pollution, the Company erected a 300-foot-tall smokestack. With the stack's completion in July 1903, everyone in the region attended a gala party. Tables were set up inside the flues for the big banquet.

The pollution lawsuits continued, and in 1918 Anaconda erected an even larger smokestack—the one that today towers more than 585 feet above the valley floor. At the time of its construction, it was probably the world's largest stack. The Washington Monument could fit inside it.

In the ensuing decades smelter workers converged on Anaconda from throughout Europe, the plains of Montana, and even the Indian reservations. All depended on the smelter, even with its frequent layoffs, strikes, and shutdowns. As longtime resident and local historian Bob Vine recalled, "Everybody would get up in the morning and then look and see if there was smoke coming out of that stack and if there was, we knew we were going to get a paycheck." The backbreaking work and pollutants took their toll on workers. As one recalled, the company would furnish new employees with three pair of leather gloves, a pair of wool coveralls, "and all the arsenic you could eat."

Anaconda's blue-collar existence came to a sudden, unexpected halt on "Black Monday," September 29, 1980. Atlantic Richfield, faced with a nationwide strike and world market problems, announced the shutdown of its Anaconda smelter and its refinery in Great Falls. One worker was overheard remarking, "Marcus Daly would have rolled over in his grave."

*Inside the Washoe Smelter.* —Anaconda–Deer Lodge County Historical Society, Anaconda

Once the shock of the shutdown wore off, Anacondans shifted gears, hoping to bolster the tourist trade. The site of the original smelter became part of a Superfund cleanup site, where work began on a golf course, with smelter tailings slag in the "sand traps." Golf champion Jack Nicklaus designed the course. He came to Anaconda for groundbreaking ceremonies, hit several golf balls from the slag, and pronounced the stuff "playable."

### PHILIPSBURG

The loop of Montana 1 west of I-90 is known as the Pintler Scenic Route. Traveling northwest from Anaconda, drivers wind past Georgetown Reservoir, a popular fishing lake created by a dam built in 1905 to supply water for the Anaconda smelter. The highway then drops into the fertile Flint Creek valley. Native Americans used the large deposits of flint here for their arrows. Later, cattle ranchers moved in from the Deer Lodge Valley.

Late in 1864 prospector Hector Horton spotted a promising outcrop of lead in the hills above the upper valley. The following summer he returned to stake the Cordova Lode. Horton's claim and others nearby proved so rich in silver that a group of investors from St. Louis established a smelter—one of the first in Montana Territory. In 1867 teams of oxen hauled in the heavy stamps, boiler, and steam engine for the Hope Mill. One of the wagons sank so deep into a bog that freighters were forced to wait until the swamp dried up to pull it out.

The St. Louis investors also brought in one of the nation's outstanding mining experts, Philip Deidesheimer, to design and run the smelter.

*Hope Mill, Philipsburg.* —Granite County Museum and Cultural Center, Philipsburg

*Parade moves up Philipsburg's Main Street, circa 1900.* —Granite County Museum and Cultural Center, Philipsburg

Deidesheimer placed the mill near a small tributary of Flint Creek. The road to the smelter became the main street of the community that sprang up. The mill workers and their families decided to name their new town after its true founder. Since "Deidesheimerburg" proved a bit of a mouthful, they called the place Philipsburg.

For years the town and its mill led a marginal existence. Then a series of big silver strikes, beginning in 1881, rejuvenated Philipsburg. After the Northern Pacific ran a branch line up Flint Creek from Drummond, Philipsburg's future as a commercial center was assured.

## GRANITE

### Silver Bonanza

As you drive past milepost 36 near Philipsburg, a big scar is visible on the mountainside northeast of town. This is the site of Montana's (and one of the world's) richest silver-mining districts. The remains of the mines, the mills, and the town of Granite can be reached by driving about four miles up the mountain from Philipsburg on a rough dirt road.

In 1880 Philipsburg's Charles D. McLure began working the outcropping of silver ore on Granite Mountain. For two years miners had tunneled fruitlessly into the mountain. McLure's financers in St. Louis wired him that they wanted the operation shut down. McLure decided to let one last shift work the claim before giving them the bad news. That evening they hit a body of ore, which assayed out at 1,700 ounces of silver to the ton.

The silver strike on Granite Mountain could not have come at a better time. During the 1880s the federal government was buying large amounts of the metal for coinage, thus insuring a steady demand. Soon the railroads arrived, enabling the heavy metal stamps and other milling equipment to be hauled in. Granite's population swelled to more than 3,000 miners and their families. They crowded onto a mountainside so steep that the narrow main street was laid out on two levels. Many buildings tunneled into the mountain and had their front ends perched on fragile stilts.

Miners were paid four dollars a shift. Many filled their dinner buckets with the rich silver ore, which enhanced their salaries considerably. Winters in this 7,000-foot boomtown proved very harsh, and miners emerged from their work underground soaked in sweat, only to have their clothes freeze to their backs before they reached home. Pneumonia took a heavy toll.

The high altitude and hard work left many miners too tired to do much carousing. Granite had the usual quota of saloons and amusement parlors, but it also boasted a first-class reading room, a bathhouse, a fine toboggan-run down to Philipsburg, and at least four churches. One minister recalled that the men in his choir could "swear like the devil and sing like angels."

*Bi-metallic Mine, Granite.* —Granite County Museum and Cultural Center, Philipsburg

The silver vein on Granite Mountain supported two big mines—the Granite Mountain and the Bi-metallic. Each erected stamp mills for processing ore two miles down the hillside. Huge iron buckets on tramways carried ore down the mountain and fuel for the mines back up the mountain. Other mills sprang up closer to the mines. The pans in all of them ran red with the rich ruby silver. By 1890 Montana had become the nation's largest producer of silver, and the mines at Granite led the state. In the end the Granite mines produced more than $32 million in silver.

Finally, in 1893, just as the richest ore veins on Granite Mountain were beginning to run thin, a national panic hit. Worried investors lost confidence in a currency backed heavily by silver. Congress voted to end federal silver purchases. The shock led to the sudden closure of the mines on Granite Mountain, and 3,000 miners were thrown out of work overnight. Arthur L. Stone watched the exodus down the hill to Philipsburg:

It was the most complete desertion I have ever seen. . . . Wheelbarrows, go-carts and burros had their place in the procession. . . . Everyone was in a hurry and pushed and jostled to reach the bottom first.

As the parade left town, someone tied down the steam whistle at the Bi-metallic Mine. The wail echoed across the mountain until all the steam drained from the engines.

The silver crash did not turn Granite into an instant ghost town. Several years later the two big mines merged and produced a healthy profit for another decade. But by 1915 the lower levels of the mines were flooded. A fire in 1958 leveled the remaining mine buildings. Today, only a few cabins alongside piles of crumbling bricks and decaying beams mark the site of Montana's greatest silver bonanza.

I-15
# Monida—I-90
**122 miles**

## THE CENTENNIAL VALLEY

Beaverhead is at once Montana's largest and southernmost county. Its creation early in 1865 also makes it among the state's oldest. It is separated from Idaho by a portion of the Continental Divide known as the Centennial Mountains.

The 7,000-foot-high Centennial Valley runs east and west for sixty-five miles along the base of this range. The first cattle were brought into the area in 1876, thus giving the valley its name. Settlers here often manufactured whiskey for personal use. When prohibition arrived, the practice became profitable. The rugged terrain and severe weather kept law enforcement agents at bay and enabled still owners to go about their business in remote places with names like Dolly's Gap, Bull Dog Hollow, and Hidden Stills. Valley hog farmers often used the mash from the stills to fatten their animals. According to local lore, alcohol made the hogs docile and the meat more tender and flavorful.

Clark Canyon Reservoir, near the headwaters of the Beaverhead River, marks the approximate location of "Camp Fortunate." Here in August 1805, members of the Lewis and Clark expedition bargained with the Shoshoni to obtain the horses they needed to continue across the Rocky Mountains. The Shoshoni lived in poverty in the mountains between present-day Montana and Idaho. After encountering Lewis and Clark, they became shrewd traders in a hurry. The explorers paid a heavy price in weapons and trinkets to gain only twenty-nine horses. The expedition party then cached some supplies and headed west across Lemhi Pass.

# THE SOUTHERN GATEWAY

Drivers on I-15 north across Monida Pass and down the Beaverhead Valley are following the main route that led to the goldfields of Montana Territory. Throughout the 1860s and 1870s, this trail from Utah ran heavy with traffic. Everything from the sleek Concord passenger and mail coaches of Wells, Fargo & Company to big lumbering wagons laden with freight pulled by oxen moved back and forth, night and day, along this route.

Once the Union Pacific Railroad reached Utah, hundreds of wagons began embarking from the railhead at Corinne, bound for Montana. For a time it seemed that everyone from Mormon farmers to recently freed black slaves were hauling wagonloads of provisions to the hungry miners of Montana Territory. Some yoked eight teams of oxen to pull three wagons at once. Such massive trains took about a month to travel from Utah to Helena. In winter the journey could take a lot longer. In November 1871 winter came early. Freighters and their oxen were hopelessly snowed in until the following spring.

In 1867 it cost $120 to ride a Wells Fargo stage for three days from Virginia City to Salt Lake. For this price passengers got to sleep sitting up in tiny crowded coaches racing down bumpy, dusty roads. There were rest stops along the way, but travelers usually carried their own food. Wells Fargo made most of its money carrying mail and gold dust. This made them popular targets for highwaymen. Robberies, however, were not nearly as frequent as later writers of western novels made it appear. A more common occurrence was the wagon toppling off the trail; drivers seeking to make trips faster than their competitors often took foolish risks.

In spite of the best efforts of the freighting and stagecoach companies, residents of Montana's gold camps felt isolated and longed for a railroad. By the mid-1870s, the cost of hauling heavy mining and smelting equipment into Montana and ore out of the territory had grown nearly prohibitive.

Two railroads, the Northern Pacific to the east and the Utah & Northern in the south, began building toward Montana, but each encountered money problems following the national financial panic of 1873. Track-building from both directions came to a halt. Owners of the Utah & Northern demanded a big subsidy from Montana's merchants before they would extend their line. Finally, in May 1878 the Union Pacific took control of the reorganized Utah & Northern line and began laying narrow-gauge track north through Idaho.

On March 15, 1880, tracklayers crossed the Idaho border. A delegation came south from Helena to drive two silver spikes to mark the occasion. A

*A Utah & Northern train.* —Beaverhead County Museum Archives, Dillon

snowstorm delayed the ceremony for a week. In the extreme cold, on the night of December 26, 1881, a train carrying fifty passengers arrived in Butte. Montana at last had its railroad, and the southern corridor leading from Utah became even more vital.

### DILLON

In 1880, as construction crews of the Utah & Northern moved down the Beaverhead Valley, they approached the ranch of Richard Deacon. The Irish bachelor disliked the railroad and threatened to sue if it tried to condemn his strip of rich bottomland. But he offered to sell his entire place for $8,000. The railroad owners approached the merchants who had been traveling with the construction crews. The owners promised that if the businessmen bought Deacon's land and gave the railroad the right-of-way, the owners would hold up construction there for the winter.

The merchants realized that, if they established a town site at the ranch, it would become Montana's center for freight and passenger traffic all winter long. They could turn a quick profit by selling lots. They met at Deacon's ranch and had dinner. He charged them a dollar apiece for the meal. Realizing how badly they wanted to buy him out, Deacon raised his asking price another $2,500, and the deal was struck.

The founders named their new town after Sidney Dillon, the president of the railroad. That winter, as expected, the place boomed. Yet most people

*Main Street, Dillon, circa 1886.* —Beaverhead County Museum Archives, Dillon

realized that once the railroad construction crews moved northward, the town could easily disappear. It was then that a core group of merchants and Beaverhead Valley farmers and ranchers joined in a common cause. They campaigned successfully to get the county seat moved from nearby Bannack, thus assuring Dillon's permanence.

Within a decade Dillon had become the region's commercial center, but some wanted to make it more. Citizens held a mass meeting at the local skating rink to discuss plans for bringing in a teacher-training college. One speaker predicted, "Dillon will become the very Athens of the West." A hill south of town had been christened "college hill" long before the legislature voted in 1893 to locate the state teachers' college in Dillon.

Celebrations in Dillon sometimes turned unpleasant. In August 1943 the circus came to town. Just as the performing elephants were entering the tent, a bolt of lightning struck, knocking three of the huge beasts to the ground. One elephant, affectionately known as Old Pitt, died at the scene. They buried him at the county fairgrounds. Years later, during the 1979 Labor Day parade, two jet fighters from the Montana National Guard flew overhead to give the 8,000 spectators an added thrill. The wing of one low-flying jet struck a local grain elevator. The plane exploded in a fireball a block ahead of the oncoming parade. The pilot was killed, and flying debris injured several others. The carnage would have been far worse had the jet been flying toward the parade crowd instead of away from it. Although the pilots had not been authorized to fly lower than 1,000 feet, the jet struck the grain elevator at about 130 feet. The mayor of Dillon later remarked, "I guess people will remember this for a while."

## BANNACK

During the summer of 1862, tall, handsome Jack White came to the hills of southwestern Montana (then a part of Idaho Territory) searching for gold. Near the mouth of a small tributary of the Beaverhead River, White panned some promising-looking gravel. He also encountered swarms of grasshoppers, so he named the stream Grasshopper Creek. The gravel proved to be rich with gold.

Once news of White's discovery spread, hundreds of fortune seekers scrambled north from Colorado Territory. Montana's first gold rush was under way. They named the miners' camp Bannack after the tribe of Native Americans that camped nearby. The richest gold came from the rock shelves above the creek bed. The gold was so close to the surface that some prospectors began pulling up clumps of sagebrush and found gold dust among the roots. In the words of writer Dan Cushman, it was "probably the purest gold, on average, ever found in the west, or perhaps in the world."

Most prospectors were honest and hardworking, but Bannack attracted its quota of unsavory characters. Writing in April 1863, one of the camp's few women, Emily Meredith, observed:

*Beaverhead County Courthouse, A. F. Wright Store, and Bannack Hotel.*
—Beaverhead County Museum Archives, Dillon

I don't know how many deaths have occurred this winter but that there have not been twice as many is entirely owing to the fact that drunken men do not shoot well. . . . bullets whiz around so, and no one thinks of punishing a man for shooting another.

As several thousand people crowded onto Grasshopper Creek and as other discoveries were made in nearby gulches, miners petitioned Congress to form the new territory of Montana. After President Lincoln signed the act granting territorial status, Bannack became the new capital. Montana's first legislature met in December 1864 in a vacant store and unfinished log hotel. The governor's residence consisted of a building with a single room with bunk beds nailed against a wall.

Bannack's gold boom ended quickly. Montana's capital moved east to Virginia City and Bannack was deserted. In 1953 a group of Dillon citizens, eager to preserve Bannack, purchased most of the buildings for $1,000. The following summer they presented the town to the state of Montana, which has preserved it ever since as a state park. Bannack can be reached by driving east of Dillon for twenty-one miles on Montana 278 and south on a short gravel road.

Montana 43

# Chief Joseph Pass—Divide

77 miles

### THE BIG HOLE BATTLEFIELD

The Big Hole Battlefield National Monument lies just north of Montana 43, sixteen miles east of Chief Joseph Pass. On August 8, 1877, the weary Nez Perce tribe camped in this meadow on the North Fork of the Big Hole River. They called the area "Iskumtselalik Pah"—the place of ground squirrels. Tribal members felt confident that the soldiers who had chased them from their Idaho homeland were now far behind. Their leader, Chief Looking Glass, did not bother to post sentries.

Unknown to them, infantrymen and volunteers commanded by Civil War veteran Col. John Gibbon had closed in to within striking distance. After marching his men from Fort Shaw to Fort Missoula and up the Bitterroot Valley, Gibbon was eager to put a quick end to the Nez Perce menace. When his scouts spotted the camp in the meadow, he planned a surprise attack at dawn.

Around midnight the soldiers moved undetected into place along the western flank of the Nez Perce camp. At dawn Gibbon's men charged into the camp. Most of the Indians were asleep when the first shots rang out.

*Overlooking the Big Hole Battlefield.*

Much of the fighting was hand-to-hand. Soldiers shot indiscriminately into the tepees at point-blank range. Tribal member Yellow Wolf later recalled, "Some soldiers acted with crazy minds." Within twenty minutes the soldiers had gained control of the southern end of the village. To the north the Nez Perce repulsed the first attack, and many were managing to escape.

Confident of victory, Colonel Gibbon ordered his men to quit pursuing the retreating Nez Perce and to set fire to the camp. The tepees, wet with dew, did not burn easily. This gave the Indians time to rally.

As the Nez Perce charged, Gibbon, on horseback in front of his men, made an easy target. A bullet shattered his leg. The soldiers retreated up the wooded bench just west of the valley and began digging shallow rifle pits on the slope. Nez Perce marksmen inflicted horrible casualties. One lieutenant recalled hearing the "dull thud" of bullets hitting flesh. Lacking medical supplies, soldiers treated their wounds with tobacco juice before bandaging them.

As they laid siege to most of Gibbon's command, the Nez Perce also succeeded in capturing the soldiers' only field howitzer, along with their reserve supply of rifle ammunition. After nightfall the Indians began slipping away. The last warriors fired a parting volley before riding off.

They left the field littered with bodies. Gibbon's infantry lost twenty-nine men. By best estimates the Nez Perce dead numbered seventy. Ambulance wagons and doctors came from Helena, Butte, and Deer Lodge to treat the wounded soldiers. The Nez Perce carried their worst casualties on travois as they moved east.

The Missoula press called the engagement "the most gallant Indian fight of modern times." Six of Gibbon's men received the Medal of Honor. But after viewing the scene, a young aide to Gen. Oliver Howard wrote, "I have never been in a fight where women were killed, and I hope never to be."

Five-year-old Josiah Red Wolf spent most of that tragic day cowering near the bodies of his mother and baby sister. Nearly ninety years later, he participated in the groundbreaking ceremony for the National Park Service visitor center at the battlefield.

## THE BIG HOLE:
## VALLEY OF 10,000 HAYSTACKS

"We ascended a small rise and beheld an open beautiful leavel [sic] valley or plain. . . . In every direction around which I could see high points of mountains covered with snow." So wrote William Clark in July 1806 after crossing Gibbons Pass into the Big Hole Basin. Clark and his men were on their return trek across Montana. The party camped near Wisdom, where some of their horses were stolen, and near Jackson, where they boiled wild game meat in the hot springs.

This valley became a popular route for fur-trading expeditions. Beginning in the 1870s cattlemen from the Deer Lodge and Beaverhead Valleys began setting their animals to graze on the 125 varieties of wild grasses and forage plants native to the area. The stockmen found the Big Hole's winters much too severe to risk settling here permanently.

Not until the early 1880s did a few hardy homesteaders take up permanent residence in the basin. They cut and stacked huge amounts of firewood to get them through the winter. It took them until 1898 to establish the town of Wisdom.

For decades, the Big Hole has been known as "the Valley of 10,000 Haystacks." In 1910 two local ranchers invented the Sunny Slope Slide Stacker, also called the beaver slide. Ranchers throughout the West used this device to stack their hay for many years. Long after others abandoned this method of putting up hay, Big Hole ranchers continued to use the

*Beaver slide stacking hay, Big Hole Basin.* —Beaverhead County Museum Archives, Dillon

beaver slide to erect their thirty-foot stacks. Although tractors instead of horses now power the stackers, haying in the Big Hole is done much as it was in 1910.

## Montana 41
# Dillon—Twin Bridges
### 27 miles

### BEAVERHEAD ROCK

About midway between Dillon and Twin Bridges is a famous landmark of the Lewis and Clark expedition—Beaverhead Rock. The explorers were growing exhausted as they moved their boats first up the Jefferson and then the Beaverhead Rivers. Meriwether Lewis was suffering from diarrhea, and a sore on William Clark's ankle made it difficult for him to walk. Searching for the Shoshoni Indians, Lewis led a small party on foot ahead of Clark and the boats. Shallow water and rapids slowed their progress. They frequently had to drag their cumbersome boats across sandbars.

At the junction of the Big Hole and Beaverhead Rivers, Lewis attached a note to a willow instructing Clark to proceed up the Beaverhead. A beaver had removed the stick by the time Clark arrived. Clark's party forced their boats nine miles up the Big Hole before they turned back in the right direction. They named the nearby Ruby River "Philanthropy" and the Big Hole River "Wisdom." As they approached Beaverhead Rock, Lewis recorded:

> The Indian woman [Sacajawea] recognized the point of a high plain to our right which she informed us were not very distant from the summer retreat of her nation. . . . This hill she says her nation [the Shoshoni] calls the beaver's head from a conceived resemblance of its figure to the head of that animal.

Early the next morning, August 9, 1805, Lewis again set out on foot seeking the elusive Shoshoni and their horses.

## TWIN BRIDGES

The fertile area around the confluence of the Big Hole, Beaverhead, and Ruby Rivers was a natural site for a town. At least Judge Mortimer Lott and his brother John thought so in 1867. They constructed toll bridges across both the Big Hole and the Beaverhead—thus the name Twin Bridges. Not a piece of iron went into either of the 100-foot-long spans. Big wooden pins held the bridges together.

Twin Bridges grew into a prosperous trade center. As many towns fought to become sites of Montana's state institutions, Twin Bridges made a bid to gain the state normal school for the training of teachers. Dillon won the school, but the legislature voted to give Twin Bridges the state orphans' home as a consolation prize. Judge Lott donated the land; the legislature appropriated $7,500 for construction; in 1894 the home opened its doors to five children. The State Bureau of Child and Animal Protection ran the home. They designated it for the care of "orphans, foundlings, and destitute children."

By the time the place closed down in 1975, some 5,900 children had spent part of their lives here. Of that number, fewer than 5 percent were orphans. More frequently the home took in children from broken homes, neglected children, or children from parents who were too poor or too ill to care for them. Recognizing this change, the state eventually renamed the orphanage the Montana Children's Center.

Throughout its existence the center was nearly a self-sufficient community. The children worked in gardens, butchered their own beef, baked

*Montana State Orphans' Home, Twin Bridges, 1896.* —Montana Historical Society, Helena

their own bread, and cooked their own meals. They also raised livestock, made shoes, and bottled milk. The campus had an elementary school, a swimming pool, and a gym.

In 1995 about 200 alumni of the center attended a reunion at the now decaying facility. The main thing that most of them recalled was having to work very hard. Others remembered being beaten with rubber hoses or broom handles and being locked up for as long as a week for breaking rules. Another added, "The bad part was you were shown absolutely no affection." Before they left the reunion, the former residents placed a marker containing the names of the children buried in the unmarked graves at the Twin Bridges cemetery.

## Montana 287
# Twin Bridges—Ennis
### 43 miles

## LYNCH MOB: THE VIGILANTE TRAIL

As you drive between Twin Bridges and Virginia City, you are following one of Montana Territory's first travel routes. For years stagecoaches rambled through here, carrying passengers and gold between the placer camps of

Bannack and Virginia City. The route was known as the Vigilante Trail—so named because of its association with gangs of alleged bandits and the citizens who organized to exterminate them. The tale of the Vigilantes is one of the state's most deeply embedded bits of folklore. It has been repeated largely unchanged and with little critical analysis by writers for more than a century.

In brief, the story goes like this: During the earliest days of the gold camps, a well-organized band of more than 150 cutthroats imposed a reign of terror on Bannack, Virginia City, and all points in between. They committed countless robberies and murdered at least 102 people. The mastermind of the gang, which was known as "the Innocents," turned out to be the sheriff of Bannack, Henry Plummer. The outraged citizenry banded together to form the Vigilantes. Over the space of two months this secretive group of men hanged Henry Plummer, two of his deputies, and eighteen more of the worst outlaws. In doing so they freed Montana from the grip of lawlessness.

For years nearly everything written about Montana's Vigilantes episode was based on two books. Virginia City schoolteacher and newspaper editor Thomas Dimsdale wrote *The Vigilantes of Montana* right after the events took place. Nathaniel Langford wrote *Vigilante Days and Ways* several decades later. Both men had close ties to the Vigilantes and wrote the books to justify what they did. Not until a century after Montana's hanging spree did other writers begin to paint a more realistic picture of the episode.

By all accounts, Henry Plummer was a man with a shady past. He was an eloquent speaker who liked to gamble. He was handy with a gun. As a law officer in California, he went to prison for killing a man, only to be pardoned by the governor. He killed another man in Montana, but a miners' court acquitted him. In May 1863 the miners in Bannack elected

*Graves of alleged members of Plummer gang, Boot Hill Cemetery, Virginia City.*
—Thompson-Hickman Free County Library, Virginia City

Plummer their sheriff by a sizable margin. According to contemporaries, Plummer went about his duties faithfully, honestly, and efficiently.

But Plummer also had enemies. Among them were chief justice Sidney Edgerton and his nephew, a young lawyer named Wilbur F. Sanders. As leaders of the territory's burgeoning Republican Party, Edgerton and Sanders viewed the Democrat Plummer as a potential political rival. In December 1863 Sanders helped organize the Vigilantes—a band of citizens bent on speedy justice and retribution.

Operating outside the law, the Vigilantes executed a pair of suspected criminals. One of them, Red Yeager, in a futile effort to save his own skin, implicated Plummer and others in alleged crimes. With Yeager's testimony as their sole evidence, the Vigilantes hauled Plummer and his two deputies to the town gallows and hanged all three. Dimsdale's newspaper articles assured skeptics that the hangings had been justified.

During the deadly cold winter of 1864-65, the Vigilantes went about their ghastly business. Some of their victims were genuinely bad people. Others were guilty only of associating with shady characters, and some had not even kept bad company. In one instance, they surrounded the cabin of an alleged bandit known as Spanish Frank. When the man inside repelled them with gunfire, the mob blew open the door with a cannon. Seeing a young man inside under the rubble, they emptied their revolvers into him, hauled him outside, and hanged his body. They burned the cabin and threw the corpse into the fire. Two weeks later they learned that their victim was not Spanish Frank at all, but a man named Jose Pizanthia. Rather than admit their blunder, the Vigilantes simply spread the rumor that Pizanthia had been "one of the most dangerous men that ever infested our frontier."

Of the twenty-one victims, the majority had come to Montana with no known criminal records. About half were either sick, wounded, or crippled before their capture. No evidence has surfaced that any of them belonged to a criminal network. There had been no crime wave in Montana's gold camps. Several robberies had been committed, but in only one instance was the victim murdered. A miners' court convicted the culprit.

Eventually some people began to condemn what the Vigilantes were doing. By 1867, when a group of Vigilantes in Helena attempted to revive their old organization, opponents wrote them a clear public message: "You must not think you can do as you please. We are American citizens, and you shall not drive and hang whom you please." Vigilante justice did nothing to rid Montana of road agents. During the late 1860s, there were frequent robberies. Only now more of the crimes appeared to be the work of gangs.

In 1969, 105 years after the lynchings, a commission studying violence in America concluded, "the execution of Sheriff Henry Plummer in Montana" was "a miscarriage of justice." Yet the myth of this gallant secret body rescuing Montana from the Plummer "gang" will probably never die. Montana's Highway Patrol officers and vehicles continue to display the numbers 3-7-77, the mysterious symbol used by the Vigilantes.

## ALDER GULCH

### Gold Dredges

Between Alder and Virginia City the highway parallels legendary Alder Gulch. The region, with its great mounds of gravel and boulders, looks like a war zone. The desolation is the result of gold dredging that took place during the late nineteenth and early twentieth centuries.

By the late 1890s, when a team of geologists from Harvard University began looking over Alder Gulch, the creek had already been thoroughly dug up by generations of prospectors. Still, they felt that there was enough low-grade gold ore left to make a profit by employing gigantic dredges.

Gordon McKay led a group of Boston investors to form the Conrey Placer Mining Company. Soon dredges as large as ocean freighters were

*Alder Gulch gold dredge.* —World Museum of Mining, Butte

tearing up the streambed and thousands of acres of rich pastureland with their huge iron buckets. The dredges were gigantic floating sluice boxes, described by historian Clark Spence as "ugly, graceless, megalosaurian." As they crept slowly up Alder Gulch, they created their own ponds.

The first dredges were steam-driven. Later, electricity became the preferred mode of power. The electric dredges employed relatively few men. The work could be extremely dangerous. Broken bones and lacerations were common. Two men were electrocuted, another decapitated.

When McKay died, most of the profits from the dredging company went to Harvard University, and that institution earned a tidy sum from the last remnants of gold on Alder Gulch. The profit came at the expense of a devastated landscape and the destruction of what remained of historic mining camps such as Nevada City, Adobetown, and Junction.

## VIRGINIA CITY

In the spring of 1863 a party of eight prospectors, led by William Fairweather and Henry Edgar, set out to join an expedition into the Yellowstone Valley. Their plans changed after a band of Crow Indians forced them back west. On May 26 they set up camp on a small tributary of the Ruby River. Fairweather noticed an interesting piece of rimrock near the stream. He asked the others to pan here, hoping to find enough gold to buy tobacco once they returned to Bannack. By the next day the excited party had $180 worth of gold from the gulch that Edgar christened Alder because of the trees lining its banks.

In Bannack the prospectors found it impossible to keep their find a secret. More than 200 men followed them on their return trip. Alder Gulch proved far richer than even Fairweather and his friends could have imagined. Soon some 10,000 fortune seekers lined the entire length of the gulch along a continuous stretch known locally as "Fourteen Mile City." Late that first summer, prospector F. E. W. Patton observed:

> It has a growing population, living in all manner of ways and localities, some families and messes of men living in houses, some in wagons, some in tents, some in bush arbors, and some under clusters of trees. All are more engaged in searching for and obtaining gold than preparing for comfort, or for the approaching winter.

Because many of the gold seekers here were former Confederate soldiers or Southern sympathizers, they tried to give the main population center on Alder Gulch the name Varina City, after the wife of Confederate president Jefferson Davis. Then the pro-Union territorial judge allegedly declared, "No such blot as this shall stain the honor of the camp." He changed the name to Virginia City, which seemed to please both sides. Once much of the population of Bannack had moved to these new, richer diggings, the capital of Montana Territory also moved here.

Unlike so many placer finds that played out in less than a year, the gold in Alder Gulch proved longer lasting. Single claims the size of city lots sometimes produced $100,000. In less than three years prospectors removed $30 million in gold from the stream.

After a few years the easiest gold had disappeared. Whites sold their worked-over claims to Chinese miners. For the next quarter century, the Chinese immigrants shoveled tailings into wheelbarrows, pushed them across plank catwalks, and washed out the remaining gold. As in virtually every place they settled in Montana Territory, they suffered from harsh, discriminatory treatment from the white population. The territorial legislature even passed a bill prohibiting them from owning mining claims.

Once the Chinese miners left, the gold dredges arrived to take out the last bit of precious metal. By the end of the Second World War, Virginia City stagnated. But auto-borne tourists continued to visit the place. Its historic buildings had managed to escape the fires that had ravaged most other early mining camps.

A young couple from Great Falls, Charles and Sue Bovey, took special interest in the area. Avid historians and collectors, the Boveys began buying up and restoring old buildings in Virginia City. They filled some with relics from the nineteenth century. Later they purchased the site of the disappeared mining camp of Nevada City. Using the lone existing photo of the town, they reconstructed its Main Street. After Charles Bovey's death in 1978, the restored towns deteriorated rapidly. Then in 1997 Montana's legislature voted to fund the purchase of historic Virginia City and Nevada City from Bovey's heirs. The Montana Historical Society began overseeing yet another restoration effort.

## ENNIS

Across the Tobacco Root Mountains from Virginia City lies the Madison River and the town of Ennis. From its beginnings the community was a family affair. Irish immigrant William Ennis began hauling freight to Bannack and Virginia City in 1863. Seeking pastureland for his herds of oxen, he crossed into the Madison Valley. Soon he was cutting hay from the lush meadows near the river. He built a crude cabin from cottonwood logs and brought his wife and daughter to live on his new homestead.

Ennis built a more permanent house that eventually became a hotel and boarding house. The William Ennis general store opened in 1879. Mrs. Ennis taught at the town's first school. A son, William J., operated a saloon and was the town's first blacksmith. Direct descendants of Ennis served as postmasters here for eighty-four years. William Ennis died tragically in 1898 when a former friend shot him on a Virginia City street.

# Hebgen Lake—Lewis and Clark Caverns

## THE MADISON CANYON EARTHQUAKE

After it leaves Yellowstone National Park, the Madison River flows practically due north through the county bearing the same name. The Madison Valley was once a popular route for fur traders. The basin is prime cattle country and a fisherman's paradise. Near the Wyoming border, a dam backs up the upper Madison to form Hebgen Lake. In the canyon just below this dam, Mother Nature went on a tear on the night of August 17, 1959.

It was a warm, clear, moonlit summer evening at the height of the tourist season. Several hundred visitors to the Yellowstone Park region were settled in campgrounds or parked along the highway in the canyon below Hebgen Lake. At 11:37 P.M., the fault along the eastern front of the Madison Range shifted suddenly and violently. The earthquake measured 7.5 on the Richter Scale, making it by far the most severe ever recorded in Montana and one of the worst in North America.

The force of the quake caused the water in Hebgen Lake to slosh back and forth. Several times it spilled over the dam and down into the canyon. Meanwhile, on the canyon's south wall a layer of dolomite rock that had been holding up a huge bank of unstable schist suddenly gave way. Some 80 million tons of rock literally flowed down the steep canyon, instantly buried the Madison River, and shot up the other side. Boulders larger than houses came to rest thousands of feet from where they had been. As the waters of the Madison backed up behind this new natural dam, Earthquake Lake was born.

The human losses were horrifying, but not nearly as severe as the first estimates. Nine bodies were found and another nineteen wound up missing, permanently entombed in the pile of rubble left by the slide. When the slide hit, it created winds of hurricane force. A woman from Idaho, camping with her family in the canyon, recalled being awakened by the roar. When the blast of air hit them, her husband grabbed a tree for support and was strung out like a flag before he let go. She watched as one of

*Newborn Earthquake Lake after the 1959 Madison Canyon slide.* —USDA Forest Service, Northern Region

her children blew past her and the family car tumbled away. Her husband and three children did not survive.

As the water began to rise and a crack in Hebgen Dam threatened to give way, shaken victims scrambled up the steep mountainside seeking refuge. The wind had blown the clothes from many of them. As the new lake rapidly rose, it carried away the trailer of a California couple. They spent the night clinging to a treetop in the middle of the lake. Miles from the quake's epicenter, windows shattered in West Yellowstone and the chimney at the Old Faithful Inn fell through the roof. Downstream at Ennis, residents were evacuated in the early morning hours. Many feared a tidal wave might come shooting down the Madison Valley.

Through the following days, dozens of government agencies and hundreds of volunteers assisted in rescue and evacuation work. Many opened their homes to the refugees. Army engineers dug a makeshift spillway to get the Madison River flowing again. Today the rebuilt US 287 runs through the slide area and skirts Earthquake Lake. At the visitor center, you can relive the fascinating, horrifying events of August 1959.

241

## PONY

At the base of the Tobacco Root Mountains six miles west of Harrison, lies the mining town of Pony. Tecumseh Smith found the first placer gold in this region in 1867. Everyone called Smith "Pony" because of his small size. Eight years after Smith's discovery, a mother lode of gold-bearing quartz was discovered near a patch of wild berries. The Strawberry Mine and nearby operations caused the population of Pony to swell to several thousand. The local bank was finished with marble imported from Pennsylvania. In 1900 a Boston syndicate erected a big electric stamp mill. But the gold ore proved to be of such poor quality that the mill never operated. Eventually most of the mill's lumber went into sheep sheds on area ranches.

## LEWIS AND CLARK CAVERNS STATE PARK

Just north of where US 287 joins Montana 2 between Three Forks and Whitehall, a side road leads up from the Jefferson River valley to Lewis and Clark Caverns State Park. Millions of years ago, when this area was part of a large sea, a thick layer of marine-animal shells accumulated into a limestone formation. After uplifting forces formed the Rocky Mountains, acidic water seeped into the limestone, slowly dissolving it and creating a spectacular series of passages and rooms. Lewis and Clark knew nothing of these caves bearing their names. In fact, no whites set eyes on them until long after the two explorers had paddled up the Jefferson River.

In 1882 two men from Whitehall stumbled across the caverns. Ten years later, Tom Williams and Bert Pannell rediscovered the opening to the caves while hunting in the nearby hills. Several years later, Williams and a small party returned to the caves. With flickering candles for illumination, they slowly lowered themselves with ropes down the steep entrance. What they saw below enchanted them. As stories spread of great rooms with stone waterfalls and huge colorful rock formations, dozens of others soon were exploring the caves.

Dan Morrison, the owner of a local limestone quarry, took a special interest in the caverns. He built a spiral staircase in the 100-foot shaft leading down from the opening. By 1901 Morrison was advertising the caverns as his own and conducting tours. These early visitors carried their own candles. Morrison allowed each person to break off a small rock formation to keep as a souvenir. The damage is still visible today.

When others challenged Morrison's claim to the caverns, a long legal battle ensued. In 1908 the federal government made the caves a national monument. But Congress did not approve needed funds, so the caves sat undeveloped and closed. Meanwhile, Dan Morrison pressed his case in court and continued to lead unauthorized tours through the caverns until his death in 1932.

Finally, in 1937 the federal government agreed to transfer the caverns to the state of Montana. Yet, before the caves could become Montana's first state park, a lot of expensive development was still necessary. The federal government, through its Civilian Conservation Corps (CCC) was finally in a position to do the job. The CCC set up a large camp at LaHood Park in Jefferson Canyon. For six years scores of young men, many from cities back east, worked in the caves and the surrounding area.

When the job began, the caves were filled with trash, rat nests, and a huge buildup of bat guano. The odor was overpowering. Crews hauled out hundreds of buckets of debris. They trapped and removed the rats. One young worker lost his balance while perched high on a wall and fell fifty feet to his death. CCC workers also chiseled out hundreds of stairs and cut a trail to the entrance. They blasted out a new entrance to provide easier access. They also explored and discovered new large chambers. Finally the workers installed lights.

On the first Sunday of May 1941, more than 3,000 people drove to the caves for a dedication ceremony. A rainstorm canceled festivities, but many hiked up the trail from the new visitor center and toured the caverns. Today, Lewis and Clark Caverns is one of the few state parks in Montana earning a profit.

*Civilian Conservation Corps workers at Camp LaHood.* —Jefferson Valley Museum, Whitehall

# Three Forks—Butte

## WHITEHALL

Whitehall received its name from a large white house built by Major E. G. Brooke in 1865 to serve as a stage station. The town did not spring up until the Northern Pacific Railroad laid its tracks through the Jefferson Valley in 1889. A reporter from nearby Boulder wrote of the new community:

> We entered this little burg feeling that we were among thriving and industrious people. The people were not given to riotous living, whiskey drinking and general debauch usual to small new towns.

Dominating the "skyline" of Whitehall is a tall, stark smokestack. The stack is all that remains of a speculative venture that failed. Around the turn of the century, Billings had a thriving sugar beet industry. Some residents of Whitehall hoped to imitate this successful venture. After planting test plots, which proved that beets grew well here, the Amalgamated Sugar Company agreed to build a sugar factory.

Whitehall businessmen pushed everyone to buy stock in the enterprise and persuaded farmers to grow beets. In November 1917 Amalgamated began work on its factory. The following spring, the company built a fifty-room hotel and numerous houses for future factory workers. A company agent brought in 100 families of Russian immigrants to work the beet fields.

After dry summers in 1918 and 1919, beet harvests did not meet expectations. Wartime needs slowed work on the factory. Still, supporters did not give up. They formed a booster club and signed up more farmers and businessmen. The local press extolled, "Finish the yonder beet factory and soon Whitehall will be a city of 5,000 people."

Amalgamated promised to stay in Whitehall only if 3,000 acres were planted in beets in 1920. This quota went unmet, and Amalgamated began selling off bricks from the sugar plant. The local school district leased the hotel and used it for a dorm, and the railroad removed its tracks leading to the factory site. Today only the 227-foot stack remains. Some have labeled it "a monument to folly." Still, Whitehall is not alone. A similar smokestack stands on the outskirts of Hamilton, Montana—the remnant of yet another unused sugar factory.

# Butte—Helena
### 64 miles

## BASIN

*Nature's Cure*

The mining town of Basin has experienced more booms and busts than most communities its size. During the 1860s placer miners flocked to Basin Creek, but the gold quickly gave out. A decade later the town grew up around hard-rock gold and silver mines. By the century's end, high smelting prices and low silver prices forced many mines to shut down. Several bad fires burned large portions of the town, but most business owners rebuilt after each disaster.

The area's most productive mine, the Katy, lost its smelter to a fire. At the adjoining Hope gold mine, a fire destroyed the concentrator and caused seven miners to suffocate. During the 1920s, the Jib Mining Company reopened the Hope and the Katy mines, but mismanagement led to a sudden shutdown.

Following the Second World War, people began entering many of the area's mines to experience the curative power of radon gas. The lodges and restaurants of Basin and Boulder accommodated the new wave of visitors. Abandoned mines such as the Merry Widow, the Earth Angel, and the Free Enterprise found new life. As people sat in the mines to relieve their assorted aches and pains, they ignored warnings from the Environmental Protection Agency that radon caused cancer. As one mine owner remarked, "When people get relief from pain, they don't care what the government says." One mine even had a special room where dogs and cats could get treatment for their arthritis.

## BOULDER HOT SPRINGS

The town of Boulder arose as a typical 1860s mining camp. Later it evolved into a regional trade center and became the Jefferson County seat. Its primary attraction, however, has always been the many hot springs in the nearby hills.

In some ways Boulder Hot Springs is a microcosm of Montana's history. Before European settlement, Native Americans frequented the springs during their treks across the mountains. During the 1860s, gold prospector James Riley homesteaded here and built a bathhouse and tavern to serve local miners. Two decades later another owner dug a swimming pool that the Helena press called "probably the largest in the territory." He also erected

*Boulder Hot Springs resort.*

a two-story hotel that catered to weary area ranchers and weekend vacationers from Helena.

In 1909 Butte mining baron James A. Murray purchased the springs and erected a luxury resort. Murray favored California mission architecture, so the building featured stuccoed walls, arches, and fountains. The resort thrived as Butte's mines prospered. During the height of the 1930s depression, an earthquake destroyed the Olympic-size swimming pool. The resort briefly housed 140 refugee orphans from Helena whose orphanage had also been wrecked by the earthquake.

Following the Second World War, a man with the colorful moniker Pappy Smith opened the place as the Diamond S Ranch. Throughout the 1950s it entertained a generation of baby-boomer kids and their parents. Then during the hedonistic 1960s and 1970s, a series of shortsighted owners let the resort deteriorate so badly that state health inspectors finally closed it down.

In 1989 a group headed by a psychologist and author of books on addictions purchased Boulder Hot Springs and converted the place into a quiet retreat for workshops on recovery and personal growth.

### ELKHORN
From Montana 69, six miles southeast of Boulder, a good gravel road leads twelve miles north to the well-preserved mining town of Elkhorn.

Swiss immigrant Peter Wys discovered the rich Elkhorn silver lode in 1870. Helena banker Anton M. Holter and his partners built a mill and laid out a town below the mine. During the boom years of the late 1880s and early 1890s, a British syndicate ran the mine. The Northern Pacific Railroad ran a line from Boulder up Elkhorn Creek. The grade was so steep that only short trains could make the run.

The town was home to the families of Cornish, German, and Irish miners, as well as French and Norwegian woodcutters. The lumbermen kept busy providing fuel to run the mine engines and to heat the local buildings. The largest standing building in Elkhorn is the Fraternity Hall. It once housed meetings of the Masons, the Knights of Pythias, and the Cornish Glee Club. People usually ate downstairs and danced upstairs. On one occasion two revelers argued over whether the orchestra should play a square dance or a waltz. The square dancer shot and killed the waltzer. He was hanged in Boulder.

The Elkhorn Mine somehow survived the big silver collapse of 1893. During the early decades of the twentieth century, the mine closed and reopened repeatedly. By the time the Northern Pacific pulled up its tracks in 1931, the heyday of Elkhorn silver was over.

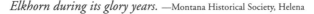

*Elkhorn during its glory years.* —Montana Historical Society, Helena

## *Last Chance Gulch*

Helena's main street is called Last Chance Gulch. The street follows the path of the stream where a quartet of prospectors known as "the Georgians" discovered gold. The historic Montana Club building marks the location of the find.

The Georgians did not intend to search for gold here. They had heard of a big discovery in southern British Columbia. En route they met other fortune seekers who informed them that the Canadian diggings had played out. They decided to cut north, via the Little Blackfoot and Prickly Pear Valleys, and try their luck in the Marias River region. After failing to find their El Dorado there, they retraced their route. On July 14, 1864, they camped on a tiny branch of Prickly Pear Creek that one of them termed their "last chance."

One of the party, Reginald Stanley, moved upstream and sank a prospect hole to bedrock. As he recalled years later, he dug up "three or four flat, smooth nuggets . . . that made the pan ring when dropped into it." When members of the party returned to Alder Gulch for supplies, several dozen men followed them back north. After they staked their claims and built cabins, the miners voted to name the place Helena after a town in Minnesota with a similar name.

During the next few years Last Chance and the neighboring gulches yielded more than $15 million in gold. Once they played out, numerous quartz gold mines in the region kept Helena booming. As hundreds crowded into the narrow gulch, they risked falling into abandoned prospect holes. Buildings often wound up propped on stilts as miners washed out the ground below.

Fire was a constant hazard. Tinder-dry wooden buildings, a scarce water supply, and a main street that acted as a natural chimney led to nine devastating fires in less than nine years. The worst, in 1874, began in a Chinese gambling house, swept through nearly every business in town, and destroyed 150 homes. Residents decided that if they could not prevent fires, they should at least try to spot them before they spread. They erected the fire tower that still stands atop a hill overlooking the gulch.

## *The Capital City*

Helena repeatedly rose from its ashes and continued to grow. In 1875 the territorial government seat moved here from Virginia City. A year later the first legislature came to town.

During the late nineteenth century some of Montana's most elegant, pretentious homes were constructed in the town's fabled westside mansion

*Montana's state capitol under construction.* —Montana Historical Society, Helena

district. Helena reputedly contained more millionaires per capita than any town in the nation. Only a few of the new rich had found their fortunes underground. Most were bankers, freighters, merchants, or lawyers. Their huge houses featured balconies, cupolas, interiors of hand-carved hardwoods, fireplaces in every room, and well-groomed lawns with fountains and statues. Today the houses are a big tourist attraction. They can be viewed best by walking through the neighborhood bounded by Lawrence, Monroe, Stuart, and Benton Streets.

In 1894 following a bribe-filled election contest, Helena defeated Anaconda as the permanent site of Montana's capital. On election night, a great bonfire illuminated Mount Helena. Everyone in town enjoyed unlimited free drinks, courtesy of copper king and Helena backer William A. Clark. After bartenders tired of pouring drinks, they simply tossed the champagne bottles to anyone still sober enough to catch them.

Four years later, two architects from Iowa won the bid to design Montana's capitol building. The elegant rotunda, designed in the mode of a nineteenth century opera house, featured a broad staircase and historical paintings around the interior of the dome. Outside, the dome was sheathed in copper—fittingly representing the industry that for decades had dominated the proceedings inside.

Besides the capitol building, two other turn-of-the-century landmarks dominate Helena's skyline. The downtown Montana Club building is a replacement of the original structure that burned in 1903. Cass Gilbert, the designer of New York's Woolworth Building, modeled the club after an Italian Renaissance palace. It housed an exclusive group of wealthy ranchers, miners, and merchants. Mark Twain, Theodore Roosevelt, and Prince Albert of Belgium have all been guests here. Until the 1930s, women were not allowed to use the building.

The twin spires of the St. Helena Cathedral tower above Warren Street. Austrian-born architect Albert O. von Herbulis designed the cathedral. It stands as one of America's finest examples of Gothic architecture. Gold-mining magnate Thomas Cruse put up much of the money to build the church. His was the first funeral to be held there.

### Earthquakes

Helena sits atop the northern end of the intermountain seismic belt. Indians warned early settlers that the earth here sometimes shook. Prior to 1935, residents had been jarred by occasional small quakes. Then, beginning October 3, 1935, and continuing for the next three months, more than 1,200 tremors jolted the area. Two of the quakes caused heavy damage, killed four people, and led to the most widespread panic in the community since the days when fires swept through Last Chance Gulch.

The first serious tremor hit just before 10 P.M. on October 18. People fled from crumbling buildings. Falling debris killed two men. A steady stream of cars flooded out of town. National Guard soldiers patrolled the streets, sometimes shooting at damaged chimneys to knock them down before they fell unexpectedly. The Northern Pacific depot, the city hall, and many schools and businesses lay in ruins.

Just as Helenans were beginning to recover from the shock of this quake, another big jolt hit just before noon on Halloween. By this time residents who had not already left town were "quake hardened." Instead of rushing into the streets to be hit by falling debris, they remained indoors until the shaking subsided. This did not help two workers on a scaffolding who were repairing damage done by the previous quake to the Kessler Brewery; both men fell to their deaths. The earthquake also completed the destruction of the new half-million-dollar high school. For the remainder of the year, students attended classes in railroad cars.

To this day, the earth beneath Helena shakes periodically. But the town's biggest commotion still takes place each odd-numbered year, when the state legislature convenes.

## The Devil's Brigade

Beginning in July 1942, Helena became home for a joint American-Canadian military unit formally called the First Special Service Force. Young dynamic Lt. Col. Robert T. Frederick commanded this elite band of commandos. He chose the mountains around Helena as the unit's training site because it had an ideal environment to prepare men for their chosen mission—an invasion of Nazi-occupied Norway. None of the hundreds of young men who converged on Fort William Henry Harrison knew their mission. Recruiters had merely promised them "a short and exciting life."

In the spirit of wartime patriotism, Helenans warmly welcomed the soldiers. When the men practiced informal hand-to-hand combat in the local bars, bartenders calmly tried to save as much of the glassware as possible. When their demolition exercises tore up abandoned mines and shattered windows in town, the mayor advised citizens that such sacrifices were necessary for the war effort. Townspeople invited the soldiers into their homes for Sunday dinners. Inevitably, many soldiers fell in love with local girls. Some 200 hasty weddings took place in spite of warnings from chaplains that the volunteers likely would not survive their dangerous mission.

Indeed, some wondered if they would even survive training exercises. They went on thirty-mile excursions through the deep snow in below-zero weather. Instructors compressed the normal three-month parachute training exercise into six days. Colonel Frederick delivered a short lecture on how to roll when they hit the ground, then slung his chute onto his back and said, "That's enough, let's go."

As the recruits trained, the Allied command decided to scrap the mission to Norway. Instead, the brigade's first mission was to the Aleutian Islands. Before the 2,300-man force left Helena in April 1943, they marched down Last Chance Gulch, where Helenans gave them a rousing, sad send-off.

Once in combat—first in the Aleutians and later in Africa and Italy—the men performed courageously and efficiently. They did their best work at night. Terrorized Nazi soldiers called them "the black devils in baggy pants." War correspondents simply called them the Devil's Brigade. As predicted, they suffered appalling casualties. Three-quarters of those in the unit were either killed or wounded.

After the war some of the men returned to Helena to live. Others came here for reunions of the Devil's Brigade. On one such occasion in 1980, the veterans dedicated a monument in Helena's Memorial Park. It featured two flags and an eagle with a scroll in its mouth. The scroll carried no inscription, possibly because the mens' private motto was "Ah, screw them Krauts."

# Helena—I–90

**62 miles**

## CONFEDERATE GULCH

Visible to the east across Canyon Ferry Reservoir as you drive between Helena and Townsend are the Big Belt Mountains. A series of small gulches have carved deep, narrow valleys on the western slopes of this range. The streams, with colorful names like Magpie, Hellgate, Avalanche, and Cave, all once ran rich in placer gold. The southernmost gulch, Confederate, was the richest of all. You can drive to it by turning north on county road 284 about two miles east of Townsend. Just under sixteen miles north, a dirt road leads up the gulch.

Confederate soldiers Washington Baker and F. M. "Pomp" Dennis had just been paroled from a Union prison when they wandered up this stream in December 1864. Here two more ex-Rebels, Jack Thompson and John Wells, joined them. Thompson washed up ten cents' worth of gold dust. This encouraged the four to move further upstream, where the gravel grew increasingly more productive. They named the stream Confederate Gulch and built four cabins to get them through the winter. The paths in the snow among the cabins formed a diamond, so they jokingly called the place Diamond City.

As word of the find spread, more prospectors trickled in. One of the less experienced men repeatedly asked a veteran miner about a good place to look for gold. Exasperated, the old-timer finally pointed to the nearest sidehill and told him to try "over yonder." The resulting discovery was the famous Montana Bar—a two-acre bench that many still believe was the most gold-laden piece of real estate ever found in the world. The gold literally clogged the sluice boxes. It was not unusual for a miner to wash more than $1,000 worth of gold from a single pan of gravel. People later recalled seeing nail kegs filled with gold dust sitting around in the open.

Diamond City finally lived up to its name, as 5,000 people congregated there. Crews dug large ditches to bring in water for hydraulic mining. They forced the water into canvas hoses and through large nozzles under tremendous pressure. It took at least six men to handle a single nozzle, which blasted out a stream of water powerful enough to knock down a brick wall. It easily removed the overburden of gravel and mud so the miners could get at the gold near bedrock. It also left an ugly mess. The tailings that washed down Confederate Gulch forced merchants in Diamond City to put their buildings on stilts and eventually relocate on higher ground.

*Hydraulic mining at Confederate Gulch.* —Montana Historical Society, Helena

By 1870 the boom had ended. Diamond City's population shrank to 255. Ten years later only four families remained here. Confederate Gulch yielded at least $15 million in gold. Exact value estimates are uncertain because many feared robbers and brought out their pay dirt secretly.

### TOWNSEND

Although Broadwater County was named after a Helena entrepreneur, the word accurately describes the upper Missouri River as it runs north across the county's entire length. In July 1805, as the Lewis and Clark expedition worked its way up that portion of the river now inundated by Canyon Ferry Reservoir, Meriwether Lewis recorded, "The grass in these extensive bottoms is green and fine. . . . The land is a black rich loam and appears very fertile."

For more than a century the small community of Townsend has based its economy on the farmers and ranchers working this rich soil. The Northern Pacific Railroad founded and named the town, built a depot, and sold lots cheap enough to encourage quick settlement. The Helena press called it "the metropolis of the Missouri Valley," and predicted it would rival Billings in importance.

The W. E. Tierney Company founded Townsend's two mainstay business establishments—a mercantile store and the Townsend House Hotel. The new hotel featured a restaurant serving oysters on the half shell. And it offered the ultimate convenience—a two-story outhouse with a wooden walk leading directly from the second floor.

## US 12
# Helena—Garrison
**46 miles**

### THE BROADWATER HOTEL AND NATATORIUM

Today, as US 12 runs through the western outskirts of Helena, not even a sign marks the site of a tourist complex that was once called one of the seven wonders of the West. But the Broadwater Hotel and Natatorium never turned much of a profit, and in its declining years it was a local eyesore.

During the 1860s Charles A. Broadwater supplied beef to miners at Bannack. He managed the successful Diamond R freight operation, founded Helena's Montana National Bank, and organized the Montana Central Railroad. Yet he is best remembered as the builder of the luxury hotel and bathing facility just west of Helena. In 1889 the press described the new palace:

> The hotel is a beautiful structure, three stories in height, covering a broad tract of ground, built on the cottage plan with broad verandas, lighted by electricity, warmed by steam, supplied by hot and cold water, furnished like a palace, and has attached to it the finest private bath houses in the world—finer than those Caesar gave to Rome.

The grounds included trees, flowers, statues, fountains, and a large artificial lake that served as a skating rink each winter. But the showcase item was the natatorium, or "aquatic theater." The imposing Moorish architectural structure stood 150 feet high. Circular trusses with no interior supports held up the shell-like building, which covered what the builders called "the world's largest swimming bath fed by natural water." Thousands of gallons of hot and cold mineral water dropped down a forty-foot-high cascade of granite boulders into the pool. Each of the 100 dressing rooms had a large stained-glass window. Promoters billed the natatorium as "the place to effectually and completely recover lost nerve force and to rebuild a debilitated system."

*Broadwater Hotel with the Natatorium in the background.* —Haynes Foundation Collection, Montana Historical Society, Helena

Broadwater died shortly after the hotel's completion, and his family ran it for about a decade. It then passed through the hands of two owners from Butte and a group of Helena investors. The Helenans tried to promote the Broadwater as a stopover for tourists driving between Yellowstone and Glacier National Parks. The idea never caught on, and the hotel closed in 1924. The bathhouse opened only in the summer. Helena's 1935 earthquake damaged the pool's plumbing so badly that the natatorium closed for good. The old hotel thrived briefly as a casino and dance hall, but a statewide crackdown on gambling in 1941 ended this revival. The once graceful building deteriorated until the 1980s, when it was finally razed.

## RIMINI

### *War Dogs*

At the eastern base of MacDonald Pass, a gravel road leads south to the old mining town of Rimini. Pronounced RIM-in-eye by the locals, it sits at the base of Red Mountain. A rich lead and zinc mine flourished here in the late nineteenth century.

During the 1930s the Civilian Conservation Corps ran a training camp from Rimini. After America entered the Second World War, the U.S. Army

*Training sled dogs and drivers, Camp Rimini.* —Montana Historical Society, Helena

found another use for the abandoned camp—dog training. By mid-1942 American aircraft were ferrying supplies and equipment across arctic regions, but when the planes went down, rescue proved extremely difficult. Transport planes began taking nine-dog sled teams as close to the crash site as possible, and from there the dogsleds carried drivers, trained medics, and equipment to the downed aircraft.

The rugged terrain, deep snow, and long winters of the Rimini area proved ideal for training these teams. The camp operated for nearly two years. It housed 15 instructors, 7 veterinarians, 150 trainees, and 800 dogs. At first the army kept the dogs in old shipping crates; later they built nicer doghouses. A slaughterhouse on the base butchered old army cavalry horses for dog food. In those times of meat rationing, horse tenderloin sometimes wound up on the tables of servicemen.

Although people were encouraged to donate their dogs to the war effort, sled dogs proved difficult to find. Few people owned Alaskan malamutes and Siberian huskies. Experienced dogsled operators were also rare. Some were veterans of Richard Byrd's antarctic expeditions. Others came from New England, where they had used dogsleds to haul tourists at ski resorts.

Once the veteran sled men shipped off to Canada and Alaska, many recruits arrived who had never seen much snow. The instructors told them that the goal of their training would be to become at least as smart as their dogs. Besides learning how to handle the dogs, the men had to learn wilderness survival skills, sled repair, and how to make leather boots for the dogs.

By the summer of 1944 the demand for sled dogs and drivers had declined to the point that the army closed the Rimini base. By then the base had served its purpose. Dogs and men trained here rescued 150 survivors of arctic airplane crashes and salvaged tons of equipment. Rimini's was a rare wartime mission—training men to save lives instead of taking them.

### MULLAN PASS

Near milepost 24, at the western foot of MacDonald Pass, a road heads northeast across Mullan Pass. It was late 1853 when John Mullan learned of the pass that eventually bore his name. Gabriel Prudhomme, a French-Indian explorer, told Mullan about this low-elevation passage across the Continental Divide.

The following March, Mullan personally demonstrated that wagons could be taken across the pass. Six years later, as he completed surveying his famous military road between Fort Benton and Walla Walla, Washington, Mullan crossed the pass just before a solar eclipse in mid-July. He recorded that the pass "is six thousand feet above the level of the sea and is evidently one of the lowest depressions in the whole range."

In 1883 construction crews for the Northern Pacific reduced the grade and elevation even further. They cut a tunnel for three-quarters of a mile at 5,500 feet above sea level. Soon trains were speeding passengers through here, just as John Mullan had predicted they would do more than three decades earlier.

### ELLISTON

Elliston, at the foot of MacDonald Pass, arose as a railroad division point and logging town. For five years, beginning in 1889, a wooden flume stretched for nine miles into the woods up the Little Blackfoot River. The flume carried cordwood down to a railroad spur east of town. From here trains took the wood to Anaconda, where it became fuel for Marcus Daly's smelter.

All winter, loggers would haul the wood, cut into four-foot lengths, and stack it near the head of the flume. With spring runoff, the short logs shot down the flume. The sides of the flume were a little less than four feet across to prevent the logs from turning sideways and jamming up. Still, watchmen had to ride horses up and down near the flume to break up jams.

In 1894 a fire leveled Elliston. The town rebuilt, only to have another fire destroy it a year later. Fortunately there was plenty of lumber available by then, because the Anaconda Company had abandoned its wooden flume.

## AVON

The first building in Avon was the Cramer House. The log structure housed construction crews for the Northern Pacific as they ran their line through here. For years after that, Avon served as a loading point for ore from nearby mines, livestock from area ranches, and lumber cut in the surrounding hills.

According to a local legend, a showman once brought a trained bear to the Cramer House to entertain the populace. The bear escaped, and for days everyone stayed indoors as he freely roamed the town. The trainer finally managed to get close enough to the bear to hand him a bottle of whiskey. As the bear swigged down the bottle's contents, the master recaptured him.

**I-15 and US 287**
# Helena—Augusta
**74 miles**

## MARYSVILLE

### The Drumlummon Mine
Thomas Cruse was one of many miners who migrated east into Montana after failing to find his fortune in California or Nevada. He scoured the hills around present Marysville until his friend and benefactor William Brown gave him an abandoned hard-rock claim. For years Cruse worked his mine alone, sinking a 500-foot shaft through solid granite to reach the mother lode. He named the mine after Drum Lummon parish in his native Ireland. He named the town that arose near the mine after Mary Ralston, one of its first residents.

Cruse was an astute businessman. He knew that only big money and modern equipment would unlock the real wealth of his mine. After re-

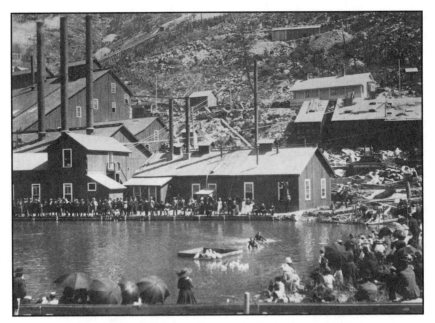

*Marysville residents cavort near the Drumlummon Mine.*
—Montana Historical Society, Helena

moving about $150,000 in gold, he sold out in 1883 to investors from London for more than $1.6 million and one-sixth interest in the Drumlummon.

Cruse then moved to Helena, where he purchased a home in the city's mansion district. He donated generously to a number of causes, including the construction of Montana's new capitol building. At age fifty he married the twenty-four-year-old daughter of U.S. Senator Thomas Carter. The new Mrs. Cruse taught her husband to read and write. In public he always walked several steps behind her, perhaps in deference to her education. After her death at an early age, Cruse raised their daughter, Mamie. Mamie, like her mother, died young after leading what contemporaries delicately called "a scandalous life."

Meanwhile, ore shipments from the Drumlummon soon averaged $80,000 a month. Then, in 1889 the owners became locked in a protracted battle with a company from St. Louis that owned an adjacent claim. Drumlummon miners followed their ore body into an area claimed by the St. Louis mine. Rival crews ignited smoke pots and built walls to drive off miners raiding their claims. It was a precursor of the sort of underground warfare that later plagued Butte. After eighteen years of litigation, the St.

Louis firm finally won. By then the Drumlummon's best ore had been removed. The mine closed for good in 1916. It had long since secured its position as Montana's richest gold mine.

Although the Drumlummon was the mainstay of Marysville's economy, there were other producing mines in the area. By 1885 about 4,000 people lived in the town. Both the Great Northern and Northern Pacific railroads were eager to tap into this wealthy mining district. The two lines raced to be the first to build up the steep grade into Marysville. The Northern Pacific arrived first, laying rails along the hillsides above the gulches. The Great Northern ran its line near the bottom of Silver Creek Valley. The Northern Pacific refused to allow its rival to build under its trestle, which crossed Sawmill Gulch near town. This forced the Great Northern to build its station an inconvenient quarter of a mile below town. It abandoned this little-used line within two years.

By 1925, when the Northern Pacific pulled out, there were only fifty families living in Marysville. Yet it refused to become a ghost town. You can reach it by cutting east from I-15 on county road 279. Drive another ten miles and take a gravel road leading west to Marysville. The remains of the Drumlummon Mine can be seen south of the road just before it enters town.

## MANN GULCH

I-15 between Helena and Great Falls parallels the Missouri River. Twenty miles north of Helena, a side road leads to a canyon that Meriwether Lewis named "the gates of the rocky mountains." After the party fought the strong current up the canyon on July 19, 1805, Lewis recorded:

> This evening we entered much the most remarkable clifts [sic] that we have yet seen. . . . Every object here wears a dark and gloomy aspect. The towering and projecting rocks in many places seem ready to tumble on us.

Mann Gulch is one of several small streams that drops into the Missouri from the rugged Gates of the Mountains Wilderness, east of the river. This nondescript little draw, which can be reached only by boat, attained infamy on August 5, 1949. On that hot afternoon, strong winds swept a small forest fire across the gulch near its mouth. The wall of fire trapped a group of smoke jumpers sent in to fight it. Thirteen young men perished. It was one of the worst tragedies in the history of fire fighting.

At the time of the Mann Gulch Fire, the art of smoke jumping was still in its infancy. As recently as 1935, a Forest Service official in Missoula had remarked that parachute jumpers were all "more or less crazy." In July 1940 Rufus Robinson and Earle Cooley became the first men to jump from an airplane into a forest fire.

*Smokejumpers prepare to board a Ford tri-motor, 1952.* —W. E. Steuerwald photo, USDA Forest Service, Missoula

*Smokejumpers descend, circa 1944.* —K. D. Swan photo, USDA Forest Service, Missoula

Missoula soon became the take-off point for hundreds of aerial assaults on small fires. Most of the young smoke jumpers were either veterans of military paratrooper corps or college students seeking adventure and a decent-paying summer job.

The sixty-acre lightning-caused fire that fifteen smoke jumpers dove toward at Mann Gulch appeared to be a routine affair. They reached the ground safely, and a district fireguard joined them. Their foreman, B. Wagner Dodge, gathered the men. They crossed to the north side of Mann Gulch and moved toward the Missouri River and the site of the fire.

Then things unraveled in a hurry. A sudden gale caused the fire to leap across the gulch into dry grass, through which it ran with lightning speed. Seeing this, Dodge had his men reverse direction and move back up the gulch. With the canyon acting as a wind tunnel, the fire blasted up the ridge.

As the exhausted crew got to within 150 yards of the top of the ridge, Dodge lit an escape fire. Over the roar of the onrushing fire, he tried to order his men to lie down inside the newly burned area. One man yelled, "The hell with this, I'm getting out of here!" Two men charged straight up the ridge. They were lucky enough to find a rock slide, where the fire burned past them. The rest of the crew ran from the fire at an angle up the ridge. They lost the race. Eleven burned to death instantly; the inferno melted their canteens. Two others died the following morning in a Helena hospital. The thirteen victims were the first smoke jumpers ever to die in a fire.

Yet something good came from the tragedy. Today every jumper trained at Missoula's Aerial Fire Depot is told about the Mann Gulch Fire. Jumpers leap into every blaze carrying the Ten Standard Orders for safely fighting fires—rules that rose from the ashes of Mann Gulch.

## AUGUSTA AND GILMAN

### A Tale of Two Towns

As I-15 angles northeast toward Great Falls, US 287 exits north and leads thirty-eight miles to Augusta. Meriwether Lewis led his small band of homeward-bound explorers through this area in July 1806. They camped on a large island in the middle of the Sun River. Near the end of the nineteenth century, more than 40,000 head of cattle grazed on the Sun River Range.

Augusta was a modest trade center in the spring of 1901 when a fire leveled its business section. Some said that Augusta had become the most moral community in Montana because the fire had destroyed all its saloons but spared the churches.

After Augusta rebuilt, an even greater threat arose in 1912, when the Great Northern Railway ran a branch line from Great Falls, up the Sun River, and across the Continental Divide. Railway officials laid the line about two miles north of Augusta. Here they surveyed a town site they named Gilman. Augusta's banker, Abraham Lincoln Bradley, relocated in Gilman and invited his merchant friends to join him. Some refused to leave Augusta. They established a new bank, and a heated rivalry began.

Most believed that Gilman with its railroad would easily overshadow Augusta, much as the establishment of Kalispell, west of the divide, had led to the demise of nearby Demersville. But residents of Augusta were fiercely loyal to their little community. After they failed to persuade the Great Northern to build a spur from Gilman, they took their cause to the Montana legislature. They secured passage of a bill that empowered the state railroad commission to force railways to build commercial spurs to towns that were up to two miles off the main line.

After a long legal battle, the Great Northern relented and extended its spur to Augusta. By then a drought and a drop in the price of cattle had ravaged the area's economy. Bradley's overextended Gilman State Bank closed in November 1923. Augusta's bank also went broke, but by then most people in Gilman realized that the new rail spur would mean the demise of their town. After another big court fight, the Great Northern

*Abandoned Gilman State Bank.*

shut down its Gilman depot. In the exodus that followed, some lifted their houses from their foundations and moved them, along with sidewalks, to Augusta. Augusta remains today what it always has been—a modest agricultural community.

# Rogers Pass—Ovando
**64 miles**

## ROGERS PASS

### Seventy Below
Montana 200 crosses the Continental Divide via 6,376-foot-elevation Rogers Pass. Meriwether Lewis chose a pass just north of here to cross the Great Divide. Decades later, the Great Northern Railway named Rogers Pass after one of the line's surveyors.

Just west of the summit of Rogers Pass, a sign commemorates an important meteorological event. Near here, in the early morning hours of January 20, 1954, an official National Weather Service thermometer recorded a temperature of seventy degrees below zero—a record low for the continental forty-eight states.

On that calm morning the skies had cleared after a week of steady snowfall. The extreme cold was causing frequent popping noises in the cabin of volunteer weather observer H. M. Kleinschmidt. About 2 A.M. he went out and checked the thermometer, which recorded only temperatures down to sixty-five below. The mercury had retreated as far as it could go into the bulb. After Kleinschmidt described the event and mailed the thermometer to Washington D.C., the Weather Service determined that the temperature had reached at least minus 69.7 degrees.

## LINCOLN
Settlement in the Lincoln area began in 1865, with the discovery of gold on a number of tiny streams several miles northwest of the present town. Prospectors Dave Culp and Tom Patterson made the find. They named the place Abe Lincoln Gulch.

A toll road across Stemple Pass to Helena was the town's main link to civilization. One winter a brawl broke out in a local saloon, and prospector John Smoot was severely wounded. Another miner set off for Helena to fetch a doctor. He kept drinking whiskey to keep warm and got lost in the mountains. Meanwhile, Smoot died.

Like so many other mining camps, the settlement on Lincoln Gulch disappeared once the gold played out. The area reverted to near wilderness until homesteaders began ranching along the upper Blackfoot River. People from Helena and Great Falls also began building summer cabins in the area. In 1919 British immigrant James L. Lambkin and his wife, Mary, purchased the tiny hotel in Lincoln. They replaced it with a larger log structure and surrounded it with small cabins for tourists.

During the prohibition era, stills from around Lincoln supplied Helena's government offices, drug stores, and the state capitol with all the liquor they could handle. In its prime, Lincoln's cottage industry produced 300 gallons of booze a month. Whenever a farmer-moonshiner went to jail for his activities, his wife ran the operation.

Lincoln's remote environs also have attracted a number of eccentrics and recluses over the years. The most infamous was Theodore J. Kaczynski, a middle-aged hermit who lived in a crude cabin about four miles south of Lincoln. He survived by eating wild game and the vegetables he grew. Occasionally he rode a bicycle to town to pick up supplies and visit the local library.

On April 3, 1996, several dozen FBI agents moved in on the cabin and took Kaczynski into custody. Lincoln residents were shocked to learn that their quiet polite neighbor was the prime suspect in a series of mail-bomb attacks that had stumped the nation's law-enforcement officials for eighteen years. Fifteen bombs constructed by the so-called Unabomber had killed three people and injured twenty-three. The evidence that agents found inside Kaczynski's cabin included a partially assembled pipe bomb.

Once news of the arrest spread, scores of reporters and television crews swarmed into Lincoln. They interviewed virtually everyone in town several times. One townsman echoed the feelings of many when he told reporters, "There are guys in Lincoln, Montana, who are scarier looking . . . who carry guns and knives. Ted was just a nice guy."

## THE CANYON CREEK FIRE

The Scapegoat Wilderness lies north of Montana 200 between Rogers Pass and Ovando. In 1988 one of Montana's worst forest and range fires shot east out of the wilderness and burned nearly to Augusta before it finally ran out of fuel and died.

The Canyon Creek Fire began when lightning struck a tree in the Scapegoat late in June. The Forest Service designated it a "prescription fire" and allowed it to burn. But fire managers underestimated the fuel buildup caused by four years of drought. Once the fire raced across the Continental Divide, crews moved in to control it.

On the night of September 6, the flames exploded. Winds up to fifty miles an hour blasted the fire across containment lines, tripling its size. A firestorm reminiscent of the great 1910 burn shot thirty miles east. It blackened nearly a quarter of a million acres and left burned hay fields and fences and dead cattle in its wake. Generally the "let it burn" policy has proven to be a successful forest-management practice. Canyon Creek proved a tragic exception.

# The Central Valleys

*We came in by way of the gap to the famous Judith Basin which was, indeed, a paradise land of plenty; game of all kinds, lots of good water and timber. What more could we want? After finding what we had searched for, our journey ended right here.*

—Mrs. Clemence Gurneau Berger

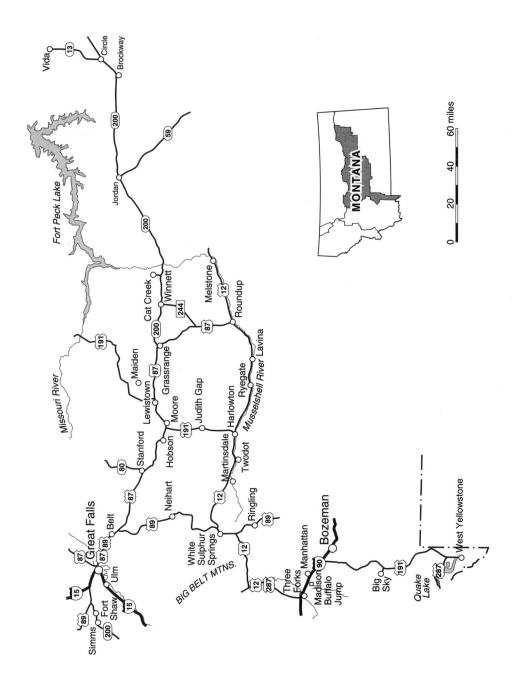

0    20    40    60 miles

Clemence Berger entered the Judith Basin in central Montana in 1879, along with a large group of Métis—people of French Canadian and American Indian lineage. Her feelings of wonder and optimism were shared by thousands of others who later took up raising stock and farming in the many lush valleys watered by tributaries entering the Missouri River from the south. Lands drained by the Gallatin, Smith, Judith, Musselshell, Big Dry, and Redwater Rivers, and dozens of lesser streams attracted hordes of eager settlers throughout the late nineteenth and early twentieth centuries.

Central Montana—that region bounded by the base of the Rockies on the west, the Missouri River on the north, the Musselshell and Gallatin Valleys on the south, and the "Big Open" region of Garfield and McCone Counties on the east—was long a bison-rich hunting ground for Native Americans. Before acquiring horses, hunters drove the bison over cliffs. Projectile points and tepee rings found at the many buffalo jumps date back several thousand years. More recently, the Crow, Blackfeet, Nez Perce, Salish, and Sioux tribes all followed the migrating herds into this region, but no tribe claimed it as their homeland.

Lewis and Clark were probably the first white explorers to view the southern tributaries of the Missouri. Although they named the Musselshell, the Judith, and the Smith Rivers, they did not take time to explore these drainages. During the early decades of the nineteenth century, a handful of fur trappers passed through the area. Permanent settlement did not come until the 1860s gold rush. As prospectors and other immigrants demanded protection from Indian raids, the military established Camp Cooke near the mouth of the Judith, Fort Shaw on the lower Sun River, Camp Baker in the Smith River valley, and Fort Ellis in the Gallatin Valley. At the same time a series of short-lived trading posts arose near the mouth of the Musselshell.

In the spring of 1867 the U.S. government began an ill-fated attempt to run a Pony Express mail route between St. Paul, Minnesota, and Helena. In central Montana this route crossed the Missouri River below the mouth of the Musselshell. It ran to the Judith Mountains, along the foothills of the Snowy Mountains through the Judith Gap, and up the Musselshell River before crossing over to Confederate Gulch. Seeking to protect their land against this invasion, the Blackfeet and Sioux attacked and robbed riders until no one was willing to travel the Musselshell route alone. As historians K. Ross Toole and Merrill Burlingame recorded, "What mail the riders did not use for warming their food, the Indians stole."

# CATTLE COUNTRY

The native tribes who managed to drive out the Pony Express could not keep white cattlemen from bringing their stock into central Montana. Beginning in 1870, Dan Floweree, Conrad Kohrs, Robert S. Ford, and others trailed big herds onto the open ranges of the Sun River valley. Soon, cattle and sheep were grazing throughout the valleys of the Musselshell, Judith, and Box Elder Rivers.

Across the region stockmen cooperated to form large roundup associations to brand and control their animals. Frontier journalist Robert Sutherlin described the 1888 spring roundup of the Musselshell Association as "a mammoth concern composed of about 100 men, 85 riders, 1,000 saddle horses and nearly a dozen tents, and represented 100,000 head of cattle." Sutherlin added, "The rapidity with which the branding and knifing was done was truly wonderful. The scene would make our humanitarian friends of the East shudder." Sutherlin witnessed this roundup after the devastating winter of 1886–87 had wiped out more than half the herds in central Montana.

That winter transformed the cattle industry. Stockmen began fencing their land and raising hay for winter feed. The area experienced even greater changes with the arrival of railroads. By the early 1890s the Great Northern and Northern Pacific transcontinental lines skirted the northern and southern edges of the region. During the first decade of the twentieth century, steel rails penetrated the valleys of the Missouri tributaries. Foremost among these lines was the last of Montana's transcontinentals, the Chicago, Milwaukee, St. Paul & Pacific Railroad (the Milwaukee Road).

# THE MILWAUKEE ROAD

Some have called the Milwaukee Road the finest rail line ever built. Others have labeled it a major mistake and a financial disaster. Each assessment is accurate. From the time it entered Montana in 1906 until its last freight train made its run in 1980, the Milwaukee operated under severe financial hardship. Forced to compete with two established rail lines, the Panama Canal, and the trucking industry, the line experienced three bankruptcies during its stormy career.

But by 1912 the Milwaukee Road was shipping freight and passengers along 818 miles of the best track in Montana. It featured well-engineered grades, concrete-lined tunnels, and all-steel bridges. Its depots—with their tall clock towers—exist today as unique landmarks in Great Falls, Butte, and Missoula. Along the Milwaukee's former route between Harlowton, Montana, and Avery, Idaho, decaying brick transformer stations stand as

*"Little Joe" electric engines at the Milwaukee Road depot in Three Forks.*
—Montana Historical Society, Helena

stark reminders of a time when the line ran boxlike orange and maroon electric locomotives along the western half of its route through Montana. Electric locomotives proved to be cleaner and more cost-efficient than steam engines. For many years toy-train companies sold engines based on the Milwaukee Road's design.

In central Montana the Milwaukee ran its rails along the Musselshell River between Melstone and Martinsdale. At the time of its construction, the line passed through a region already lined with ranches and irrigation ditches. Construction workers bridged or moved the channel of the Musselshell 117 times along this section. The company spent thousands of dollars settling damage claims pressed by ranchers.

Like its competitor rail lines, the Milwaukee Road blanketed the midwestern and eastern states with promotional literature offering discount transportation rates to those willing to settle in the vast, empty prairies along its route. One popular brochure featured an illustration of a farmer plowing up gold coins. In another flier a Montana homesteader testified, "Now as I have been in this locality for thirty years, I find that we do not have as hard winters as we did thirty years ago, and we get more rain in the summer."

During the twentieth century's second decade, the railroad's publicity scheme worked well. The valleys of central Montana filled with optimistic homesteaders. All along the Milwaukee's main line and its branches leading north to Lewistown and Great Falls, dozens of small towns sprang up

*Part of the Milwaukee Road's campaign to lure settlers to its central Montana route.* —Western Heritage Center, Billings

to serve the new population. Most did not survive the drought and ensuing exodus of settlers throughout the 1920s and 1930s. In 1923 alone, eight banks failed in Wheatland County. Today even the railroad that created central Montana's homestead boom is gone. But some of the communities it built have survived and grown in a diversified economy combining agriculture with mining, oil, and tourism.

Montana 200
# Simms—Great Falls
32 miles

## SIMMS

The community of Simms was a product of the Sun River Irrigation Project, which began diverting water and selling forty-acre plots to homesteaders in 1908. An engineer for the U.S. Reclamation Service platted Simms and the downstream town of Fort Shaw. Founders wisely constructed a two-story school right in the center of town. In 1916 the Simms *Enterprise* boasted, "Simms has no saloon and refuses to have one and this fact has won recognition and a unique position for it." The Sun River Valley State Bank, which opened in 1913, closed for good in 1937—the same year that the Rural Electrification Administration (REA) brought electricity to the town.

The Sun River flows east to its junction with the Missouri at Great Falls. Its grass-rich valley was long a popular hunting ground for Native Americans. The region is dotted with numerous buffalo jumps, or *pishkins,* used by ancient hunters before the arrival of the horse. Later, members of the Crow and Blackfeet tribes fought a number of bloody battles for control of this excellent hunting ground. And still more recently, the valley supported up to 600,000 head of open-range cattle.

## FORT SHAW

The U.S. Army established Camp Reynolds in June 1867 about five miles above the place where the Mullan Road crossed the Sun River. A year later, they renamed the fort in honor of Col. Robert G. Shaw, who was killed during the Civil War while commanding the 54th Massachusetts Volunteers—a regiment of African American soldiers.

As headquarters for the military district of Montana, Fort Shaw served as the territory's chief fort. Infantrymen stationed here guarded the Mullan Road, maintained telegraph lines, and escorted survey parties. Fort Shaw

*Fort Shaw Indian School girls' basketball team, 1903.* —Montana Historical Society, Helena

soldiers also participated in the infamous Baker Massacre of Blackfeet Indians on the Marias River and in the bloody Big Hole Battle during the Nez Perce War.

In 1891 the army abandoned the post. A year later its buildings began housing an Indian school. During the early 1900s the school had more than 300 students and 17 teachers. It also boasted one of the finest girls' basketball teams ever to play the game. Illinois native Sadie Campbell coached the team to a state championship in 1903. They defeated teams from Butte, Helena, and Missoula, as well as teams from each of the state's big universities. Later the team traveled to the World's Fair in St. Louis. Along the way they played local girls' teams in exhibition games. To raise money, the young women donned native costumes and staged Indian dances, charging spectators fifty cents each. In St. Louis the girls defeated every team they played, including several men's teams. Between 1902 and 1906 the team won every game except one—a contest in which they were forced to play by girls' rules.

## GREAT FALLS

"The grandest sight I ever beheld." This is how Meriwether Lewis described the Great Falls of the Missouri River after first gazing at the spectacle on June 13, 1805. Lewis sat atop rocks below the falls for four hours staring into "a perfect white foam which assumes a thousand forms in a moment." He then spent the rest of the day in a vain attempt to find an easy portage around the series of falls. The next morning he sent Joseph Field downstream with a message for William Clark and the rest of the party announcing that he had at last found the elusive Great Falls.

The expedition spent an entire month making the torturous portage around the eighteen miles of rapids and waterfalls that today flow past the city of Great Falls. Pushing crude cottonwood carts with rounded trunk slabs for wheels, the party trudged across ground churned up by bison herds and filled with prickly-pear cactus that cut into their feet. Grizzly bears raided their meat supply at night. Violent rain and hailstorms drenched them. The exhausted men frequently collapsed into a dead sleep. Yet, Lewis recorded, "no one complains, all go with cheerfullness."

In the weeks they spent here, Lewis and Clark carefully surveyed the entire region. Near one falls Lewis discovered a midstream island where an eagle had placed a nest atop a cottonwood tree. It was William Clark who first encountered what he described as "the largest fountain spring I ever saw," with water boiling up from under rocks near the river's edge and falling eight feet into the Missouri. On July 15 the party left the area in eight canoes, all "heavily laden."

*The Great Falls of the Missouri prior to construction of dam and power plant.*
—Cascade County Historical Society, Great Falls

A year later Lewis and a smaller party took only four days to portage the falls on their return trip. Today, River Drive in Great Falls runs adjacent to the Missouri, where Lewis and Clark viewed the upper falls. Clark's large "fountain spring" is now Giant Springs State Park. In this park a first-rate interpretive center, opened in 1998, commemorates the Corps of Discovery's sojourn in the area. The Great Falls can be reached by taking US 87 five miles north from downtown Great Falls and then driving east six miles on the Ryan Dam Road. Power dams have robbed all the falls of much of their original grandeur.

### Paris Gibson

For seventy years after Lewis and Clark portaged around the falls of the Missouri, the region remained pristine. In 1880 Fort Benton merchant Paris Gibson visited the falls after he had read about them in Lewis and Clark's journals . Gibson had already grown rich and gone broke as a flour and wool merchant in the Minneapolis area. He moved to Montana at age forty-nine and was well on his way to earning another fortune when he and his son explored the falls. Gibson later recalled his impressions:

> I could readily understand the feelings of Captain Lewis as he gazed upon this scene 75 years before. . . . I had never seen a spot as attractive

*Paris Gibson.*
—Cascade County
Historical Society,
Great Falls

as this. . . . I had looked upon this scene for a few moments only when I said to myself, here I would found a city.

In the summer of 1883, Gibson and others platted the town site and named it Great Falls. A year later Gibson's old friend from his years in Minneapolis, James J. Hill, visited the site and informed Gibson of his plans to extend his rail line westward. With Hill's money and a transcontinental railroad connecting the new town to Eastern markets, Gibson envisioned a "new Minneapolis" on the banks of the upper Missouri.

For the next forty years Paris Gibson labored tirelessly to make his vision a reality. He lured investors and industry into the town. He boosted dryland farming in the surrounding region to bring in settlers and to produce raw material for the town's factories. By 1888, when Gibson became its first mayor, Great Falls already had more than 2,000 citizens. Two years later the population had doubled.

Unlike most founders of western cities who were mere boosters seeking fast money, Gibson wished to make his city a place "of unsurpassed beauty and attractiveness." He made sure residential neighborhoods had wide,

*Amalgamated Copper Company's Great Falls smelter.* —Cascade County Historical Society, Great Falls

geometrically regular streets lined with trees and punctuated by large parks. He argued that grass and trees would make "the modest home of the workingman as attractive as the more pretentious home of the wealthy merchant." Parks, he felt, would lead "intelligent people" to live in Great Falls.

As a state legislator Gibson tried unsuccessfully to make Great Falls the site of a single state university. His town suffered another blow when Hill decided to extend his line to the coast due west from Havre and not through Great Falls. Great Falls never became the vast city Gibson had envisioned. But the town still celebrates his legacy. A 1979 booster pamphlet noted that Paris Gibson's spirit still serves as a "guide for making Great Falls a better place to live."

Even though it never became another Minneapolis, Great Falls emerged in the early twentieth century as one of Montana's leading industrial centers. In 1890 the first power dam backed up the Missouri River at Black Eagle Falls. The hill above the dam became the site of the copper-smelting complex of the Boston and Montana Company. In 1901 the Amalgamated Copper Company took over the smelter. Eight years later, what was called the highest chimney in the world puffed its first smoke from the smelter. A postcard describing the structure noted that it would require a hen laying an egg every day for 730,000 years to supply enough eggs to fill the stack. The smelter closed in 1980. Two years later, when crews demolished the stack, more than 40,000 people watched the event.

### Cowboy Artist

Among those lured to live on the tree-lined streets of Great Falls were artist Charles M. Russell and his wife, Nancy. If Montana has a patron saint, it is probably Charlie Russell. Russell's art graces the state capitol and the Montana Historical Society museum, and his buffalo-skull logo appears on Montana's license plates. His is the only statue of an artist in Washington D.C.'s Statuary Hall.

The son of a wealthy St. Louis industrialist, Russell was a precocious boy who preferred hanging out with the Mississippi riverboat men and fur traders rather than going to school. Russell longed to live on the wild western frontier. His father finally relented and let him visit a friend's Montana sheep ranch in 1880, just before Russell turned sixteen. He remained in Montana for most of the rest of his life.

From his years on the Mississippi, Russell enjoyed sketching and modeling crude figures from wax and clay. He was a failure as a sheepherder in Montana, partly because he spent too much time drawing and modeling and ignored the sheep. After spending two years under the tutelage of latter-day mountain man Jake Hoover, Russell became a night wrangler on

*Charlie and Nancy Russell.* —Cascade County Historical Society, Great Falls

the Judith River. He worked for twelve years for various cattle outfits in central Montana, but he never became a skilled cowboy. As he later wrote, "I was neither a good roper nor rider. . . . I lived to play and I'm playing yet."

He continued to paint and draw. In the spring of 1887 he hastily sketched what became perhaps his most famous work of art—a picture of a single starving steer with wolves lurking in the background. He entitled it "Waiting for a Chinook." It became popular in Helena, where businessmen renamed it "The Last of the Five Thousand." Throughout his cowboy days, Russell regarded his art as a mere hobby. He gave away his work to his many friends or painted pictures for saloon and store owners to pay off his debts. He indulged in frequent drinking binges and cavorted in Helena's red-light district. Later tales about his sojourn among the Blood Indians in Canada were exaggerated. Russell stayed only three months in a cabin in Canada and spent relatively little time among the Blackfeet.

Not until 1893—when he visited the world's fair in Chicago, where three of his paintings were displayed—did Russell decide to make art his career. Three years later he married Nancy Cooper, a girl still in her teens. She became his financial advisor and manager. Russell accurately described

*B-17 bombers await shipment from Great Falls.* —Cascade County Historical Society, Great Falls

their partnership: "She is the business end and I am the creative. . . . She lives for tomorrow and I live for yesterday."

Nancy demanded and got increasingly higher prices for her husband's artwork. The couple built a house at the corner of Thirteenth Street and Fourth Avenue in Great Falls. Out back he built a studio from telephone poles that he called his "shack." In this single room, with its stone fireplace and a roof strewn with elk horns, he sat before his canvasses on a backless kitchen chair with a cigarette between his lips. The art he created here was soon being exhibited and sold from New York to Rome.

In many ways the urbane lifestyle Charlie and Nancy Russell led seemed to run counter to his art and writing. He romanticized the rugged, unspoiled frontier of Native Americans, mountain men, and cowboys. He frequently groused about city life and the demise of the frontier. Yet the Russells lived in Montana's most urban of towns and spent an increasing amount of time in California among their movie-star friends.

Following Russell's death in 1925, the artist's home and studio became a historic site. The city of Great Falls later funded a museum, next to his studio, which today houses a fine collection of his art.

### Malmstrom Air Force Base

On the east end of Second Avenue North in Great Falls is the main gate to Malmstrom Air Force Base. Beginning in early 1942 Great Falls became a staging area for shipments of airplanes and cargo to the Soviet Union through the Lend-Lease Act. From here some 8,000 fighters and bombers took off for Alaska and eventual delivery to Russia, flying across treacherous arctic wasteland. Early in the war it was recognized that the Great Falls municipal airport was inadequate for such a massive undertaking, so the military constructed East Base on land east of town. The army air force used this facility to train B-17 bomber pilots.

During the war, construction of the 2,000-acre base (along with work on a highway to Alaska) helped bring Great Falls out of the Great Depression. In 1948 the base served as the nation's only training center for the pilots who flew C-54 cargo planes during the historic Berlin airlift. During the early 1950s jet fighters began roaring over town. In 1955 they renamed the base after Col. Einar A. Malmstrom, a World War II ace pilot who had been killed when his trainer jet crashed near Great Falls a year earlier.

During the early 1960s the Air Force phased out the fighter planes at Malmstrom, and the base became headquarters for the 150 Minuteman nuclear missiles located throughout central Montana. The missiles made Great Falls a primary cold-war target zone and the site of antiwar protests each year on Easter.

I-15
# Great Falls—Cascade
27 miles

## CASCADE

Cascade began as a stop on the Montana Central Railroad in 1886. The old post office, Dodge, changed its name to Cascade when the railroad arrived. The town was a supply point for farmers and ranchers in the Chestnut Valley to the north. Cascade once was slated to be the county seat for a proposed county called Dearborn. But Dearborn County never was, and Cascade remained a small railroad stop. During prohibition all eleven saloons in Cascade shut down. A bootleg joint known as the Bucket of Blood allegedly operated from a shack near town.

## ST. PETER'S MISSION

St. Peter's Mission was located about fifteen miles due west of Cascade. The mission was the last of several attempts by the Jesuits to establish a religious center among the Blackfeet.

In 1862 they constructed a mission on the north bank of the Missouri near present Great Falls. Constant skirmishes between the Blackfeet and prospectors heading west forced the Jesuits to move their mission to its final location near Bird Tail Rock.

During the late 1870s the Jesuits erected stone buildings to house a school for boys at St. Peter's. In 1883 Louis Riel, the French Canadian leader of the Métis Red River Rebellion in Canada, served as one of the teachers at the school. Riel lived here for only about a year before he returned to Canada, where he was convicted of treason and executed.

Later, Ursuline nuns came to teach at St. Peter's. In 1891 they moved into a three-story stone convent known as Mount Angela. St. Peter's became a school for girls. The first Catholic residents of Great Falls depended on the priests and nuns from St. Peter's for church services and religious education. A fire in 1918 destroyed the girls' school, but by then the Ursulines had established a new school in Great Falls.

**Montana 22 and US 89**
# Great Falls—Ringling
**118 miles**

## BELT

In 1877 John K. Castner, a former mule skinner on the Fort Benton–Helena route, discovered an outcrop of coal in the hills near Belt Creek and developed one of the first commercial coal mines in Montana. He hauled the coal in freight wagons to Fort Benton for use in the steamboats and homes there.

It was in Fort Benton that Castner met Mattie Bost, a former slave from North Carolina who was working as a laundress. Castner and Mattie were married in Helena, and the couple moved to a crude log cabin on the creek near Castner's coal mine. This cabin became the Castner Hotel—the nucleus of the new town of Belt.

Mattie ran the hotel and served meals to stagecoach passengers on the Great Falls-to-Lewistown route. Her meals, consisting of vegetables from her garden and meat of wild game, which she hunted herself, became famous throughout the region. Mattie also worked in her husband's coal mine and later bought a large ranch near Belt. Throughout her life Mattie donated food to needy townspeople. When she died she left her sizable estate to charity.

In the early 1890s the Anaconda Company became interested in the Belt coalfields. Marcus Daly's agent, P. J. Shields, filed claims on much of the land surrounding the town and leased Castner's mine. Soon the Ana-

*Castner Street, Belt, with Anaconda's coal mines in background.*
—Cascade County Historical Society, Great Falls

conda Company erected coke ovens, furnaces, a coal-washing plant, tipples, and houses for the new immigrant miners.

At their peak the Anaconda coal mines in Belt employed more than 1,000 miners. Daily they produced more than 2,500 tons of coal that traveled to the smelters in Anaconda and Great Falls via a branch of the Great Northern Railway.

In its heyday Belt was like a miniature Butte. Miners here came from most of the nations of Europe and settled in ethnic communities with names like French Coulee, Coke Oven Flat, Finlander Row, and Slav Town. A slack dump near town caught fire and smoldered for years. It cast a pall of sulfurous gas over the valley, killing trees and plants and turning the houses black. The saloons on Castner and Bridge Streets ran night and day. On paydays deputy sheriffs were assigned to each saloon to act as referees when fights broke out and to check for guns, knives, and blackjacks.

Once the railroads converted to diesel power and the Anaconda smelters began using natural gas for fuel, coal production in Belt came to a halt. The town became a quiet railroad stop. That quiet was rudely disrupted on the afternoon of November 26, 1976, when tanker cars on a Burlington Northern freight train jumped the tracks on the viaduct over the road leading into town. The resulting explosions and fires hurled tanker cars high into the air and ravaged the section of town near the tracks. The careening tankers smashed into storage tanks at the nearby Farmers Union Oil Company. Burning fuel oil from the ruptured cars sent a wall of flames down Castner Street. Alert firemen managed to divert this flaming flow into Belt Creek. The fire leveled nine buildings and killed two people. Thousands of gallons of oil polluted Belt Creek for miles downstream.

## MONARCH, NEIHART, AND BARKER

### Mining Towns

As it winds through the Little Belt Mountains, US 89 parallels the route of James J. Hill's Montana Central Railroad branch line, which ran from Great Falls to the mining towns of Monarch, Neihart, and Barker. In later years excursion trains on this route were known as "fish trains." They dropped off fishermen at their favorite holes on Belt Creek in the morning and picked them up on the return trip.

In the forested canyon between Monarch and Neihart, the dumps and remains of the once-rich silver mines can still be seen from the highway. James L. Neihart and his two partners discovered the first pay dirt in this region in the early 1880s. An area newspaper described the infant town of Neihart as having "twenty-four to twenty-five houses with roofs and as many more without, and a number of tents." Silver ore shipped from here was so rich that it still yielded $200 a ton after mine owners had paid the $100-a-ton charge to freight it to Omaha, where it was smelted.

Still, the mines were beginning to languish when the Montana Central's rails reached Neihart in November 1891. A brass band planned to greet the first train, but the subzero temperatures made instruments impossible to play. Instead, blasts of powder in the nearby hills signaled the event. Dignitaries drove a spike made of silver from the nearby Queen of the Hills Mine. The area's forty silver mines boomed until the 1893 silver panic. Yet even with the drop in silver prices, mines in the Little Belt Mountains produced well into the twentieth century.

## WHITE SULPHUR SPRINGS

James Scott Brewer, a native of Virginia, built the first house in the Smith River valley in a spot he called Trinity Springs. Later the Flathead Indians told him of nearby hot springs that they used as "medicine waters," and Brewer moved there. By 1872 he had constructed a bathhouse, stables, a general store, and a twelve-by-twelve-foot plunge. As one early settler along the upper Musselshell River recalled, "Jim Brewer . . . cleaned out the spring, built a house over it, charged the boys 75 cents each for a bath, sold whiskey and ran one hell of a place."

*White Sulphur Springs, 1886.* —Montana Historical Society, Helena

In 1877 Brewer sold his springs to Dr. William Parberry, a physician from nearby Confederate Gulch. Parberry had been sending his patients to Brewer's springs to soak away their ailments in the hot sulphur waters. When he took over, he renamed the place White Sulphur Springs and replaced Brewer's cabin with a brick hotel, complete with reading rooms and a billiard saloon.

As a community arose around the springs, the local newspaper boasted White Sulphur as "the Saratoga of the West," an "Eldorado of ease and elegance, where cool breezes kiss away the burning rays of the summer sun and a panacea for human ills gushes forth from mother earth." Guests discovered that water from one of the springs made a "first-class chicken soup." Parberry also found the water to be good for heating sheep dip. White Sulphur Springs emerged as the main recreation spot for the Confederate Gulch miners, the farmers of the Smith Valley, and soldiers from nearby Camp Baker.

The fortunes of White Sulphur Springs began to decline after a syndicate purchased the resort and many town lots in 1883. They ignored maintenance at the resort and boosted the price of lots so high that many chose to build on the outskirts of town. Attempts to lure a railroad failed. As area silver mines declined in the late 1890s, people lost interest in visiting hot-springs resorts. White Sulphur's population dropped sharply. In 1910 local civic leaders raised enough money to construct a railroad connecting the town to the new Milwaukee Road to the south. But even this failed to revive the resort.

Despite the resort's misfortunes White Sulphur managed to thrive as an agricultural and commercial center for a wide region. Today the town's most conspicuous landmark is a large stone house on the highest hill in town. Locals have long referred to the place as "the castle." Merchant Byron Roger Sherman designed and built the structure in 1891. Sixteen-oxen teams pulled the massive wagons that hauled the granite for the house from the Castle Mountains, twelve miles to the southeast. Sherman also constructed White Sulphur's first light plant. Power came to town via bare wires supported on spruce poles. Sometimes birds got tangled in the wires, shorting out all of the lights in town. After Sherman moved to California, his castle rented out as apartments for a time, before the building deteriorated. In the 1960s the local historical society began renovating the house and converted it into an excellent museum.

### FORT LOGAN

Originally known as Camp Baker, Fort Logan sits near the Smith River, eighteen miles northwest of White Sulphur Springs. The army constructed the post to protect miners and ranchers and to guard the Carroll Trail from the Blackfeet. Later they renamed the fort to honor a soldier killed by Nez Perce at the Battle of the Big Hole. The post featured a unique, eight-sided, log blockhouse that enabled troops to fire outward from all angles. Even though the military abandoned Fort Logan in 1880, its blockhouse still stands on private property visible from the road.

### CASTLE

The mining camp of Castle received its name from the turret-like spires above the town. Lafe Hensley and his three brothers developed the rich silver deposits in the area during the late 1880s. At its peak an estimated 2,000 miners and other fortune seekers filled Castle and nearby camps. Mines such as the Yellowstone, the Cumberland, and the Great Eastern made Castle one of Montana's richest silver producers. The boomtown contained a brass band, four newspapers that succeeded each other in rapid order, three smelters, fourteen saloons, and three brothels, including one called Minnie's Sporting House.

Castle fell victim to the 1893 depression. Even the arrival four years later of Richard Harlow's "Jawbone Railroad" failed to revive the town. Many of Castle's abandoned buildings are still standing. They are on private land along a dirt road, seven miles north of Montana 294, about midway between Martinsdale and Ringling.

Probably Castle's most famous citizen was Anna Robinson. As she waited tables at her mother's boardinghouse, Anna entertained the miners with her singing. She became known as "the Belle of the Castles," and many acclaimed her as the most beautiful girl in Montana. Eventually Anna wound up starring in Broadway plays in New York. She had many rich suitors and eventually married a European aristocrat. After her husband gambled away the couple's fortune, Anna left him and returned to the stage. Bad investments continued to plague her, and Anna wound up dying impoverished in New York's state hospital for the insane.

## RINGLING

The town of Ringling began as the farm community of Leader. Around 1910 residents renamed it after John Ringling, the youngest of the five Ringling brothers who had gained renown as the owners of America's largest circus. After Ringling purchased thousands of acres in the valley for raising cattle, he constructed a railroad linking White Sulphur Springs to the Milwaukee Road main line near Leader.

Rumors flew that Ringling and his brothers planned to make the area winter quarters for their circus. Anticipating quick wealth to be made from such a venture, Leader changed its name, and people in White Sulphur Springs helped Ringling fund his railroad. Ringling impressed many with his plans to restore White Sulphur's resorts to their glory days by extending his railroad north to Great Falls and south to Yellowstone National Park.

But John Ringling proved to be more a boaster than a builder. Few of his grandiose schemes were realized. After he lost interest in his ranches, he turned them over to his heavy-drinking nephew, Richard. Despite the bad habits that led to his early death, Richard managed to gain control of 200,000 acres of Montana ranch land on which he ran thousands of sheep and cattle. He also built one of the West's largest dairy barns.

Ringling's White Sulphur Springs & Yellowstone Park Railroad never extended beyond its original twenty-three miles along the upper Smith River, and it never made much of a profit. Still, it operated into the 1970s, hauling livestock, logs, and wood pulp. In its final years, there were so many derailments along the decaying line that a repair truck often accompanied trains to place the engine back on the rails. Meanwhile, Ringling suffered from a series of bad fires. By the 1940s author Ivan Doig recalled that the town consisted of "a spattered circle of houses around several large weedy foundations." It has changed little since then.

# Raynesford—Lewistown
**71 miles**

## RAYNESFORD AND GEYSER

The community of Raynesford and the adjacent town of Geyser both boomed with the arrival of a branch of the Great Northern that built southeast from Great Falls to Billings in 1906. The Great Northern purchased land from rancher Edmund Huggins for the Raynesford town site. Railroad officials agreed to name their new town after Huggins's youngest daughter, Henrietta Raynesford. The railroad constructed a depot, a pumping station, and a bunkhouse to house its section crews.

Geyser began in the early 1880s as a stage station on the Great Falls–Lewistown route. Pioneer rancher George Hay told the men mapping the stage route that they would have to fence off nearby mud springs to protect their stock. When he showed the stage line officials the springs, Hay pushed a twenty-foot pole into the mud. When he pulled it out, water and mud shot into the air. They named the new station Geyser in honor of this natural phenomenon.

## COLD-WAR SENTINELS

If you look south near milepost 24, between Geyser and Stanford you will see a large, square area surrounded by a formidable chain-link fence. Buried in a silo beneath this section of land is one of 200 Minuteman nuclear missiles that lie hidden beneath the wheat fields and grasslands of north-central Montana.

In July 1963, after two years of construction, 150 Minuteman sites were declared operational. Later, fifty more were added to the 341st Missile Wing, headquartered at Malmstrom Air Force Base. Some of the missiles had been ready for firing during the 1962 Cuban Missile Crisis if they had been needed. President John F. Kennedy referred to them as his "ace in the hole."

Each silo is eighty-four feet deep and twelve feet across. Twenty launch-control centers, buried sixty feet underground house the personnel who watch the missiles. More than 2,000 miles of underground communication cables connect the launchers. The silos themselves contain no people, but they are guarded by electronic equipment so sensitive that a rabbit hopping nearby will light up warning lights at a control center. The missiles themselves, which have been upgraded periodically, carry warheads with the explosive power of 5 million tons of TNT. During the cold-war era, each missile was targeted to a specific Soviet city.

At first area residents welcomed the construction jobs that the silos brought to central Montana. But most were also a bit uneasy over the realization that Montana's missile zone would be a primary target if a shooting war with the Soviets were ever to break out. Many assumed the attitude of a Great Falls businessman who, in 1969, told the *New York Times,* "The whole thing is just like a pain that stays with you for a long time. After awhile you just don't think about it much."

## STANFORD

Stanford began in 1875 as a stage station on the route between Billings and Fort Benton. Like most towns in this area, it had to relocate once the Great Northern line arrived. One building that housed a large dance hall got stuck halfway between town sites. It stood alone on the landscape for a week before it could be dislodged and moved the rest of the way. As the railroad brought a flood of homesteaders to the new town, many stayed in a tent city adjacent to the stockyards. Needless to say, they were most eager to move from there to their new farms.

Stanford is the county seat of Judith Basin County. The struggle to create this county and make Stanford its seat lasted ten years, beginning in 1913. It was one of Montana's longest, most expensive, most bitter county-division fights. Geyser newspaperman H. S. Thurston drove for twelve hours through deep snow to Lewistown to verify his signature on the petition that created the county. Then five towns entered the contest for the new county seat, and a long series of lawsuits began. Stanford and Hobson each spent $25,000 in legal costs before Stanford won out.

## DENTON

Denton can be reached most easily by driving twenty-three miles north from Stanford on Montana 80 and 81. The town arose in 1913 as the main division point on the Milwaukee Road's branch line between Great Falls and Lewistown. By July of that year the Great Falls *Tribune* reported, "Lumber is being transformed into buildings as fast as it can be put on the ground, and although four lumber yards have been established, their stock is being converted into buildings as fast as they can get it in."

The boomtown was the center of a failed movement to create a new county named Banner. In anticipation, the local hotel even changed its name to the Banner. Sometimes entire neighborhoods of homesteaders arrived. A group from Iowa settled south of town in an area they named the Iowa Bench. Another group from Washington created their namesake bench east of town. Denton managed to survive the crop failures of the 1920s even though the local bank shut down.

Over the years, one of the town's most successful "crops" has been twin children. At least forty-eight sets of twins have lived in this small town; in 1966 alone there were seven sets of twins enrolled in the small local school district.

## UTICA

Utica, nestled on the Judith River about five miles south of Windham, served as headquarters for the big Judith Basin roundup of the 1880s. At its peak, the Judith Basin pool of ranchers ran more than 70,000 head of cattle on the open range here. Each fall, up to 500 cowboys converged here, making it the liveliest place in central Montana. The cowboys raced their horses on the town's only street and caroused in the local saloons. Among the many cowhands who came here from the Midwest was Charlie "Kid" Russell.

## HOBSON

The first community in the Hobson area was the stagecoach station of Philbrook, located on the south side of the Judith River. When the railroad arrived, rancher S. S. Hobson purchased land for a new town site near the tracks. At first the new town also called itself Philbrook. Backers of Hobson wanted the town named after him. The railroad named the new

*Judith Roundup, Utica, circa 1885. Charles Russell is probably on the fourth horse from the right.* —Montana Historical Society, Helena

town Hobson, but the post office retained the name Philbrook. Some suggested changing the name of the place to Hobbrook, Philson, or Brookson to stop all the arguing. Finally, in 1912 the postmaster relented and changed the name to Hobson.

As homesteaders crowded into the area, Hobson prospered. The product of its flour mill was called "the Pride of the Judith." Many in town were less proud of the house of ill-fame that operated from a tar-paper shack near the stockyards on land the Milwaukee Road rail line owned. Leaders of the local womens' club urged the Milwaukee officials to evict the two sisters running the place. After the railroad men refused to comply, a fire of mysterious origin burned the house to the ground. Undaunted, the sisters built a larger house on a solid foundation on the same railroad land. Faced with the prospect of a permanent business, the club women pressed the Milwaukee to shut down the house, and the company finally agreed. Then, to the shock of many, the sisters put their house on wheels and moved it to the main street of town, right across from the post office. Refusing to admit they had been evicted, the owners said they had simply moved to get closer to their clientele.

## LEWISTOWN

Lewistown is located near the geographic center of Montana and is the largest city in Fergus County and the eight counties surrounding Fergus. Peter Koch erected the first permanent structure here in 1873. Bozeman merchants had heard rumors that the federal government planned to make central Montana the reservation for the Crow Indians. In anticipation they had Koch build a trading post. When the rumors proved false they quickly sold out to Alonzo Reed and John Bowles.

Reed and Bowles proved to be two of Montana's most unsavory businessmen. First they moved their trading post several miles to get away from the watchful eye of the U.S. Army, which had established Camp Lewis nearby. Then for years they carried on an illegal, but lucrative, trade in liquor and firearms with area Indians. The trading post, known as Reed's Fort, became an overnight stop for freighters on the Carroll Trail. But most travelers chose not to linger here for long because Reed was a jealous man and an excellent shot. Reed and Bowles's partnership ended in a drunken fistfight between the two owners. Reed closed the post in 1880.

By then more civilized settlers were arriving. Among the first were a group of Métis who had been wandering for years in northeastern Montana and North Dakota. Sawmills along the region's streams and the discovery of gold in the nearby Judith Mountains brought in more people.

Shortly after platting the town site, citizens of Lewistown staged their first Independence Day celebration. They planned to hold a parade and race horses. The unplanned events of that day in 1884 made the celebration long-remembered.

Sometime around noon, two notorious horse thieves—Charles Fallon and Charles Owens—also known as Rattlesnake Jake—rode into town. After quenching their thirst in a local saloon, the pair wandered into the crowd at the racetrack. Here Rattlesnake Jake hit the butt of his revolver on the face of a young man named Bob Jackson. In the ensuing fracas, people started shooting. After a running gunfight through the business district, the outlaws made their last stand near the tent of a local photographer. They kept shooting until they could no longer stand up. It took nine bullets to bring Jake down and another five to kill Fallon. The photographer made a nice profit selling souvenir pictures of the corpses.

As Lewistown grew, its wooden buildings gave way to structures made from the area's native sandstone. Around the turn of the century a group of skilled stonemasons from Croatia settled in Lewistown. Once here, they erected many unique churches, public buildings (including the courthouse), and business establishments. Many of these structures of hand-cut stone still stand today, giving Lewistown one of the most attractive historic districts in the state.

One of the town's sandstone buildings, the county high school, was built amid anger and controversy, and it fell the same way. In 1903, just after they laid the school's cornerstone, the Croatian stonemasons walked off the job after the contractor refused to recognize their union. Nonunion carpenters complained of threats from the striking masons. Once the strike ended, armed guards patrolled the construction site to protect the workers.

Fifteen years later the high school became the center of a sordid series of events. During the years of America's involvement in the First World War, racism and mass hysteria disguised as patriotism ran rampant in Montana. Nowhere was it more pronounced than in Lewistown, where the mayor declared, "With our sacred honor and our liberties at stake, there can be but two classes of American citizens, patriots and traitors."

At least a quarter of those living in Fergus County at the time were foreign-born, including a sizable German population. During the war years many of these people were harassed and forced to prove their loyalty. Anyone suspected of uttering pro-German remarks or questioning the war effort was hauled before a citizens committee and even jailed under provisions of Montana's harsh new sedition law.

*Stonemason crew of Croatian immigrants poses before beginning work on the Masonic Temple in Lewistown.* —Brenner's Studio Collection, Lewistown

*Methodist Church, Lewistown, one of many buildings erected by Croatian stonemasons.* —Brenner's Studio Collection, Lewistown

In late March 1918 mob violence exploded in Lewistown when hundreds of demonstrating townspeople broke into the high school, took out all the German textbooks, and threw them into a bonfire. Because the school's principal had hesitated in giving up the books, the mob forced him to kiss an American flag and declare his loyalty. They forced nine others suspected of disloyalty to carry a flag up and down Main Street. The crowd nearly lynched one local resident because he had refused, on religious grounds, to buy war bonds.

A month later arsonists poured gasoline throughout the high school building and burned it to the ground. The "patriots" blamed German sympathizers for the fire, but no one ever discovered the identity or motives of the arsonists. After the fire, men patrolled the streets with rifles. The disaster sobered Lewistown's residents. No further mob action took place.

*Fergus County High School prior to 1918 fire.* —Brenner's Studio Collection, Lewistown

# Lewistown—Fred Robinson Bridge

## THE CARROLL TRAIL

Between Lewistown and Roy, US 191 follows a portion of the historic Carroll Trail. This short-lived route was the brainchild of Helena merchants seeking a cheaper, easier way to ship goods to Montana's gold camps than via the established routes running north from Utah or up the Missouri River to Fort Benton.

The new route opened in 1874. Construction on the Northern Pacific had stalled in North Dakota, so the railroad agreed to contract with a steamboat company to haul goods from Bismarck to the junction of the Musselshell and Missouri Rivers. From here, ox-drawn wagons owned by the Diamond R Freighting Company would carry the provisions west to Helena. The new trail, along with a town near the mouth of the Musselshell, was named after Matthew Carroll, an official of the Diamond R. The army stationed soldiers in Camp Baker, near present White Sulphur Springs, and at Camp Lewis, near present Lewistown, to protect travelers on the trail.

From the time it opened, problems plagued the Carroll Trail. One early traveler recorded that, when wet, the road became "a greasy, slippery, fathoming mass of clinging mud." The steamboat line that contracted to haul the goods to Carroll proved unreliable. Freight wagons took up to thirty days to travel the route. And during the second year of operation Sioux war parties attacked Camp Lewis, the town of Carroll, and freighters along the trail. All of this led to the abandonment of the Carroll Trail.

### MAIDEN AND GILT EDGE

Just north of milepost 10 on US 191, the Maiden Canyon Road leads east eight miles to the mining camp of Maiden. The gravel road then winds down a narrow canyon to Gilt Edge. A better road leads to Gilt Edge north from US 87, east of Lewistown.

In 1880 a group of prospectors led by "Skookum Joe" Anderson discovered gold along Maiden Gulch in the heart of the Judith Mountains. Within a year several thousand people rushed in and Maiden became known as "the Queen City of the Judith Basin." Because the town lay within the boundaries of the Fort Maginnis Military Reservation, no one could claim legal title to the land. "Lot jumping" became a common practice until townspeople persuaded the army to redraw the borders to exclude Maiden

*New Year celebration, Maiden, 1885.* —Brenner's Studio Collection, Lewistown

from its lands. During the four years in which the mining camp flourished, at least $5 million in gold and silver came from mines around Maiden. The town also had its share of bigotry. On one occasion a band of thirty masked men, which the local newspaper approvingly called "the klan," rode into Maiden's small enclave of Chinese residents. At gunpoint they forced the immigrants to leave the camp.

The mining boom at nearby Gilt Edge did not arrive until nearly ten years after Maiden's heyday. The low-grade limestone could not be mined at a profit until one of the nation's first cyanide-process mills was installed here in 1893.

Within a few months after the mill began operating, the company failed to meet its payroll. To appease the angry miners, company officials paid them off in worthless "Gilt Edge checks." After merchants demanded payment for this counterfeit paper, the county sheriff closed down the mine and mill. This threw everyone in town out of work, and many miners turned to cattle rustling to feed their families. The mine's two managers, meanwhile, tried to slip out of town with a wagon loaded with gold bullion. The sheriff arrested one of the men near Great Falls. The other partner boldly returned to Gilt Edge, where he narrowly escaped a lynch mob. The Gilt Edge mining operation survived this shaky start and ultimately produced more than $10 million in gold and silver.

# The DHS Ranch

Northeast of Gilt Edge on Ford's Creek, near the southeast slopes of the Judith Mountains, lie the sites of Fort Maginnis and the DHS Ranch. Neither site is marked, and both are on private land.

Granville Stuart—a pioneer prospector, merchant, writer, and cattle rancher—founded the DHS Ranch on Ford's Creek in the spring of 1880. Stuart claimed the land after a long search for a suitable ranch for the Pioneer Cattle Company, owned by Stuart, Samuel T. Hauser, and two other partners. From his vantage point near the southeast base of the Judith Mountains, Stuart observed, "The whole country clear to the Yellowstone is good grass country. . . . This is an ideal cattle range."

After wandering with his brother James through much of Montana Territory and dabbling in a variety of occupations, Granville Stuart finally struck it rich in the cattle business. Yet early on he foresaw the forces that would eventually destroy him and many other big cattlemen when he observed, "In five or six years the ranges will begin to exhaust."

In 1884 Stuart helped organize the Montana Stock Growers' Association. Among its first tasks, the association sought to rid the Missouri River country of cattle rustlers and horse thieves. A secretive vigilante group known as "the Stranglers" based its operations at the DHS Ranch. No one will ever know how many men the vigilantes executed. Estimates run from eighteen to sixty. Most of the deaths occurred in a big gunfight at an abandoned wood yard near the mouth of the Musselshell River in July 1884. Here a gang of rustlers led by John Stringer fought it out with a vigilante band led by Stuart. Seven outlaws died of gunshot wounds or were burned alive inside their cabin.

The 1886-87 winter wiped out a sizable portion of the DHS herd. Veteran cowhand Teddy Blue Abbott, who was working the DHS at the time, recalled, "The snow crusted and it was hell without the heat." Although the ranch survived the winter, Stuart went bankrupt. The other owners replaced him as manager of the DHS. After serving a brief stint as U.S. ambassador to Paraguay and Uruguay, Stuart wound up working in Butte as a librarian.

## Fort Maginnis

The military established Fort Maginnis on the upper hay meadow of the DHS Ranch in 1880 to protect Judith Basin settlers from the Blackfeet and Sioux. By the time of its construction the tribes had been confined to reservations. Neighboring ranchers found the soldiers more annoying than the Indians. After just ten years the army abandoned the fort.

*Officers' quarters, Fort Maginnis.* —Brenner's Studio Collection, Lewistown

## ROY

Roy's golden era lasted for about five years. In 1912 the Milwaukee Road railway ran a feeder line through the area and platted a new town site. A barn loft served as the first rooming house. The railroad reached town in the spring of 1914. Soon trains were bringing in cars filled with immigrants. Settlers pitched tents in town while they waited to establish their homesteads, so the town commons resembled a traveling circus.

After drought hit in 1918 local businesses began burning down. Some speculated that the fires were set on purpose. Despite their adversity, those who chose to stick it out in Roy remained optimistic. A book written to celebrate the town's diamond anniversary noted, "One thing that has not changed among those that remain is their unshakable belief in tomorrow."

## THE FRED ROBINSON BRIDGE

During the 1920s, as automobiles replaced horses as Montana's chief mode of transportation, residents in Fergus County began to lobby for a bridge across the Missouri River and a road running to Malta. The 250 miles of Montana's Missouri was probably the nation's longest span of unbridged river. As crews extended highways north from Lewistown and south from Malta, officials picked out a bridge site (where US 191 crosses the Missouri River).

The Second World War halted all road construction, and it was another dozen years before work began on the bridge. At the August 16, 1959, dedication ceremony Montana state senator Fred L. Robinson, for whom the bridge was named, supplied free food for the big crowd. After more than 10,000 people showed up, airplanes were dispatched to fly in more food.

# Lewistown—Circle
## 197 miles

### GRASS RANGE

Grass Range arose as a stagecoach stop along the road from Lewistown to Maiden and Fort Maginnis. In the fall of 1881 a prairie fire started near here and blackened more than 500 square miles of grassland. Granville Stuart later recalled, "For ten days every available man in the country with wet gunny bags fought the flames with desperation." After the Milwaukee Road railway's branch line arrived in 1913, the town filled with homesteaders. In its prime, Grass Range had ten restaurants and three hotels. Its bank managed to hold on until 1931, before collapsing under the weight of unpaid loans to area farmers and ranchers. By the 1960s only three businesses remained open on Main Street.

### THE N BAR RANCH

On Montana 19/US 87 south of Grass Range at milepost 25, a gravel road turns west and leads up Flatwillow Creek to the extensive stock-raising operations of the N Bar Ranch. The N Bar is one of the nation's oldest continuously running ranches; its headquarters on the Flatwillow has been here for over a century.

The N Bar brand began in Nebraska, where Henry and Zeke Newman established a large ranch on the Niobrara River. In the early 1880s they drove their stock to ranges on the Powder River and north, near the mouth of the Musselshell. The 1886-1887 winter devastated the Newmans' herd. Helena mining magnate Thomas Cruse, who owned a sheep ranch on Flatwillow Creek, bought the N Bar's surviving cattle, along with the rights to use the brand. Over the next quarter century, Cruse expanded his land holdings to about 19,000 acres. He also controlled water holes and rangeland as far east as Jordan. The ranch on Flatwillow was largely self-sufficient, boasting its own commissary, blacksmith shop, and lumber mill.

Once homesteaders began fencing off central Montana's rangeland, Cruse sold his ranch to businessmen from Helena and Lewistown. The new owners planned to subdivide it into 100-acre homesteads. Their scheme failed to attract buyers. In 1930 Jack and Gene Milburn purchased the N Bar. They built the ranch into the 40,000-acre spread that today dominates the Flatwillow Valley.

## WINNETT

In 1909 Walter Winnett erected a log cabin saloon to serve the employees on his large ranch. After homesteaders began arriving Winnett opened a general store. Then, in 1914 the Milwaukee Railroad Land Company platted a town and sold lots. Winnett's most storied building was the Montana Hotel. The original building served as a warehouse on Walter Winnett's Ranch. Then he decided to convert it into a hotel, but he changed his mind in the middle of construction and made it an opera house instead. In the ensuing years the building served first as a hotel, then as a school dorm, then a hotel again, then a school dorm again, and finally as the home of a local minister. The school district razed the building in 1960 and some of the lumber went into the new Baptist church.

By 1919 Winnett appeared destined to decline along with most of the other drought-stricken small towns in eastern Montana. Then explorers struck oil at nearby Cat Creek, and hordes of people flooded back into town. By the summer of 1921 Winnett's thirty hotels and rooming houses were jammed. One hotel housed rented beds in a tent, for which they charged not by the day, but by the shift. Oil flowed to Winnett on a pipeline laid on top of the ground. From here it was pumped into railroad tank cars. At the peak of production in 1921, three oil trains a day departed from Winnett.

Eventually Standard Oil gained control of much of the area's oil production. One pipeline driven out by Standard placed a sign near its loading dock that read, "Here lies the Independent Pipeline with no oil to transport. A half million dollar tribute to the unscrupulous, smothering, false propaganda of the Standard monopoly." As production peaked Winnett became the county seat of newly formed Petroleum County. Then the Cat Creek field began to dry up, the drought continued to drive away homesteaders, and a 1929 fire leveled much of Winnett's business district. The population stabilized at around 400.

### Cat Creek Oil Field

Near milepost 153 a winding gravel road leads north from Montana 200 to the Cat Creek oil field. In 1920, amid these badlands a group of oilmen from Montana, Oklahoma, and Wyoming struck a small pool of some of the nation's richest crude oil.

When drillers began sinking a well in the late fall of 1919, the road to Cat Creek was a set of wagon tracks leading to a few scattered homesteads. Winter came early with one of the worst blizzards anyone could recall. In January the crew struck not oil, but warm artisan water. As the water hit the freezing air it formed a small glacier around the rig. The drillers fought the water flow, trying to cap the well. Their wet clothing quickly froze to their bodies, forcing frequent dashes to the cookhouse to thaw out.

But the crew kept drilling, and eventually they struck oil. One driller, Curly Meek, later recalled:

> They tried to keep it a little quiet because it was all government land. . . .
> When I sent a wire to . . . the president of the company in Denver, I sent
> it to him in code. The wire read "Pine trees grow tall here, come ye men
> of war." Everyone tried to get me drunk and everything else to try to
> find out if they got a well.

Inevitably the news spread and, by spring, other companies scrambled to place drilling equipment throughout the remote site. At first the field had no storage tanks, so the oil flowed into a coulee. People came in to stare at the big pool and to take any oil they needed free of charge. It was so rich that it could be used directly in farm tractors and Model T Fords.

Tar-paper shacks housing the wildcat drillers soon dotted the hills and gullies of the Cat Creek basin. By the end of 1921 nearly seventy wells were pumping oil, and several dozen companies were sinking new wells.

*Cat Creek oil field, 1920s.* —Brenner's Studio Collection, Lewistown

Water for the drillers had to be hauled in by horses. Water sold for a dollar a barrel, which, at the time, was also the going rate for a barrel of oil.

During the early excitement optimists predicted that the oil field would stretch to the Judith Mountains and beyond the lower Musselshell River. But the pool proved to be only about a mile wide and six miles long. As oil crews hit more and more dry holes, the boom died quickly. Mergers eliminated the smaller companies and, by the late 1930s the Continental Oil Company controlled virtually the entire Cat Creek field.

## MOSBY

In 1904 William and Mary Mosby relocated their rural post office to the east side of the Musselshell River at a place called Half-breed Crossing. They renamed the place Mosby and began operating a ferry. Eventually a wooden bridge replaced the ferry, and when it washed out in the early 1920s angry farmers in Garfield County pressed officials of Fergus County on the west shore to replace it.

In the 1930s a new steel bridge was erected. At the gala dedication celebration, couples danced the night away along the entire length of the bridge. During the 1950s and 1960s, a refinery at Mosby converted crude oil from the Cat Creek field into gasoline and jet fuel. Today Mosby sits largely abandoned. Even the post office moved to the west side of the Musselshell.

## JORDAN

"Isolated" and "remote" are the adjectives usually employed to describe Jordan. In 1930 a radio station in New York called it "the lonesomest town in the world." No railroad ever built through Jordan. A state highway and telephone lines did not arrive here until the 1930s. A diesel-powered light plant supplied electricity until the Rural Electrification Administration (REA) finally installed power lines in 1952. The nearest town of any size is Miles City, eighty-five miles southeast via Montana 59.

Arthur Jordan left his native England at age fourteen, stowing away on a ship. Two years later he wound up in Deadwood, Dakota Territory, and in the summer of 1896, he established a homestead along the tree-lined Big Dry River. As area cowboys dropped by his log shack to visit, Jordan began stocking supplies for them.

On one occasion Jordan and his family left town to visit friends on the Powder River. On their return they were surprised to find that the locals had turned the post office into a saloon. Jordan promptly furnished some logs to erect a separate saloon building, which he recalled, "was the source of much trouble in the new town." Drunken cowboys habitually shot up Jordan's store as well as the town's only restaurant.

Cattle thieves from the Missouri Breaks frequented Jordan, giving it a reputation as the toughest town in eastern Montana. Arthur Jordan recalled a trial in the county seat of Glendive in which the judge could not decide how to punish the convicted prisoner. The county attorney suggested that he be sentenced to live in Jordan for six months because "that would be punishment enough for any man." No woman could be persuaded to teach school in this rugged outpost, so the first teacher was a card player known as Gambler Brown. If fishing in the Big Dry River looked good, Brown dismissed school for the day and headed for the water.

The eroded badlands surrounding Jordan proved to be a treasure trove for paleontologists. Beginning around the turn of the century, scientists unearthed bones of triceratops and a rare *Tyrannosaurus rex* skeleton. The museum in Jordan displays several of these fossil finds.

## JUSTUS TOWNSHIP

### *Standoff*

Because of both its promise and its remoteness, the American West has often lured individuals and groups with unique, eccentric, and bizarre beliefs and lifestyles. From mountain men to religious colonies, from gangs of outlaws to self-styled militiamen, Montana has had its share of interesting folks.

Isolated Garfield County was a haven for livestock thieves in the 1890s. A century later this region sheltered another band of individualists who chose to operate outside the rules of society. They called themselves "Freemen." For several years in the mid-1990s, the Freemen worked from a base known as Justus Township, located on a ranch about thirty miles west of Jordan. Here they conducted seminars on how to defy government at all levels, mainly by writing bogus checks. They justified their action with a combination of conspiracy theories, Biblical quotations, and offbeat interpretations of American law.

After the Freemen piled up nearly $2 million in bad debts and threatened the life of a federal judge, FBI agents surrounded the ranch on March 25, 1996. Because similar sieges at Waco, Texas, and Ruby Ridge, Idaho, had ended in tragedy, federal officials acted cautiously. They were prepared to wait for the suspected criminals to surrender peacefully. Meanwhile, the Freemen nailed a copy of the Declaration of Independence to a fence post, labeled the federal government a "corporate prostitute," and flew an American flag upside down above the ranch house.

Along with more than 600 federal agents came a swarm of news-media people. Jordan became the focus of nationwide attention each day that the siege dragged on. After more than two months of this disruption of their lives, many Jordan area residents had had enough. More than 200 people signed a petition urging the FBI to use "reasonable force" to end the siege.

Finally, in early June, the FBI cut off the ranch's electricity and moved up three armored cars. Then, after eighty-one days, the remaining sixteen Freemen surrendered. It was termed the longest standoff in modern American history, but bloodshed had been avoided. Montana legislator Karl Ohs, who helped negotiate the surrender, termed the Freemen "individuals, all with different agendas." One woman, who had been with the Freemen but grew disenchanted and left before the siege ended, called Justus Township "as close to hell as I ever want to get."

## BROCKWAY

Brockway received its name from the three brothers who founded the town. It did not take off until the much-belated arrival of the Redwater Branch of the Northern Pacific Railroad in 1928. After that, Brockway became one of the nation's leading grain-shipping centers, often loading more than a million bushels of wheat a year onto railroad cars.

## McCONE COUNTY

Between Brockway and Circle, Montana 200 parallels the Redwater River. This tributary of the Missouri has long watered some of the richest grassland in the state. Vast herds of bison once grazed here. Later some of Montana's largest cattle outfits trailed their herds into this region. The first cattle came via trail from Texas. With the completion of the Northern Pacific's main line in 1883, cowboys unloaded the cattle in Glendive and drove them north. The basin's grassland proved ideal for raising sheep also. At one time, sheepherders' wagons lined both sides of the Redwater every summer.

Even though McCone County lacked a railroad, during the height of eastern Montana's homestead boom immigrants flocked here. The open range yielded to barbed wire. More than a dozen new towns sprang up. Settling on 320-acre plots in a single township were a factory worker from Michigan, a college graduate from New York, a lumberjack from Wisconsin, a minister from Indiana, a lawyer from North Carolina, and a sheepherder from Norway. All shared the dream expressed by one Redwater homesteader who later recalled, "Most of us came west as young married couples because we wanted to make our own start. . . . It was an adventure to build a new home in a new land, even though the home was a shack."

# CIRCLE

Circle enjoyed two boom eras. The first came in 1928, when the railroad finally reached here. The second arrived in 1951, when the first Williston Basin oil wells began producing. Peter Rorvik established the first store at the Circle Ranch in 1905. Ranchers chipped in to pay Rorvik to carry their mail to and from Glendive, whenever he went there to get goods for his store.

Like so many Montana towns, Circle relocated to be near a prospective railroad. A contractor from Glendive used a Reeves steam tractor to haul the hotel, bank, schoolhouse, and other buildings to the new town site platted by the Great Northern. But the railroad never arrived.

Frustrated by constant delays and the empty promises of the Great Northern, businessmen in Circle looked south. They persuaded the Northern Pacific to run a branch line from Glendive through Circle and Brockway. Today Montana 200 generally follows the route of the Redwater Branch Railroad. On June 2, 1928, the line was completed and Circle held a gala parade and barbecue. Three trains decorated with banners reading "First Train into the Redwater" brought in 1,500 passengers. In all, 10,000 people showed up. News crews shot film of the event, which was shown in theaters throughout the nation. It was probably the last such railroad-opening celebration staged in Montana.

*The first Northern Pacific train reaches Circle, June 1928.*
—Frontier Gateway Museum, Glendive

The railroad created a renewed homestead boom, but this one did not last long. Circle slid into the 1930s depression along with the rest of eastern Montana. By 1932 trains were running only twice a week. Many of them brought in carloads of Red Cross relief food, along with tons of grasshopper bait.

On Friday the thirteenth in July 1951, Shell Oil Company drillers struck oil northeast of Circle. The local newspaper later recorded, "Almost overnight our little city was swarming with oil men and lease hounds." The railroad installed an oil-loading dock at the Circle freight yard. Here trucks transferred the crude oil into tanker cars. Four years later a pipeline began carrying the oil south to refineries in Wyoming, and Circle's loading facility shut down.

## VIDA

### Wind Power

Montana 13 leads thirty miles north from Circle to Vida. This tiny homestead community gained renown as the home of one of Montana's first radio stations. During the 1920s station KGCX entertained listeners with newscasts, weather reports, and dance music played by the Vida Syncopators.

Vida gained even wider recognition as a result of the experiments of local brothers Joe and Marcellas Jacobs. Decades before the REA brought power into this area, the Jacobs brothers had wired their parents' ranch house, using a gasoline generator as a power source. Soon they began building wind-powered generators. The turbine wind generators worked so well that neighboring farmers purchased them for their own lighting systems.

As the Jacobs Wind Electric Company expanded, the brothers decided to move their operation to Minneapolis, Minnesota, to be closer to their parts suppliers. They marketed the device using a fleet of a dozen trucks that toured county fairs throughout the Midwest. In 1933 Admiral Richard Byrd installed a Jacobs generator to provide power for his settlement at the South Pole.

The Jacobs brothers shut down their factory in 1956. By then, REA lines had replaced wind generators on most farms and ranches. Yet even today, some people use rebuilt Jacobs wind generators, invented on the plains of eastern Montana.

# Melstone—Harlowton

## THE MUSSELSHELL RIVER

At Melstone, US 12 joins the Musselshell River about where the stream takes a ninety-degree turn to flow due north toward the Missouri River. The highway follows the Musselshell for 145 miles along its easterly course from its headwaters near Bair Reservoir. It also follows near the same route as the defunct Milwaukee Road rail line.

The first mention of the river comes in the journals of Lewis and Clark, but for years prior to the expedition's arrival at its mouth, Indians had found freshwater mussels in its bed. Lewis described the Musselshell: "from appearances it might be navigated with canoes a considerable distance, its bed is coarse sand and gravel principally with an occasional mixture of black mud." Lewis wrongly speculated that the river's headwaters were near the Yellowstone River.

### ROUNDUP

Even though it has a cowtown name, Roundup was primarily a coal-mining town. In 1882 buffalo hunter James McMillan and his wife erected a small store and saloon beneath steep rimrocks near the confluence of Half Breed Creek and the Musselshell River. Nearby was a grassy tableland that became a popular gathering place for ranchers and cowhands. On this flat, where the present-day town of Roundup sits, cattlemen from up and down the Musselshell gathered for their annual roundup.

The Bull Mountains rise just south of the Musselshell near Roundup. When the Milwaukee Road began surveying its rail route through here in 1906, it sent two company officials to prospect for coal. According to one local story, a rancher told the officials that he had spotted a big vein of coal near Roundup, while he was wading the river to retrieve a duck he had shot.

Because it was about the only decent coal vein along the railroad's proposed transcontinental route, the Milwaukee did not waste time. It formed the Republic Coal Company, which began mining in 1907, even before the rails reached Roundup. Wagons pulled by twelve-horse teams hauled the first boilers, pumps, and other mine equipment north from Billings. A settlement known as Coal Camp arose on the flats above old Roundup. A long double-decked bunkhouse held a hundred miners. The new camp stole the name Roundup from the neighboring settlement.

The big mines south of Roundup were known simply as Number One, Number Two, and Number Three. Mine Number One proved short-lived. Mine Number Three displaced it, and by 1918 this mine employed 600 men, who mined enough coal to fill a railroad car every twelve minutes. But Mine Number Two, located three-and-one half miles to the south, proved to be the most productive and longest lasting. In 1909 the *Anaconda Standard* called Number Two "the most modern and expensive plant that is known in the coal mining world." It also boasted the deepest vertical shaft—some 287 feet below the surface—of any coal mine west of the Mississippi.

Coal in the Bull Mountains lay along steep hillsides in horizontal seams less than ten feet thick. As a result most mining was done by the "room-and-pillar" method. Miners took coal from large rooms using timbers to prop up the ceilings. Falling rock was a frequent hazard that crushed miners. Roundup's mines were known to be the most dangerous in the state.

*Coal miners and horses, Republic Coal Company Number 3 Mine near Roundup.*
—Musselshell Valley Historical Museum, Roundup

Mules and horses hauled the coal deep inside the mines to the shafts, where power hoists lifted it to the surface. At the mine in Klein, south of Roundup, the animals stayed in an underground stable, so many never saw the light of day. One mule, named Dinah Miner, spent nearly her entire life underground. When she was brought to the surface, they found that she was totally blind. Whenever an animal died in the mine, they hauled the carcass to a nearby coulee to be fed to the coyotes. In 1930 electric locomotives replaced the mules and horses.

Like all of the big western mining towns, Roundup attracted immigrant miners from many European countries. The largest ethnic groups came from the Yugoslavian republics of Croatia and Slovenia. They settled either in Roundup, at a place known as Camp Three, or in Klein, near the Number Two Mine. Here they lived in four-room houses with unique peaked roofs, built and owned by the Republic Coal Company, who charged the miners ten dollars a month for rent. Some of these company houses are still scattered around the Roundup-Klein area. One man, who grew up at Camp Three, recalled:

> We were as poor as church mice. We had a large garden, made sauerkraut in a fifty gallon barrel. . . . We did all the work while dad worked in the . . . mine. We were so poor, we even had to steal our coal by picking up the chunks that fell along the railroad track from moving cars.

More than seventy saloons operated in the Musselshell County coal towns. They were the main social centers for the men and off-limits to women. During prohibition some of the saloons remained open, and many miners earned extra money by manufacturing and selling wine and other varieties of moonshine liquor. A raid by federal agents uncovered some batches that tested as high as 111 proof.

From the beginning, the big mines in Roundup were solidly unionized. Several prolonged strikes occurred, but none led to violence. Tony Boyle, the onetime national president of the United Mine Workers, once operated a mine near Roundup. After the Milwaukee Road rail company converted to diesel power, demand for Roundup coal dropped sharply. Eventually the Republic Company sold its Klein Mine. The mine closed for good in 1956.

## LAVINA

In 1882, as the Northern Pacific built west up the Yellowstone Valley, Fort Benton merchant Thomas C. Power realized that a whole new trade region would soon be opened up. Because Power expected central Montana to attract many settlers, he hired Walter Burke to lay out a new stage route from Fort Benton to the new railroad boomtown of Billings.

Burke and his men blasted out stumps, bridged rivers, and constructed seventeen stage stations along the 220-mile route. Of all the stage stops, Burke's favorite was the one where the route bridged the Musselshell River. He named the stop Lavina to honor a former sweetheart. Apparently no one ever recorded Mrs. Burke's thoughts about this arrangement. Burke later recalled, "We put up stage stables, mess house, bunk house for the men to sleep in, a store, and of course my saloon. That was the biggest business of them all." Soon Concord coaches were carrying passengers and mail in three directions from Lavina to the new communities of Billings, Lewistown, and Roundup.

When survey crews for the Milwaukee Road rail line came up the Musselshell in 1907, they chose a new town site a mile downstream. During its homestead-era boom years, Lavina called itself "the White City." Neat, white-painted buildings lined both sides of Main Street. The first issue of the Lavina *Independent* proclaimed, "as the town is composed absolutely of progressive, clean minded and vigorous citizens, nothing but the utmost impossibility will retard its future growth." Today the Milwaukee's rails and most of the white buildings are long gone, but the town still has its two landmark business establishments—the two-story Adams Hotel and the brick building housing the Slayton Mercantile Company.

## RYEGATE

Ryegate is another homestead-era boomtown along the Milwaukee rail route. It grew up in a rye field, on one of the Musselshell Valley's oldest cattle ranches. By the time people living in this region managed to create Golden Valley County in 1920, drought was beginning to cripple central Montana's economy. Ever optimistic, the Ryegate boosters launched a bid to make their town the new county seat. They composed a long jingle sung to the tune of "Marching through Georgia," which went in part:

> Ryegate is the city where they market lots of wheat
> Ryegate is a city that has never known defeat
> Ryegate is the city that should be the county seat
> The best town in Golden Valley County!

Ryegate's population has long remained around 300—about what it was during the years of the big wheat boom.

Eight miles south of Ryegate is a broad, isolated basin known as Big Coulee Valley. On this spring-fed grassland John T. Murphy established one of Montana's premier cattle operations, the 79 Ranch, also called the

Montana Cattle Company. Unlike most of the open-range cattle barons, Murphy chose to purchase, rather than to lease, the land for all his home ranches. At its peak in the early 1890s, the 79 shipped seven trainloads of cattle to the Chicago stockyards each year.

## HARLOWTON

From its founding at the dawn of the twentieth century, until the Milwaukee Road pulled up its tracks in Montana in the early 1980s, Harlowton was the epitome of a Montana railroad town. Its founder and namesake was Richard A. Harlow, the builder of the Montana Railroad. It was here that the Milwaukee Road switched from steam power to electric power on its westward line. The Milwaukee's roundhouse and shops dominated the local economy. The Star Hotel was once the Milwaukee crew's hotel. Harlowton's hospital once belonged to the Milwaukee. The local museum houses a fine collection of Milwaukee Road memorabilia, and a beautifully restored box-electric locomotive graces the corner of Central Avenue and Second Street.

Attorney Richard Austin Harlow settled in Helena in 1886 and began investing in railroads and real estate. He grew obsessed with running a rail line east from Helena to the rich silver mines of Castle. With financial backing from a friend in New Jersey, Harlow hired crews who began laying rails up the rugged Sixteen Mile Creek Canyon. Harlow later recalled this construction:

> Trouble was the normal condition. The owners of the little ranches that we crossed held us up with shotguns. The ranchmen along the route hesitated to sell us supplies, fearing they would not get their money.

As it turned out, the ranchers' fears were justified. Throughout his career Harlow operated on a shoestring. His reputation for smooth talk and empty promises to both his creditors and workers earned his railroad the nickname the Jawbone. One man who worked on the Montana line's grading crew recalled, "I worked that whole season and waited another year to get my pay."

By the time the Jawbone Railroad reached the Castle area in 1896, the price of silver had long since plummeted. To recoup his losses, Harlow looked east hoping to tap into the rich agricultural and livestock district of the upper Musselshell River. In 1900 his rails reached the large sheep camp known as Merino. On high ground just west of here Harlow's chief engineer, Arthur Lombard, mapped out a new town site and named it in honor of his boss. Three years later Harlow extended his line north through the Judith Gap to Lewistown.

*General Electric locomotives on the Milwaukee Road, circa 1915.*
—Montana Historical Society, Helena

Crises plagued the Jawbone Railroad throughout its twelve-year existence. Obsolete equipment traveled over poorly built roadbeds. Breakdowns and accidents stranded passengers on remote prairies for days. On one occasion railroad officials published the following announcement: "The passenger train scheduled to arrive in Lewistown three weeks ago last Monday will arrive tomorrow evening." To nearly everyone's relief, the Milwaukee Road bought out the Jawbone in 1909, rebuilt most of the track, and made it part of its transcontinental system.

With the arrival of the Milwaukee, Harlowton flourished. Shortly before the rails reached here, a fire leveled twenty-four business establishments on the main street. The disaster enabled merchants to relocate closer to the new depot. A. C. Graves built a big hotel on a bluff just above the depot. He used stone quarried from a hill behind the hotel. Because a new ordinance required fireproof construction, others took advantage of the local sandstone too.

The Milwaukee launched a national advertising campaign and brought hundreds of homesteaders into the Musselshell Basin. Harlowton's population neared the thousand mark and included a sizable community of Japanese-born railroad workers and business owners.

In 1916 the Milwaukee completed electrification of the 438 miles of its line between Harlowton and Avery, Idaho. Harlowton became known as the place "where electricity replaces steam." The Milwaukee ran North

America's longest electrified line. It employed the world's largest electric locomotives—built by General Electric, the monsters weighed in at 282 tons. One famous early passenger, Thomas A. Edison, accurately described the electric line: "You ride with ease. . . . It is the very last word in transportation."

The Milwaukee Road, along with its new, big grain elevators, made Harlowton Montana's second-largest grain-shipment center. It became the county seat of the appropriately named Wheatland County. The drought hit in 1919, and only about six inches of rain fell on Harlowton during the entire year. The resulting depression lingered for two decades. By 1940 Wheatland County owned more than 86,000 acres of foreclosed farmland.

US 191

# Harlowton—Moore

39 miles

### JUDITH GAP

The Judith Gap is a low pass between the Big Snowy Mountains on the east and the Little Belt Range to the west. Here US 191 follows a historical route that Native Americans, fur traders, freighters, stockmen, and homesteaders traveled between the Musselshell and Yellowstone Valleys to the south and the Judith Basin to the north. In 1853 railroad surveyor Lt. John Mullan viewed the Judith Valley from a high hill and estimated that 200,000 buffalo blanketed the area.

The town of Judith Gap was a product of the Great Northern Railway, which built a branch line through here from Great Falls to Billings in 1908. The railroad laid out the town as a division point. It constructed a depot, repair buildings, a water tank, a coal dock, and a large roundhouse. Its strategic location and railroad facilities made Judith Gap the largest of the newly established homestead-era towns in central Montana. Restaurants and saloons remained open day and night to serve the crews of the eight passenger trains and several freight trains that ran through Judith Gap every day. One of the saloons featured a live eagle in a cage hanging from the ceiling and kept a black bear penned outside.

### UBET

Near milepost 23 in the small community of Garneil, is a historical marker commemorating the old stage stop of Ubet and the pioneers of

*Ubet House.* —Brenner's Studio Collection, Lewistown

central Montana. A. R. Barrows founded Ubet in the early 1880s, when he erected a house, barn, saloon, ice house, and hotel. Ubet lay at the crossroads of two important stagecoach and wagon roads—the Carroll Trail, running between the Missouri River and Helena, and the trail connecting Fort Benton and Great Falls with the new railroad town of Billings.

Barrows's standard reply to travelers asking to spend the night was "you bet"—hence the name. Although Barrows used sawdust to insulate the hotel from the area's gale-force winds, the Ubet House was still a cold place to stay. But the food served here gained a reputation as the finest in central Montana. The chief cook was Barrows's wife Alice. She and her three children ran the place after his death in 1885. Barrows' son, John, later recalled:

> Ubet was a one-man town. There were no private residences. . . . It served not on account of its buildings alone, but because the hotel service was held to a very high standard by a family which had a great capacity for making friends though small capacity for making money.

In 1903, just as the railroad built through the Judith Gap, the Ubet House burned down. Garneil arose nearby, established by a family of temperance advocates. Deeds to lots here contained a clause forbidding the erection of a saloon. Ed Beach owned land just south of town and had no aversion to liquor. South Garneil, with its three saloons, quickly sprang up there.

# Harlowton—US 89

## TWODOT

No town in Montana has a more interesting-sounding name than Twodot. George R. "Two Dot" Wilson established a ranch here and eventually grazed cattle across thousands of acres in Meagher and Sweet Grass Counties. His livestock all sported a simple brand—two dots, one on top of the other. When Richard Harlow pushed his Jawbone Railroad through the Musselshell Valley, Wilson set aside 140 acres for a new town near the rails and built a hotel.

After the Milwaukee Road took over the Jawbone route and electrified its line, it erected Substation 1 in Twodot. The substations were simply large transformers that converted the alternating current to direct current to power the electric locomotives. One night a windstorm caused the transformer to explode. The resulting fire destroyed the substation, the post office, the fire station, and Twodot's only two bars. Twodot became the only substation on the Milwaukee line without an enclosed transformer room. Most residents missed the bars more than the railroad building.

## MARTINSDALE

### The Sheep Baron

Martinsdale, near the North and South Forks of the Musselshell, arose in 1877 as a stop on the Carroll Trail. It gained renown as the location of the home ranch of Montana's famous sheep rancher, Charlie Bair. Bair ran away from home as a teenager and wound up working as a brakeman on the Northern Pacific run between Billings and Helena. An astute businessman, Bair did odd jobs in Helena and ran a check-cashing service for his fellow railroad workers. By 1890 he had saved enough money to buy a sheep ranch near Lavina.

Bair constantly expanded his holdings and invested in new business ventures. By 1895 he owned a ranch near Billings where he ran 40,000 sheep. Three years later, during Alaska's Klondike gold rush, Bair sold his entire flock and journeyed north. Although he invested in gold property in the Yukon Territory, he made his real fortune selling a machine, invented by a friend that could quickly thaw frozen ground, making hydraulic mining much easier. He returned to Montana a millionaire.

Bair plowed much of his fortune back into the sheep business. He leased a large section of the Crow Indian Reservation. His holdings peaked around

315

*Charles M. Bair,*
*sheep baron.*
—Parmly Billings
Library, Billings

1910, when he was running some 300,000 head and declared to be the largest sheep grower in North America. That same year, Bair shipped a million and a half pounds of wool to Boston on a single forty-seven-car train. He had the train cars emblazoned with letters three feet tall proclaiming the shipment "the largest wool clip grown by one individual on the North American Continent."

After he lost his lease on the Crow Reservation, Bair purchased a small ranch near Martinsdale. He expanded his acreage during the dry 1920s and 1930s, as busted homesteaders were glad to sell out to him rather than give up their land for delinquent taxes. Throughout his long life Bair personally supervised operations on his ranches. He could often be seen in his white shirts and tailored suits branding or shearing sheep.

Bair spent much of his time in Billings, where he sometimes rented out an entire floor of the Northern Hotel for parties that lasted several days. Just before prohibition became law, Bair and several friends bought up the hotel's entire stock of liquor. And he loved fast horses and fast cars. He hired a chauffeur as soon as the first car he drove refused to respond to his command of "whoa." Until his death in 1943, Bair sped among his far-flung holdings, cigar clenched in his teeth, urging his driver to go faster.

Bair and his daughters, Marguerite and Alberta, filled their Martinsdale ranch house with antique furniture and artwork purchased during their frequent excursions to Europe. Alberta Bair was as flamboyant as her father. She donated much of the family fortune to charities throughout Montana. Following Alberta's death at age ninety-seven, the Bair house, with its luxurious trappings, became a museum. The guided tour takes about an hour.

I-90
# Three Forks—Bozeman
**30 miles**

### THREE FORKS
The Missouri Headwaters State Park, just north of I-90 near the town of Three Forks, is a very important place in Montana's history. Here, at the confluence of the three streams that form the Missouri River (the Madison, Gallatin, and Jefferson Rivers), the Lewis and Clark Corps of Discovery camped for about a week in late July 1805. William Clark and three of the men walking ahead of the boats got here first. Clark left a note attached to a stick for Lewis and proceeded to explore the westernmost fork, because it appeared to lead into the mountains.

Lewis, meanwhile, arrived with the rest of the party and concluded, "believing this to be an essential point in the geography of this western part of the Continent I determined to remain . . . until I obtained the necessary data." He named the forks the Gallatin, the Madison, and the Jefferson in honor of the secretary of the treasury, the secretary of state, and the president, respectively. Upon the party's return, President Jefferson asked them why it had taken so long to name a river after him. Someone replied diplomatically that they had waited to find a river worthy of bearing his name.

For many years prior to Lewis and Clark's arrival here, the hub of the forks of the Missouri had been a popular hunting and gathering place for all the region's Native American tribes. After Lewis and Clark's expedition, white traders gravitated to this fur-rich area. The most prominent trapper to make his mark here was John Colter. Colter parted company with Lewis and Clark as the party descended the Missouri River in 1806. The party had encountered members of a trapping expedition who persuaded Colter to go back up the Yellowstone River with them.

Colter wound up trapping for a group led by Manuel Lisa, based at a new post at the confluence of the Big Horn and Yellowstone Rivers. Traveling alone, he extensively explored present south-central Montana and north-western Wyoming. He was the first white "tourist" to view the geysers of today's Yellowstone National Park.

But it was at Three Forks where Colter experienced his greatest adventure. In the summer of 1808 he and his partner John Potts encountered a band of about 800 Blackfeet. The Blackfeet were angry because Colter had sided with the Salish and Crow during an earlier battle. The Indians killed Potts. They stripped Colter naked and signaled to him to run away. When many of the younger warriors began chasing him, Colter knew he was in a race for his life. He managed to seize the spear of his closest pursuer and kill him. When he reached the Madison River, he dove in and hid among drifting logs. After the Blackfeet gave up searching for him, Colter began his 200-mile trek back to Lisa's post. When he arrived, haggard and starving, his friends did not recognize him.

Despite his brush with death, Colter returned several times to Three Forks country. In 1810 he was among a group who erected a trading post here. After Indians attacked the post and killed several traders, Colter left for good, declaring, "I will leave the country day after tomorrow and be damned if I ever come to it again." The other partners also soon abandoned the post.

The modern community of Three Forks is the latest of four towns that sprang up in the Missouri headwaters region. The first, known as Gallatin City, arose in 1862 on the west bank of the Missouri, just above the mouth of the Gallatin. The founders hoped to make it a major river port. They offered free land to whoever brought in the first steamboat. Apparently none of them had studied the travels of Lewis and Clark. After they learned that the Great Falls blocked upstream navigation on the Missouri, they vacated the place.

Many who left Gallatin City moved their cabins to a new site two miles south on the Madison River. This second Gallatin City became a county seat for a time, but it did not last much longer than its predecessor. A town founded by James Shedd on the Jefferson River proved more permanent. Beginning in the mid-1860s Shedd erected a series of cottonwood-log toll bridges across the Madison, the Jefferson, and many of the region's swamps. He established a hotel near his Madison Bridge that became a popular overnight stagecoach stop.

In 1880 Shedd sold out to a pair of Englishmen: Asher Paul and Michael Hanley. They renamed the place Three Forks and built a much larger hotel. Several years later another British syndicate purchased the hotel, bridges, and several thousand nearby acres. After their cattle-raising operation proved a bust, they turned the area into what they called a "colony." Others referred to it as "Montana's original dude ranch." Agents in England contacted wealthy nobility with headstrong sons. They told them that their colony in the Montana wilds was perfectly suited for domesticating wild young men. Many were eager to ship their sons west for awhile. Once they were in Montana, the spoiled young men did more hell-raising than reforming. They were horrible shots with rifles, so they used shotguns. Their favorite pastime was riding through town around midnight, firing their guns wildly to "wake up the blooming duffers of Americans."

The present town of Three Forks grew up as a division point on the Milwaukee Road rail line in 1908. John Q. Adams, the town's founder, also built the landmark hotel—the handsome, white Sacajawea Inn. At one of the first city council meetings, members voted to limit the number of saloons to six. Within two years there were fourteen. Once the Milwaukee electrified its line through here, it pulled out its repair facilities. Then drought forced many area homesteaders to leave, and Three Forks languished. Today it thrives on agriculture and the tourist trade.

*Three Forks Hotel and stage station, 1880s.* —Gallatin County Historical Society, Bozeman

## TRIDENT

The cement plant and small community of Trident can be reached by a road leading four miles north of the Missouri Headwaters State Park. Area limestone mine operator Dan Morrison established the factory here among limestone bluffs that lined the Missouri River. A group of Mormons from Ogden, Utah, helped Morrison finance the venture. In 1910, following a prolonged fight, the Utah group wrested control of the operation from Morrison. They began producing a product with the unlikely name of Red Devil Cement. For a time Trident was a town where only American citizens were allowed to live. The Italians, Slavs, and other immigrants who made up most of the workforce resided in dirt-floor shacks at a nearby place derisively referred to as "Wop Town." People of the two communities frequently mingled on Saturday nights while they boiled their clothes to rid them of lice. In 1917 the Ideal Cement Company purchased the plant.

## THE MADISON BUFFALO JUMP

Take the Logan interchange off I-90 and drive seven miles south to reach the Madison Buffalo Jump. It is one of the finest examples of a *pishkin*—a place where native people stampeded herds of bison off a precipice. A good kill here would provide a tribe with enough food and clothing to last an entire year. Early Americans may have used this site for as long as 4,000 years before they acquired horses in the eighteenth century.

## MANHATTAN AND AMSTERDAM

The first white settlement in the Manhattan area was a stagecoach stop known as Hamilton. When the Northern Pacific Railroad arrived, the town moved north to the track and adopted the name Moreland. In 1890 a group of wealthy brew masters from New York learned that the soil and climate of the lower Gallatin was ideal for raising barley. They organized the Manhattan Malting Company. Among the founders was Jacob Rupert, the owner of the New York Yankees baseball team.

The investors purchased thousands of acres of benchland from the Northern Pacific and organized an irrigation company to bring in water. They got Moreland to change its name to Manhattan and erected a big malt house. Next to the malt house they built what was called the largest grain elevator between St. Paul and Seattle. Soon malt manufactured here went to breweries throughout Montana, the eastern U.S., and the great beer centers of Europe, where it was always highly prized.

The company sent agents to the Netherlands to bring in new barley farmers. These Dutch immigrants founded the nearby community of

*Manhattan Malting Company's grain elevator and malt house.*
—Gallatin County Historical Society, Bozeman

Amsterdam. Most of the new settlers were members of the Christian Reformed Church, and they built one of the largest rural churches west of the
Mississippi. The era of prohibition destroyed Manhattan's lucrative malting industry and forced the farmers to begin raising other crops.

### BELGRADE

Railroad magnate Henry Villard had several Serbian investors in his
Northern Pacific line. As a gesture to them, he named a siding west of
Bozeman after the Serbian capital, Belgrade. When the Serbs later came
here aboard Villard's golden-spike excursion train, they disembarked and
saw nothing but waving grass in all directions. "My God," one of them
declared, "and this is Belgrade."

But Belgrade had an ambitious booster, Thomas Buchanan Quaw, who
predicted, "we may expect the place to develop into a second Helena." The
town grew steadily as the center of a rich grain-growing region. By the turn
of the century, it contained five big elevators and claimed to be the largest
grain-shipping station on the Northern Pacific west of Minneapolis. Then
in 1913 the Milwaukee Road ran a rail spur northwest from Bozeman,
tapping into Belgrade's wheat country. Farmers no longer had to haul their

grain by wagon and wait all day to unload. Belgrade's boom era had come to an end. Today it thrives as a bedroom community for Bozeman and the home of that town's airport.

## BOZEMAN

Mountains surround virtually the entire lower Gallatin Valley. Because no big gold strikes took place in this immediate area, it seems an unlikely place for one of Montana's earliest white settlements. But land here proved extremely fertile, and soon the basin, with its hub city of Bozeman, became the granary for the mining camps west of here.

John M. Bozeman, the town's namesake, was one of the West's foremost trailblazers. When Bozeman was twelve years old, his father left his family and headed to the California goldfields; his family never heard from him again. A dozen years later, in 1860, John Bozeman left his wife and three daughters and headed to the Colorado goldfields. His family never saw him again, either.

Bozeman never cared much for mining, especially after he failed to strike it rich in either the Colorado or Montana Territories. He sought his fortune leading others to the goldfields. By 1863 he and a partner, John Jacobs,

*John M. Bozeman.*
—Gallatin County
Historical Society,
Bozeman

began looking for a more direct route between the Oregon Trail and the Montana diggings. During their first exploration trek, a band of Indians stole their provisions. They nearly starved making their way south to the Platte River and civilization. This did not shake their resolve, and soon Bozeman and Jacobs were leading a wagon train northwest from the Platte in Wyoming. A companion described Bozeman as "active, tireless, and of handsome stalwart presence. . . . He had no conception of fear."

Bozeman's route ran through the heart of the last decent hunting grounds of the Crow, Sioux, and Northern Cheyenne. Indians forced Bozeman's first wagon train to turn back. Undaunted, Bozeman and a small party proceeded west to Virginia City. They crossed the divide between the Yellowstone and Gallatin Rivers where William Clark had passed decades earlier. A companion named it Bozeman Pass. Bozeman took several more wagon trains up the new route, which came to be called the Bozeman Trail. Mountain-man-turned-guide Jim Bridger led others along a parallel route through the canyon and past the mountains northeast of Bozeman, both of which today bear his name.

The Bozeman Trail did not last long as a travel route. As Black Elk of the Ogalala Sioux later observed, the white men "wanted to have a road up through our country to the place where yellow metal was, but my people did not want the road. It would scare the bison and make them go away, and it would let the other white men come in like a river."

The U.S. Army established a string of forts along the trail, but they could not keep the Cheyenne and Sioux from harassing the wagon trains. Soldiers who ventured too far from the protective forts found themselves under attack. In 1867 the army abandoned its posts, and the "Bloody Bozeman" trail fell into disuse. Today I-90 parallels portions of the route near the Montana-Wyoming border and between Reed Point and Bozeman.

John Bozeman, meanwhile, settled down in the town he helped to start. He was elected a probate judge, established a farm, and helped build the town's first hotel. Then, in April 1867 Bozeman and a friend set out east, hoping to secure a contract to sell flour to the army at Fort C. F. Smith. Near present Livingston, the pair encountered a small band of Indians, probably Blackfeet. Shooting broke out, and Bozeman took two bullets to the chest. They proved fatal. His remains were later buried in the town that had taken his name.

From its beginnings, Bozeman prospered as a service center for area farms and mines. Fort Ellis, built three miles east of town, provided protection from possible Indian raids. John Bogert, a mayor in the 1880s, aptly described Bozeman:

From the first its growth has been slow, but in many respects healthy and strong. It has never been what might be called a 'hurrah' town nor has it ever indulged in extravagant expectations in regard to its future; consequently, it has never passed through an exciting or fictitious boom and its consequent paralyzing reaction.

Bozeman's conservative bent was apparent to the writer of the 1930s Works Progress Administration (WPA) guidebook for Montana, who noted that ordinances prohibited dancing after midnight and outlawed drinking beer while standing. As a result, the local bars were equipped with stools.

### Montana State University

Political horse trading during the 1893 session of Montana's legislature led to the choice of Bozeman as the site of Montana's land-grant agricultural college. Still, it was appropriate that the school ended up in the heart of the state's richest farm belt. Prominent Bozeman businessmen—led by Nelson Story, Peter Koch, and Walter Cooper—worked hard to bring the college to Bozeman.

The first classes met in a crude wooden building that had formerly housed a roller skating rink. Construction of a permanent campus began on county land that had previously been designated as the site for the poor farm.

*Original home of Montana State University.* —Renne Library Archives, Montana State University, Bozeman

From the beginning, the school's administrators pushed a curriculum strong in engineering, agriculture, and the mechanical arts.

James Reid, the school's president during most of the 1890s, sought to wed an emphasis on science with his own Christian moral principles. Each Monday morning he presided over campuswide assemblies that included lectures on ethics and devotional exercises. Reid sought to eliminate dances, which he called "the most hurtful and demoralizing form of amusement among students."

He brought on the ire of local merchants when he crusaded to shut down Bozeman's red-light district. But he had the merchants' support when he fired three faculty members who had questioned his brand of leadership. This incident, according to historian Merrill Burlingame, marked the beginning of "a forty-five year spree of star chamber proceedings, book burning, suppression of academic freedom and the firing, without hearings, of both professors and presidents."

Throughout its first five decades, the college worked closely with the Anaconda Company and other corporate interests in Montana to turn out efficient, conforming engineers devoted to their employers. The school's personnel service rated students on all aspects of their character. A bad character rating could discredit students and cast a cloud over their future. Still, many students secretly disobeyed campus rules, such as those that forbade both smoking and getting married.

Then, during the two decades after the Second World War, college president Roland R. Renne transformed this small backward school into a major university. A devoted New Dealer and a product of Wisconsin's progressive education system, Renne saw the role of the university as a central agent of democracy. Graduates, he felt, should serve all of society, not just the corporations. As he worked to strengthen the liberal arts curriculum, Renne encountered opposition from Montana's corporate masters. But under his firm hand the school's physical plant expanded enormously and enrollment soared to more than 5,000 students.

Still, Montana State University retained its reputation for conservatism. Even Renne blocked the appearance of controversial speakers on campus. During the 1960s, though students voiced opposition to the war in Vietnam, their protests were mild compared to what took place elsewhere. A former administrator recalled, "We had an interesting situation where students would transfer from MSU to Missoula to get where the action was, and students from Missoula would come here to get away from the action."

*Yellowstone-bound tour buses at Gallatin Gateway Inn.* —Gallatin County Historical Society, Bozeman

US 191
# Bozeman—West Yellowstone
**91 miles**

### GALLATIN GATEWAY

On the west side of US 191, south of Bozeman and north of milepost 76, is the turnoff to Gallatin Gateway. The earliest town here was called Salesville, named after lumberman Zacharia Sales, who erected a sawmill in the 1860s. Sales established lumber camps up the Gallatin Canyon and floated ties down the river for use on the Northern Pacific.

After the lumber mills shut down, Bozeman business interests established a short electric-rail line from Bozeman to Salesville, hoping to push it up the canyon to Yellowstone Park. When the Milwaukee Road acquired this line, they decided not to build up the rugged Gallatin Canyon. Instead they opened the Gallatin Gateway Inn in 1927. Tourists arriving here were called "Gallagaters." After their brief stay in the inn, the Milwaukee loaded them onto yellow buses that took them up the canyon road to the park.

# GALLATIN CANYON

Between Bozeman and West Yellowstone, US 191 runs up the scenic, pristine Gallatin Canyon. This area, nestled between the Madison and Gallatin Ranges, has remained largely unspoiled, in spite of the best efforts of some who have sought to dam or dredge the river, drill oil, or log off the timber.

Early trappers spilled into the canyon from the Three Forks area, and prospectors came here from the big mining camps just to the west. But they remained only briefly, failing to strike it rich. During the early 1900s, Bozeman capitalist Walter Cooper established a company that cut thousands of railroad ties up the canyon along the tributaries of the Gallatin River. Lumbermen placed the ties behind retaining dams on the small streams. In the spring they dynamited the dams and drove the ties down the Gallatin.

Once it became apparent that no rail line would ever run up the canyon, valley interests began pushing to improve the road. The Bozeman press described the earliest trail as "a dizzy bridle path." Ranchers pasturing their cattle here had to drive the animals single-file along treacherous ledges. Work crews finally widened the route, and a stream of cars soon ran south to West Yellowstone and the park. Many of the first autos had

*Karst's Resort, Gallatin Canyon.* —Gallatin County Historical Society, Bozeman

327

gravity-fed gas tanks. This forced drivers to back up some of the steeper hills, to enable gasoline to reach their engines.

As an improved road brought in tourists, some of the canyon's pioneer homesteaders established dude ranches. Among the more prominent resort owners were Thomas Michener, Sam Wilson, and Pete Karst. Cabins usually rented for twelve dollars a week. For another six dollars dudes gained the use of a horse.

Karst's Resort, which for years nestled on the highway near milepost 55, featured dog races, a golf course, and a swimming pool heated from a boiler salvaged from an abandoned gold mine. Pete Karst cleared off the slope across the river from the resort and installed Montana's first ski tow. Skiers grasped a wire cable as an old automobile engine propelled them to the top of the hill. During prohibition, most people knew that Karst's was a place where they could easily purchase liquor. Karst later recalled, "it was pretty good bootleg; no one ever went blind."

## BIG SKY SKI RESORT

A road leads west off US 191 near milepost 48 to the Big Sky Ski Resort. Big Sky was the pet project of Montana native Chet Huntley, who gained fame as a television newscaster. Built with the financial backing of some of America's largest corporations, the resort opened in 1973. Inadequate facilities, poorly designed ski runs, and frequent power failures all helped cause the resort to lose money during its early years. Eventually it came to take on the look and feel of larger ski complexes in Colorado—a mountainside cluttered with big luxurious condos and lodges that some people love and others regard as an eyesore.

### Kidnappers

In July 1984 the ski resort at Big Sky provided the opening scene of a real Wild West drama that captured the attention of the nation for much of the following year. Don Nichols was an experienced woodsman and a self-styled mountain man. He shared many of the habits and character flaws of the early-day trappers and explorers of Montana. He distrusted virtually everyone and shunned civilization, choosing to live in the mountains along with his son Dan. Don Nichols had promised to find his son a woman, if the boy agreed to remain living with him in the wild.

In midsummer 1984 near Big Sky, the Nicholses came upon Kari Swenson, a world-class biathlete. They forced her from the trail and, throughout the following day, moved her to several hidden camps where they chained her to trees. When two would-be rescuers arrived, Dan panicked and accidently shot Swenson in the chest. Don shot and killed one of the searchers, then the kidnappers fled west into the Madison Mountains, leaving Kari Swenson alone and bleeding. Fortunately searchers found her and got her to a hospital in time.

For the next five months, the Nicholases eluded posses, holing up in the mountains they knew so well. Some in the media romanticized the father and son as rugged mountain men. Others, led by Swenson's parents, denounced them as common criminals. Finally, in mid-December, a rancher spotted campfire smoke just north of the bridge where Montana 84 crosses the Madison River. He alerted Madison County sheriff Johnny France, a former rodeo champion, who went into the Nicholses' camp alone and captured them without firing a shot.

The following summer, the Nicholses' trial took place in Virginia City's historic courthouse. Marc Racicot, who later became governor of Montana, was the state's prosecuting attorney. Father and son each received prison sentences. Dan's sentence was much lighter because the jury felt he acted under the influence of his father. Sheriff France briefly basked in the glow of a hero-worshiping nation. But some of his fellow law officers accused

*Union Pacific officials inside the railroad's dining hall, West Yellowstone, circa 1920.*
—Gallatin County Historical Society, Bozeman

him of grandstanding, and he lost his bid for reelection. Kari Swenson recovered, again participated on America's biathlon team, and became a veterinarian. After his parole, Dan Nichols attended college, got married, and began working with developmentally disabled adults. His father remained imprisoned and embittered.

## WEST YELLOWSTONE

The remote forests along the western edge of Yellowstone National Park seem an unlikely place for a railroad town to spring up, but that is exactly what happened at West Yellowstone. In 1907 the Union Pacific extended its Oregon Short Line branch east to here from Idaho. The railroad hoped to capture some of the Yellowstone tourist trade that the Northern Pacific had long monopolized with its line from Livingston to the park's northern boundary.

The Union Pacific erected a handsome stone depot and a first-class dining hall. Tourists arriving here usually hopped into elegant four-horse Concord coaches that carried them through the park. The first residents here were squatters on U.S. Forest Service land. It took a sixteen-year political and court battle for them to gain title to the lots they had built on.

Today West Yellowstone is known as America's snowmobile capital. Thousands tour the park each winter on snow machines. But during its early decades, West Yellowstone lay dormant and nearly isolated each winter. Bobsleds, horse-drawn toboggans, and dogsleds all brought mail here during the long winters.

# THE YELLOWSTONE BASIN

*The Crow country is a good country. The great spirit has put it exactly in the right place; when you are in it you fare well; whenever you go out of it, whichever way you travel, you fare worse. . . . It has snowy mountains and sunny plains; all kinds of climates, and good things for every season.*

—Arapooish, chief of the Crow

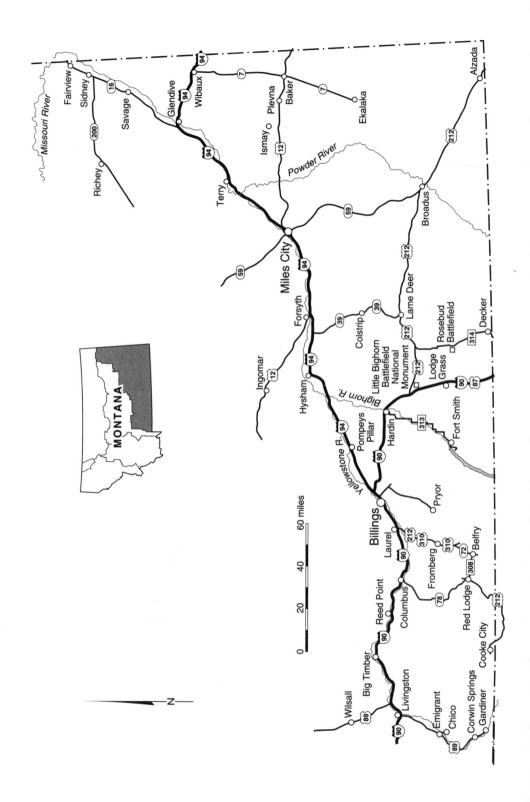

The "Crow country" that Chief Arapooish described in the 1830s encompassed the Yellowstone River drainage in Montana. After flowing into the state from its headwaters in Yellowstone National Park, the Yellowstone River runs north and then northeast for 440 miles before joining the Missouri just across the North Dakota border. Its waters still flow freely, unimpeded by major dams. Like the Yellowstone itself, its main tributaries—the Stillwater, Clarks Fork, Bighorn, Rosebud, Tongue, and Powder Rivers—arise in the high mountains of southern Montana and northern Wyoming. All of these water- and grass-rich valleys once teemed with wild game. It was, indeed, a country filled with "good things for every season."

By the time the first European explorers arrived, the Crow dominated the Yellowstone River basin. Like the whites, they were relative newcomers. Stone Age hunters began roaming these plains at least twelve thousand years ago. The earliest nomads came on foot, stalking mammoths and giant bison. Their weapons were short spears that they hurled with a device called an *atlatl*. Over time, these Yellowstone hunters learned how to stampede bison over cliffs in communal drives. This method served generations of native people quite well until the Crow acquired horses around the mid-1700s—about the time they migrated into the Yellowstone country.

*Lower Yellowstone River between Miles City and Forsyth.*

# EXPLORATION

From the time of the earliest European explorers, the Yellowstone was known as "the river of the yellow rock." French explorer Pierre Gaultier de Varennes de la Verendyre, along with two of his sons, possibly led the first party of white explorers to enter the Yellowstone Basin. Details of their exploration are sketchy and speculative. In the late spring of 1742 according to some accounts, the la Verendyre expedition, comprising only seven men, reached the Yellowstone River somewhere northeast of present Miles City. They spent about twenty days traversing the region between the Bighorn and Powder Rivers.

Another Frenchman, Francois Antoine Larocque, led a more extensive exploration of the basin in 1805. Larocque and two companions spent much of the summer traveling with a band of Crow hunters. Like Lewis and Clark, he kept daily journals with detailed descriptions of the plants, animals, and native peoples he encountered. After watching Crow hunters scalp and mutilate the bodies of two enemy scouts, Larocque decided to leave the Yellowstone Basin in a hurry. The incident, he noted, "made me shudder with horror at such cruelties."

A year later, on July 15, William Clark's party reached the Yellowstone near present-day Livingston. They spent the next eighteen days riding and floating down the river. Unlike Larocque, they did not encounter the Crow, but it was likely Crow hunters who stole all their horses. Clark and most of the men floated the river in two crude, cottonwood-log canoes lashed together. Another small contingent, led by Sergeant Nathaniel Pryor, lost their horses and braved the Yellowstone in two bullboats—buffalo hides stretched over willow frames. Although Clark named many of the tributary streams and landmarks in the Yellowstone River area, only a few—including Pompey's Pillar, Pryor Creek, Clarks Fork, and the Shields River—retain those names today.

In the decades following Clark's voyage, many fur trappers traversed the Yellowstone Basin. Most left no record of their travels, and the region remained the domain of Native Americans. One early visitor, Jesuit priest Pierre Jean De Smet, recorded that the Yellowstone country was "the battleground where the Crows, the Blackfeet, Sioux, Cheyennes, Assiniboins, Aricaras, and Minnetarees fight out their interminable quarrels, avenging and revenging without respite their mutual wrongs."

In the spring of 1859 the U.S. government sent another survey party into the Yellowstone country. The expedition, led by Captain W. F. Raynolds and his lieutenant, Henry E. Maynadier, had instructions to explore the region as thoroughly as possible and to map the best travel routes. Guided by legendary mountain man Jim Bridger, the Raynolds party spent most of two summers traversing the entire drainage. They reached the Yellowstone near the mouth of Rosebud Creek, where Raynolds observed "over 50 square miles was visible, literally black with buffalo." He correctly predicted that "the sight was one which in a few years will have passed away forever."

Raynolds also concluded that the Yellowstone Valley "affords peculiar facilities for a railroad." Lieutenant Maynadier, whose party descended part of the Yellowstone in a foul-smelling bullboat they facetiously named the Rose of Cashmier, declared that the river was suitable for steamboat navigation.

## COMMERCE

During Montana's gold rush in the mid-1860s, several flotillas of Mackinaw boats transported miners and their goods down the Yellowstone from near present-day Livingston. One contemporary described the crafts as "little better than rafts." They frequently grounded on sandbars or crashed on rocks. Indian hostilities soon ended these downstream voyages.

Likewise the steamboat era on the Yellowstone River, which began about a decade later, was short-lived. The Yellowstone, with its many rapids and divided channels, proved more difficult to navigate than the upper Missouri. Still, from the mid-1870s to the early 1880s steamboats such as the *Josephine,* the *Far West,* and the *Yellowstone* chugged up and down the river.

During the U.S. military's campaign against the Cheyenne and Sioux, steamboats frequently transported and ferried soldiers and supplies. In one of the most noted runs down the Yellowstone River, veteran river man Grant Marsh piloted the *Far West,* laden with wounded soldiers from the Little Bighorn battle, from the mouth of the Bighorn River to Bismarck, Dakota Territory, in just over two days.

Miles City, near the mouth of the Tongue River, emerged as the Yellowstone's chief river port. Although boats ventured beyond here, only a few made it as far upstream as Coulson, near the present site of Billings. In 1882 the rails of the Northern Pacific extended up the Yellowstone Basin, and the riverboat era here came to an end.

By the time the railroad arrived, white hunters had nearly wiped out the vast herds of bison that had so astounded Lewis and Clark. In their place came thousands of cattle, turned loose to graze on grasslands that had once fed the buffalo. Except on a short stretch east of Billings, the Northern Pacific tracklayers worked along the south bank of the Yellowstone. The line's division points, spaced at 100-mile intervals, became some of the Yellowstone Valley's most important towns. Glendive, Forsyth, Billings, Laurel, and Livingston all flourished as rail shipping centers. As construc-

*Northern Pacific railroad car designed to lure new settlers.* —Western Heritage Center, Billings

tion crews reached these places, the towns bustled with excitement. Teamster Walter Cameron recalled arriving in Glendive: "Nearly everyone of our bunch who had money enough to buy liquor got gloriously soused and gun plays and fist fights were common."

Even after the arrival of the railroad, agricultural development in the Yellowstone Valley moved slowly. Until the turn of the century the region was considered better suited for stock raising. In 1907 another railroad, the Milwaukee Road, reached the Yellowstone River near Terry and built through the valley to Forsyth before cutting northwest to the Musselshell River. Both the Milwaukee and Northern Pacific launched high-powered promotional schemes to lure homesteaders. In 1900 total wheat acreage near the Yellowstone Basin amounted to around one square mile. By 1920 wheat covered more than 450 square miles in the valley. Large federal irrigation projects south of Sidney and east of Billings at Huntley lured more farmers.

## THE YELLOWSTONE TRAIL

Shortly after the Milwaukee railroad arrived, the automobile began rivaling the train as a transportation mode. Today's I-94 from Terry to Billings and I-90 west of Billings follow one of America's pioneer automobile routes: the Yellowstone Trail.

The Yellowstone Trail began as a modest scheme of businessmen in Ipswich and Aberdeen, South Dakota, to build a better road across the twenty-six miles separating their towns. It quickly grew into a plan to construct a quality road to carry tourists from Minneapolis to Seattle, with an important side route from Livingston to Yellowstone National Park.

The Yellowstone Trail Association adopted a unique logo consisting of a black arrow painted on a yellow background. These markers appeared on rocks, telephone poles, and even buildings along the route. The association declared May 22 1914 as Trail Day. In dozens of communities, people showed up with picks and shovels to help grade and gravel their section of the road. By 1920 the Yellowstone Trail had become one of the nation's most heavily traveled interstate roadways. On Montana's first road maps it was designated Highway Number 1. A guide to the Trail called it "the most comfortable long summer drive known to man." This historic route forms the nucleus of our tour of the Yellowstone country.

US 89
# Gardiner—Wilsall
**84 miles**

## THE ROAD TO WONDERLAND

US 89 from Gardiner to Livingston follows the upper Yellowstone River through the beautiful Paradise Valley—the earliest tourist corridor to Yellowstone National Park. From the time the first government surveyors unveiled the wonders of Yellowstone to the nation, officials of the Northern Pacific Railroad recognized that the region could lure in thousands of tourist passengers on their planned transcontinental rail line. They helped to persuade Congress to set aside Yellowstone as the nation's first national park in 1872.

Shortly after the Northern Pacific's main line reached Livingston in 1883, it ran a branch fifty-two miles up the Yellowstone River toward the park. In that first year alone, nearly 20,000 Yellowstone-bound tourists changed trains at Livingston. A land dispute with the people of Gardiner led the railroad to stake out the terminal of Cinnabar, four miles to the north. For nearly nine decades, the Northern Pacific called itself the Yellowstone Park Line. Its promotional literature labeled the park "Wonderland."

Tourist runs along the Yellowstone branch were often slow and casual. One early passenger wrote that his train stopped once to pick up a package left in a field, once to retrieve some buttermilk that a little girl had brought for the passengers, and finally to enable the engineer to draw his pistol and bag a prairie chicken.

In 1915 government officials opened Yellowstone Park to automobile traffic. At about the same time, construction crews, often comprised of convicts from the Montana State Prison, completed work on the Yellowstone Trail auto route from Livingston to the park. Workers cut part of the road through the solid rock of Yankee Jim Canyon. From then on, the proportion of auto-bound tourists reaching Yellowstone climbed steadily. In September 1965 the last passenger train left Gardiner.

## GARDINER

Gardiner received its name from Johnston Gardiner, an early-day Yellowstone country fur trapper. Although there have been lucrative gold and coal mines nearby, Gardiner's economy has always centered around the Yellowstone Park tourist trade. Shortly after its founding in 1883, Gardiner consisted of 200 people living in tents and log shacks. Here park tourists could find diversion in the town's thirteen saloons and six houses of ill-fame. Because Yellowstone's boundary ran along the sidewalk line in front of their buildings, businessmen could build on only one side of Gardiner's main street.

Every tourist season thousands of motorists pass under Gardiner's Theodore Roosevelt Arch. Near the beginning of its construction, in April 1903, the arch's namesake President came to Gardiner and laid the cornerstone. More than 4,000 people witnessed the event. The Livingston press called it "the crowning day of glory in the existence of the little border town."

For two weeks President Roosevelt toured the park with a small party. Newspaper reporters were banned from the tour and sat cooling their heels on the Presidential train, parked at the Cinnabar railhead. Near the end of their stay, one reporter grumbled, "Well, thank goodness this blooming town will be wiped off the map when we leave." Cinnabar's post office closed down within a month after the President departed.

## JARDINE

A steep gravel road leads to the old mining camp of Jardine, five miles northeast of Gardiner. From the first placer gold find on Bear Gulch in 1865, mines in this area experienced a series of booms and busts. Early attempts to get at the gold through a powerful hydraulic system proved fruitless.

In 1898 Englishman Harry Bush, with big ambitions and big outside capital, erected a stamp mill to process ore. He also built several hotels, three general stores, and a school. The mill operated at a loss for months, until miners hit a rich gold vein. To celebrate, Bush staged a big ball,

*President Theodore Roosevelt at the cornerstone-laying ceremony for Roosevelt Arch, Gardiner, 1903.* —Yellowstone National Park Archives

complete with a feast of buffalo meat and an ample supply of liquor. Bush's big spending eventually pushed his mine into receivership. The Bear Gulch mines operated under a series of different owners until a fire destroyed the Jardine mill in 1948.

## THE CUT COMPOUND

Nine miles north of Gardiner, where Corwin Hot Springs flows into the Yellowstone River, a physician opened a health spa and resort. After the hotel and bathhouses burned in 1916, new owners operated a dude ranch here for many years. In 1981 members of a California-based religious sect, the Church Universal and Triumphant, purchased the Corwin property along with the nearby 12,000-acre Royal Teton Ranch. After acquiring even more land, the church moved its headquarters to its new home in the Paradise Valley.

Elizabeth Claire Prophet led the church as a self-proclaimed "Messenger of the Ascended Masters." Among the "Ascended Masters" were Christ, Buddha, Pope John XXIII, and Prophet's late husband, Mark. The religion was a unique mix of Christian fundamentalism, conservative patriotism, and Far Eastern philosophies. From the time of the sect's move into Montana, many neighboring residents expressed concern over its secretive nature and its members' fanatical devotion to their leader.

When the church drilled a well to tap the hot springs, Yellowstone officials saw a threat to the park's geysers. Concerns increased when the church began erecting a massive bomb shelter in preparation for Prophet's predicted nuclear cataclysm. A leaky storage tank for the shelter contaminated the area with petroleum fuel. And in 1989 two CUT officials, including Prophet's second husband, Ed Francis, received sentences to federal prison after being convicted of conspiring to acquire enough automatic weapons and ammunition to outfit an army of 200.

An infuriated Park County commissioner declared, "These people have lost all meaning of the word church." Prophet, meanwhile, told a reporter: "We are going to continue to be good neighbors. We just want to be treated like ordinary people."

## YANKEE JIM CANYON

Between mileposts 13 and 17, US 89 passes through Yankee Jim Canyon. James George, or "Yankee Jim," camped in the narrow canyon in 1871 and began charging a toll to travelers on the narrow road, the only feasible route between Livingston and Yellowstone Park. He also erected a crude roadhouse and bar, where he entertained travelers with his tall tales.

When construction crews for the Northern Pacific reached Jim's place in 1883, he greeted them with his buffalo gun. After long bargaining sessions, the railroad purchased the right-of-way, but Jim never forgave the Northern Pacific for ruining his toll-road business. He tried unsuccessfully to sue the railroad, and greeted passing trains by shaking his fist and cursing at the engineers. The Park County sheriff once remarked:

> He puts in an average of about five days lapping up corn juice and telling the whoppingest lies ever incubated on the Yellowstone and ten days of neutralizing the effects of them by talking and living religion.

## EMIGRANT

Emigrant is the location of Park County's earliest mining camp. Prospectors discovered placer gold here in 1863. The camp, consisting of tents and log huts, was known as Yellowstone City. Provisions in the remote camp often ran short. During one harsh winter residents were reduced to eating the gum from area pine trees. Within three years the gold played out.

## LIVINGSTON

Located at the bend where the Yellowstone River turns east, Livingston owed its birth and rapid early growth to the Northern Pacific Railroad.

The first white settlement in the area arose four miles downstream from the present town. Here, Amos Benson built a trading post and ran a ferry during the 1870s. Benson's Landing sold supplies to soldiers and liquor to the Indians.

In July 1882 Joseph McBride arrived with orders from his employer, the Northern Pacific, to establish supply stores for the railroad's approaching construction crews. Wagons unloaded seventy tons of merchandise just south of present Livingston, and the town of Clark City was born. By the time the rails reached here in November the town had forty-four business houses, thirty of which were saloons. Many pulled up stakes as soon as the rail workers moved west.

Once the first trains arrived, the Northern Pacific surveyed a new town site, which they named in honor of Johnston Livingston, a railroad director from St. Paul, Minnesota. When the railroad announced plans to build here its largest roundhouse between Minnesota and the West Coast, Livingston's future was assured. Within a year Livingston boomed with more than 2,000 residents, making it the largest town in the Yellowstone Basin.

*Northern Pacific roundhouse and repair shops, Livingston, 1947.*
—Warren McGee private collection

Livingston was clearly a company town. The Northern Pacific laid it out, sold the lots, and provided the livelihood for most of its residents. By 1900 the railroad had erected a machine shop, car shops, and a fifteen-stall roundhouse. But the Northern Pacific's crowning achievement in Livingston was its elaborate $75,000 depot completed in 1902. Designed by the same architectural firm that had laid out New York's Grand Central Station, the Italian-style depot for decades accommodated passengers as they changed trains to head south to Yellowstone National Park. After Amtrak discontinued its runs through central Montana in 1979, the structure was converted to a railroad museum. It remains one of Montana's premier architectural landmarks.

As a town filled with railroad workers, Livingston gained a reputation for toughness. As late as 1912 schoolboys carried pistols to class. The local red-light district on South B Street flourished, until police closed it down after the Second World War. During the district's heyday, women working here abided by strict rules. They could not drink in public and were not allowed in residential areas after dark.

The worst of many notorious saloons was the Bucket of Blood. Kitty Leary, more widely known as Madame Bulldog, ran this establishment.

*The historic Northern Pacific depot, Livingston.*

Standing six feet tall and weighing nearly 200 pounds, Madame Bulldog announced, upon opening her saloon that she would stand for "no damn foolishment." To avoid paying the wages of bouncers, she threw out trouble-makers herself. According to local lore, she once removed an equally tough female patron, Calamity Jane, after Jane slapped a male customer and fired a shot through the ceiling. When asked why Jane had not fought back after being thrown out, a witness observed, "Calamity was tougher'n hell, but she wasn't crazy!"

Many of Livingston's railroad workers were strong union men. During the 1894 strike against the Pullman Company, the infant American Railway Union refused to handle trains with Pullman cars. Virtually all rail traffic on the Northern Pacific came to a halt. Company owners persuaded the federal government to use federal troops to move the trains. Most Montanans, especially the citizens of Livingston, sympathized with the strikers.

The arrival of troops caused the strike to turn violent. Several Northern Pacific bridges were burned. On July 10 a train filled with soldiers commanded by Captain B. C. Lockwood pulled into Livingston. At the depot a crowd of 700 curious locals met the train. Lockwood dismounted, struck one civilian in the stomach, and rushed about shouting orders to the crowd. He struck a rail worker with his saber. Fights broke out between union and nonunion workers. After the mayor questioned his high-handed tactics, Lockwood responded by calling the mayor a son-of-a-bitch and declared, "I am running this town."

Citizens of Livingston held a mass meeting at the opera house, where they denounced the troops and drafted a telegram of protest to federal officials. The army later investigated the incident and declared Lockwood's actions to be "entirely justifiable" under the circumstances. The strike ended in defeat for the Pullman workers. In Livingston the Northern Pacific refused to rehire many of those who had walked off their jobs.

### CLYDE PARK AND WILSALL

The Shields River is the only significant tributary entering the Yellowstone from the north. Beginning in the 1870s, stockmen brought in their herds to graze in the rich valley grassland. They sold beef to the Crow Reservation.

Clyde Park arose near a post office located at a crossroad among several ranches. One of the ranches had an imported Clydesdale stallion—hence the name. When the Northern Pacific ran a branch line up the Shields Basin in 1912, Clyde Park filled with homesteaders. The town's population peaked at 752, before hard times hit both the railroad and area wheat farmers.

Wilsall arose as the northern terminus of the Northern Pacific's branch line from Livingston. The first railway station was a boxcar on the track. During the early 1900s wheat boom, the town's three grain elevators were filled to capacity.

I-90
# Livingston—Laurel
**100 miles**

## WIND POWER

On the benchland between Livingston and Big Timber, the annual average wind speed is around sixteen miles an hour—the highest of any measuring station in America. Gusts over ninety miles an hour are frequent. They have been known to blow freight trains off the tracks.

During the late 1970s, when oil prices skyrocketed, entrepreneurs eyed the Livingston bench as a potential wind-generating farm. A number of firms and even the city of Livingston erected a variety of experimental wind generators mounted atop fifty-foot towers. Most were visible from the freeway. Virtually all the generators encountered the same problem— the wind was too strong. Gusts sped the propellers at tremendous speeds, blowing generators to pieces, or toppled the towers, scattering the expensive equipment across the bench.

Once oil supplies became plentiful again, energy prices dropped. The project failed to attract needed investors. Firms found the power rates in California more attractive, and several huge wind farms went up in that state. Only a few of the windmills on the Livingston bench remain standing. Three can be seen near milepost 336, on the south side of I-90.

### SPRINGDALE

#### Hunter's Hot Springs

The tiny community of Springdale was once the site of one of Montana's busiest health resorts. For generations Crow Indians journeyed to the hot springs here to ease their bodily aches. They even bathed their horses in the water to cure their sore backs. When Dr. Andrew Jackson Hunter came across the springs while on a gold-prospecting expedition, he promptly named the springs after himself.

Hunter hoped to construct a resort to rival those back east, but Indian hostilities forced him to postpone his plans until 1883. In that year he erected a two-story hotel in time to accommodate tourists arriving via the newly completed Northern Pacific Railroad. In a promotional pamphlet Hunter claimed that waters here could cure everything from syphilis to colic. At the turn of the century Butte magnate James A. Murray purchased the resort and built the large Hotel Dakota. Murray's grand resort failed to make money in the sparsely populated region, and in 1932 the Dakota burned to the ground.

## BIG TIMBER

Big Timber received its name from the large grove of cottonwood trees that grew near the site where Big Timber Creek and the Boulder River flow into the Yellowstone River from opposite directions. William Clark called the place Rivers Across. The first white settlement here was a stage station near the mouth of Big Timber Creek. In 1882, when the Northern Pacific arrived, the community of Dornix flourished on a railroad spur on the south bank of the Yellowstone. Later the railroad relocated the town to higher ground along the main line and renamed it Big Timber.

A lynching marred the town's first year. A rejected suitor shot a young schoolteacher three times. She survived the attack, but he was not so lucky. A mob of masked men broke into the general store, where he was being held. They strung him up from a store beam and riddled his body with bullets.

*Fleeces from Reed Point arrive at Big Timber for shipment, circa 1890.*
—Montana Historical Society, Helena

The rich grassland at the foot of the Crazy Mountains and up Boulder Creek to the south proved ideal for raising sheep. Big Timber flourished as one of the nation's largest wool-shipping points. In 1895 alone, nearly 5 million pounds of wool left here via the Northern Pacific. Six years later William Whitfield built Montana's first woolen mill here. The mill gained renown as a producer of fine blankets. Gold mines on the upper Boulder River added to the region's wealth.

Over the years the wind belt between Livingston and Big Timber has produced catastrophic fires in both towns. The worst in Big Timber came on Friday, March 13, 1908. Sparks from a passing locomotive ignited grass near the local stockyards. Strong winds spread the flames into the business district. The fire quickly destroyed most of three business blocks and five residential blocks. The Livingston Fire Department rushed in aboard a freight train and helped put out the blaze before it consumed the entire town. At the height of the fire, one local hotel owner decided that it would be a good idea to have fire insurance. He dashed about town in a vain attempt to find an agent to write him a policy.

### REED POINT

During the 1990s, Reed Point gained a measure of notoriety for an annual Labor Day sheep drive down the town's Main Street. But during Reed Point's early years, it had more enduring claims to fame. In 1915 wheat grown by an area farmer was judged Montana's best at the State Fair. High between the town's two grain elevators, a banner proudly proclaimed, "Reed Point, the Prize Wheat Town of Montana."

At the same time, residents were growing record-setting vegetables. During the 1915 growing season, the local newspaper told about a nineteen-pound beet, potatoes weighing three pounds each, a "mammoth turnip," and a squash "bigger than a washtub." The Northern Pacific purchased many of the area's giant potatoes for their dining cars.

In 1914 a group of ladies in Reed Point organized a baseball team that challenged and beat a team made up of local businessmen. Four years later, Montana's first all-woman jury participated in a legal case here.

### COLUMBUS

Horace Countryman, a pioneer Montana miner and merchant, established a trading post and stage station near present Columbus in 1875. Countryman came here to take advantage of trading opportunities with the new Crow Agency, located up the Stillwater River near present Absarokee. Known as Eagle's Nest, Countryman's stout log building had

*Sandstone quarry, Columbus, 1904.* —Haynes Foundation Collection, Montana Historical Society, Helena

loopholes where sharpshooters could ward off any attacking Cheyenne or Sioux. Later, customers changed the place's name to Sheep Dip because of the foul-tasting liquor that Countryman sold. In the words of Col. J. I. Allen, who traded here:

> Countryman was chief of the town. In addition to the hotel, he owned the toll road and ferry, with a saloon as a sideline. These enterprises yielded hundreds of dollars weekly. . . . It was also rumored that he had a pretty fair idea of where the Indians were getting their whiskey supply.

By the time the Northern Pacific reached here in 1882, the settlement was known as Stillwater. Eventually the railroad renamed the town Columbus to avoid confusion with another Stillwater along its line in Minnesota.

Columbus grew slowly until around the turn of the century when Ben Hager decided to establish a quarry in the sandstone bluffs north of town. The rock here proved easy to cut and work to a smooth surface, making it ideal building material. In 1899 the State of Montana contracted with the Columbus quarry to provide stone for the new capitol building in Helena.

A group from Helena soon bought the quarry and vastly expanded its operation. Manager Mike Jacobs went to Chicago and recruited skilled, Italian-immigrant masons. Huge wooden beams equipped with winches and pulleys hoisted the cut stone slabs from the hillsides. Horses provided most of the power. The Northern Pacific ran a spur line to the quarry. Stone from here went into federal buildings in Butte, Helena, and Billings; a high school and Masonic temple in Missoula; and a hotel and high school in Havre. The Northern Pacific used waste stone from the quarry as riprap on its roadbeds. The expert stonecutters also carved scores of cemetery headstones and fancy facades for brick buildings throughout the state.

In 1910 the Columbus quarry lost a bidding war with a granite quarry near Boulder to gain the contract for the state capitol annex. Much of the cutting and stone-moving equipment was moved from Columbus to the new quarry. By then, new construction materials were replacing stone, and many of the original masons were aging or dying, leaving no one to carry on their work. For the next three decades, a local firm used the remaining cut blocks from the quarry to manufacture headstones.

## PARK CITY

In 1882 a group of seventy-eight people from Ripon, Wisconsin, formed a colony and headed to the Yellowstone Valley aboard prairie schooners. The local land company lured the colonists to Billings. Once there, they found that the company was asking more for land than they were willing to pay, so they proceeded twenty-three miles up the Yellowstone River and platted a town. They christened it Rimrock after the bluffs to the north. But after they planted gardens and trees, they decided Park City was a more suitable name. Reputedly, the name change so angered the general manager of the Northern Pacific that he chose nearby Laurel rather than Park City to locate the line's roundhouse and engine shops.

After an initial boom, Park City languished. Many of the original colonists sold their land and moved away. Then Billings erected a sugar beet refinery, and the richest land around Park City blossomed with a new cash crop. At the same time, new homesteaders began growing wheat on the region's drylands. A description of the town in 1913 boasted:

> There are no poor people in Park City. The affirmation of community interests . . . has brought about friendly communications with all the outside towns, and has instilled a spirit of peace and happiness in its people.

# Columbus—Cooke City
**114 miles**

## RED LODGE

Nestled near the foot of the mighty Beartooth Mountains, Red Lodge arose as a stagecoach stop in 1884 and blossomed as a coal-mining town. Entrepreneurs from Bozeman formed the Rocky Fork Coal Company to tap into the rich coal veins, and Henry Villard extended a branch of his Northern Pacific Railroad south from Laurel to the mines. By 1890 trains were bringing in hundreds of immigrant miners and hauling out coal to be used by the railroad and by the Anaconda Company's copper smelters.

Young, single coal miners, rowdy cowboys, and a scattering of Crow Indians made early Red Lodge an exciting place. John "Liver Eating" Johnston served as the town's first constable. According to local lore, Johnston once settled a saloon brawl by picking up the two fighting miners—one under each arm—and carrying them outside, where he laid them across a hitching pole and banged their heads together.

Throughout the first two decades of the twentieth century, mine production increased, and Red Lodge grew steadily to a peak population of 5,500. Irish, German, Slavic, English, and Italian miners all found their way here, but the largest ethnic group came from Finland, where most had been tenant farmers.

Red Lodge was very much a company town. Besides providing jobs, the mine owners meddled in local elections, furnished crude housing for the miners and their families, and fired anyone who opposed their policies too strongly. A literal social hierarchy existed as the Rocky Fork Coal Company officials built large houses on the bluff overlooking town. Below them lived the master mechanics, and at the bottom the miners lived in two-room houses in their various ethnic communities. The first company manager was driven around town in a fine carriage drawn by white horses.

Greed and racial prejudice led to horrible working conditions for the immigrant miners. Native-born Americans and those who spoke English held the safest, highest-paying jobs. Company officials and Montana's Inspector of Coal Mines were openly hostile toward foreigners. Fires, poison gas, and cave-ins led to frequent deaths and serious injuries. Most of the victims were eastern-Europeans. Company managers attributed the accidents to the carelessness of the victims and paid no compensation to the miners or their families.

In self-defense the miners joined unions. Several strikes shut down the coal mines and eventually produced higher wages, shorter working hours, and slightly safer mines. Unfortunately, prolonged strikes in 1919 and 1922 led to the steady decline of coal mining in the Red Lodge area. The Northern Pacific discovered that coal could be mined more cheaply in open-pit mines at Colstrip. In 1924 the big West Side Mine shut down; six years later the East Side Mine closed.

Prohibition, along with the closure of the mines, led to a new industry in Red Lodge—moonshine liquor. Old-time residents recalled that during the 1920s they merely had to walk outside and smell the air to determine who was making whiskey or wine. The illicit brew found ready markets as far away as Chicago and San Francisco. It often left town in containers labeled "syrup."

Hard times in Red Lodge forced the town's many ethnic communities out of their isolation. As they stood in common bread lines, members of once-rival national groups began participating in each other's celebrations. Beginning in the early 1950s the people of Red Lodge inaugurated a Festival of Nations to celebrate their many rich traditions. The nine-day event continues to attract tourists each August.

### The Greenoughs

Visitors are also lured to Red Lodge by a ski area at nearby Willow Creek and by one of Montana's largest annual rodeos. Begun in 1929, the Red Lodge Rodeo enjoyed early success because of the fame of the family of Ben and Myrtle Greenough.

A runaway from a Brooklyn orphanage, Ben Greenough began ranching in the Red Lodge area long before the town's founding. He won Montana's first bronco-busting contest. Five of his eight children were successful rodeo riders. Son Turk won national fame as a saddle-bronc rider. In the 1930s, an era when women participated in the same events as men, sisters Alice and Marge Greenough attained world fame riding bulls and bucking horses in nearly every state in the Union. A rodeo accident in El Paso broke Alice's ankle so badly that it had to be held together with ivory pegs. This did not prevent her from winning bronc-riding titles in Boston and New York. She even rode bulls in Spain, later recalling, "I came out of a little old steel-constructed chute, and I'd ride the bull. Then they would go ahead and use him in the bullfight and kill him."

*Champion
bronco rider
Alice Greenough.*
—Carbon County
Historical Society,
Red Lodge

## THE BEARTOOTH HIGHWAY

Between Red Lodge and Cooke City, US 212 crosses the 11,000-foot Beartooth Plateau. It is one of America's most spectacular auto routes. The surrounding mountains are part of the Abasaroka-Beartooth Wilderness, created in 1978.

In August 1882 Gen. Philip H. Sheridan led the first organized expedition to cross this rugged region. Following an inspection tour of Yellowstone National Park, Sheridan—along with 128 soldiers and civilians—took a shorter return route to the railhead at Billings. The party made good time, traveling along unmarked game trails. The only mishap occurred when a mule slipped from the trail and had to be rescued from a pine tree.

As the mines declined in Red Lodge, local leaders began lobbying Congress to fund construction of a highway to Cooke City and Yellowstone Park. They knew that the road would bring in hundreds of summer vacationers. During the 1920s, tourists were already exploring the Beartooths on horseback from isolated dude ranches such as Camp Sawtooth, Camp Beartooth, and Richel Lodge.

Early in 1932, Congress passed the bill to create the road at a cost of $2.5 million. Construction began that summer. Because of short working seasons, it took five years to complete the job. Two workers lost their lives—one died in an accidental powder explosion and the other was jerked into a rock crusher. Construction crews gave some of the road's landmarks colorful labels, including Frozen Man's Curve, Lunch Meadow, and the Mae West Curve. For many years members of the Red Lodge Chamber of Commerce served motorists free beverages from a roadside snowbank that they called the Top o' the World Bar.

## COOKE CITY

Situated between the Beartooth Mountains and Yellowstone National Park, Cooke City serves the needs of thousands of vacationers each year. The town began as a mining camp following the discovery of placer gold in 1869. A band of Indian raiders forced the camp's founders, Adam "Horn" Miller and James Gourley, to take cover in their prospect holes.

None of the entrepreneurs in Cooke City's New World Mining District grew rich, mainly because the camp failed to attract a railroad. Attempts to construct rails from the west through Yellowstone Park, and from the east via Red Lodge, came up empty. During long winters, bored miners played marathon cribbage matches in the town's thirteen saloons. One New Year's Day an avalanche swept through the camp, killing two miners. One of the bodies was not recovered until the following Fourth of July, when the snow finally melted. One longtime resident recalled, "Everybody who lived in Cooke those days was more or less a character. They had to be to stay there."

Today the burned trees on the hills just above Cooke City provide ample evidence of the 1988 forest fires that nearly destroyed the town. The fires that swept through Yellowstone Park and much of the Northwest that year were the most destructive since the 1910 holocaust. They blackened more than one-third of the land inside Yellowstone before mid-September snowstorms finally doused the embers. Because U.S. Forest Service and National Park Service officials were following a "let burn" policy, they did not begin fighting some of the lightning-caused blazes until late July. Eventually the fires proved beyond the control of the 25,000 firefighters who stood on hundreds of miles of fire lines.

Ironically, the fire that forced the evacuation of Cooke City and nearby Silvergate resulted from a backfire deliberately set to prevent the larger Storm Creek fire from sweeping through the area. On the day of the evacuation, one resident recalled that it "looked like a war zone, with columns of

*Early Cooke City.* —Carbon County Historical Society, Red Lodge

soldiers marching down Main Street and bombers dropping retardant on the fires which raged out of control above town on the ridgeline."

In the long run, Yellowstone's massive fires did much to rejuvenate the park's forests. Today visitors see a brand new forest rising from the ashes.

US 212 and Montana 72
# Red Lodge—Laurel
**44 miles**

## BEARCREEK

### *Mine Disaster*

Montana 308 between Red Lodge and Belfry runs through the old coal-mining towns of Washoe and Bearcreek. Although the last mine here closed in 1970, some of Montana's richest coal beds still lie just below the surface. Extensive mining did not begin here until 1906, when a railroad came south from Bridger. Miners representing the same nationalities found in Red Lodge quickly moved in, and by 1920 more than 7,000 people lived in the narrow valley. Montana's inspector of coal mines once remarked that there was enough coal in the Bearcreek Field to meet the needs of the entire state for 500 years.

*Bearcreek, 1918.* —Carbon County Historical Society

Several companies operated big mines in the area, but the most productive was Smith Mine Number 3. Even after the other mines shut down, the Smith Mine remained active. Production here rose markedly during the early 1940s to meet the demands of a nation at war.

When the miners began their shift on the morning of February 27, 1943, they were in high spirits. It was a Saturday, so they knew they would be earning time-and-a-half pay. At about 9:30 A.M. the lift operator heard a muffled explosion and felt the force of a tremendous wind. He telephoned the surface: "There's something wrong down here. I'm getting out!" Of the seventy-seven men who entered the Smith Mine that morning, only three came out alive.

Scores of rescue workers came from Butte, Roundup, and other mining towns. A later investigation determined that most of the miners died from the effects of poisonous gases and a lack of oxygen after the explosion. No one will ever know what set off the blast, but safety precautions in the mine had been lax. The miners used open-flame lamps, and smoking was permitted underground. Most of the victims died instantly, but amid the devastation rescuers found a message scrawled on a wall: "Good bye wives and daughters. We died an easy death. Love from us both be good."

### BELFRY

F. A. Hall, the chief builder of the rail line from Bridger to the Bearcreek coalfields, founded Belfry. He named the town after his main financial backer, Dr. William Belfry. For years the town served as headquarters for the Montana, Wyoming & Southern Railroad. The removal of the rails in the 1950s dealt the town a crippling blow. Yet Belfry and its fine school held on. The nickname for the local teams was a natural—the Bats.

## BRIDGER

Mountain man and guide Jim Bridger led wagon trains to Bozeman and Montana's goldfields in the 1860s. Wagons forded the Clark's Fork of the Yellowstone near here, and it became known as Bridger Crossing. After the railroad arrived, Bridger became an important shipping center for area farmers.

## FROMBERG

The first town in this area was Gebo, named after Sam Gebo, the man who discovered coal here. The Northern Pacific extended a spur line to the coalfields. The richer coal in the Red Lodge area soon overshadowed the Gebo mines, but by then the nearby town of Fromberg was flourishing. Fromberg arose as an agricultural center for the fruit and vegetables grown in the lush Clark's Fork Valley. The town boasted a big brick-making factory. The plant received a boost in 1911, when the Great Western Sugar Company ordered 4 million bricks to construct its refinery in Billings. During the 1920s Fromberg was the home of a famous tourist camp. The camp offered motorists gas, wood, water, lights, and shade, all free of charge.

## LAUREL

Laurel has long been one of Montana's most important railroad and petroleum centers. It did not start out that way. In 1883 a guidebook for the Northern Pacific called the town nearest here, known as Carlton, an "unimportant station . . . west of Billings."

All of that changed in 1906. By that year, James J. Hill controlled three major railroads—the Great Northern, the Northern Pacific, and the Chicago, Burlington & Quincy. He decided that the spacious area near where the Clarks Fork joins the Yellowstone River offered an ideal location for major railroad facilities. He spent over a million dollars to create the largest rail yards between St. Paul and Seattle.

Laurel's rail structures included machine shops, an ice-making plant, loading docks, a huge water tank, and a roundhouse with fifty-five stalls. In 1909 the Great Northern extended a line south to Laurel. Five years later the Burlington reached here from the south. By then many of the products of Montana's farms and mines were leaving the state through Laurel.

Although Laurel grew quickly, it was not a typical Montana boomtown. No one came here to get rich quick, but most did well working for the railroad or growing sugar beets in the surrounding valleys. Among the first farmers were a group of German immigrants who had earlier farmed in Russia's Volga River valley. They worked the beet fields each summer and lived in town during the winter.

Laurel's status as a rail center led to the construction of its big oil refinery in 1930. The town proved to be the ideal point for refining crude from newly developed fields near Cody, Wyoming, and shipping the products in tank cars in all directions. Laurel Leaf was the brand name of gasoline produced here. The sulfur content of the gasoline proved so high that it could not meet legal requirements. The refinery went bankrupt trying to solve the problem. It reopened several years later after better sources of crude were discovered.

### Nez Perce Escape

About seven miles north of Laurel on county road 532, a small stone marker commemorates the site of a skirmish during the 1877 Nez Perce War. After crossing the Yellowstone River near present Laurel, the Nez Perce headed north toward a dry trough in the rimrocks known as Canyon Creek. Hotly pursuing them were several hundred cavalrymen led by Col. Sam Sturgis. Indian sharpshooters managed to hold back the charging soldiers, and the tribe once again beat back their tormentors and continued north toward Canada. The Nez Perce suffered light casualties. Three cavalrymen were killed, and a mule suffered major damage after the soldiers fired a howitzer while it was still mounted on the animal's back.

## I-90
# Laurel—Wyoming Border
**121 miles**

### COULSON

On the east side of Billings, just west of where I-90 crosses the Yellowstone River, is Coulson Park—an open area on the north bank of the river. One of the steep bluffs just south of the river here is known as Sacrifice Cliff. According to legend, a number of young Crow Indians rode to their deaths off this cliff in a vain attempt to halt a smallpox epidemic.

Coulson Park was once the site of the bustling Yellowstone River town of Coulson, named after the owners of a steamboat line. Perry W. McAdow founded the town in 1877, erecting a sawmill and store here. For five years,

*Street scene in Coulson.* —Parmly Billings Library, Billings

until the arrival of the Northern Pacific Railroad, Coulson flourished as a riverboat port and stage station. Legendary steamboat pilot Capt. Grant Marsh first brought his boat, the *Josephine,* up the Yellowstone River to this area in 1875. Marsh once boasted, "I can take my boat where there's a heavy dew."

On the high ground north of town, Coulson residents established Boothill Cemetery. It allegedly began with the grave of a cowboy who made the mistake of calling another man a liar. By 1882 the Coulson newspaper noted, "Of all the graves up on the hill, we have yet to chronicle the occupancy of one who departed this life through the medium of disease." Among those buried at Boothill were the local sheriff, gunned down while intervening in a domestic dispute; a man thrown from his horse during an Independence Day race; two men killed by the Nez Perce; a judge who was run over by a train; and a prostitute who walked into the Yellowstone River after muttering, "Here goes nothing."

Coulson residents usually hauled the body of the deceased to the cemetery in a wagon. After a very brief ceremony, everyone made a mad dash back to town, where they drowned their sorrows in the nearest saloon.

Once during the rush to town a man was thrown from his horse and killed. This necessitated another quick funeral, followed by a drinking spree. Today Boothill Cemetery has been restored. It sits right off the airport road (Montana 3), just west of where Main Street intersects.

After the Northern Pacific arrived and decided to locate the town of Billings on the alkali flats two miles to the west, Coulson declined. Hoping to save their town, merchants established a horse-drawn trolley to Billings. Even though the price of the trolley ride included a free beer from Coulson's brewery, the town could not survive.

## BILLINGS

### *The Magic City*

Like so many of Montana's railroad towns, Billings sprang up virtually overnight on the flats north of the Yellowstone River. Montana's largest town, Billings has long been known as "the Magic City" because of its rapid early growth.

As the Northern Pacific construction crews moved up the Yellowstone, a group of businessmen, mostly railroad officials, formed the Minnesota & Montana Land & Improvement Company. Early in 1882, in an area known as Clark's Fork Bottom, they platted a town and named it after Frederick Billings, a former president of the Northern Pacific. The town's two long main streets—Minnesota and Montana Avenues—paralleled the railroad. Northern Pacific publicist E. V. Smalley noted that eastern speculators buying lots in Billings "knew no more about the valley of the Yellowstone than about that of the Congo."

Speculation and inflated real-estate prices led to an early falling-out between Northern Pacific officials and Herman Clark, the president of the Billings realty company. Railroad leaders blamed Clark's price gouging for driving off hundreds of potential settlers. They threatened to sue Clark for not building the railroad depot according to their specifications. The Northern Pacific refused to use the cheap depot Clark built and erected one of their own.

Despite such misunderstandings, more than 1,000 people called Billings home by the end of the town's first year. The forty-mile-long Big Ditch was soon bringing irrigation water to Billings and surrounding farmland. Many residents lived in tents and wagons. Streets often were a muddy quagmire, which the local press described as "too deep to wade and hardly enough to swim." Garbage dumped on a slough northeast of town gave off a stench that told travelers when they were nearing Billings.

Following the initial boom, Billings encountered hard times. A series of big fires destroyed many of the original wooden buildings. The severe winter of 1886-1887 nearly crippled the town's livestock-shipping business.

A lynching in 1891 did nothing to improve Billings's reputation. On a warm July night a mob of locals stormed the jail and seized a man accused of killing a popular saloon keeper. They hanged him from a telephone pole near the railroad tracks and left the body in full view of passengers arriving the next morning. The following year, Billings constructed a building near the rimrocks intended for a state prison. Then the Montana legislature decided to locate Montana's penitentiary in Deer Lodge, and the structure in Billings became a country club.

During the first two decades of the twentieth century, Billings prospered once more. The arrival of thousands of homesteaders onto the plains of eastern Montana bolstered Billings's status as a supply, processing, and shipping center for a vast agrarian hinterland. The town's population reached 14,000 by 1913. In 1906 the Billings Sugar Company erected a large beet-processing plant. The Great Western Sugar Company later took over the factory, and it gradually expanded to become one of the largest in the nation. Billings acquired a sizable population of Mexican nationals who came to harvest and process sugar beets.

A lucky few made big fortunes in Billings. Preston B. Moss came here from Missouri and became head of the town's largest bank. After his bank weathered the 1893 crash, Moss built an elegant twenty-five-room man-

*Montana Avenue and the Billings Brewing Company sign, Billings.*
—Western Heritage Center, Billings

*Trucks near the Yale Refinery, Billings.* —Western Heritage Center, Billings

sion. The Moss home at 914 Division Street is now a museum, featuring guided tours throughout the summer. Moss also financed the construction of the Northern Hotel and rebuilt it after the original structure burned down in 1940.

The largest store in town was the Yegan Brothers Mercantile. Calamity Jane once clerked in the big sandstone building until she pulled a knife on a customer and was dismissed. For years the Billings Brewing Company stood as a prominent downtown landmark. A huge lighted sign atop the building featured a bottle filled with beer that tipped and poured it into a glass.

Another boom came after the discovery of oil in southern Montana and northern Wyoming in the late 1940s. Carter Oil and Conoco both constructed refineries in Billings. These joined the Yale Oil Company, which had built the town's first refinery in 1929. Yale produced "Super Powered Litening Gasoline," which advertisements called "distinctively a 100 percent Billings Product." By the 1970s Billings stood as Montana's premier urban center, and *Money* magazine chose it as one of America's top ten small cities.

## HARDIN

The town of Hardin was born after the Chicago, Burlington & Quincy Railroad pushed its line north through the Crow Reservation. Eager to develop agriculture along its line, the railroad gave the Lincoln Land

Company of Nebraska the task of locating a trading center. In 1904 Congress opened to white settlers a "ceded strip" of Crow land between the Yellowstone River and the present reservation boundary. Two years later the company platted the Hardin town site at the confluence of the Bighorn and the Little Bighorn Rivers. Bob Anderson, the builder of the town's first hotel, regained much of the money he paid out in wages to his construction workers by selling them liquor from a tent near the construction site.

The anticipated population boom never came to Hardin. The town's small white population, moreover, often displayed a hostile attitude toward the reservation Crow who used Hardin as a source for supplies. Hardin's economy received a big boost in 1936 when the Holly Sugar Company constructed a large modern beet refinery here. The factory, which featured its own coal-fired generating plant, employed more than 250 people. After Holly shut down the refinery in 1970, area beet farmers were forced to begin shipping their crops west to Billings.

## THE WHEAT KING

Much of the Crow Reservation land just south of Hardin has long been part of what was once called "the world's largest wheat farm." The farm sprang up as the brainchild of a true agricultural entrepreneur, Thomas D. Campbell.

Born in a sod farmhouse in North Dakota, Thomas Campbell was always fascinated with machinery. He grew convinced that only through mechanization could the vast acreages on the Great Plains achieve their true potential. After America entered the First World War, the demand for food products skyrocketed. Recognizing opportunity, Campbell persuaded federal officials to support his scheme to grow large acreages of wheat on western Indian reservations. He then secured a $2 million loan from a group of prominent bankers led by J. P. Morgan.

With the money, Campbell founded the Montana Farming Corporation. At a time when most of the nation's wheat was being produced on small farms, using horses or tiny tractors, Campbell thought in much larger terms. He secured leases on thousands of acres on the Fort Peck and Crow Reservations. He purchased 50 plows, 60 grain drills, 100 grain wagons, and 34 Altman Taylor tractors. These monster machines, weighing thirteen tons with eight-foot-high wheels, could pull a plow, disc, grain drill, and packer all at once. On one occasion Campbell's workers established a record by using fifteen Altman Taylors to plow, disc, and plant a 640-acre field in sixteen hours without a single mechanical failure.

*Altman Taylor tractors setting the world plowing and planting record at the Campbell wheat farm.* —Montana Historical Society, Helena

The drought that hit Montana's plains following the First World War prevented Campbell's operation from making a profit for the first four years. His Eastern banker friends abandoned the venture. Undaunted, Campbell simply bought them out and kept plowing ground and planting wheat. By 1923, when the rains returned, he had more than 110,000 acres under cultivation. His Crow Reservation farm stretched forty-two miles north to south.

Thomas Campbell's "wheat factory" weathered the Great Depression and prospered. Campbell's methods gained him worldwide recognition. He advised government officials in Russia, England, and France on how to bolster their nations' wheat production. In Montana, Campbell gained a reputation as a fair boss, even though the Montana Farmers Union criticized him for working men for only two months a year before dropping them. The Crow made him an honorary member of the tribe, giving him the name Ahwagoda-Agoosh (Known All Over the World).

## LITTLE BIGHORN BATTLEFIELD

With the possible exception of the Battle of Gettysburg, no military engagement on American soil has received as much attention from historians and a fascinated public as the clash that took place on June 25, 1876, on the hills just east of Montana's Little Bighorn River. On that day, a large, combined force of Sioux and Cheyenne fighting men defeated five companies of the U.S. 7th Cavalry commanded by Lt. Col. George Armstrong Custer. The battle lasted less than two hours. None of the 210 men under Custer's command survived.

The Battle of the Little Bighorn was one of several engagements that summer resulting from the U.S. military's effort to force the Sioux and Cheyenne nations to return to their reservations. The Indians' refusal to comply with the wishes of the whites was a reaction to repeated violations of treaties, particularly after the whites discovered gold and rushed illegally onto Sioux land in the Black Hills.

In many ways Custer personified nineteenth-century white racism in America. In leading his small force into a camp of several thousand Indians, he brashly underestimated both the ability and the desire of the natives to fight back. Writing just after Custer's column marched off to battle, a reporter with the unit reflected this arrogant attitude:

> The General is full of perfect readiness for a fray with the hostile red devils, and woe to the body of scalp-lifters that comes within reach of himself and brave companions in arms.

The reporter was among those who wound up with a lifted scalp.

The myth of Custer began as soon as news of the battle stunned the nation. Books written by Custer's long-living widow, Elizabeth, elevated the commander to near sainthood. Beginning with Buffalo Bill's Wild West Show, dozens of plays and motion pictures portrayed Custer and his men bravely fighting to the end against overwhelming odds, in a "last stand" on Custer Hill. Poems, novels, and paintings all further embellished the myth.

At the battle site the army marked the field graves of the dead soldiers. Later they transferred the bodies to Custer Hill and put in place the imposing granite marker that still stands. White interpreters at the battlefield told tourists of the brave soldiers who sacrificed their lives to help open the West. In the reenactments of the battle, Indians simply participated in a white man's story. In 1926 reporters at the fiftieth anniversary of the event termed the battle a "massacre" and a "temporary victory of the red man's savagery."

Not until the late 1960s and the awakening of America's civil-rights movement did attitudes begin to change. Spurred by the book *Custer Died for Your Sins* and the movie *Little Big Man,* many began seeing the events at the Little Bighorn from a different perspective. During the 1976 centennial celebration of the battle, 150 Native Americans led by Russell Means of the American Indian Movement staged a dramatic protest. As a symbol of the Indian's distress, they carried an American flag upside down. They circled the crowd, chanting and beating drums.

*American Indian Movement demonstrators at Little Bighorn Battle centennial, June 25, 1976.* —Hal Stearns private collection

Traditional interpretations of the battle came under scrutiny during the early 1980s. Following a prairie fire at the site, a team of archaeologists and historians scoured the battlefield, using metal detectors. After unearthing thousands of artifacts—mostly spent shell cartridges—they pieced together a story of the battle far different from most earlier versions. Once Custer's men encountered overwhelming odds they panicked, and all organized resistance ended. The end came with the soldiers either in wild flight or complete disarray. This description of the soldiers' behavior corresponded with long-ignored Native American oral accounts of the battle.

Finally, after an effective campaign by Native Americans and their supporters, Congress in 1991 authorized an Indian memorial at the battlefield. They also agreed to change the site's name from the Custer Battlefield to the Little Bighorn Battlefield National Monument. Testifying at a hearing on behalf of the name change, Crow leader Barney Old Coyote argued, "The fact is that this has always been, is now, and always will remain Crow Country. . . . Custer lived here less than 36 hours."

## THE CROW RESERVATION

As it runs north and south between Hardin and the Wyoming border, I-90 passes through the large Crow Indian Reservation. Like most of Montana's reservations, the Crow is the final product of a series of treaties, each of which reduced the domain of a once-great nation.

The Crow trace their tribal origin to the region near Lake Winnipeg, Canada. They were part of the Hidatsa, a large tribe of agrarian people. Sometime during the late 1300s they began a slow migration southwest, into present North Dakota and eastern Montana. In the mid-eighteenth century the Crow split from the main Hidatsa tribe and came to rely primarily on bison for their food supply. In their own language, the Crow are called *Absarokee*, which means "children of the large-beaked bird." Because their sign-language gesture for the tribal name was made by flapping their arms like a bird, whites and other tribes called them Crow.

From the time they first encountered the whites, the Crow sought to establish and maintain friendly relations with the new invaders. Because they were perpetually at war with the Blackfeet and the Sioux, they needed allies. Early trappers described them as shrewd traders and skilled horse thieves. Unlike many other tribes, they were usually able to avoid alcohol, calling it "white man's fool water." Crow scouts assisted the U.S. Army in its wars against the Sioux, Cheyenne, Blackfeet, and Nez Perce.

Despite such help, in 1882 the U.S. government again reduced the Crow reservation. Their old reserve stood in the way of the oncoming Northern Pacific Railroad. Two years later the government forced 130 Crow families to move from their tribal headquarters in the Stillwater Valley to the flat country along the Little Bighorn. The move ended the Crow's life as hunters, and soon disease wiped out many of the tribe's young people.

The lone act of defiance against the Crow's new, confining life on the reservation came in 1887. A small band of young Crow, led by a man known as Sword Bearer, returned to the Crow Agency eager to celebrate a horse-stealing expedition against the Blackfeet. They rode through town firing rifles into the air. Sword Bearer pointed his rifle at an Agency official. Fearing a general uprising, hundreds of troops poured into the reservation. After a brief skirmish in which one soldier was killed, most of the Crow surrendered. Sword Bearer escaped, only to be killed later by a member of the tribal police force.

Following this incident the great Chief Plenty Coups began to assert his authority over the tribe. Throughout the next century of reservation life, the Crow managed to maintain their traditional close family structures. In the 1990s nearly three-quarters of the Crow still spoke their native language—a much higher proportion than Montana's other tribes.

## Fort C. F. Smith and Yellowtail Dam

About twenty-five miles due west of Lodge Grass, the massive Yellowtail Dam backs the Bighorn River into the reservoir that inundated the scenic Bighorn Canyon. Just downstream from the dam, on the east bank of the river, is the site of Fort C. F. Smith. Soldiers erected this remote post in 1866 to protect travelers on the Bozeman Trail. A year later on a hot August day, a large band of Sioux, Cheyenne, and Arapaho attacked soldiers and civilian hay cutters about three miles downstream from the fort. For eight hours the small group lay behind crude log barricades and valiantly fought off the Indians' repeated charges. Finally the Indians broke off the attack, and the men returned to the fort, having suffered only three casualties.

Yellowtail Dam was named after the renowned leader of the Crow tribe, Robert Yellowtail. Ironically, Yellowtail strongly opposed the dam and led the prolonged court battle against the project. After earning a law degree through correspondence courses, Robert Yellowtail emerged as the Crow tribe's leading defender against the various onslaughts of the U.S. government. In 1934 he became the first Indian superintendent of his own tribe. He encouraged the Crow to preserve their heritage, and he resurrected the tribal fair and summer powwow.

Yellowtail's biggest fight came in the 1950s over the proposed dam in the Bighorn Canyon. Among his opponents were government officials, energy company executives, and even many members of his own tribe. The decision to sell the site at a bargain price left the Crow divided for years. Afterward an embittered Yellowtail declared, "It's the same old story. To hell with the Indians, take their land and talk afterwards."

## Pryor

### Chief Plenty Coups

The tiny community of Pryor lies in the remote western end of the Crow Reservation. It is the site of the home and burial place of one of the Crow tribe's greatest chiefs, Plenty Coups.

Aleek-chea-ahoosh (Plenty Coups) was born in 1848 near present Billings. As a boy he had a vision that advised him to be like a chickadee—a good listener who develops his mind. Still, his prowess as a warrior elevated Plenty Coups to chief status. He influenced his people to cooperate with the whites, later recalling, "Our decision was reached not because we loved the white man . . . but because we plainly saw that this course was the only one which might save our beautiful country for us."

The course Plenty Coups advised his people to take proved wise. The Crow managed to retain a portion of their tribal homeland. Although he

*Plenty Coups, chief of the Crow.* —Montana Historical Society, Helena

could neither read nor write, Plenty Coups learned to speak English and eloquently argued the Crow cause several times in the nation's capital. He advised young people of his tribe, "With education you are the white man's equal; without it you are his victim."

Plenty Coups chose to live and farm with a small band of close followers on upper Pryor Creek. Before his death he willed his property to the federal government so it could become a public park. Today a museum stands near his cabin and burial site in the shadow of the Pryor Mountains.

**I-94**
# Billings—Miles City
**145 miles**

## HUNTLEY PROJECT

The best way to reach both the Huntley Project Museum and the National Historic Landmark at Pompey's Pillar is by taking Montana 312 east from US 87, just north of Billings. The highway runs through the corn, wheat, and sugar beet fields irrigated by the Huntley Project ditch.

The Yellowstone River town of Huntley arose in 1877 as a riverboat port, stage stop, and post office. Big business developed here in liquor, furs, and buffalo hides. In 1882 the arrival of the Northern Pacific Railroad led the entire town to relocate south of the river. Stockman M. F. Trask ran sheep in the surrounding countryside. He declared that the land, covered with sagebrush and greasewood, was "not worth a chaw of tobacco."

But others saw that the region held promise, if only irrigation water could be brought in. In 1904 the Crow Indians sold the land to the U.S. government. A year later the government authorized the Huntley Project— one of the first federal irrigation projects built under terms of the 1902 Reclamation Act. Work on the Yellowstone diversion dam, ditches, and tunnels went slowly at first. Bad weather, labor difficulties, and delays in the arrival of materials caused several contractors to go broke.

Finally, in the summer of 1907 the first irrigation water entered the main canal. Soon settlers were breaking ground on forty-acre irrigated plots. Eventually the project covered 33,000 acres and included the small towns of Huntley, Worden, and Ballantine. Many of the new farmers had immigrated here from Germany and Russia. As they encountered problems making the annual payments required by the project, the government gradually extended their loan period. Some were paying off their farms into the 1970s. Today residents of the Huntley Project district remain a close-knit community and stage a big picnic each July on the anniversary of the opening of the project.

### POMPEY'S PILLAR

Pompey's Pillar is clearly visible from I-94 near milepost 23. It was also clearly visible to William Clark and his party as they floated down the Yellowstone River on July 25, 1806. After arriving here during a rainstorm, Clark climbed the 200-foot rock outcropping and later recorded, "from its top had a most extensive view in every direction." Clark christened it Pompey's Tower after Sacajawea's infant son, Jean Baptiste Charbonneau, whom Clark affectionately called Pomp. Later, amid some ancient pictographs on the tower's northeast face, Clark carved his name and the date. The inscription remains preserved today behind shatterproof glass. It is Montana's only surviving physical evidence of the Lewis and Clark Corps of Discovery.

The Crow Indians called this sandstone block "where the mountain lion lies." Clark was not even the first white man to view the tower. A year earlier fur trapper Francois Antoine Larocque had described it as "a whitish perpendicular rock." In the ensuing years others carved their names into the rock.

In 1873 American soldiers accompanying a railroad survey crew camped near the base of the tower. As many of the men bathed in the Yellowstone River near the rock, a Sioux war party opened fire on them. One of the officers, George Armstrong Custer, later wrote: "The scampering of naked men up the hill was very comical."

### BIGHORN

Almost from the time that William Clark floated past here in 1806, the confluence of the Bighorn and the Yellowstone Rivers has been a popular trading and gathering place. In the summer of 1807 entrepreneur Manuel Lisa and nearly sixty men arrived here aboard keelboats from St. Louis. Somewhere near the mouth of the Bighorn, they built the first trading post on the Yellowstone. Known variously as Lisa's Fort, Fort Manuel, and Fort Raymond, it was probably the first building erected by white men in Montana.

Difficulties with the Indians forced the traders to abandon the post after only four years. Over the next several decades, Fort Benton, Fort Henry, Fort Van Buren, and Fort Cass each enjoyed brief lifespans at this site. In the summer of 1875 veteran frontiersman Fellows D. Pease erected a trading post on the Yellowstone's north bank, below the mouth of the Bighorn. From the beginning, the Sioux harassed the traders here and eventually laid siege to the outpost. Troops finally came from Fort Ellis near Bozeman to rescue the beleaguered survivors.

By late 1877, the army was well on the way to driving the Sioux from the Yellowstone country. Steamboats were frequently plying the river to the mouth of the Bighorn. Junction City arose here as a wide, open river port, complete with fourteen saloons and three dance halls. It died shortly after the arrival of the railroad. The small community of Bighorn, on the Yellowstone's south side developed when the Northern Pacific built through here. It did not grow substantially until 1906, when this area, long part of the Crow tribal lands, was opened to homesteaders.

### HYSHAM

The county seat of Treasure County, Hysham began as a siding along the Northern Pacific where the railroad unloaded goods for Charles J. Hysham, owner of the Flying E cattle outfit. In 1906, after an executive order removed the area from the Crow Reservation, a general store and school sprang up here. Ada Channel, who taught at the school, was one of

*Yucca Theater, Hysham.*

the few women who played a big role in establishing a Montana town. The Hysham town site was platted on forty acres of Channel's homestead.

Hysham's landmark building is the Yucca Theater. It is indeed unusual to find a Spanish-style stucco structure on the plains of eastern Montana. The theater's designer and builder, Dave Manning, worked in southern Colorado and New Mexico as a young man. After running the Yucca as a silent movie house for a short time, Manning moved his family into the back section of the building. Manning also gained renown as one of America's longest-serving state legislators. Beginning in 1932 he represented this area in Helena for fifty-two years. Today the theater-turned-home contains memorabilia from Manning's political career.

## FORSYTH

Buffalo hunter Peter Jackson was probably the first white resident of present Rosebud County. In the spring of 1883 a riverboat loaded more than 10,000 buffalo hides from Jackson's landing just east of Forsyth. In 1882 the Northern Pacific built its tracks up the Yellowstone River. Railroad officials viewed the area at the mouth of Rosebud Creek as a perfect location for a minor division point. It lay midway between the line's two new towns of Glendive and Billings. Because the owner of land here refused to sell out, the Northern Pacific located its new town several miles farther west on Thomas Alexander's homestead.

They named the town after Col. James W. Forsyth of the 7th Cavalry. Town builders platted Forsyth as a smaller version of Glendive and Billings. The railroad right-of-way divided the town, and a single row of business lots faced the tracks. The railroad with its roundhouse furnished a number of jobs, but Forsyth grew very slowly until the turn of the century.

In 1901 the Northern Pacific launched its promotion to lure homesteaders onto its land in Montana and North Dakota. During the next decade Forsyth's population shot from around 200 to nearly 1,400. The town became the county seat for the new Rosebud County. In 1908 the Milwaukee Road rails arrived on the north side of the river opposite Forsyth. From here its tracks angled northwest toward the lower Musselshell River. Although Forsyth remained a Northern Pacific town, the Milwaukee brought hundreds of new homesteaders into northern Rosebud County—more customers for the merchants of Forsyth.

In 1913 at the height of the homestead boom, the people of Rosebud County erected one of Montana's most beautiful courthouses. The Neoclassical-style building—with its copper dome—also became the center of a scandal that ended in the indictment of two county commissioners. The problems arose when the commissioners voted to enhance the plans for the building *after* the construction bids had already been made. This led to

*Rosebud County Courthouse, Forsyth.*

a cost overrun of more than $45,000—a sizable amount of money in a relatively poor county.

The Forsyth newspaper accused the commissioners of hiding behind a "dark curtain of silence" regarding their overspending. When Judge Charles Crum convened a grand jury to investigate the affair, he ordered the sheriff to take possession of the new building. But the construction company foreman and the county's building superintendent held the building's keys and refused to turn them over to the sheriff. The foreman hid inside the building behind locked doors. Deputies broke in through a window and finally persuaded the foreman to come out of his hiding place between the building's roof and ceiling. Judge Crum found both the foreman and the building superintendent to be in contempt of court. After several years of litigation, charges against the commissioners were dismissed.

After the drought hit eastern Montana in 1918, Forsyth's fortunes plummeted. All three of the town's banks eventually closed their doors. Some of Rosebud County's smaller towns disappeared completely. Forsyth, aided by its railroad jobs, managed to weather the Depression. The town emerged as a popular stop for auto-borne tourists traveling the Yellowstone Trail and its successor, US 10. For many years, Forsyth Springs, a rest area just west of town, catered to their needs.

## FORT KEOGH

Just west of Miles City is the site of Fort Keogh. In the aftermath of the Little Bighorn Battle, the army regarded the mouth of the Tongue River as a strategic site for a post. Construction began in 1877, after soldiers spent a cold winter in damp drafty huts at Tongue River Cantonment. They built Fort Keogh on a level prairie two miles west of the junction of the Tongue and Yellowstone Rivers.

Nelson A. Miles, the fort's first commander, was one of the West's most successful military leaders. His superiors put up with his huge ego and abrasive personality because soldiers under his leadership consistently won victories over the Sioux, Cheyenne, and Nez Perce. Miles preferred to fight during the winter because the weather reduced the mobility of the Indians. During the frigid 1877 winter, soldiers under Miles repeatedly defeated the Sioux and Cheyenne, and forced them back onto their reservations.

Following the subjugation of the Indians, soldiers remained stationed at Fort Keogh for three more decades. Among the units that served here with distinction was the 25th Infantry Regiment, composed of African American soldiers. In 1910 the army converted Fort Keogh into the nation's largest remount station, and for the next decade local cowboys broke horses and trained them for military use. Military regulations forced them to treat

*Fort Keogh soldiers cutting ice on the Yellowstone River.* —Range Riders Museum, Miles City

the horses gently. As one cowboy remarked, "almost any day you can see the cowpunchers at Keogh handling big, sturdy cavalry mounts like they were sick kittens." Following the First World War the army abandoned Fort Keogh, and it became a federal range and livestock experiment station.

## MILES CITY

One of the earliest white settlements on the Yellowstone River, Miles City sprang up late in 1876, after commander Nelson Miles grew so disgusted with the civilian loafers and gamblers at his Tongue River Cantonment that he ordered them to leave. They set up two tent saloons and a gambling hall where Miles had drawn a marker, two miles east of the post. To show that they harbored no hard feelings, they invited Miles to a dinner of wild game and liquor. They decided to name the town after Miles, whom they toasted as "our future President."

A year later, after the soldiers moved to the new Fort Keogh, Miles City relocated on the east bank of the Tongue River. A portion of the trail running between the fort and Bismarck, Dakota Territory, became Main Street. Miles City boomed as a trade center for a wide region along the lower Yellowstone. Each spring steamboats brought passengers and supplies up the Yellowstone and hauled thousands of buffalo hides to eager markets downstream.

From its beginnings, Miles City was a boisterous, tough town. In March 1880 the local press proudly declared: "We have 23 saloons in our town, and they all do a good business. We are to have one church soon." The town's first jail was a stockade that was far from escape-proof. An armed guard, assisted by the sheriff's pet bear, watched over prisoners around the clock.

In the early 1880s the Northern Pacific Railroad arrived along with many substantial cattle, sheep, and horse outfits. As Miles City filled with cowboys, sheepherders, hide-hunters, soldiers, and railroad workers, early judge D. S. Waide described the scene as "utterly demoralized and lawless." The judge added, "There are on an average about a half-dozen fights every night. Almost every morning drunken men can be seen lying loose about the city."

A well-known saloon, Charlie Brown's, was the polling place for Miles City's most infamous election. In 1882 the town had about 1,200 people, including women and children. Yet it took the judges five days to count the 1,700 ballots, including many from a precinct known as Wooley's Ranch, which to this day has never been located.

Not surprisingly, the town's red-light district flourished. The most prominent madam, Mag Burns, sent out engraved invitations to the grand opening of her establishment. One local prostitute, called Connie the Cowboy Queen, had a dress embroidered with cattle brands. It was said that the brand of every outfit between the Yellowstone and Platte Rivers could be found on her dress. Miles City's parlor houses did not close for good until a state attorney general's order shut them down in the 1960s.

Amid all of the town's chaos, there emerged signs of permanence and order. In 1883 six Ursuline nuns arrived from Ohio and erected a convent. Each year most of Montana's prominent ranchers congregated in Miles City for the annual meeting of the Montana Stock Growers' Association. The event, first held in a local roller-skating rink, featured a parade with a military band, a big banquet, and a ball on the final evening.

Miles City has long been an important place for rounding up and trading wild horses. Beginning with the first Miles City Roundup in 1914, the town also became a prominent rodeo center. From these traditions came the annual bucking-horse sale. The event, held late each May, has been described as a sort of "cowboy Mardi Gras."

Although the Northern Pacific ran through Miles City, it bypassed the town when it established its division points. Miles City did not become a big railroad center until the arrival of the Milwaukee Road's transcontinental line in 1907. The Milwaukee made Miles City a division headquarters and erected a roundhouse and repair shops. During the early 1900s homestead boom Miles City's land office was among the busiest in eastern Montana. The influx of homesteaders and railroad workers caused the town's population to more than triple. The 1980s departure of the Milwaukee dealt the local economy a big blow.

During the 1960s and 1970s, Miles City gained a measure of national recognition as the home of the nation's smallest television station. KYUS (pronounced KAY-use by the locals) was literally a mom-and-pop business, operated by Dave and Ella Rivenes. The owners wrote, produced, and performed two and a half hours of local news and programming daily. Everyone in Miles City tuned in to find out what their neighbors were doing.

US 212
# Crow Agency—Alzada
166 miles

### THE ROSEBUD BATTLE SITE

To reach the site of the Rosebud Battle, take Montana secondary road 314 twenty miles south from Busby, and then the gravel road a mile and a half to the west. It was here, near a bend on upper Rosebud Creek that Brig. Gen. George Crook and some 1,300 soldiers, Crow and Shoshone scouts, and assorted miners and packers were camped on June 17, 1876. The force was part of a large-scale effort by the U.S. Army to force the Cheyenne and Sioux back onto their reservations.

That morning, the soldiers in the valley saw their scouts gallop into the camp from the hills to the north. Following in close pursuit was a huge force of Cheyenne and Sioux. As Crook later recalled, "The singing of the bullets above our heads speedily convinced us that they had called on business."

For the next six hours, soldiers and Indians engaged in a fierce battle that ebbed and flowed over a ten-square-mile area. One of the soldiers observed later:

> The Indians proved then and there that they were the very best cavalry soldiers on earth. In charging towards us they exposed little of their persons, hanging on with one arm around the neck and one leg over the horse, firing and lancing from underneath the horses' necks, so that there was no part of the Indian at which we would aim.

The battle proved indecisive. The Indians, tired after riding from their camp on the Little Bighorn, simply broke off the engagement. Casualties were light on both sides despite the intensity of the fight. Eight days later these same tribesmen met the cavalry force of George Armstrong Custer in a more famous conflict.

## THE NORTHERN CHEYENNE RESERVATION

Between Busby and Ashland, US 212 crosses the Northern Cheyenne Indian Reservation. The Cheyenne share their Algonquian language origins with the Blackfeet, Arapaho, and Gros Ventre. Sometime in the 1400s they migrated from Canada's Great Lakes region into present northern Minnesota, where they were farmers. As white pressure forced them west onto the Great Plains, they took up hunting. Around 1830 the tribe split, and the more numerous Southern Cheyenne moved to Colorado's Arkansas River basin.

Repeated treaty violations by the whites led the Northern Cheyenne to ally with their longtime enemies, the Sioux. Together they defeated Custer at the Little Bighorn. Their victory was short-lived. Once the military subdued them, the U.S. government forced most of the Cheyenne to live with their southern tribesmen in Indian territory, i.e., Oklahoma.

This arrangement did not work out. On the morning of September 10, 1878, 300 Northern Cheyenne, led by Chiefs Little Wolf and Dull Knife, slipped off the reservation and began the long journey north to the Yellowstone country. Their tragic exodus was similar in many ways to the Nez Perce trek of the preceding year. They repeatedly outmaneuvered and eluded the soldiers sent to capture them. In Nebraska the small band split, with Dull Knife surrendering at Fort Robinson. Many died while resisting military efforts to send them back to Indian territory. Eventually Little Wolf and about 125 followers reached Fort Keogh. General Miles allowed them to remain here, with another Northern Cheyenne band under Chief Two Moons.

By then, many Northern Cheyenne families were beginning to settle along the upper Tongue River and the tributaries of upper Rosebud Creek. They had already established a de facto reservation when an executive order in November 1884 set aside the Tongue River Reservation, just east of the Crow Reservation, as the Northern Cheyenne's new homeland.

Plagued by hunger and high unemployment, the Northern Cheyenne on the reservation have steadfastly resisted attempts by the U.S. government to assimilate them with neighboring tribes and to exploit the rich coalfields that lie beneath most of the reservation. Into the 1990s the tribe or individual tribal members retained control of nearly all of the reservation's land.

*Gathering near the mission door at St. Labre.* —L. A. Huffman photo, Montana Historical Society, Helena

During the late 1960s the tribe signed leases with several coal companies. Later they felt that the leases were unfair and that mining threatened their environment and tribal integrity. After years of legal battles, Congress finally passed legislation to cancel the leases. At the height of the dispute, the American Indian Movement hoped to enlist the Northern Cheyenne into their cause. But, after visiting the reservation and observing the tribe's well-established militancy, a movement organizer concluded, "The Northern Cheyenne don't need AIM."

### THE ST. LABRE MISSION

The St. Labre Mission lies across the Tongue River from Ashland. The impressive modern building complex is vastly different from the original three-room log structure that served as the mission's first headquarters in 1884. Father John Eyler and three Ursaline nuns established the mission and school. Poverty and poor health plagued their early efforts in this place, appropriately named for Saint Joseph Labre—the poorest of God's poor.

## POWDER RIVER COUNTRY

Broadus is the only town of any size on Montana's Powder River. The first white explorers to enter this region found the Powder River country most foreboding. Explorer and fur trader Francois Antoine Larocque came through here in 1805 and recorded:

*N Bar crossing, Powder River.* —L. A. Huffman photo, Montana Historical Society, Helena

The current of the river is very strong and the water so muddy it is scarcely drinkable. The savages say that it is always thus and that it is for this reason that they call the river Powder.

More than fifty years later, after viewing the badlands surrounding the Powder, railroad surveyor Capt. W. F. Raynolds concluded, "I doubt if a single section of land in sight would produce sufficient to furnish an ordinary family with a respectable meal."

Not until the early 1880s, following the extermination of the bison herds, did the grasslands along the Powder River begin to attract stockmen. Among the first to arrive was Englishman Oliver Wallop. He experimented in raising draft horses and thoroughbreds, before he took his outfit south into Wyoming. In 1880 the Niobrara Cattle Company brought in cattle bearing its famous N Bar brand. Its big ranch along the Powder dominated the economy until the first homesteaders began arriving.

## BROADUS

Broadus may be the only town in Montana named after a genuine working cowhand. Oscar Broaddus arrived here in 1885, serving as a range foreman and roundup boss for the N Bar. He repeatedly tried to save enough money to buy his own ranch, only to squander it in the saloons and gambling parlors of Miles City. Eventually Broaddus bought and sold several ranches in the Powder River country, including one at the site of the town bearing his name. He married a widow with four children, and the couple had four more children. Probably for this reason, Broaddus built the area's first schoolhouse.

The influx of homesteaders led to the creation of Powder River County in 1919. There were no real towns in the new county so it was difficult to find a county seat. Oscar Broaddus had long since sold his ranch at the present Broadus town site to settler George Trautman. Trautman's widow donated eighty acres near her farm for a county seat. The town was named for the original owner of the place, but only after one of the d's had been dropped from his last name.

An old dance hall was converted into a courthouse. When the first bank opened, the owner had to carry the currency in his coat pocket until a safe arrived. No railroad ever reached this area. From the town's founding, citizens campaigned for improved roads instead of a railroad. Mrs. Trautman donated a right-of-way for a highway, and one of the first business establishments was Shorty's Garage. Still, current US 212, which runs through town, was not paved until the late 1950s. The early gravel road was so poor that one homesteader west of town planted sunflowers in a very large pothole to serve as a warning to motorists.

## THE REYNOLDS BATTLE SITE

Montana 391, a gravel road that parallels the west bank of the Powder River, leads to the site of the Reynolds battleground, about 36 miles southwest of Broadus. A stone monument bearing the names of the four soldiers killed here sits on the east side of the road overlooking the site, which is on private land.

Here on March 17, 1876, soldiers under the command of Col. Joseph J. Reynolds attacked and burned an encampment of Cheyenne led by Chief Two Moon. Reynolds's column of men had split off from a much larger army that had moved north from Fort Fetterman under the command of Gen. George Crook.

Even though they had ignored government orders to return to their reservation, Chief Two Moon and his people felt that they were at peace with the whites. They were on a buffalo hunting trip when they camped in a grove of cottonwoods on the west side of the Powder River. The attack took the encampment by surprise.

In spite of heavy fighting that lasted for several hours, only two Indians and four soldiers died in the battle. The Cheyenne retreated to nearby hills, where they watched in dismay as the soldiers burned their lodges and captured their horses. Many of the tepees were so full of powder and ammunition that they exploded, sending lodgepoles sailing high into the air.

The Cheyenne mounted a countercharge and managed to recapture their horses. Reynolds, eager to rejoin Crook's main column, broke off the fighting and retreated. He was convinced that his men had destroyed the camp of legendary Chief Crazy Horse.

After they salvaged what they could from their burned-out encampment, Two Moon and his people began a freezing two-day trek northeast, where they joined forces with Crazy Horse. The unprovoked attack embittered the Cheyenne and strengthened their alliance with the Sioux. For his failure to hold the village until Crook arrived and for allowing the Indian horses to escape, Colonel Reynolds was court-martialed and stripped of his command for a year. Three months later, at the Little Bighorn, the Cheyenne gained a measure of revenge.

### ALZADA

The town of Alzada began in 1877, when Lewis M. Stone built a saloon and store at a spot where a military telegraph line crossed the Little Missouri River. The town, then known as Stoneville, was an important station on the stage route between Deadwood, Dakota Territory, and Miles City. According to local lore, Stone once offered a cowboy a drink in his saloon by placing a bottle of strychnine and a glass of water on the bar and telling him, "Mix it to suit yourself."

During the early 1880s the hills and badlands of southeastern Montana became a popular place for large cattle and horse ranches to graze their stock. Rustlers also found the area quite lucrative. During a snowstorm on February 14, 1884, the streets of Stoneville formed the scene of a shootout between a sheriff's posse and members of a gang of horse thieves led by George Excelbee. The outlaws managed to escape, but not before they killed a sheriff. Stray bullets also struck and killed two cowhands who had wandered into the street to get a better look at the melee. The posse later cornered one gang member at a nearby ranch, where they riddled him with bullets.

**Montana 39 and US 12**
# Lame Deer—Sumatra
**107 miles**

### COLSTRIP

Much of eastern Montana lies on top of one of the world's largest coalfields—a deposit known as the Fort Union Formation. The first coal in this formation to be mined extensively was near the town of Colstrip. In 1924 labor difficulties plagued the mines of the Northern Pacific Railroad

*Shovel at Northern Pacific's Colstrip mine, 1929.* —Montana Historical Society, Helena

near Red Lodge. To end its dependence on Red Lodge coal, the railroad turned to a rich seam of coal lying just beneath the surface, south of Forsyth.

The Northern Pacific ran a branch line from Forsyth. Strip-mining involved dynamiting and removing the soil "overburden," digging up the coal, and loading it into railroad cars. Because its own labor force was unionized, the Northern Pacific turned to a private contractor to do the mining. The company strung a power line from Billings to the work site to run the huge electric shovels.

It was the nation's first totally electrified open-pit mine. The gigantic dragline shovel could remove up to seven tons of coal or overburden in each bite. The railroad soon found that mines here could produce more than five times the amount of coal per shift as its old underground mines.

The railroad built the company town of Colstrip near the mines. Colstrip had houses and barracks for the miners, a mess hall, and a general store. There was also an indoor skating rink, a golf course, and a swimming pool, consisting of a mine pit filled with water from underground springs.

For thirty-four years both the Northern Pacific and its contractor profited from the Colstrip mines. Finally, in 1958 the Northern Pacific switched to diesel power. The coal mines shut down, and Colstrip nearly became a ghost town.

Then, in the late 1960s the Montana Power Company, which had purchased the mineral leases for the Colstrip area, began mining coal here to feed a power plant in Billings. When the nation seemed to be running short of oil in the 1970s, many viewed Montana's low-sulphur coal as an alternative energy source. Montana Power's subsidiary, the Western Energy Company, erected two huge coal-fired power plants near Colstrip. At the same time, trains began hauling coal from here for use by utilities in the Midwest.

In the early 1980s, as Western Energy built two more even larger power plants, Colstrip's population soared to 7,000. Gradually, modern, permanent housing replaced the trailers that had housed the construction workers.

As Colstrip's economy flourished, the town became the symbol and focal point of a debate over the environmental damage that strip mines and coal-burning power plants were causing. Many feared that eastern Montana would become a "national sacrifice area" to meet the nation's hunger for cheap energy. Montana's legislature passed one of the nation's highest coal severance taxes, along with strict laws forcing the coal-producing companies to reclaim the land once the coal had been mined.

## VANANDA, INGOMAR, SUMATRA

### Railroad Towns

As it cuts across northeastern Rosebud County, US 12 passes through the remnants of three towns—Vananda, Ingomar, and Sumatra. All three arose as products of the Milwaukee Road rail line and the early twentieth century homestead boom.

The railroad erected coal docks and water towers at all three towns. New schools gave them a sense of permanence. The most impressive school was the two-story brick structure built in 1920 at Vananda. The boarded-up building still dominates the prairie skyline here. Vananda also had a large reservoir south of town that served as a water source for the railroad. Residents swam in it in summer and skated on it in winter, until the Milwaukee let it run dry.

For several decades Ingomar claimed the title of "sheep shearing capital of North America." The town's big shearing shed could hold up to 4,000 sheep and keep up to fifty shearers busy at once. A big, single-cylinder engine powered the clippers and a long belt that carried the fleeces to a sacking area. During the operation's peak years, the Milwaukee hauled 2 million pounds of wool a year from Ingomar.

Homesteading in northern Rosebud County proved challenging because much of the land was very difficult to till. The 1920s drought caused many to leave. Sumatra enjoyed a brief revival following the Second World War, when several wildcat oil wells began producing in the area. Other wells struck a pool of very hot water. These artificial geysers provided a few area ranches with a reliable natural source of heat.

# Miles City—Ekalaka
### 112 miles

## ISMAY

Ismay arose at the junction of Sandstone and O'Fallon Creeks, along a popular livestock and stagecoach trail. Once the Milwaukee Road built train tracks through here in 1907, the town grew rapidly. Many of the homesteaders came here from Wisconsin, where farming had been much less challenging. During the dry years, they tried and failed to raise corn, flax, and potatoes on their land. Many left town via the Yellowstone Trail highway—a crude dirt road that became a sea of mud whenever it rained.

The Milwaukee Road named Ismay after an official's two daughters, Isabelle and May. Following the 1912 sinking of the steamship *Titanic,* many residents wanted to change the town's name: they had learned that a passenger named Ismay had pushed his way into a lifeboat ahead of women and children. By 1990 Ismay's population was down to thirty-one people, making it Montana's smallest incorporated town. In an effort to bolster their town's fortunes, residents decided to change its name to Joe, Montana, in honor of the popular professional football player. Although signs welcome visitors to Joe, Montana, highway maps still call it Ismay.

## PLEVNA

Another homestead-era Milwaukee railroad boomtown, Plevna was unique because it was established by immigrants from Russia. The town received its name from a city in Bulgaria captured by Russian forces in 1877.

## BAKER

Baker sits at the crossroads of US 12 and Montana 7. In the late 1870s and early 1880s two stage routes crossed near here. The heavily traveled trail between Fort Abraham Lincoln and Fort Keogh ran north of here, and the Custer Trail ran south from Wibaux through the present town site.

In 1907 Milwaukee Road rail crews noticed a livestock watering hole along their proposed route and decided it would be a fine location for a reservoir to supply water for their steam engines. The rails reached here late in 1907, and a few area ranchers soon began setting up businesses in hastily built shacks at the camp that was then called Lorraine. Later they renamed the town after the Milwaukee's chief construction engineer, A. G. Baker.

Soon the railroad was bringing in hordes of new homesteaders. One pioneer recalled:

> Miles and miles of wire and posts were sold and everywhere could be seen those bright new wagons with "Rock Island" or "Studebaker" painted along their shiny dark green sides.

Early Baker had a flour mill, a flax mill, a brickyard, and a cigar factory that advertised that it could make cigars of any size or strength. Businessman Charlie Ferris specialized in erecting twelve-by-sixteen-foot tar-papered shacks on homestead sites. For $200 he and his boys could assemble one in less than a day.

In 1915 a homesteader drilling for water north of town struck one of Montana's largest natural-gas fields. His well caught fire and burned for years before being capped. Eventually a pipeline carried gas from here to Glendive, Miles City, and east to the Black Hills area.

Oil from the nearby Baker Dome took a little longer to develop. The casing on the first drilling rig tore loose and dropped into the test hole. Crews wasted six months and a sizable sum of money trying to drill around and through the smashed metal before they gave up. Although a few wells operated during the decade before World War II, the real boom came when the Shell Oil Company began pumping oil from the Cabin Creek Field.

## MEDICINE ROCKS STATE PARK

A dozen miles north of Ekalaka, motorists on Montana 7 encounter a group of fascinating rocks. The sandstone formations, laid down on a floodplain 70 million years ago, were long a popular gathering place for Native American hunters. The Indians called them "medicine rocks." They carved and painted inscriptions on them. Theodore Roosevelt sometimes camped here while herding cattle. He called the formations "fantastically beautiful." Today the area is a state park.

## EKALAKA

In 1884 Claude Carter was hauling a load of logs across Russell Creek when his wagon bogged down in the mud. He reportedly declared, "Hell, any place in Montana is a good place to build a saloon." Carter's Old Stand Saloon, with its dirt floor and a plank for a bar, served drinks to cowboys in Montana's southeast corner for several decades.

*Old Stand rival Orlando Osgood Saloon, Ekalaka, circa 1905.*
—Cady photo, Carter County Museum, Ekalaka

The town that grew up around Carter's saloon was originally called Puptown, perhaps because its streets were often filled with dogs. Later the local postmaster decided to rename it Ekalaka. Ijkalaka, an Ogalala Sioux, was the wife of David Russell, the first white man to settle in the region. Her name means "one who wanders."

During the early 1880s cattlemen discovered the lush grasslands surrounding Ekalaka. Pioneer rancher John Clay described the area:

> What a wondrous country it was for grass! Never before or since have I
> seen such fat calves and it took two men all of their time to rastle them.

Later, sheepherders and homesteaders moved in even though Ekalaka lay forty miles from the nearest railroad.

In 1920, as drought brought hard times to the homesteaders, prohibition killed the Old Stand Saloon. The local newspaper printed the establishment's obituary in a column edged in black: "Death came peacefully in the presence of a few fond mourners whose hearts were too full for utterance."

It was also during the 1920s that Nicholas Kalafatich, a master stone-mason from Poland, supervised construction of several fine buildings using sandstone quarried east of town. Among those buildings was a garage that later became the Carter County Museum. The museum houses one of Montana's finest collections of fossils. Southeastern Montana has been a popular area for fossil hunters ever since 1904, when a team of paleontologists from Chicago's Field Museum unearthed a triceratops skull west of Chalk Buttes. Today dinosaur bones discovered in Carter County grace the collections of museums throughout the United States.

## I-94
# Miles City—Wibaux
**104 miles**

## KILLING FIELDS

As it parallels the Yellowstone River, I-94 passes through an area once filled with huge herds of bison. During the early 1880s it was the scene of the slaughter of the last great bison herd in the United States. From the town's founding in 1876, Miles City became Montana's biggest shipping center for buffalo hides. The first hides went down the Yellowstone River on steamboats. Once the Northern Pacific arrived, in 1881, much larger loads of hides could be hauled out and the hunters nearly doubled their kill rate.

Most of Montana's bison hunters drifted north from the southern Great Plains, where they had perfected the art of mass slaughter. They worked in the winter, when the hides were in their best condition and the animals were less mobile. Using Sharps rifles, they simply stood near the herd and shot down the animals like cattle. They skinned the bison quickly, before the hide froze to the carcass. They warmed their hands by plunging them into the buffalo entrails as they worked, then left the meat to rot. One hunter reportedly killed 107 animals in a single "stand."

The northern Plains bison herd, once estimated at 1½ million animals, disappeared after just a few hunting seasons. By the fall of 1883 they were gone. For years the hunters refused to acknowledge what they had done. They sat around in the saloons of Miles City, Terry, and Glendive waiting for the big herds to return from hiding in Canada. Veteran cow puncher Teddy Blue Abbott described them:

> The buffalo hunters didn't wash, and looked like animals. They dressed
> in strong, heavy warm clothes and never changed them. You would see

three or four of them walk up to a bar, reach down inside their clothes and see who could catch the first louse for the drinks.

## TRAIN WRECK

Between mileposts 166 and 167 to the northeast across the Yellowstone River, a tiny stream named Custer Creek flows out of the Little Sheep Mountains. A Milwaukee Road rail bridge spans the creek, just before it joins the Yellowstone. At this crossing, just after midnight on June 19, 1938, there occurred the worst commercial transportation disaster in Montana's history.

That evening, an unusual, slow-moving black cloud hovered over the headwaters of Custer Creek and dumped six inches of rain in only three hours. Still, at around 10:30 P.M. a track inspector noticed that the creek at the railroad bridge was running only slightly higher than normal. Rainstorms had slowed the progress of the Milwaukee's Olympian Express, but by the time it reached the bridge it was moving at just over fifty miles an hour.

The flash flood and the train hit the bridge at almost exactly the same time. The locomotive and the tender made it across just as the bridge gave way. As the other cars went into the raging torrent, they pulled the engine backward. A mail car piled on top of the locomotive, killing the engineer and four crew members.

One passenger-filled sleeper car shot directly into the river. Another sleeper hung on the remnants of the bridge just long enough to enable the passengers to escape, before it also plunged into the swirling floodwaters. Porter Lewis Williams calmly herded the passengers out of the teetering car and was praised as a hero. Later he said, "I can't see why everyone is making a fuss because I . . . told the passengers which door to leave from. I do that every time the train stops."

Four cars remained on the track on the east side of the bridge, their passengers uninjured. A telegrapher for the Northern Pacific on the opposite side of the Yellowstone River noticed that the Milwaukee train was long overdue, and he had heard an explosion. He wired Miles City for help. Because the Yellowstone River cut off the location of the disaster from the highway, it took rescuers a long time to arrive. Some of the bodies washed down the Yellowstone as far as Glendive and Sidney.

Of the 165 passengers and crew members aboard the Olympian, 47 died and 75 were injured. It was listed as one of the five worst railroad disasters in American history. An investigation judged the wreck to be "an act of God." The train station nearest the accident scene was called Saugus.

*Aftermath of crash of Milwaukee Road's Olympian Express, Custer Creek, June 1938.*
—Range Riders Museum, Miles City

After the disaster, people sometimes canceled their trip after learning that the train would be passing through here. The Milwaukee finally changed the name of the place to Susan.

## TERRY

Terry is named after Gen. Alfred H. Terry, a commander during the U.S. Army's war against the Sioux and Cheyenne. In 1877 as the army pursued the Sioux in this area, buffalo hunter J. W. Montague built a dugout south of the present town site. He offered soldiers food and lodging. Others supplied fuel wood for the Yellowstone River steamboats. One steamboat, the *Osceola*, wrecked near the mouth of the Powder River during a fierce storm. The captain recalled, "We were caught in an open prairie country . . . and the storm came down on us like an avenging fiend."

Terry was still a tiny village when the Milwaukee Road ran its tracks up the Yellowstone River in 1907 and launched a big advertising campaign to bring in homesteaders. One flier confidently declared, "On these lands immense crops of grain, hay and vegetables can be raised without irrigation, and they are rapidly being settled up."

Among the earliest settlers to take up land near Terry were the Englishman Ewen Cameron and his wife Evelyn. In 1893 they moved to a ranch south of Terry, where Ewen planned to raise polo ponies and export them to England. Evelyn Jephson Cameron was a well-bred member of a wealthy London family. To the chagrin of her relatives in England, she relished life in the wilds of eastern Montana. She once wrote, "Manual labor is about all I care about. . . . I like to break colts, brand calves, cut down trees, ride, and work in the garden."

Ewen's polo-pony gambit went bust after many of the horses died en route to England. From then on, the Camerons had to struggle to survive. To make ends meet, Evelyn took in boarders, sold vegetables that she raised, and cooked for roundup crews. And, using a mail-order camera, she taught herself photography.

Evelyn began taking glass-plate photographs of her neighbors and the wildlife near the ranch. She took dozens of pictures of cowboys, sheepherders, farm wives, and homesteaders as they went about their daily chores. For a short time, she worked out of a hotel room in Terry, where she took formal photos of children, weddings, and other celebrations among the ethnic groups that were arriving in Terry to take up homesteading. Among her eager customers were the tough sheep-shearing crews who worked in the sheds near Terry's railroad tracks.

*Evelyn Cameron mounting photographs in her ranch house.*
—Evelyn Cameron Collection, Montana Historical Society, Helena

Following Ewen's death in 1915, Evelyn ran the ranch alone for thirteen years. By the time she died, her photography, as well as her many charitable deeds, had earned her friends throughout much of eastern Montana. Evelyn Cameron's photographs, together with the daily diaries she kept, provide one of the most detailed records available of life on the Great Plains. A building next to the historical museum in Terry houses an exhibit of her photos.

With the possible exception of Evelyn Cameron, Terry's most famous 1920s citizens were the members of the Terry Cowboy Band. The band began in 1909 as the Terry Cornbelt Band. Members were all either local businessmen or area cowhands. Soon the band was playing for concerts and parades in the small towns of eastern Montana. Then, in 1927 they gained national fame after they secured an invitation to play for President and Mrs. Calvin Coolidge on the occasion of his fifty-fifth birthday.

A caravan of autos hauled band members to the "summer White House" in the Black Hills. Once there, they serenaded the Coolidges with a special song they had written for the occasion. The band adopted the slogan "Cal's Our Pal and She's Our Gal." They presented the president with a big pair of cowboy chaps with his name on them. According to one band member, after the president donned his new duds, "He took each step slowly, seeming to know the great disaster that would befall him if he should lock his spurs together while coming down the stairs."

*The Terry Cowboy Band.* —Prairie County Museum, Terry

## GLENDIVE

On July 31, 1806, returning members of the Corps of Discovery under William Clark camped near the Yellowstone River seven miles upstream from present Glendive. Here Clark spotted "a white bear and the largest I ever saw." The men shot the grizzly four times, but were unable to kill it.

A later hunter in the area had better luck. In 1854 Irish nobleman Sir George Gore arrived on the Great Plains with a retinue of 112 horses, 14 hounds, 6 wagons, and more than 40 employees. Veteran mountain man Jim Bridger served as the party's guide. Over the next two years, by Gore's estimate, the hunting expedition slaughtered 40 grizzly bears, 2,500 bison, and countless deer, elk and antelope. The wanton destruction of animals led an Indian agent to file an official complaint. On his trek through Montana in 1856, Gore crossed a small tributary of the Yellowstone, which he named Glendive.

Beginning in 1873 the area near the mouth of Glendive Creek served as a supply depot for soldiers who arrived here aboard steamboats. The birth of the town of Glendive awaited the approach of the Northern Pacific Railroad. In 1880 a group led by Maj. Lewis Merrill formed the Yellowstone Land and Colonization Company and platted the town.

Throughout its history Glendive has remained primarily a railroad town. Henry Douglas and David Mead, who opened the town's first general store, offered to furnish the bricks for a roundhouse. In return the Northern Pacific made Glendive a division headquarters for 525 miles of track between Mandan, North Dakota, and Livingston. Besides the roundhouse, the railroad built a large brick depot, a machine shop, a powerhouse, and a three-story hospital. The businesses lining Merrill Avenue all faced the railroad track, and one grocery store even had a spur line running to its back door.

During the last two decades of the nineteenth century, cowboys herded thousands of cattle to the big stockyards in Glendive for rail shipment. Several big outfits ran cattle on the open range of Dawson County. The largest by far was the XIT. Beginning in 1890 the XIT trailed cattle from its home ranch in Texas onto the grasslands of Dawson County, where it had acquired grazing rights to more than 2 million acres.

By the time the XIT left Montana around 1910, the Glendive area was filling up with homesteaders. In 1900 Dawson County had fewer than 2,500 residents. Twenty years later the same area—now carved into six counties—was home for more than 25,000 people. Former railroad workers and ranchers along with foreign immigrants all became dryland wheat farmers.

*Northern Pacific rail yards and depot, Glendive.* —Frontier Gateway Museum, Glendive

Glendive suffered along with the rest of eastern Montana through the drought and depression decades. All four of the town's banks managed to stay open because the millionaire owner of the largest bank publicly pledged every penny he had in order to keep his bank solvent. At the height of the Depression, the town fathers even raised enough money to build a public swimming pool. During the late 1930s the federal government constructed the Buffalo Rapids Project, which brought irrigation water to farms along the Yellowstone River between Glendive and Miles City.

Beginning in the early 1950s Glendive and many other communities near the Montana–North Dakota border basked in the prosperity of the newly discovered Williston Basin oil field. In July 1951 Shell Oil Company hit a gusher near Richey. Several months later, a Texaco well within sight of Glendive struck oil.

Drilling rigs sprang up like mushrooms across a 100-mile stretch of prairie. The title of a 1952 article in *Business Week* magazine accurately summarized Glendive's new boom: "Find Oil and Everyone Comes to Town." More than a thousand new residents picked up their mail at the post office's general-delivery window. Most lived in one of the 500 new trailer houses hastily brought into town. By mid-decade the region was producing more than a million gallons of oil per month.

Oil brought high-paying jobs to Glendive. It also made the town's economy dependent on the fluctuations of the world market. During the

1970s Arab oil embargo Glendive flourished. A decade later, after an oil-supply glut depressed prices, many businesses pulled out of town or went broke.

## WIBAUX

### *The Cattle King*

Wibaux is one of just two places in Montana where the county and county seat share the same name. (Missoula is the other one.) The town and county bear the last name of one of Montana's premier cattlemen, Pierre Wibaux.

Born in Roubaux, France, Wibaux was the well-bred son of a family that amassed a fortune in the textile industry. While visiting England, young Wibaux learned of the money that many British investors were making in cattle ranches on the American plains. Defying his enraged father, Wibaux left for America in 1892 at age twenty-four.

*Pierre Wibaux, cattle king.* —Montana Historical Society, Helena

In Chicago, Wibaux studied the entire beef industry, from the raising of cattle to the packing of meat. While there he met fellow Frenchman and cattle baron the Marquis de Mores. He accompanied de Mores to the Montana-Dakota border country. In an area rich with grass and water in the Beaver Valley, Wibaux staked out his ranch. Later he wrote his brother in France:

> You can't imagine this country from a business point of view. If a man is intelligent, has courage and can see things clearly, he can make money. Only the lazy and stupid fellows remain poor here.

When Wibaux arrived in eastern Montana in 1883, Mingusville, located in the Beaver Valley along the Northern Pacific route, was a popular cattle-shipping point. On weekends cowboys filled the saloons and recklessly shot up the town. One storekeeper reportedly built a sidewalk in front of his building using the empty cartridge shells he picked up from the street.

At first Wibaux entered into a partnership with one of Mingusville's founders, Gus Grisy. Grisy soon proved to be a shiftless drag on the operation, and Wibaux dissolved the partnership. Wibaux had accumulated a modest herd of cattle bearing his W Bar brand when the horrible winter of 1886–87 devastated the region's cattle industry.

Nearly two-thirds of the cattle in the borderland region perished. But the W Bar herd fared much better. As Wibaux wrote home, "The cattle acclimated or raised in this country have relatively well borne this ordeal. Our cattle have been much favored." When most of the big cattle outfits began selling off the remnants of their herds, Wibaux secured investment money from France and began buying up cattle at bargain prices. From these tough survivors he built a herd that grew to more than 65,000 animals. Eventually he ran cattle from the Powder River to as far north as the Big Dry and Redwater Rivers in the Missouri drainage.

Wibaux also made money investing in banks, mines, and a Chicago insurance firm. He was the main person behind the petition drive to change the name of Mingusville to Wibaux. After Wibaux died in 1913 his family, acting on his wishes, erected the large statue of him that today stands on the western edge of his namesake town, gazing toward his old ranch. The office where Wibaux transacted much of his business is the main building of the town's museum complex.

In the years following Pierre Wibaux's death, two events briefly brought excitement to the town. In the summer of 1916 a strong wind blew over a circus wagon, freeing the ostriches. Local cowboys roped and returned all the birds except one, which perished when it ran into a barbed-wire fence.

In 1929 a flash flood shot down the Beaver Valley and destroyed many of the buildings in town. The Methodist minister and his wife drowned when the torrent carried away their house.

# Glendive—Fairview
### 66 miles

## INTAKE

Intake arose as the site of the big diversion dam for the Lower Yellowstone Irrigation Project. The dam began diverting water from the Yellowstone River into its system of canals in 1909. Three years later, crews using mules and horses finished digging a network of nearly 400 miles of canals and drainage ditches. Typhoid fever plagued the workers.

Settlement in the project area was slow at first. Ranchers in the area were reluctant to convert to raising irrigated crops. Then, in 1925 the Holly Sugar Company erected its refinery in Sidney. Shortly after that, one visitor recorded that the valley had been turned into "a lush oasis, green with alfalfa, sugar beets, feed grains, and other forage crops."

## SAVAGE

The Lower Yellowstone Irrigation Project stimulated growth in the homestead-era boomtown of Savage. Savage was named after a railroad official from Billings. Its name could just as easily have stemmed from the fact that nearby hills and draws provided bandits and cattle rustlers with excellent hiding places. In the spring of 1884, just south of here, a band of seven masked outlaws attacked a military paymaster carrying $10,000 in cash. They killed one of the escorting soldiers and wounded two others, but failed to find the cash. One of the soldiers had hidden it aboard an ambulance wagon.

## SIDNEY

Sugar beets and oil have long been the economic mainstays of Sidney. Trappers Jimmy Crane and "French Joe" Seymour built the first cabin near the town site in 1876. A contemporary described Crane as "a dead shot with a rifle, an ardent lover of whiskey and an expert at draw poker, but aside from these he had no religious accomplishments worth speaking of."

In 1888 the town petitioned for a post office. The local justice of the peace decided to name it Sidney after the six-year-old son of a couple boarding at his home. For years, staunch local opposition kept saloons out of

*Holly Sugar Company refinery, Sidney.* —Montana Historical Society, Helena

Sidney. Town site owner E. A. Kenoyer included a clause in commercial property deeds forbidding buyers from selling liquor on their premises. When the saloons eventually arrived, they proved to be more like social clubs than the rowdy establishments that graced most other towns in Montana. Sidney voted to close its saloons in 1915—years before the rest of the state enacted prohibition.

Citizens had difficulty bringing a railroad into Sidney. To persuade the Northern Pacific to extend a branch line north from Glendive, local landowners offered the railroad a free right-of-way. Augustus Vaux, the owner of the largest store in Sidney, offered to construct a grain elevator near the depot. Amid much fanfare, the branch line finally arrived in 1912. Sidney staged a big parade, with visitors from other area towns marching through town carrying banners bearing the names of their communities.

By the time the railroad reached Sidney, the homestead boom was giving birth to many communities. By 1926 Richland County contained eighty-one school districts. Of even greater importance to Sidney's future, the Holly Sugar Company decided to build a refinery here. Workers rushed to complete the plant in time for the 1925 beet harvest. A brick company in nearby Fairview ran shifts day and night to manufacture the 2 million bricks needed for the new refinery. Much of the equipment came from a dismantled sugar plant in Anaheim, California.

Sidney's refinery enabled area farmers to grow a cash crop. It provided seasonal employment for many others. Beet by-products, including the tops, pulp, and molasses, proved excellent for fattening livestock. While most eastern Montana towns were losing people during the lean 1920s and 1930s, Sidney's population nearly doubled to 3,000. Farmers brought migrant workers from Mexico to thin and harvest the beets.

Sidney's growth received another boost in the 1950s following the discovery of the big Williston Basin oil pool. Because of the international oil shortage, the 1970s proved to be Sidney's biggest growth decade. Oil workers often lived in hotel rooms in shifts. Local officials imposed a limit on camping in the park north of town to prevent it from becoming a city of tents. As big trucks hauled drilling rigs across nearby farmland, disputes arose between the landowners and the oil companies. The farmers resented the ugly roads and black pits scarring their pastures.

The oil boom ended in the early 1980s. Unemployment in Sidney skyrocketed. In spite of the change in Sidney's fortunes, the local historical society managed to complete the beautiful Mondak Heritage Center building. Today it is one of the finest museums and art centers in the state.

## LAMBERT AND RICHEY

### Branch Line Towns

Montana 200 west of Sidney leads to the small towns of Lambert and Richey. Both communities prospered when the Great Northern ran a branch line south from Bainville. The tracklayers reached Lambert first, in November 1914. By the time the rails arrived, homesteaders had already taken up claims on government land. Many had come in covered wagons. Some of the early settlers spent their first winter in dugout shelters in the area's hills.

Two years later, in December, the tracklayers reached Richey. Richey was one of Montana's few homestead-era towns named after a real homesteader. Clyde Richey also served as the first postmaster here in 1911. When the railroad came, the town celebrated with Steel Day. More than 1,500 people showed up to partake in a free barbecue, picture shows, and a dance. They roasted the steer in a big pit at the town's main intersection.

During the years of bumper wheat harvests, nearly a million bushels of grain filled Lambert's three giant elevators. During the boom the town had two banks and four lumber yards. Lambert began to decline after it lost the county-seat election to Sidney. In 1927 a fire leveled an entire block, and the town voted to disincorporate. Another fire four years later destroyed most of the remaining businesses. Still, in 1971—long after its best years—Lambert with its 102 citizens had three representatives in Montana's poorly apportioned state legislature.

During its prime, Richey claimed to be the nation's second largest wheat-shipping town. Farmers came here from up to fifty miles in all directions to store their bumper crops. After they built a bridge across the Missouri River at Wolf Point and the Northern Pacific ran its branch line north from Glendive to Circle, Richey's big trade radius shrank considerably.

## FAIRVIEW

On August 2, 1806, William Clark and the last members of the Corps of Discovery to leave Montana floated down the Yellowstone River south of present Fairview. They shot one more big grizzly bear just before they crossed into present North Dakota.

Lewis Newlon, a native of Nebraska, built a sod house on the town site of Fairview in 1903. He platted three blocks on his homestead and named it Fairview. He offered lots for a dollar apiece to anyone willing to establish a business there. Newlon had few takers, until the railroad arrived in 1912. During the 1920s Fairview boasted a creamery, a cheese plant, and a pickle cannery.

On May 2, 1929, four robbers armed with sawed-off shotguns stole $4,500 from the Fairview State Bank. They locked nine bank employees and customers in the vault. It took the county sheriff just eight days to round up all four robbers. In handing each of them forty-year prison sentences, the judge remarked, "While we want to encourage industry up and down the valley, we don't want to encourage this kind of industry."

# SELECTED BIBLIOGRAPHY

Only a portion of the several hundred sources I consulted for this book are listed below. Most of Montana's counties and towns have at least one published history available. Commemorative issues of local newspapers were also helpful. I extensively used the back files of Montana's excellent historical journal, *Montana: The Magazine of Western History*; some of the more interesting articles are cited below. Numerous articles in the popular *Montana Magazine* also proved useful, particularly the well-written pieces by historian Dave Walter.

## GENERAL WORKS

Alt, David and Donald W. Hyndman. *Roadside Geology of Montana*. Missoula, Mont.: Mountain Press, 1986.

Bryan, William L., Jr. *Montana's Indians: Yesterday and Today*. 2nd ed. Helena, Mont.: American and World Geographic Publications, 1996.

Burlingame, Merrill G., and K. Ross Toole. *A History of Montana*. 3 vols. New York: Lewis Historical Publishing Co., 1957.

Emmons, David M. "The Price of 'Freedom': Montana in the Post-Anaconda Era." *Montana: The Magazine of Western History* 44 (fall 1994): 66–73.

Federal Writers' Project of the Work Projects Administration. *Montana: A State Guide Book*. New York: Viking Press, 1939.

Fritz, Harry W. "The Origins of Twenty-First-Century Montana." *Montana: The Magazine of Western History* 42 (winter 1992): 77–81.

Hampton, Bruce. *Children of Grace: The Nez Perce War of 1877*. New York: Henry Holt and Co., 1994.

Hidy, Ralph W., Muriel E. Hidy, Roy V. Scott, and Don L. Hofsommer. *The Great Northern Railway: A History*. Boston: Harvard Business School Press, 1988.

Howard, Joseph Kinsey. *Montana: High, Wide, and Handsome*. New Haven: Yale University Press, 1943.

Kittredge, William. "The War for Montana's Soul." *Newsweek,* April 15, 1996, 43.

Lavender, David. *Let Me Be Free: The Nez Perce Tragedy*. New York: Harper Collins, 1992.

———. *The Way to the Western Sea: Lewis and Clark Across the Continent*. New York: Harper and Row, 1988.

Malone, Michael, Richard Roeder, and William Lang. *Montana: A History of Two Centuries.* Rev. ed. Seattle: University of Washington Press, 1991.

Malone, Michael P. "The Close of the Copper Century." *Montana: The Magazine of Western History* 35 (spring 1985): 69–73.

Malone, Michael P., and Dianne G. Dougherty. "Montana's Political Culture: A Century of Evolution." *Montana: The Magazine of Western History* 31 (winter 1981): 44–58.

Miller, Don, and Stan Cohen. *Military and Trading Posts of Montana.* Missoula, Mont.: Pictorial Histories Publishing Co., 1978.

Montana Historical Society. *Not in Precious Metals Alone: A Manuscript History of Montana.* Helena, Mont.: Montana Historical Society, 1976.

Moulton, Gary E., ed., *The Journals of the Lewis and Clark Expedition.* 11 vols. Lincoln, Nebr.: University of Nebraska Press, 1987.

Renz, Louis T. *The History of the Northern Pacific Railroad.* Fairfield, Wash.: Ye Galleon Press, 1980.

Schwantes, Carlos A. *Railroad Signatures Across the Pacific Northwest.* Seattle: University of Washington Press, 1993.

Shirley, Gayle C. *More than Petticoats: Remarkable Montana Women.* Helena, Mont.: Falcon Press, 1995.

Spence, Clark C. *Montana: A Bicentennial History.* New York: W. W. Norton and Co., 1978.

Toole, K. Ross. *Montana: An Uncommon Land.* Norman, Okla.: University of Oklahoma Press, 1959.

## THE NORTHERN CORRIDOR

Aasheim, Magnus. *Sheridan's Daybreak: A Story of Sheridan County and Its Pioneers.* Great Falls, Mont.: Blue Print and Letter, 1970.

Brown, Mark. *Before Barbed Wire.* New York: Henry Holt and Co., 1956.

Chittenden, Hiram Martin. *History of Early Steamboat Navigation on the Missouri River: Life and Adventures of Joseph LaBarge.* 2 vols. New York: Francis P. Harper, 1903.

Dalich, Tony. "Shelby's Fabled Day in the Sun: Dempsey vs. Gibbons, Fourth of July, 1923." *Montana: The Magazine of Western History* 15 (summer 1965): 2–23.

Daniels County Bicentennial Committee. *Daniels County History.* Great Falls, Mont.: Blue Print and Letter, 1977.

Diamond Jubilee Committee. *Plentywood Portrait: Toil, Soil, and Oil.* Plentywood, Mont.: Herald Printing, 1987.

Douma, Don. "Second Bonanza: The History of Oil in Montana." *Montana: The Magazine of Western History* 3 (fall 1953): 18–30; 4 (winter 1954): 42–51; 4 (spring 1954): 42–49: 4 (summer 1954): 45-49.

Dusenberry, Verne. "The Rocky Boy Indians." *Montana Magazine of History* 4 (Winter 1954): 1–15.

Ewers, John C. *The Blackfeet: Raiders on the Northwestern Plains.* Norman, Okla.: University of Oklahoma Press, 1958.

Farr, William E. "Sollid Wants to See You: George Sollid, Homestead Locator." *Montana: The Magazine of Western History* 29 (Spring 1979): 16–27.

Flannery, Regina. *The Gros Ventres of Montana.* Washington D.C.: Catholic University of America Press, 1953.

Floerchinger, Dorothy, and Alicia O'Brien. *Conrad: 75 Years of Pride and Progress.* Conrad, Mont.: The Independent Observer, 1985.

*Footprints in the Valley: A History of Valley County, Montana.* 3 vols. Shelby, Mont.: Promoter Publishing, 1991.

Hill County Bicentennial Commission. *Grit, Guts, and Gusto: A History of Hill County.* Havre, Mont.: Hill County Bicentennial Commission, 1976.

Historical Book Committee. *Railroads to Rockets: Diamond Jubilee, Phillips County, Montana.* Malta, Mont.: Historical Book Committee, 1962.

Horner, John R., and James Gorman. *Digging Dinosaurs.* New York: Workman Publishing, 1988.

Johnson, Dorothy M. "Durable Desperado: Kid Curry." *Montana: The Magazine of Western History* 6 (spring 1956): 22–31.

Liberty County Museum. *Our Heritage in Liberty.* Chester, Mont.: Liberty County Museum, 1976.

Lucht, Gary. "Scobey's Touring Pros: Wheat, Baseball, and Illicit Booze." *Montana: The Magazine of Western History* 20 (summer 1970): 88–93.

Montana, Monte. *Monte Montana: Not Without My Horse.* Auga Duke, Calif.: Double M, 1993.

Overholser, Joel. *Fort Benton: World's Innermost Port.* Fort Benton, Mont.: Joel Overholser, 1987.

Phillips County Historical Society. *The Yesteryears.* Malta, Mont.: Phillips County Historical Society, 1978.

Pratt, William C. "Rural Radicalism on the Northern Plains, 1912–1950." *Montana: The Magazine of Western History* 42 (winter, 1992): 42–55.

Saindon, Bob, and Bunky Sullivan. "Taming the Missouri and Treating the Depression: Fort Peck Dam." *Montana: The Magazine of Western History* 27 (summer 1977): 34–57.

Sharp, Paul F. *Whoop-Up Country: The Canadian-American West, 1865–1885.* Helena, Mont.: Historical Society of Montana, 1955.

Thompson, Erwin N. *Fort Union Trading Post: Fur Trade Empire on the Upper Missouri.* Williston, N. Dak.: Fort Union Association, 1994.

Vestal, Stanley. *The Missouri.* New York: Farrar and Rinehart, 1945.

Vichorek, Daniel N. *The Hi-Line: Profiles of a Montana Land.* Helena, Mont.: American and World Geographic, 1993.

Vindex, Charles. "Radical Rule in Montana." *Montana: The Magazine of Western History* 18 (winter 1968): 2–18.

Walter, Dave. "The Baker Massacre." *Montana Magazine,* March/April 1987, 61–68.

Wilson, Gary A. *Honky-Tonk Town: Havre's Bootlegging Days.* Helena, Mont.: Montana Magazine, 1985

## THE CROWN OF THE CONTINENT

Brimlow, George F. "Marias Pass Explorer, John F. Stevens." *Montana Magazine of History* 3 (summer 1953): 39–44.

Buchholtz, C. W. "The Diary of Albert 'Death-on-the-Trail' Reynolds, Glacier National Park, 1912–1913." *Montana: The Magazine of Western History* 35 (winter 1985): 48–59.

———. "The Historical Dichotomy of Use and Preservation in Glacier National Park." Master's thesis, University of Montana, 1969.

———. *Man in Glacier.* West Glacier, Mont.: Glacier Natural History Association, 1976.

De Santo, Jerome. "Drilling at Kintla Lake: Montana's First Oil Well." *Montana: The Magazine of Western History* 35 (winter 1985): 24–37.

———. "The Legendary Joe Cosley." *Montana: The Magazine of Western History* 30 (winter 1980): 12–27.

———. "Missing in Glacier: The Disappearance of the Whitehead Brothers in 1924." *Montana: The Magazine of Western History* 39 (summer 1989): 54–69.

Diettert, Gerald A. *Grinnell's Glacier: George Bird Grinnell and Glacier National Park.* Missoula, Mont.: Mountain Press, 1992.

Glacier Park Foundation. *A History of Many Glacier Hotel.* Minneapolis: Glacier Park Foundation, 1985.

Glacier Park Inc. *Glacier/Waterton Commentary Manual, Bus Drivers–Tour Guides.* West Glacier, Mont.: Glacier Park, Inc., 1991.

Grinnell, George Bird. "The Crown of the Continent." *The Century Magazine,* September 1901, 660–72.

Hanna, Warren L. *Montana's Many-Splendored Glacierland.* Seattle: Superior Publishing, 1976.

———. *Stars over Montana: Men Who Made Glacier National Park History.* West Glacier, Mont.: Glacier Natural History Association, 1988.

Houk, Rose. *Going-to-the-Sun: The Story of the Highway Across Glacier National Park.* West Glacier, Mont.: Glacier Natural History Association, 1984.

Ober, Michael J. "Enmity and Alliance: Park Service-Concessioner Relations in Glacier National Park, 1892–1961." Master's thesis, University of Montana, 1973.

———. "The CCC Experience in Glacier National Park." *Montana: The Magazine of Western History* 26 (summer 1976): 30–39.

———. "Glacier's Skyland Camps." *Montana: The Magazine of Western History* 23 (summer 1973): 30–39.

Olsen, Jack. *Night of the Grizzlies.* New York: G. P. Putnam's Sons, 1969.

Rinehart, Mary Roberts. *Through Glacier Park: Seeing America First with Howard Eaton.* Boston: Houghton Mifflin, 1946.

Robinson, Donald H. *Through the Years in Glacier National Park: An Administrative History.* West Glacier, Mont.: Glacier Natural History Associaton, 1960.

Walter, Dave. "Avalanche on Going-to-the-Sun Road." *Montana Magazine,* July/August 1983, 47–50.

## THE LOGGING FRONTIER

Bicentennial Committee, Bonner School. *A Grass Roots Tribute: The Story of Bonner, Montana.* Missoula, Mont.: Gateway Printing, 1976.

Burk, Dale. *The Clearcut Crisis: Controversy in the Bitterroot.* Great Falls, Mont.: Jursnick Printing, 1970.

Davis, Deborah J. "Gumboot Gamblers: Tales of the Cedar Creek Gold Rush." Manuscript, 1987. Superior, Mont., Mineral Museum and Historical Society, 1987.

Dunbar, Seymour, and Paul C. Phillips, eds. *The Journals and Letters of Major John Owen, Pioneer of the Northwest, 1850–1871.* 2 vols. New York: Edward Eberstadt, 1927.

Elwood, Henry. *Kalispell, Montana and the Upper Flathead Valley.* Kalispell, Mont.: Thomas Printing, 1980.

Fahey, John. *The Flathead Indians.* Norman, Okla.: University of Oklahoma Press, 1974.

Farr, William. "The Big Ditch: Irrigation in the Bitterroot Valley." *Montana Historian* 6 (June 1976): 34–43.

Glover, James M. *A Wilderness Original: The Life of Bob Marshall.* Seattle: The Mountaineers, 1986.

Graetz, Rick. *Montana's Bob Marshall Country.* Helena, Mont.: Montana Magazine, 1985.

Howard, Helen Addison. *Northwest Trail Blazers.* Caldwell, Idaho: Caxton Printers, 1963.

Johnson, Olga W. *Flathead and Kootenay: The Rivers, the Tribes, and the Region's Traders.* Glendale, Calif.: Arthur H. Clark, 1969.

Kidder, John. "Montana Miracle: It Saved the Buffalo." *Montana: The Magazine of Western History* 15 (spring 1965): 52–67.

Manning, Richard. *Last Stand: Logging, Journalism, and the Case for Humility.* Salt Lake City: Peregrine Smith Books, 1991.

McAlear, J. F., and Sharon Bergman. *The Fabulous Flathead: The Story of the Development of Montana's Flathead Indian Reservation.* Polson, Mont.: Reservation Pioneers, 1962.

Merriam, H. G. *The University of Montana: A History.* Missoula, Mont.: University of Montana Press, 1970.

Morrow, Delores. "Our Sawdust Roots: A History of the Forest Products Industry in Montana." Manuscript, 1973. Missoula, Mont., Mansfield Library, University of Montana.

Mullan, Capt. John. *Report on the Construction of a Military Road from Fort Walla Walla to Fort Benton.* Washington D.C.: U.S. Government Printing Office, 1863.

Mullan, Pierce C. "Bitterroot Enigma: Howard Taylor Ricketts and the Early Struggle Against Spotted Fever." *Montana: The Magazine of Western History* (winter 1982): 3–13.

Murphy, James E. *Half Interest in a Silver Dollar: The Saga of Charles E. Conrad.* Missoula, Mont.: Mountain Press, 1983.

Powell, Ada. *The Dalys of the Bitter Root.* Hamilton, Mont.: Ada Powell, 1989.

Rader, Benjamin. "The Montana Lumber Strike of 1917." *Pacific Historical Review* 36 (May 1967): 189–207.

Robbin, R. C. *Flathead Lake: From Glaciers to Cherries.* Bigfork, Mont.: The Bigfork Eagle, 1985.

Schafer, Betty, and Mable Engelter. *Stump Town to Ski Town: The Story of Whitefish, Montana.* Caldwell, Idaho: Caxton Printers, 1973.

Smead, W. H. *Land of the Flatheads: A Sketch of the Flathead Reservation, Montana.* St. Paul: Pioneer Press, 1905.

Spencer, Betty Goodwin. *The Big Blowup: The Northwest's Great Fire.* Caldwell, Idaho: Caxton Printers, 1958.

Spritzer, Donald E. *Waters of Wealth: The Story of the Kootenai River and Libby Dam.* Boulder: Pruett Publishing, 1979.

Stevensville Historical Society. *Montana Genesis.* Missoula, Mont.: Mountain Press, 1971.

Stone, Arthur L. *Following Old Trails.* Missoula, Mont.: Missoulian Publishing, 1913.

Venn, George A. "The Wobblies and Montana's Garden City." *Montana: The Magazine of Western History* 21 (fall 1971): 18–30.

Wilson, Joan Hoff. "Peace Is a Woman's Job, Jeannette Rankin and American Foreign Policy: The Origins of Her Pacifism." *Montana: The Magazine of Western History* 30 (winter 1980): 28–41.

———. "Jeannette Rankin and American Foreign Policy: Her Lifework as a Pacifist." *Montana: The Magazine of Western History.* 30 (spring 1980) 38–53.

## THE MINING FRONTIER

Adams, Duncan. "Montana Superfund Sites: Hopeful or Hopeless?" *Montana Magazine* (September 1994): 80–90.

Bakken, Gordon Morris. "Was There Arsenic in the Air? Anaconda versus the Farmers of Deer Lodge Valley." *Montana: The Magazine of Western History* 41 (summer 1991): 30–41.

Bayne, Nedra. "The Broadwater: Relic of Elegance." *Montana: The Magazine of Western History* 19 (summer 1969): 58–66.

Beaverhead County History Book Association. *The History of Beaverhead County.* Logan, Utah: Herff-Jones, 1990.

Broadwater County Historical Society. *Broadwater Bygones: A History of Broadwater County.* Bozeman, Mont.: Color World of Montana, 1977.

Chadwick, Robert A. "Montana's Silver Mining Era: Great Boom and Great Bust." *Montana: The Magazine of Western History* 32 (spring 1982): 16–31.

Christopherson, Edmund. *The Night the Mountain Fell: The Story of the Montana-Yellowstone Earthquake.* West Yellowstone, Mont.: Yellowstone Publications, 1962.

Cushman, Dan. *Montana: The Gold Frontier.* Great Falls, Mont.: Stay Away Joe Publishers, 1973.

Davis, Jean. *Shallow Diggins: Tales from Montana's Ghost Towns.* Caldwell, Idaho: Caxton Printers, 1962.

Davison, Stanley R., and Rex C. Myers. "Terminus Town: The Founding of Dillon, 1880." *Montana: The Magazine of Western History* 30 (fall 1980): 16–29.

Edgerton, Keith. "A Tough Place to Live: The 1959 Montana State Prison Riot." *Montana: The Magazine of Western History* 42 (winter 1992): 56–69.

Fischer, Karen. "Training Sled Dogs at Camp Rimini, 1942–1944." *Montana: The Magazine of Western History* 34 (winter 1984): 10–19.

Hammond, Helen. *Garnet: Montana's Last Gold Camp.* Missoula, Mont.: Acme Press, 1983.

Jackson, W. Turrentine. "Wells Fargo Stagecoaching in Montana." Parts 1–4 *Montana: The Magazine of Western History* 29 (winter 1979): 40–53; (spring 1979): 38–53; (summer 1979); 56–68 (fall 1979): 52–66.

Karsmizski, Kenneth W. "The Lewis and Clark Caverns: Politics and the Establishment of Montana's First State Park." *Montana: The Magazine of Western History* 31 (fall 1981): 32–45.

Kent, Phillip. *Montana State Prison History.* Deer Lodge, Mont.: Powell County Museum and Arts Foundation, 1979.

Maclean, Norman. *Young Men and Fire.* Chicago: University of Chicago Press, 1992.

Malone, Michael P. *The Battle for Butte: Mining and Politics on the Northern Frontier, 1864–1906.* Seattle: University of Washington Press, 1981.

Mather, R. E., and F. E. Boswell. *Vigilante Victims: Montana's 1864 Hanging Spree.* San Jose: History West Publishing, 1991.

Montana Writers' Program of the Work Projects Administration. *Copper Camp: Stories of the World's Greatest Mining Town, Butte, Montana.* New York: Hastings House, 1943.

Nolon, Edward W. "'Not Without Labor and Expense' The Villard-Northern Pacific Last Spike Excursion, 1883." *Montana: The Magazine of Western History* 33 (summer 1983): 2–11.

Pace, Dick. *Golden Gulch: The Story of Montana's Fabulous Alder Gulch.* Virginia City, Mont.: Dick Pace, 1962.

Paladin, Vivian, and Jean Baucus. *Helena: An Illustrated History.* Norfolk, Va.: Donning Co., 1983.

Powell County Museum and Arts Foundation. *Powell County: Where It All Began.* Deer Lodge, Mont.: Powell County Museum and Arts Foundation, 1989.

Spence, Clark C. *The Conrey Placer Mining Company: A Pioneer Gold-Dredging Enterprise in Montana, 1897–1922.* Helena, Mont.: Montana Historical Society Press, 1989.

Vine, Bob. *Anaconda Memories, 1883–1983.* Butte, Mont.: Artcraft Printers, 1983.

Wolle, Muriel Sibell. *Montana Pay Dirt: A Guide to the Mining Camps of the Treasure State.* Athens, Ohio: Sage Books, 1963.

# THE CENTRAL VALLEYS

Barrows, John R. *Ubet*. Caldwell, Idaho: Caxton Printers, 1936.

Burlingame, Merrill G. *Gallatin County's Heritage, 1805–1976*. Bozeman, Mont.: Gallatin County Bicentennial Committee, 1976.

Cascade County Historical Society. *Stone Age to Space Age in 100 Years*. Great Falls, Mont.: Cascade County Historical Society, 1981.

Cronin, Janet, and Dorothy Vick. *Montana's Gallatin Canyon: A Gem in the Treasure State*. Missoula, Mont.: Mountain Press, 1992.

Dereleth, August. *The Milwaukee Road: Its First 100 Years*. New York: Creative Age Press, 1948.

Donovan, Roberta. *The First 100 Years: A History of Lewistown, Montana*. Lewistown, Mont.: Lewistown News Argus, 1994.

Goeghegan, Patrick. "The Ringling Years: A Circus Empire in the Smith River Valley." *Montana Magazine*, March/April 1986, 14–18.

Grosskopf, Linda. *On Flatwillow Creek*. Los Alamos, N. Mex.: Exceptional Books, 1991.

Jordan, Arthur J. *Jordan*. Missoula, Mont.: Mountain Press, 1984.

Kennedy, Ethel Castner, and Eva Lesell Stober. *Belt Valley History, 1877–1979*. Belt, Mont.: Ethel Kennedy, 1979.

Malone, Michael P. "The Gallatin Canyon and the Tides of History." *Montana: The Magazine of Western History* 23 (summer 1973): 2–17.

McCarter, Steve. *Guide to the Milwaukee Road in Montana*. Helena, Mont.: Montana Historical Society Press, 1992.

McMillan, Marilyn. "An Eldorado of Ease and Elegance: Taking the Waters at White Sulphur Springs, 1866–1904." *Montana: The Magazine of Western History* 35 (spring 1985): 36–49.

Musselshell Valley Historical Museum. *Roundup on the Musselshell*. Roundup, Mont.: Roundup Record-Tribune, 1974.

Petroleum County Public Library. *Pages of Time: A History of Petroleum County*. Lewistown, Mont.: News Argus Printing, 1990.

Rackley, Barbara Fifer. "The Hard Winter, 1886–1887." *Montana: The Magazine of Western History* 21 (winter 1971): 50–59.

Reese, William S. "Granville Stuart of the DHS Ranch, 1879–1887." *Montana: The Magazine of Western History* 31 (summer 1981): 14–27.

Righter, Robert W. "Reaping the Wind: The Jacobs Brothers, Montana's Pioneer Windsmiths." *Montana: The Magazine of Western History* 46 (winter 1996): 38–49.

Roeder, Richard B. "Charles M. Russell and Modern Times." *Montana: The Magazine of Western History* 34 (summer 1984): 2–13.

———. "A Settlement on the Plains: Paris Gibson and the Building of Great Falls." *Montana: The Magazine of Western History* 42 (fall 1992): 4–19.

Rostad, Lee. "Early Railroading in Central Montana." *Montana Magazine*, September/October 1979, 64–70.

——— *Mountains of Gold, Hills of Grass: A History of Meagher County*. Martinsdale, Mont.: Bozeman Fork Publishing, 1994.

Rydell, Robert, Jeffrey Safford, and Pierce Mullan. *In the People's Interest: A Centennial History of Montana State University.* Bozeman, Mont.: Montana State University Foundation, 1992.

Silliman, Lee. "The Carroll Trail: Utopian Enterprise." *Montana: The Magazine of Western History* 24 (spring 1974): 2–17.

Simpson, Ross W. "Church Universal and Triumphant, C.U.T." *Montana Magazine* July/August 1990: 22–31.

Swenson, Janet Milek. *Victims: The Kari Swenson Story.* Boulder: Pruett Publishing, 1989.

Taliaferro, John. *Charles M. Russell: The Life and Legend of America's Cowboy Artist.* Boston: Little, Brown and Co., 1996.

Three Forks Area Historical Society. *Headwaters Heritage History.* Butte, Mont.: Artcraft Printers, 1983.

White, W. Thomas. "Paris Gibson, James J. Hill, and the 'New Minneapolis:' The Great Falls Water Power and Townsite Company, 1882–1908." *Montana: The Magazine of Western History* 33 (summer 1983): 60–69.

Zellick, Anna. "Fire in the Hole: Slovenians, Croatians, and Coal Mining on the Musselshell." *Montana: The Magazine of Western History* 40 (spring 1990): 16–31.

———. "Patriots on the Rampage: Mob Action in Lewistown, 1917–1918." *Montana: The Magazine of Western History* 31 (winter 1981): 30–43.

## THE YELLOWSTONE BASIN

Abbott, E. C. *We Pointed Them North: Recollections of a Cowpuncher.* Norman, Okla.: University of Oklahoma Press, 1955.

Anderson, Paul. "There Is Something Wrong Down Here: The Smith Mine Disaster, Bearcreek, Montana, 1943." *Montana: The Magazine of Western History* 38 (spring 1988): 2–13.

Annin, Jim. *They Gazed on the Beartooths.* 3 vols. Billings, Mont.: Reporter Printing and Supply, 1964.

Baker, Don. *Next Year Country: The Story of Eastern Montana.* Boulder: Fred Pruett Books, 1992.

Barsness, Larry. *Heads, Hides, and Horns: The Compleat Buffalo Book.* Fort Worth: Texas Christian University Press, 1985.

Billings Gazette. *Yellowstone on Fire.* Billings, Mont.: Billings Gazette, 1989.

Brown, Mark H. *The Plainsmen of the Yellowstone.* New York: G. P. Putnam's Sons, 1961.

Brown, Mark H., and W. R. Felton. *The Frontier Years.* New York: Bramhall House, 1965.

Clawson, Roger. *Pompey's Pillar: Crossroads of the Frontier.* Billings, Mont.: Prose Works, 1992.

Drache, Hiram. "Thomas D. Campbell: The Plower of the Plains." *Agricultural History* 51 (January 1977): 78–91.

Dusenberry, Verne. "The Northern Cheyenne: All They Have Asked Is to Live in Montana." *Montana Magazine of History* 5 (winter 1955): 23–40.

Evans, William B., and Robert L. Peterson. "Decision at Colstrip: The Northern Pacific Railway's Open-Pit Mining Operation." *Pacific Northwest Quarterly* 61 (July 1970): 129–36.

Fox, Richard Allen, Jr. *Archaeology, History, and Custer's Last Battle: The Little Big Horn Reexamined.* Norman, Okla.: University of Oklahoma Press, 1993.

Green, Jerome A. "The Hayfield Fight: A Reappraisal of a Neglected Action." *Montana: The Magazine of Western History* 22 (fall 1972): 30–43.

Heidenriech, C. Adrian. "The Native Americans' Yellowstone." *Montana: The Magazine of Western History* 35 (fall 1985): 2–17.

Hoxie, Frederick E. *Parading Through History: The Making of the Crow Nation in America, 1805–1935.* Cambridge, England: Cambridge University Press, 1995.

Huntley Project History Committee. *Sod 'n Seed 'n Tumbleweed; A History of the Huntley Project.* Ballantine, Mont.: Huntley Project History Committee, 1977.

James, H.S. *Geologic and Historic Guide to the Beartooth Highway, Montana and Wyoming.* Helena, Mont.: Montana Bureau of Mines and Geology, Special Publication 110, 1995.

Jensen, Joyce. *Pieces and Places of Billings History: Local Markers and Sites.* Billings, Mont.: Western Heritage Center, 1994.

Lampi, Leona. "Red Lodge and the Festival of Nations." *Montana: The Magazine of Western History* 11 (summer 1961): 20–31.

Lass, William E. "Steamboats on the Yellowstone." *Montana: The Magazine of Western History* 35 (fall 1985): 26–41.

Lucey, Donna M. *Photographing Montana, 1894–1928: The Life and Work of Evelyn Cameron.* New York: Alfred A. Knopf, 1991.

MacDonald, Marie. *Glendive: The History of a Montana Town.* Glendive, Mont.: Gateway Press, 1968.

McLemore, Clyde. "Fort Pease: The First Attempted Settlement in Yellowstone Valley." *The Montana Magazine of History* 2 (January 1952): 17–32.

Mondak Historical and Art Society. *Focus on Our Roots: The Story of Sidney and Surrounding Area.* Sidney, Mont.: Mondak Historical and Art Society, 1989.

O'Brien, Bob R. "The Roads of Yellowstone, 1870–1915." *Montana: The Magazine of Western History* 17 (summer 1967): 30–39.

Prairie County Historical Society. *More Wheels Across Montana's Prairie.* Terry, Mont.: Prairie County Historical Society, 1976.

Raynolds, Bvt. Brig. Gen. W. F. *Report on the Exploration of the Yellowstone River.* Washington D.C.: Government Printing Office, 1868.

Rostad, Lee. *Fourteen Cents and Seven Green Apples: The Life and Times of Charles Bair.* Great Falls, Mont.: C. M. Russell Museum, 1992.

Utley, Robert M. "Whose Shrine Is It? The Ideological Struggle for Custer Battlefield." *Montana: The Magazine of Western History* 42 (winter 1992): 70–74.

Vaughn, J. W. *The Reynolds Campaign on Powder River.* Norman, Okla.: University of Oklahoma Press, 1961.

Welsh, Donald. "Pierre Wibaux, Cattle King." Pamphlet. Reprint, State Historical Society of North Dakota, Bismarck, 1953.

White, W. Thomas. "Boycott: The Pullman Strike in Montana." *Montana: The Magazine of Western History* 29 (fall 1979): 2–13.

Whithorn, Doris. *Twice Told Tales on the Upper Yellowstone.* Livingston, Mont.: Doris S. Whithorn, 1994.

Wiltsey, Norman B. "Plenty Coups: Statesman Chief of the Crows." *Montana: The Magazine of Western History* 13 (fall 1963): 28–39.

Wright, Kathryn. *Billings: The Magic City and How It Grew.* Billings, Mont.: K. H. Wright, 1978.

Zupan, Shirley, and Harry J. Owens. *Red Lodge: Saga of a Western Area.* Red Lodge, Mont.: Carbon County Historical Society, 1979.

# INDEX

A & S Industries, 22
Abasaroka-Beartooth Wilderness, 351
Abbott, Teddy Blue, 297, 386
Abe Lincoln Gulch, 264
Absarokee, 346
Adams, John Q., 319
Adams Hotel, 310
Adobetown, 238
Adolf, Chief, 144
Aerial Fire Depot, 262
African Americans, 55, 106, 225, 273, 372
AIM. *See* American Indian Movement
Albert, Prince of Belgium, 250
Alberton, 142–43
Alder Creek, 37
Alder Gulch, xi, 5, 197, 198, 237–39, **237**
Alexander, Thomas, 371
Allard, Charles, 169, 170
Allen, (Col.) J. I., 347
Alexander, Chief, 144
Altman Taylor tractor, 361, **362**
Altyn, 117–18
Alzada, 380
Amalgamated Copper Co., xiii, 213,
    214, 216, 278
Amalgamated Sugar Co., 244
American Bison Society, 171
American Fur Co., xi, 4, 16, 20, 54
American Indian Movement, 363, **364**,
    377
American Legion, xiv, 95
American Protective Association, 215
American Railway Union, 343
Amsterdam, 320–21
Amtrak, 342
Anaconda, xii, xiv, 8, 11, 176, 188, 202,
    210, 211, 213, 217–20, 249, 257, 283
Anaconda Co., xii, xiv, 7–10, 133, 149,
    153, 163, 174–76, 188, 199, 210–
    20, 282, 283, 325, 349
Anaconda smelter, 8, 11

Anderson, Bob, 361
Anderson, "Skookum Joe," 295
Antelope, **10**
Ap-ah-ki, 114
apex law, 214
Apgar, 100
Apgar, Dimon, 112
apples, 185–87
Arapaho tribe, 39, 376
Arapooish, Chief, 331
ARCO. *See* Atlantic Richfield Co.
Aricara tribe, 334
Arlee, Chief, 144
Armstrong, (Capt.) M. W., 98
Army Corps of Engineers, 87
Aronson, Hugo, 70
Arrow Lake, 109
Ashland, 376–77
Ashley Creek, 174
Assiniboine tribe, 6, 15, 20, 22, 23, 31,
    38–40, 84, 334
Astor, John Jacob, 4
Astoria, 174
Atlantic Richfield Co., xiv, 10, 199, 210,
    216, 219
Audubon, John James, 121
Audubon Society, 123
Augusta, 262–65
Avalanche Creek, 101
Avalanche Creek campground, 106
Avery, Idaho, 270, 312
Avon, 258

Babb, 123
Bainville, 20, 397
Bair, Alberta, 316
Bair, Charles M., 315–17, **316**
Bair, Marguerite, 316
Bair Reservoir, 307
Baker, 383–84
Baker, A. G., 384

411

Baker, (Bvt. Col.) Eugene M., 6, 68
Baker, Charles, 59
Baker, Isaac G., 56
Baker, Washington, 252
Baker Dome, 384
Baker Massacre, xii, 6, 67, 68, 274
Ballantine, 368
Bannack, xi, 5, 198, **198**, 207, 227–29,
    **228**, 235, 236, 238, 239
Banner County, 289
Barker, 284
Barrette, Louis, 141
Barrows, A. R., 314
Barrows, Alice, 314
baseball. *See* Scoby Giants
Basin, 245
Basin Creek, 245
basketball, Fort Shaw Indian School girls'
    team, 274, **274**
Beach, Ed, 314
Bear Creek, 91, 92, 201–2
Bearcreek, xiv, 353–54, **354**
Bear Gulch, 198, 200, 338, 339
Bearmouth, 200–201, **201**
bears. *See* grizzly bears
Bear's Paw Battle, 6, 43–45. *See also* Nez
    Perce tribe
Bear's Paw Mountains, 43, 49, 51
Beartooth Highway, xiii, 351, 352
Beartooth Mountains, 349, 352
Beartooth Plateau, 351
Beaton, George "Blackie," 112
Beaverhead County, 224
Beaverhead River, 5, 197, 228, 232, 233
Beaverhead Rock, 232, 233
Beaverhead Valley, 225–27
beaver slide, 231–32, **232**
Beaverslide, 78
Beaver Valley, 394
beets. See sugar beets
Belfry, 354–55
Belfry, (Dr.) William, 354
Belgrade, 321–22
Belknap, 173
Belly River, 126
Belt, 282–84, **283**
Belt Creek, 284
Belton, 85, 86, 94, 99, 100, 105–7, 116
Benetsee, 197
Benson, Amos, 341

Benson's Landing, 341
Benton, Thomas Hart, 54
Berger, Clemence Gurneau, 267, 269
Berkeley Pit, 11, 210, 216
Berlin Airlift, 281
Bielenberg, John, 207
Big Bear, 51
Big Belt Mountains, 252
Big Coulee Valley, 310
Big Ditch, 185–86, **186**
Big Dry, 31
Big Dry River, 269, 302, 394
Big Hole Basin, 194
Big Hole Battle, xii, 229–31, 274, 286.
    *See also* Nez Perce tribe
Big Hole Battlefield National Monu-
    ment, 229–31, **230**
Big Hole River, 197, 229, 233
Big Hole Valley, 231, 232
Bighorn River, 317, 333, 334, 361
Big Mountain Ski Resort, 155–57, **156**
Big Muddy Creek, 21, 26
Big Open, 269
Big Sandy, 41, 52–53, **52**
Big Sky Ski Resort, 328
Big Snowy Mountains, 313
Big Timber, 344–46, **345**
Big Timber Creek, 345
Bigfork, 164, 174
Bighorn, 369
Bighorn Canyon, 366
Bighorn River, xi, 317, 333–35, 361,
    366, 369
Billings, 78, 244, 254, 288, 289, 310, 313–
    16, 335, 336, 348, 351, 355, 356, 358–
    60, **359**, 366, 367, 371, 381, 382
Billings, Frederick, 204, 358
Billings Brewing Co., **359**, 360
Billings Sugar Co., 359
Billy the Kid, 171–72
Bi-metallic Mine, 223, **223**
Bindler, A. J., 119
Birch Creek, 77
Bird Tail Rock, 282
bison, 7, 75, 169–71, 320, 335, 386;
    bison range, *see* National Bison Range
Bitter Root, 187
Bitter Root Inn, 187, **187**
Bitterroot Mountains, 131, 135, 137,
    138, 140, 141, 180, 182, 192

bitterroot plant 182, 183
Bitterroot River, 43, 133, 146, 180, 181, 185, 188, 194
Bitterroot Stock Farm, 187
Bitterroot Valley, xii, 131, 132, 135, 144, 182–85, 188, 190, 229
Bitterroot Valley Irrigation Co., 185, 187
Black Eagle Falls, 278
Black Elk, 323
Blackfeet Agency, 75, 77, 91, 92
Blackfeet Reservation, 29, 51, 74–76, 84, 88, 100
Blackfeet tribe, 3, 6, 15, 18, 20, 39, 51, 54, 63, 64, 66–68, 73, 74, 76, 78, 84, 85, 89–91, 114, 117, 119, 121, 125, 132, 169, 173, 174, 269, 273, 274, 279, 281, 297, 318, 323, 334, 365, 376. *See also* Piegan tribe
Blackfoot City, 137
Blackfoot River, 136, 145, 175, 176–77, 181, 197, 265
Black Sox scandal, 28
Blaine County, 42, 43
Blood tribe, 279
Bloody Knife, 26
Bloom Cattle Co., 35
Bob Marshall Wilderness Area, 178–80. *See also* Marshall, Bob
Bodmer, Karl, viii, xi, 16
Bogert, John, 323
Bole, William, 52
Bonner, xiii, 153, 174–77, **175**
Bonner, Edward L., 149, 175
Boone and Crockett Club, 123
Boothill Cemetery, 357–58
bootlegging, 47–48, 126, 224, 265, 309, 328, 350. *See also* prohibition.
Boston and Montana Co., 278
Boulder, 244–47, 348
Boulder Hot Springs, 245–46, **246**
Boulder River, 345, 346
Bourke-White, Margaret, 34
Bovey, Charles, 239
Bovey, Sue, 239
Bowles, John, 291
Bowman Lake, 97, **98**
Box Elder River, 270
Boyle, Tony, 309
Bozeman, 190, 291, 321–27, 355, 369
Bozeman, John M., xii, 5, 322–23, **322**

Bozeman Pass, 204, 323
Bozeman Trail, 5, 323, 366
Bradley, Abraham Lincoln, 263
Brandvold, Marion, 79
Brewer, James Scott, 284
Brewster Brothers Transportation Co., 114
Bridger, 353, 355
Bridger, Jim, 323, 334, 355, 391
Briggs, Charles, 151
British Northwest Expedition, 84
Broaddus, Oscar, 378, 379
Broadus, 377–79
Broadwater, Charles A., 198, 254, 255
Broadwater County, 253
Broadwater Hotel and Natatorium, 254–55, **255**
Brockway, 304, 305
Brooke, (Maj.) E. G., 244
Brown, "Kootenai," 126
Brown, William, 258
Browning, 76, 77
Bryan, William Jennings, 7
Bucket of Blood, 342
bucking-horse sale, 374
Buffalo Bill's Wild West Show, 363
Buffalo Rapids Project, 392
bullboat, 16
Bullhook Bottoms, 45
Bullion Mine, 138
Bull Mountains, 307, 308
bull train, 66
Burd, Julian, 77, 78
Burk, Dale, 192
Burke, Walter, 310
Burlingame, Merrill, 269, 325
Burlington Northern Railroad, 29, 283
Burns, Mag, 374
Busby, 376
Bush, Harry, 338
Butte, xiii, xiv, 5, 8, 32, 133, 147, 163, 175, 176, 187, 189, 199, 209–17, **212**, **215**, 231, 246, 255, 259, 297, 348, 354
Butte Oil Co., 99, 100
Buttrey, Frank A., 48–49
Buttrey's Department Store, 48–49, **48**, **49**
Bynum, 78–79
Byrd, (Adm.) Richard, 306

Cabin Creek Oil Field, 384

Cabinet Gorge, 171
Cabinet Mountains, 154
Calamity Jane, 343, 360
Camas Prairie Hot Springs, 172–73, **172**
Cameron, Evelyn, 388–90, **389**
Cameron, Ewen, 388–90
Cameron, Walter, 336
Camp Baker, 269, 285, 286, 295
Camp Beartooth, 351
Campbell, Alicia, 162
Campbell, Gordon, 64
Campbell, Sadie, 274
Campbell, Thomas D., 361, 362
Campbell wheat farm, 361–62, **362**
Camp Cooke, 269
Camp Disappointment, 73
Camp Fortunate, 224
Camp Lewis, 291, 295
Camp Reynolds, 273
Camp Sawtooth, 351
Camp Three, 309
Canadian Pacific Railroad, 57, 66
Cantonment Jordan, 136
Cantrell, "Floppin' Bill," 38
Canyon Creek, 118, 265, 266, 356
Canyon Ferry Reservoir, 253
capital, competition to become, 218,
    219, 249
capitol building, 249, **249**, 348
Cargill, W. G., 69
Carignano, Joseph, 169
Carlton, 355
Carroll, Matthew, 295
Carroll Trail, 286, 291, 295, 314, 315
Carson, Kit, 194
Carter, Claude, 384
Carter, Thomas, 259
Carter County Museum, 386
Carter Oil, 360
Cascade, 281
Cassidy, Butch, 40, **41.**
Castle, 286, 311
Castle Mountains, 286
Castner, John K., 282
Castner, Mattie, 282
Cat Creek, 300–302, **301**
cattle industry, xii, 7, 29, 36, 270
CCC. *See* Civilian Conservation Corps
Cedar Creek, 141, 142
Centennial Mountains, 224

Centennial Valley, 224
Champion International Corporation,
    176, 193
Channel, Ada, 369, 370
Charbonneau, Jean Baptiste, 368
Charles M. Russell National Wildlife
    Refuge, 38
Charlo, Chief, xii, 143–44, **143**, 145,
    182, 184
cherries, 164
Chester, 57–60
Chester Trading Co., 59–60, **60**
Chestnut Valley, 281
Cheyenne tribe, xii, 6, 334, 335, 347, 362–
    66, 372, 375, 379, 380, 388. *See also*
    Northern Cheyenne tribe
Chicago, Burlington & Quincy Railroad,
    355, 360
Chicago, Milwaukee, St. Paul & Pacific
    Railroad. *See* Milwaukee Road
Chief Joseph Pass, 227
Chief Mountain International Highway,
    125
chiefs, Indian. *See under individual names.*
Chinese Americans, 55, 141, 161, 239,
    296; rail workers 171, 204
Chinook, 36, 39, 42–43, 45, 57
*Chippewa,* 17, 54
Chippewa tribe, 22, 50–52
Chittenden, Hiram M., 17, 54
Choteau, 77, 78
Chouteau County, 16, 31, 57
Christian Reformed Church, 321
Church Universal and Triumphant, 339–
    40
Cinnabar, 337, 338
Circle, 305–6, **306,** 398
Circle C, 35, 37, 70
Civilian Conservation Corps, 24, 87,
    **105,** 105–6, **243**
Civil War, 5
Clark, Herman, 358
Clark, William, 181, 231, 232, 275, 317,
    323, 334, 345, 368, 369, 391, 398. *See
    also* Lewis and Clark expedition
Clark, William Andrews, xiii, 8, 176,
    198, 210, 211–12, 213, 218, 249
Clark Canyon Reservoir, 224
Clark City, 341
Clarke, Malcolm, 67

Clark Fork River, 131, 132, 134–36, 142, 143, 145–46, 171, 173, 181, 197, 200, 206, 210

Clark Fork Valley, 131, 139

Clarks Fork of the Yellowstone River, 333, 334, 355

Clay, John, 385

clear-cutting, 192–93, **192**

Clearwater Forest, 138

Clearwater River, 177, 181

Clyde Park, 343, 344

coal, 9, 10; in Belt 282, **283**; in Bearcreek 353, 354; in Colstrip 380–82, **381**; on Northern Cheyenne Reservation 377; in Red Lodge 349, 350; in Roundup 307–9, **308**; severance tax on, xiv, 9

Coal Bank Landing, 52

Coburg, 30

Coeur d'Alene, Idaho, 134, 136

Coeur d'Alene Forest, 138

Collins, Mike, 61

Colstrip, 350, 380–82, **381**

Colter, John, 317, 318

Columbia Falls, 153, 163

Columbia Gardens, 215

Columbia Gorge, 131

Columbia River, 173, 174

Columbus, 346–48, **347**

communism, 24–25, 147, 148

Confederate Gulch, 198, 252, **253**, 269, 285

Conley, Frank, 207, 208

Connie the Cowboy Queen, 374

Conrad, 68, 70–72

Conrad, Alicia, 159–62, **160**

Conrad, Charles E., 56, 70, 159–61, **159**

Conrad, John, 56

Conrad, William G., 56, 69–70, 75, 159–61

Conrad brothers. *See* Conrad, Charles E. *and* William G.

Conrad Mansion, 161–62, **161**

Conrad National Bank, 161

Conrey Placer Mining Co., 237, 238

conscientious objectors. *See under* World War II

Constitutional Convention of 1972, xiv, 9

Continental Oil Co., 302, 360

Cooke City, 351–53, **353**

Cooley, Earle, 260

Coolidge, Calvin, 111, 123, 390

Coonsah, 91

Cooper, Walter, 324, 327

copper, xiv, 8, 178, 199, 209–20. *See also* Anaconda Co.

copper kings, war of, 8. *See also* Daly, Marcus, *and* Clark, William Andrews

Coram, 163

Cordova Lode, 220

Corinne, Utah, 225

Corvallis, 185, 188

Corwin Hot Springs, 339

Cosley, Joe, 126–28, **127**

Cosley Lake, 126

Coulson, 335, 356–58, **357**

Coulson Park, 356

Council Grove, 142, 144

Countryman, Horace, 346, 347

county splitting, 31

Cox, Sidney, 149

Cracker Lake, 117

Craighead, Edwin, 149

Cramer Gulch, 133

Cramer House, 258

Crane, Jimmy, 395

Crazy Horse, Chief, 380

Crazy Mountains, 346

Cree tribe, 15, 35, 50–52

Crook, (Brig. Gen.) George, 375, 379. *See also* Rosebud Battle

crosses, white roadside, xiv, 94–95

Crow Agency, 346

Crow Reservation, 315, 316, 343, 360–62, 365–67, 369, 376

Crow tribe, 3, 6, 20, 182, 238, 269, 273, 291, 318, 323, 333, 334, 344, 349, 356, 361, 362, 365–68, 375

Crum, (Judge) Charles, 372

Cruse, Mamie, 259

Cruse, Thomas, 250, 258, 259, 299

Cuban Missile Crisis, 288

Culbertson, 21

Culbertson, Alexander, 20, 21, 54

Culbertson, Jack, 21

Culp, Dave, 264

Culver Military Academy, 97

Curry, Kid, 38, 40–41, **41**

Cushman, Dan, 198, 228

Custer, Elizabeth, 363

Custer, (Lt. Col.) George Armstrong, 114, 121, 363, 364, 369, 376. *See also* Little Bighorn, Battle of
Custer Creek, 387
*Custer Died for Your Sins,* 363
Custer Hill, 363
Custer Trail, 383
Cut Bank, 72–74, **73**
Cut Bank Chalet, 90
Cut Bank Creek, 73
Cut Bank Pass, 84, 85
CUT church. *See* Church Universal and Triumphant
Cutter, Kirtland, 161

Daly, Marcus, xii, 8, 175, 176, 187–90, **188**, 210, 212, 213, 217–19, 257
Daly mansion, 189
Daniels County, 27
Darby, 132, 133, 185, 186, 192
Darby Lumber Co., 193
Davis, Jefferson, 238
Dawes Act, 164
Dawson County, 31, 391
Dawson Lumber Co., 154
Day, Victor, 69
Deacon, Richard, 226
Deaf Charlie, 40
Dearborn County, 281
DeBorgia, 139
Deer Lodge, xii, 134, 198, 202, 206, 207, 209, 231, 359. *See also* Montana State Prison
Deer Lodge Valley, 197, 199, 206, 207, 210
Deidesheimer, Philip, 221, 222
Demers, Telesphore J. "Jake," 157
Demersville, 157–60, **158**, 263
Dempsey, Jack, xiii, 61–63, **63**
Dennis, F. M. "Pomp," 252
Denton, 289, 290
Depew, Harry, 151
Depression, Great. *See* Great Depression
De Smet, (Fr.) Pierre Jean, xi, 183, 334
de Trobriand, (Gen.) Philippe Regis, 68
Devil's Brigade, 251
DHS Ranch, 297
Diamond City, 252, 253
Diamond Ranch, 21
Diamond R Freight Co., 254, 295

Diamond S Ranch, 246
Dick the Diver, 171, 172
Dillon, 198, 226–29, **227**, 232, 233
Dillon, Sidney, 226
Dimsdale, Thomas, 235, 236
Dinah Miner. *See under* mules
dinosaurs, 79
Dirty Shame Saloon, 28
Dixon, 169
Dixon, Joseph M., xiii, 191, 208
Dodge, B. Wagner, 262
dogs. *See* sled dogs
Doig, Ivan, 287
Donaldson, John, 28
Dornix, 345
Doty, John, 84
Douglas, Henry, 391
Dow, Edward, 104
dredge mining, 5, 237–38, **237**
Drumlummon Mine, 258–60, **259**
Ducat, Roy, 108
Duck Lake, 123
Dull Knife, Chief, 376
Dunn, Paul, 109
Dupuyer, 77, 78
Durfee, E. H., 31
Dutch Henry, 26
Dutton, 65, 72

Eagle's Nest, 346
Eaheart, Floyd, 95
Earling, Albert J., 142
Earth Angel Mine, 245
Earthquake Lake, 240, **241**
earthquakes, xiii, 240, 241, 250, 255
East Glacier, 83, 86, 88–90, 94, 114, **115**
Eastside Highway, 185, 187
Eaton, Howard, 125
Eddy, Richard A., 175, 176
Edgar, Henry, 238
Edgerton, Sidney, 236
Edison, Thomas A., 313
Egg Mountain, 78, 79
Ekalaka, 384–86, **385**
Elkhorn, 7, 198, 246, **247**
Elkhorn River, 247
Ellison, 257, 258
Elrod, Morton J., 164
Emery, Rowe, 115, 116
Emigrant, 340

Emrick, E. B., 70
Ennis, 239–41
Ennis, William J., 239, 240
Environmental Protection Agency, 210
Essex, 93, 94, 161
Eureka, 132, 151–53
Eureka Lumber Co., 153
Evarts, William, 204
Excelbee, George, 380
Exeter, 40, 41
Eyler, Fr. John, 377

Fairfield, 79
Fairmont Hot Springs, 211
fair-trials bill, 8, 214
Fairview, 396, 398
Fairview State Bank, robbery of, 398
Fairweather, William, 238
Fallon, Charles, 292
Farlin, William L., 211
Farmer-Labor Party, 25
Farr, Hiram, 174
Farr, William, 75
*Far West,* 335
Felsh, Happy, 28
Fergus County, 291, 292, 298, 302
Fergus County High School, 294, **294.**
    *See also* Lewistown
Ferris, Charlie, 384
Festival of Nations, 350
Fiedler, Leslie, 149
Field, Joseph, 275
Fields, Reuben, 73
Fifty Mountain, 124
Finlay, Francois 197
fire. *See* forest fires
Fisher, Arthur, 199
Fisk, James Liberty, 17
Fitzpatrick, Tom, 194
Flathead Irrigation Project, 165, 166
Flathead Lake, 1, 133, 157, 162, 164,
    **165**, 173, 178
Flathead Reservation, xi, 51, 131, 157,
    164–66, 168–70, 171, 173. *See also*
    Salish tribe
Flathead River, 94, 131, 159; North Fork,
    *see* North Fork of the Flathead River
Flathead tribe. *See* Salish tribe
Flathead Valley, 132, 159
Flatwillow Creek, 299

Flint Creek, 197, 220, 222
floods of 1964, 77, 94
Floweree, Dan, 270
Flying E, 369
Flying U, 78
Flynn, Elizabeth Gurley, 147
Ford, Robert S., 270
Ford's Creek, 297
Forest City, 142
forest fires: of 1910, xiii, 137–40, **138,**
    154; in Canyon Creek, 265, 266; in
    Glacier National Park, 96, 97, 120,
    121; in Mann Gulch, 260–62; in
    Yellowstone National Park, xiv, 352,
    353
Forest Service. *See* U.S. Forest Service
Forsyth, 335, 336, 370–72, 381
Forsyth, (Col.) James W., 371
Forsyth Springs, 372
Fort Abraham Lincoln, 383
Fort Assinniboine, xii, 45, 49–50, **50,**
    52, 91
Fort Belknap, 39
Fort Belknap Reservation, 37–40, **39**
Fort Benton, xi, 4, 5, 16–18, 54–57, **55,**
    64–66, **67,** 70, 121, 134–36, 197,
    257, 276, 282, 289, 295, 309, 310,
    314, 369
Fort Buford, 22
Fort Cass, 369
Fort C. F. Smith, 323, 366
Fort Connah, 167
Fort Custer, xii
Fort Ellis, xii, 269, 323, 369
Fort Fetterman, 379
Fort Fizzle, 181–82
Fort Henry, 369
Fort Keogh, xii, 6, 44, 372, **373,** 376, 383
Fort Leavenworth, 45
Fort Lewis, 54
Fort Logan, 6
Fort Maginnis, 295, 297, **298,** 299
Fort Manuel, 369
Fort McKenzie, xi, 16
Fort Missoula, xii, 147, 229
Fort Owen, 183–85
Fort Peck, 31, 32
Fort Peck Dam, xiii, 10, 30–35, **33**
Fort Peck Reservation, 21–23, 30, 361
Fort Piegan, 16

Fort Raymond, 369
Fort Shaw, xii, 68, 229, 269, 273, **274**
Fort Shaw Indian School, 274
Fort Union, xi, 16, 20–21, 74
Fort Union Formation, 380
Fort Van Buren, 369
Fort William Henry Harrison, 251
Fortine, 153
France, Johnny, 329
Francis, Ed, 340
Frederick, (Col.) Robert T., 251
Fred Robinson Bridge, 298, 299
Free Enterprise Mine, 245
Freemen, xiv, 303–4
French Charley, 154
Frenchtown, 144
Fromberg, 355
fur traders, 4

Galata, 60
Galbraith, Jack, 115
Gall, 22, 27
Gallatin Canyon, 326–28
Gallatin City, 318
Gallatin Gateway, 326
Gallatin Gateway Inn, 326, **326**
Gallatin Mountains, 327
Gallatin River, 269, 317, 318, 323, 327
Gallatin Valley, 322
Gallup City, 70
Gambler Brown, 303
Garden Wall, 102, 120
Gardiner, 337, 338
Gardiner, Johnston, 338
Garfield, (Gen.) James A,. 144
Garfield County, 269, 302, 303
Garneil, 313, 314
Garnet,199, 201–3, **203**
Garnet Mountains, 202
Garrison, 135, 203
Garrison Junction, 207
Gates of the Rocky Mountains, 260
Gaucher, Peter, 183
Gebo, 355
George, James "Yankee Jim," 340
Georgetown Reservoir, 220
Georgia Peace Society, 148
Geyser, 288
Ghekiere family, 19
Giant Springs State Park, 276

Gibbon, (Col.) John, 229–31
Gibbons, Tommy, xiii, 61–63, **63**
Gibbon's Pass, 181, 231
Gibson, James, 78
Gibson, Paris, 276–78, **276**
Gignilliat, Fred, 97
Gignilliat, Leigh, 98
Gignilliat, (Col.) L. R., 97–99
Gilbert, Cass, 250
Gildart, Bert, 109
Gildford, 58
Gilman, 263, 264
Gilman State Bank, **263**
Gilmore, Debby, 43
Gilt Edge, 295, 296
Glacial Lake Missoula, 131
Glacier National Park, 74, 76, 81–128,
    255: avalanches in, 111–13, **113**;
    chalets in, 88, 90, 104, 117; Civilian
    Conservation Corps in, 105–6, **105**;
    conservation efforts in, 87– 88;
    exploration of, 84–85; flood of 1964
    in, 94;  forest fires in, 96–97, 120–
    21; founding of, 85–86, 123;
    geologic formation of, 83–84; grizzly
    bears in, 107–9, **108**; horse tours in,
    123–25; mining near, 117–18; Native
    Americans in, 84; oil in, 99–100,
    117–18; railroad promotion of, 86,
    88–90; Skyland camp, 97; tour buses
    in, 114–16, **115**; U.S.-Canadian
    boundary survey of, 125–26.
Glacier Park Hotel, 88, **89**, 107
Glacier Park Saddle Horse Co., 97, 123,
    125
Glacier Park Transportation Co., 115–16
Glasgow, 30, 31, 35, 41
Glasgow Air Base, 30
Glendive, 303–5, 335, 336, 371, 384,
    386, 387, 391–93, **392**, 398
Glendive Creek, 391
Goathaunt, 124
Going-to-the-Sun Chalet, 90
Going-to-the-Sun Road, 86, **87**, 94, 100–
    103, **101**, **103**, 106, 107, 111–113
gold, discovery of, xi, 5. *See also* Alder
    Gulch *and* Grasshopper Creek
Gold Creek, 197, 203–5
Golden Valley County, 310
Goos, Ida, 81

Gore, Sir George, 391
Gourley, James, 352
Grand Union Hotel, 57
Granite, 7, 199, 222–24, **223**
Granite Mountain, 222–24
Granite Mountain Mine, 223
Granite Park, 120
Granite Park Chalet, 90, 107–10
Grant, Ulysses S., 144, 205
Grant Creek, 147
Grant-Kohrs ranch, 206–7, **206**
Grasshopper Creek, xi, 5, 197, 198, 228, 229
Grass Range, 299
Graves, A. C., 312
Great Bear Wilderness Area, 94
Great Depression, 25, 32, 74, 90, 106, 166, 207, 281, 306, 362
Great Falls, viii, xiv, 11, 61, 64, 151, 167, 176, 202, 219, 239, 263, 265, 271, 274–83, 287–89, 296, 313, 314
Great Falls & Canada Railway, 61
Great Falls of the Missouri River, 3, 16, 274–77, **275**
Great Falls smelter, xiv, 11, **277**, 278
Great Northern Railway, xii, 7, 17–19, **18**, 21, 23, 27, 30, 40, 45, 57, 60, 61, 70, 73, 76, 78, 132, 151, 153–55, 162, 163, 260, 263, 270, 283, 288, 289, 305, 313, 355, 397; in Glacier National Park, xii, 84–86, 88, 90, 91–94, 99, 104, 106, 107, 116, 119, 121, 123; in Kalispell area, 157–60
Great Northwest Log Haul, 192, 193
Great Western Sugar Co., 355, 359
Greeley, William, 139
Greenough, Alice, 350, 351
Greenough, Ben, 350
Greenough, Marge, 350
Greenough, Myrtle, 350
Greenough, Turk, 350
Gregson Springs, 211
Grinnell, Elizabeth, 123
Grinnell, George Bird, 40, 85, 114, 121–23, **122**
Grinnell Glacier, 121–23, **122**
Grisy, Gus, 394
grizzly bear, 16, 107–9 **108**, 275
Gros Ventre tribe, 3, 6, 15, 38–40, 376
Grote, Floyd, 167

Gunsight Lake, 90
Gunsight Pass 107, 122
Gunther, John, 3
Guthrie, A. B., Jr., 78

Hager, Ben, 347
Half-breed Crossing, 302
Hall, Charles, 30
Hall, F. A., 354
Hamilton, 185, 187–91, 219
Hamilton, Alfred, 66
Hammond, Andrew B., 175, 176
Hanks, Camilla. *See* Deaf Charlie
Hanley, Michael, 318
Hardin, 360, 361, 365
Harlem, 30, 38–40
Harlow, Richard A., 286, 315, 311
Harlowton, 270, 311–13
Harrison, 242
Harvard University, 237, 238
Haugan, 139
Hauser, Samuel T., 297
Havre, xii, 17–19, 29, 45–49, **46**, 52, 57–59, 78, 91, 278, 348; underground Havre, 45, 48
Havre Bunch, 47
Hay, George, 288
Hays, 38
Haystack Creek funnel, 111–13, **113**
haystacks, 231, 232
Healy, John J., 66
heap roasting, 209
Heaven's Peak, 120, 121
Heavy Breast, Chief, 89
Heavy Runner, Chief, 68
Hebgen Lake, 240
Hedges, Cornelius, 195, 197
Heimes, Joseph, 127
Heinze, Fritz Augustus, xiii, 8, 213–14, **213**
Helena, xii, xiii, 5, 8, 18, 135, 167, 197–99, 204, 213, 218, 231, 236, 246, 248–52, 254, 255, 259, 262, 264, 265, 279, 282, 295, 311, 314, 315, 321, 348; mansion district, 249
Helgeson, Julie, 108–10
Hellgate, 132, 145, 185
Hell Gate Canyon, 133, 137, 181
Hellgate Trading Post, 145
Hellgate Treaty, xi, 144, 164

Hell-roaring Ski Club, 155
Hensley, Lafe, 286
Hidatsa tribe, 365
Hidden Lake, 106, 126
Higgins, Christopher P., 145, 149
Highway Commission. *See* Montana
    Highway Commission
Highway Patrol. *See* Montana Highway
    Patrol
Hi-line, 19, 20, 30, 31, 36, 40, 42, 47,
    48, 57, 60, 70
Hill, James J., 7, 17–19, 35, 45, 75, 85,
    86, 88, 89, 91, 92, 132, 155, 159,
    160, 162, 277, 278, 284, 355
Hill, Louis, 86, 88–90, 104, 111, 114,
    119, 123
Hill County, 47
Hingham, 58
Hobson, 289–91
Hobson, S. S., 290
Hoecken, Adrian, 78, 168
Holly Sugar Co., 361, 395–97, **396**
Holter, Anton M., 247
homesteaders, 9, 10, 19–20, **19**, 24, 42,
    57, 58, 165, 166, 271–73, 304, 391,
    392, 397
Honky Tonk, 46, 47
Hoover, Jake, 278
Hoover, J. Edgar, 111
Hope Mill, 221, **221**
Hope Mine, 245
Hornaday, William T., 171
Horner, Jack, 78, 79
Horse Plains, 171
Horton, Hector, 220
Hotel Dakota, 345
Hot Springs, 172–73, **172**
Howard, Joseph Kinsey, 8, 213
Howard, (Gen.) Oliver O., 45, 181, 231
Howe, Charlie, 107
Hudson's Bay Co., 114, 167, 173, 206
Huggins, Edmund, 288
Hungry Horse Dam, 163
Hunter, (Dr.) Andrew Jackson, 344
Hunter's Hot Springs, 344, 345
Huntley, 336, 368
Huntley, Chet, 328
Huntley Project, xiii, 367–68
Hysham, 369–70, **370**
Hysham, Charles J., 369

ice ages, 83, 84
Ideal Cement Co., 320
I. G. Baker & Co., 57
Ijkalaka, 385
Imassees (Little Bear), 51, 52
Indian Reorganization Act, 76
Indians. *See individual tribes*
Indian Wars, 6
Industrial Workers of the World, xiii, 9,
    25, 147, 153, 162, 176, 216
Ingomar, 382
Innocents, 235
Intake, 395
Inverness, 58
Iron Mountain, 142
Iroquois tribe, 183
Isaak Walton Inn, 93
Ismay, 383
IWW. *See* Industrial Workers of the World

Jackson, 231
Jackson, Billy, 114
Jackson, Bob, 292
Jacobs, Joe, 306
Jacobs, John, 322
Jacobs, Marcellas, 306
Jacobs, Mike, 348
Jacobs Wind Electric Co., 306
Japanese Americans, 312
Jardine, 338–39
Jawbone Railroad, 286, 311, 312, 315
Jay Cooke and Co., 204
Jeannette Rankin Brigade, 148
Jefferson, Thomas, 317
Jefferson County, 245
Jefferson River, 197, 232, 317, 318
Jefferson Valley, 242, 244
Jennings, 151
Jesuits, 144, 168, 169, 183, 281, 282
Jib Mining Co., 245
Jocko Reservation, 144
Jocko River, 145, 171
Jocko Valley, 144
Joe, 383
Johnson, James Augustine, 61, 63
Johnston, John "Liver Eating," 349
Jones, B. Walter, 151
Joplin, 58, 63
Jordan, 299, 302–4
Jordan, Arthur, 302, 303

Joseph, Chief, 44, 45, 181, 182. *See also*
  Nez Perce tribe
*Josephine,* 335, 357
Juach, Henry, 26
Judith Basin, 269, 290, 313
Judith Basin County, 289
Judith Gap, 269, 311, 313, 314
Judith Mountains, 269, 291, 295, 296,
  302
Judith River, 270, 279
Junction, 238
Junction City, 369
Justus Township, 303–4

Kaczynski, Theodore J., 265
*Kaimin,* 149
Kalafatich, Nicholas, 386
Kalispell, 106, 132, 153, 155, 158–63, 263
Kalispel tribe. *See* Pend d'Oreille tribe
Karst, Pete, 328
Karst's Resort, 327–28, **327**
Katy Mine, 245
Kearns, Jack "Doc," 61
keelboat, 16
Kennedy, John F., 288
Kenoyer, E. A., 396
Kent State University, xiv, 150
Kerr Dam, 165, 166
Kessler Brewery, 250
Kevin, 64
Kevin-Sunburst Field, xiii, 64–65, **65**
Kimmerly, Mary, 160
Kintla Lakes, 97, 99
Kipp, Joseph, 68, 70, 76
Kittredge, William, 11
Klein, 309
Klein, Fred, 112
Kleinschmidt, H. M., 264
Kneivel, Robbie, 35
Koch, Elers, 137
Koch, Peter, 291, 324
Kohrs, Augusta, 207
Kohrs, Conrad, 198, 206, 207, 270
Kohrs house. *See* Grant-Kohr ranch
Koons, Michele, 109
Kootenai River, 132, 133, 151–52, **152**,
  154, 173
Kootenai Valley, 132
Kootenay House, 173
Kootenay Lake, 152
Kremlin, 58

Kullyspel House, 174
Kutenai tribe, 3, 84, 91, 103, 132, 144,
  151, 154
KYUS, 375

Labre, St. Joseph, 377
Lady of the Rockies, 216–17
LaHood Park, 243, **243**
Lake Como, 185
Lake Koocanusa, 151
Lake McDonald, 85, 99, 101, 104–6,
  107, 109, 111
Lake McDonald Hotel, 104–6
Lake Pend Oreille, 174
Lambert, 397
Lambert, Harry, 165
Lambert's Landing, 165
Lambkin, James L., 265
Lambkin, Mary, 265
LaMousse, Young Ignace, 183
Landa, Leonard, 109
Landusky, 36–38, **37**, 41
Landusky, Powell "Pike," 37
Langford, Nathaniel, 235
Larocque, Francois Antoine, 334, 368, 377
Last Chance Gulch, xii, 197, 198, 248,
  250, 251
Latati, 169
Laurel, 335, 348, 349, 355–56
Laurel Leaf, 356
Lavina, 309–10, 315
Leader, 287
Leadville, Colorado, 212
Leary, Kitty. *See* Madame Bulldog
Leckie, Alice Jean, 100
Ledger, 70
Lee, Leroy, 217
Lee Metcalf Wildlife Refuge, 185
Leighton Act, 31
Lemhi Pass, 197, 224
Lend-lease Act, 281
Lethbridge, Alberta, 64
Levine, Louis, 149
Lewis, John E., 104
Lewis, Meriwether, 3, 15, 16, 53, 67, 72,
  74, 84, 181, 232, 253, 260, 262,
  264, 274, 317. *See also* Lewis and
  Clark expedition
Lewis and Clark Caverns State Park, xiii,
  242, 243

Lewis and Clark expedition, xi, 3–4, **4**, 29, 131, 197, 231, 253, 260, 269, 307; across Lolo Pass, 180, 181; at Beaverhead Rock, 232, 233; at Great Falls, 274–76; at Missouri headwaters, 317; at Travelers Rest, 180, 181; clash with Blackfeet, 72, 73; crosses Rocky Mountains, 224; on Missouri River, 15, 53; on the Marias, 67; on Yellowstone River, 334, 368, 391, 398
Lewis overthrust, 83, 125
Lewistown, 271, 282, 288, 289, 291–95, **293**, 299, 310–12
Libby, 133, 151–53, **152**, 154, 193
Libby Creek, 154
Libby Dam, 151
Libby Lumber Co., 154
Liberty County, 58, **58**, 59
license plates, xiii, xv–xvii, **xv**
Liebig, Frank, 107
*Life* magazine, 34
Lincoln, 264–65
Lincoln, Abraham, 5, 229
Lincoln Land Co., 361
Linderman, Frank Bird, 52
Lisa, Manual, xii, 317, 369
Lisa's Fort, 369
Little Belt Mountains, 284, 313
Little Bighorn, Battle of, xii, 6, 335, 362–64, 372, 380
Little Bighorn Battlefield National Monument, 362–64, **364**
Little Bighorn River, 361, 362, 365, 375
*Little Big Man,* 363
Little Blackfoot River, 136, 206, 248, 257
"Little Joe" engine, 271, **271**
Little Rocky Mountains, 35, 36, 40
Little Wolf, 376
Livingston, 323, 330, 334, 335, 337, 338, 340–44, **341**, 346, 391
Livingston, Johnston, 341
Lockwood, (Capt.) B. C., 343
Lodge Grass, 366
Lodgepole, 38, 40
Logan, Harvey. *See* Curry, Kid
Logan, William R., 100, 126
Logan Creek, 111, 127
Logan Pass, 87, **87**, 100–103, 106, 111
log drives, 176–77, **177**
Lolo, 180

Lolo Canyon, 182
Lolo Creek, 144, 180
Lolo Hot Springs, 181
Lolo National Forest, 137, 140
Lolo Pass, 43, 179–82
Lolo Trail, 181–82
Loma, 53
Lombard, Arthur, 311
Lone Walker, Chief, 114
Longabaugh, Harry. *See* Sundance Kid
Looking Glass, Chief, 44, 229
Lookout Pass, 135, 137
Lorraine, 384
Lost Trail Pass, 180, 182, 194
Lott, John, 233
Lott, Mortimer, 233
Louisville, 142
Louisville Bar, 141
Lower Works, 219
Lower Yellowstone Irrigation Project, 395
Lozeau, Adolph, 141
lumber industry, 132–34, **133**, 152, 153, 174–78, 192, 193

MacDonald Pass, 257
Madame Bulldog, 342–43
Madison Buffalo Jump, 320
Madison Mountains, 240, 327, 329
Madison River, 197, 239–41, 317, 318, 329
*Maiasaura,* 79
Maiden, 295–96, **296**, 299
Maiden Gulch, 295
Malmstrom, (Col.) Einar A., 281
Malmstrom Air Force Base, xiii, 280–81, **280**, 288
Malone, Michael, 213
Malta, 30, 35–36, 41, 298
Malta Plan, 36
Manhattan, 320–21
Manhattan Malting Co., 320–21, **321**
Mann Gulch, 260–62
Manning, Dave, 370
Manning, Richard, 193
Mansfield, Mike, 9
Many Glacier, 83, 88, 90, 115, 117 119–21, **118**
Many Glacier Hotel, 89, 119–21, **120**
Margaret Hotel, 175
Marias Pass, 84–86, 91–94, **92**, 116, 132, 163

Marias River, xi, xii, 3, 6, 16, 52, 67, 68, 72, 75, 248, 274
Marsh, (Capt.) Grant, 335, 357
Marshall, Bob, 178–80, **178**. *See also* Bob Marshall Wilderness Area
Martin, Tom, 167
Martinsdale, 271, 286, 315–17
Marysville, 199, 258–60, **259**
Mather, Stephen, 119–20
Maximilian of Weid-Neuweid, viii, xi, 16
Maynadier, Henry E., 334, 335
Mayville, 142
McAdow, Perry W., 356
McBride, Joseph, 341
McCarthyville, 93
McCone County, 269, 304
McCoy Gulch, 133, **133**
McDonald, Angus, 167
McDonald, Duncan, 167
McDonald Creek, 111
McGinnis, David R., 60
McGovern, Tom, 162
McKay, Dan, 31
McKay, Gordon, 237
McKenzie, Kenneth, 20
McLaughlin, Will, 120
McLure, Charles D., 222
McMillan, James, 307
McNab, James, 26
Mead, David, 391
Meagher County, 315
Means, Russell, 363
Medicine Lake Wildlife Refuge, 24
Medicine Rocks State Park, 384
Meek, Curly, 301
Meek, Joe, 194
Melstone, 271, 307
Meredith, Emily, 228
Merino, 311
Merrill, (Maj.) Lewis, 391
Merry Widow Mine, 245
Metcalf, Lee, 9. *See also* Lee Metcalf Wildlife Refuge
Métis, 269, 282, 291
Michael Davitt Mine, 214
Michel, Chief, 144
Michener, Thomas, 328
Mickel, E. O., 23
Middle Fork of the Flathead River, 105
Midvale, 88

Milburn, Gene, 300
Milburn, Jack, 300
Miles, (Col.) Nelson A., 6, 43–45, 114, 372, 373, 376
Miles City, 6, 175, 302, 334, 335, 372–75, 378, 380, 384, 386, 387, 392
Milk River, 7, 17, 19, 29, 30, 35, 36, 39, 45, 49, 51, 169
Milk River Resettlement Project, 36
Miller, Adam "Horn," 352
Milltown, 176, 210
Milwaukee Railroad Land Co., 300
Milwaukee Road, xiii, 7, 79, 132, 138, 140–42, **206**, 270–73, **272**, 285, 287, 289, 291, 298, 299, 307, 309, 311–13, 315, 319, 321, 326, 336, 371, 374, 375, 382–84; 1938 wreck, xiii, 387, 388, **388**; electrification of, 143, 271, **271**, 312, **312**
Mineral County Museum, 134
Mingusville, 394
Minnesota & Montana Land & Improvement Co., 358
Minnesota-Montana Road, 17
Minnetaree tribe, 334
Minnie's Sporting House, 286
Minuteman nuclear missiles, xiv, 71, 281, 288, 289
Mission, 66, 87
missionaries, 168–69, 183–84
Mission Mountains, 168, 177
Mission Valley, 169
Missoula, 132, 133, 139, 142, 143, 145–51, 169, 174, 179, 187, 201, 260, 348
Missoula Mercantile Co., 175
Missoula Ministerial Association, 141
Missouri Breaks, 37, 303
Missouri Headwaters State Park, 317, 320
Missouri River, xi, 4, 15, **15**, 13–17, 19, 20, 31, 32, 44, 49, 52, 53, 57, 167, 197, 260, 262, 269, 273, 277, 278, 281, 295, 298, 307, 314, 317, 333, 398
Moe, Tommy, 157
Moen, Oscar, 164
Molumby, Loy, 61
Monarch, 284
Mondak Heritage Center, 397
Monida Pass, 225
Monroe, Hugh, 113, 114, 116
Montague, J. W., 388

Montana, Monte, 23–24, **23**
Montana Bankers' Association, 167
Montana Bar, 252
Montana Cattle Co., 310
Montana Central Railroad, 254, 281, 284
Montana Children's Center, 233–34, **234**
Montana Club, 248, 250
Montana Farmers Union, 9, 362
Montana Farming Corporation, 361
Montana Highway Commission, xiii, 95
Montana Highway Patrol, xiii, 237
Montana Historical Society, 178, 239
Montana Hotel, 300
Montana Improvement Co., 175
Montana National Bank, 254
Montana National Guard, 227
*Montana Post*, xii, 6
Montana Power Co., xiii, 165, 382
Montana Railroad, 311, 312. *See also*
    Jawbone Railroad
Montana State College, 190
Montana State Prison, 207–9, 338
Montana State University, 324–25, **324**
Montana Stock Growers' Association,
    297, 374
Montana Territory, xi, 5, 199, 229, 239
Montana Western Railroad, 69
Montana, Wyoming & Southern
    Railroad, 355
Moody, W. I., 185
Moon, Nicholas, 160
Moreland, 320
Mores, Marquis de, 394
Morgan, J. P., 361
Morrison, Dan, 242, 243, 320
Morrison, "Slippery Bill," 93
Mosby, 302
Mosby, Mary, 302
Mosby, William, 302
Moss, Preston B., 359, 360
motion pictures, 163
Mountain Chief, 67
Mount Allen, 122
Mount Angela, 282
Mount Helena, 249
Mount Jackson, 114, 122
Mount Piegan, 102
Mount Reynolds, 122
Mount Sentinel,149
Mount Stimson, 122

Muldoon, Lloyd "Mully," 155
mules, 66, 90, 102, 121, 309, 351, 356,
    395; Dinah Miner, 309
Mullan, (Lt.) John, xi, 5, 54, 132, 134–
    36, **135**, 181, 183, 197, 257, 313
Mullan Pass, 136, 204, 257
Mullan Road, xi, 5, 54, 132, 134–37,
    143, 145, 185, 200, 273
Murphy, John T., 310
Murray, James A., 246, 345
Murray, James E., 9
Museum of the Northern Great Plains, 57
Museum of the Plains Indians, 76
Museum of the Upper Missouri, 57
Musselshell Association, 270
Musselshell River, 269–71, 284, 295,
    297, 299, 302, 307, 310, 311, 313,
    315, 336, 371
Mussigbrod Mine, 203, **203**
Myles, Jerry, 209

Nancy Hanks Mine, 202
Nashua, 29
Natawistacha, 20
National Bison Range, 169–71, **170**
National Guard. *See* Montana National
    Guard
National Park Service, 86, 94, 98, 101,
    105, 109, 119, 111, 123, 207, 231
National Weather Service, 264
Native Americans. *See individual tribes*
Nature Conservancy, 79
N Bar, 378, **378**
N Bar N, 29
N Bar Ranch, 299–300
Neihart, 7, 284
Neihart, James L., 284
Neils, Julius, 133, 154
Nelson, Martin, 36
Nesbit, Richard, 98
Nevada City, 198, 238, 239
New Deal, 10, 25
Newlon, Lewis, 398
Newman, Henry, 299
Newman, Zeke, 299
New World Mining District, 352
Nez Perce tribe, xii, 6, 49, 165, 167,
    180–82, 269, 357, 365, 372; Chief
    Joseph and flight of, xii, 181–82; in
    Big Hole Battle, xii, 229–31, 274,

286; at Canyon Creek, 356; surrender of, at Bear's Paw xii, 6, 43–45

Nichols, Dan, 328–30

Nichols, Don, 328–30

Nicklaus, Jack, 220

Nick the Barber 171, 172

Niobrara Cattle Co., 378

nitro shooters, 64

Nixon, Richard, 70, 71, 150

Noffsinger, George, 123

Noffsinger, W. N., 123

Nonpartisan League, 9, 24

North Fork of the Flathead River, 87, 96, 99, 163

Northern Cheyenne Reservation, 376, 377

Northern Cheyenne tribe, 6, 323, 376, 377

Northern Hotel, 316, 360

Northern Pacific Hospital, 190

Northern Pacific Railroad, 7, 57, 132, 137, 138, 147, 157, 159, 171–73, 175, 199–201, 222, 225, 244, 247, 253, 257, 258, 260, 270, 295, 304, 305–6, **305**, 309, 315, 320, 321, 326, 335–37, **336**, 340–50, **341, 342**, 355, 357, 358, 365, 368–71, 374, 380, 381, 386, 387, 391, **392**, 394, 396, 398; last-spike ceremony, 203–6, **205**

North Star Mine, 151

North West Co., 173

North-Western Coal & Navigation Co., 64

Northwest Mounted Police, 56, 66

Northwest Survey Expedition, 135

Noxon, 139

Nyack, 94

Ober, Michael, 90

O'Bill, Bob, 216

O'Brien, John, 162

O'Fallon Creek, 383

Ohio Dan, 171, 172

Ohs, Karl, 304

oil, xiv, 10; in Baker area, 384; Cat Creek Field, 300–302, **301**; Cut Bank Field, **73**, 74; in Billings area, 360; in Glacier National Park, 99, 100, 118; in Sweetgrass Hills, 63–65, **65**; in Williston Basin, 392, 393; in Pondera County, 70

Oilmont, 64

Old Coyote, Barney, 364

Old Faithful Inn, 241

Old North Trail, 77

Old Stand Saloon, 384, 385

Olympian Express, 387–88, **388**

O'Neal, Dan, 201

One-Eyed Molly, 27

Opheim, 27

Oregon Short Line Railroad, 330

Oregon Trail, 323

Orphans' Home, Montana State, 233–34, **234**

Osgood Saloon, 385, **385**

Ovando, 265

Owen, John, xi, 183–84

Owen, Nancy, 184

Owens, Charles "Rattlesnake Jake," 292

Pablo, Michel, 169, 170

pack animals. See mules

Paliser, Cap. John, 84

Palladino, Lawrence, 185

Panic of 1893, 7

Pannell, Bert, 242

Pantzer, Robert, 149, 150

Pappy Smith, 246

Paradise, 171

Paradise Valley, 337, 339

Parberry, Dr. William, 285

Park City, 348

Park County, 340

Parker, Robert Leroy. See Cassidy, Butch

Park Hotel Co., 87, 105

Park Service. See National Park Service

Patterson, Tom, 264

Patton, F. E.W., 238

Paul, Asher, 318

Pearl Harbor, 148

Pease, Fellows D., 369

Pease, (Lt.) W. A., 68

Peck, (Col.) Campbell Kennedy, 31

Pegasus Gold Corporation, 36

Pend Oreille Lake, Idaho, 131

Pend d'Oreille tribe, 144, 164–65, 169

People's Publishing Co., 24

Pershing, John J. "Blackjack," 50

Peter Kiewit Construction Co., 71

Petroleum County, 300

Philbrook, 290

Philipsburg, 220–22, **221**

Phillips, Benjamin Daniel, 35, 36

Phillips County, 36
Piegan tribe, 73–75, 84, 103, 114, 121, 132
Pinkerton, William, 41
Pintler Mountains, 217
Pintler Scenic Route, 220
Pioneer Cattle Co., 297
*pishkins,* 273, 320
Pizanthia, Jose, 236
Plenty Coups, Chief, 365–67, **367**
Plentywood, 21, 24, 28
*Plentywood Herald,* 25
Plevna, 383
Plum Creek Timber Co., 193
Plummer, Henry, xii, 235–37
Polebridge, 96, **96**
Pollock, William, 50
pollution, 209, 210, 219
Polson, 157, 165–66, **165**
Polson, David, 165
Pompey's Pillar, 334, 367–69
Pondera, 70
Pondera County, 70
Pondera Oil Field, 70
Pony, 242
Pony Express, 29, 269, 270
Poplar, 32
Poplar River, 22, 26
Populist Party, xii, 7
Portland Exposition, 88
Potts, Benjamin, 5
Potts, John, 318
Powder River, 299, 333, 334, 377–79, **378**, 394
Powder River County, 379
Powell, Floyd, 209
Power, Thomas C., 56, 134, 309
Prairie Inn, 59
Prentice, George, 155–57, **156**
Price, Ray, 112
Prickly Pear Creek, 248
Prickly Pear Valley, 197
Priest Buttes, 78
Primrose Substation, 143
Prince of Wales Hotel, 116
*Producers News,* 24–25
prohibition, 10, 46–48, 126, 224, 265, 281, 309, 321, 328, 350, 385
Prophet, Elizabeth Claire, 339, 340
Prudhomme, Gabriel, 257

Pryor, Nathaniel, 334
Pryor Creek, 334, 367
Pryor Mountains, 367
Public Health Service. *See* U.S. Public Health Service
Pulaski, Ed, 138
Pullman Co., 343
Pumpelly, Raphael, 85
Puptown, 385
Pyle, Ernie, 34, 83

Quaw, Thomas Buchanan, 321
Queen of the Hills Mine, 284

race horses, 188–90. *See also* Daly, Marcus
Racicot, Marc, 329
radio, 48, 49
radon, 245
railroad ties, 327
Rainbow Lodge, 98, 99
Ralston, Mary, 258
Rankin, Jeannette, xiii, 10, **146**, 147–48
Rarus Mine, 214
Rasmussen, Lillie Klein, 42
Rattlesnake Creek, 145
Ravalli, 157, 170
Ravalli, (Fr.) Anthony, 133, 183–84, **184**
Ravalli County, 184
Rawn, (Capt.) Charles, 182
Raynesford, 288
Raynesford, Henrietta, 288
Reynolds, (Capt.) W. F., 334–35, 378
REA. *See* Rural Electrification Administration
Reclamation Act of 1902, 368
Reclamation Service. *See* U.S. Reclamation Service
Red Bench Fire, 96–97, **96**
Red Eagle Lake, 124
Red Lodge, 349–53, 355, 381
Redwater Branch Railroad, 305
Redwater River, 269, 304, 394
Red Wolf, Josiah, 231
Reed, Alonzo, 291
Reed Point, 345, 346
Reed's Fort, 291
Reid, James, 325
Reid, Tom, 26
Reil, Louis, 282

Reil Rebellion, 51
Renne, Roland R., 325
Republic Coal Co., xiii, 307–9, **308**
Reynolds, Albert, 126
Reynolds, (Col.) Joseph J., 379–80
Reynolds, Minnie J., 147
Reynolds Battle, 379–80
Reynolds Peak, 126
Richel Lodge, 351
Richey, 392, 397–98
Richey, Clyde, 397
Richland County, 396
Ricketts, Howard T., 190–91
Riley, James, 245
Rimini, 255–57
Rimrock, 348
Rinehart, Mary Roberts, 124–25, **124**
Ringling, 286–87
Ringling brothers (John and Richard), 287
Risberg, Swede, 28
Rising Wolf Peak, 116
Rivenes, Dave, 375
Rivenes, Ella, 375
Robbin, R. C., 164
Robbin brothers, 164
Robinson, Anna, 286, 287
Robinson, Fred L., 299
Robinson, Rufus, 260
Rocky Boy, Chief, 51
Rocky Boy's Reservation, 50–52
Rocky Fork Coal Co., 349, 350
Rocky Mountain Front, 77
Rocky Mountain Laboratories, 190–91, **191**
Rocky Mountain spotted fever. *See* spotted fever
Rocky Mountain Trench, 131
rodeo, 23, 350
Rogers Pass, 3, 264
Ronan, 166–67, **166**
Ronan, (Maj.) Peter, 166
Ronan State Bank, 167
Roosevelt, Franklin D., 24, 25, 32, 116–17, **116**
Roosevelt, Theodore, xiii, 92, 171, 250, 338–39, **339**, 384
Roosevelt County, 22
Rorvik, Peter, 305
Rosebud Battle, 375–76
Rosebud County, 370–72, 382

Rosebud County Courthouse, 371–72, **371**
Rosebud Creek, 333, 335, 370, 375, 376
Ross, Alexander, 194
Ross, Kenneth, 153, 176
Ross' Hole, 131, 180, 194
Roundup, xiii, 307–10, 354
Roy, 295, 298
Royal Teton Ranch, 339, 340
Ruby River, 233, 238
Rudyard, 58
Ruhle, George C., 103
Rupert, Jacob, 320, 321
Rural Electrification Administration, 273, 302
Russell, Charles M., 4, 52, 125, 278–80, **279**, 290, **290**
Russell, David, 385
Russell, Nancy, 278–80, **279**
Russell Art Museum, 280
Russell Creek, 384
Ryan Dam, 276
Ryegate, 310–11

Sacajawea, 197, 233, 368
Sacajawea Inn, 319
Saco, 30, 35
Safeguard antimissile system, 70–72, **71**
St. Francis Xavier Church, 169
St. Helena Cathedral, 250
St. Ignatius, 167–69, **168**
St. Joe River, 138
St. Labre Mission, 377, **377**
St. Mary Lakes, 85, 90, 113–14
St. Mary's Mission, xi, 133, 183–84
St. Patrick's Day, 215
St. Paul, Minneapolis & Manitoba Railroad, 18, 35, 91
St. Paul Pass, 140, 141
St. Peter's Mission, 281–82
St. Regis, 132
St. Regis River, 132, 135–38
Saleesh House, xi, 174
Sales, Zacharia, 326
Salesville, 326
Salisbury, Rodney, 25
Salish tribe, xii, 3, 84, 91, 103, 131, 132, 135, 136, 144, 145, 165, 169, 180, 182–85, 269, 318
Salmon Lake, 177

SALT. *See* Strategic Arms Limitation Treaty
Saltese, 139
Samatra, 82
Sanders, Wilbur Fisk, 148, 236
Sanders County, 172
Sandstone Creek, 383
sandstone quarry, 347–48, **347**
Saugus, 387
Savage, 395
Savoy, 30
Scapegoat Wilderness, 265
Schenck, Ed, 155–57, **156**
Schuller, Edith May, 141
Schultz, James Willard, 84, 121
Scobey, 21, 27, 28
Scobey Giants, 28–29, **28**
sedition law, 292
"See America First," 86
Seeley Lake, 176
Seven Block, 69, 70
79 Ranch, 310
Seymour, "French Joe," 395
Sharp, Paul, 56, 66
Shaw, (Col.) Robert G., 273
Shedd, James, 318
Sheep Dip, 347
Shelby, xiii, 57, 60–63, **62**, 67, 68, 71, 78
Shelby, Peter P., 61
Shell Oil Co., 384, 392
Shellrock Manor, 163
Shepherd, Charley "Old Shep," 158
Sherburne, J. H., 76
Sherburne Lake, 118
Sherburne Mercantile, **76**
Sherburne Reservoir, 117
Sheridan, (Gen.) Philip, 68, 351
Sheridan County, 23–26, **26**
Sherman, Byron Robert, 286
Sherman Castle, 286
Shields, P. J., 282
Shields River, 334, 343
Shoshoni tribe, 197, 224, 232, 233, 375
Sidney, 336, 387, 395–97
Silcox, F. A., 153
silicosis, 216
Silver Bow Creek, 197, 210, 211
Silver Creek Valley, 260
Silvergate, 352
Simms, 273
Simpson, George, 194

Sioux tribe, xii, 6, 15, 20, 23, 27, 31, 269, 295, 297, 323, 334, 335, 347, 362–66, 369, 372, 375, 376, 380, 388
Sisson, Edward O., 149
Sisters of Providence, 168
Sitting Bull, Chief, 22, 27
Sixteen Mile Creek, 311
Skinner, Cyrus, 145
Skyland Camp, 97–99, **98**
Slayton Mercantile Co., 310
sled dogs, 255–57, **256**
Sleeping Buffalo, 35
Slem-hi-key, 144
Smalley, E. V., 358
Smart, Lee Jr., 209
Smead, W. H., 129, 131
Smith, Jedediah, 193
Smith, Tecumseh, 242
Smith and Boyd Saloon, 27
Smith Mine, xiv, 354
Smith River, 269, 284, 286, 287
smoke jumpers, 260–62, **261**. *See also*
forest fires
Smoot, John, 264
Snake River, 194
Snowshoe Mine, 154
Snowy Mountains, 269
Snyder, George E., 104
Sohon's Pass, 135
Sollid, George, 72
Sollid, Sam, 72
Somers, 162, 163
Somers Lumber Co., 133, 177
Somes, Sam, 118
Soo Line, 27
Spanish Frank, 236
Speculator Mine, xiii, 216
Spence, Clark, 4, 238
Spencer, Roscoe Roy, 191
Sperry, Lyman B., 85, 107
Sperry Chalet, 90
Sperry Glacier, 107
Spokane, Wash., 139, 147, 153
spotted fever, 190–91
Springdale, 344–45
Standard Oil, xiii, 8, 213–14, 300
Stanford, 289
Stanford, (Col.) James T., 69
Star Hotel, 311

steamboats: on Flathead Lake, 157, 165, **165**; on Flathead River, 163; on Lake McDonald, 104; on Kootenai River, 151–52, **152**; on Missouri River, xi, 17, 54–57, **56**; on Yellowstone River, 335, 373
Steinbeck, John, 3
Stemple Pass, 264
Stevens, Isaac I., 17, 74, 84, 91, 135, 143–45, 185
Stevens, John F., xi, 91–93, **92**
Stevensville, xi, 183–86
Stewart, Samuel,153
Stiles, Charles W., 191
Stillwater, 347
Stillwater River, 333, 346, 365
Stimson, Henry L., 125
Stimson Lumber Co., 154
Stone, Arthur L., 145, 223
Stone, Lewis M., 380
Stone Child, Chief, 51–52, **51**
stonemasons, 292, **293**
Stoneville, 380
Stoney Indians, 84
Story, Nelson, 324
Stranglers, 38, 297
Strategic Arms Limitation Treaty, 71
Strawberry Mine, 242
Stringer, John, 297
Stuart, Granville, 38, 197, 297, 299
Stuart, James, 197, 297
Sturgis, (Col.) Sam, 356
sugar beets, 42, 43, 244, 348, 356, 359, 361, 395–97
Sullivan, Jean, 112
Sunburst, 64
Sundance Kid, 40
Sun River, 262, 269, 270
Sun River Irrigation District, 79, 273
Sun River Valley State Bank, 273
Superfund cleanup area, 209–10, 220
Superior, 134, 141–42
Survant, John, 35
Susan, 387
Sutherlin, Robert, 270
Swamp Creek, 139
Swan Lake, 162, 177, 178
Swan Mountains, 177
Swan River, 133, 178, 263
Swan Valley, 177

Sweetgrass, 64
Sweet Grass County, 315
Sweet Grass Hills, 59–61, 64, 75
Sweet Grass Hills Treaty, xii, 22
Swenson, Kari, 328–30
Swiftcurrent Lake, 89, 119
Swiftcurrent River, 121
Swiftcurrent Valley, 117, 118, 120
Swift Dam, 77
Sword Bearer, 365

Taft, 139–41, **140**
Taft, William Howard, 86
Talbott, James A., 163
Tammany, 189, 218. *See also* race horses
Taylor, Charles E., 24–25
10th Calvary, 50
Terry, xiii, 336, 386, 388–90
Terry, (Gen.) Alfred H., 388
Terry Cowboy Band, 390, **390**
Teton County, 78, 79
Teton River, 78
Theodore Roosevelt Arch, 338, **339**
Theodore Roosevelt Highway, 93
Thompson, David, xi, 173, 174
Thompson, Jack, 252
Thompson Falls, xi, 173–74
Thompson River, 172
Thorpe, Jim, 173
Three Forks, 242, 317–19, **319**, 327
Three Forks Hotel, 319, **319**
341st Missile Wing, 288
Thurston, H. S., 289
Tinkham, A. W., 84
Tobacco Plains, 132
Tobacco River, 152
Tobacco Root Mountains, 239
Tongue River, 333, 335, 372, 373, 376
Tongue River Cantonment, 372, 373
Tongue River Reservation, 376
Toole, John, 177
Toole, K. Ross, 1, 8, 269
Top o' the World Bar, 352
Townsend, 198, 252–54
Townsend House Hotel, 254
traffic accidents, 95
Trafton, Robert M., 35
Trailer, Kid, 26–27
train robberies, 200–201
Trask, M. F., 368

Trautman, George, 379
Travelers Rest, 180–81
Treasure County, 369
Trident, 320
Trout Creek, 139
Trout Lake, 107–9
Troy, 133, 151, 154
Turkey Track, 70
Twain, Mark, 250
Twin Bridges, 232–34
Twodot, 315
Two Medicine, 116–17
Two Medicine River, 73, 77
Two Moon, Chief, 379, 380

Ubet, 313–14, **314**
Unabomber, xiv, 265
Union Pacific Railroad, 225, 330
United Mine Workers, 309
United Nations, 87
University Heights, 186
University of Montana, xiv, 134, 146–
 51, **150**, 164; Biological Research
 Station, 164
Ursuline nuns, 168, 282, 374, 377
U.S. Forest Service, 137, 141, 179, 180,
 192, 330
U.S. Public Health Service, 181, 190
U.S. Reclamation Service, 273
US 2, 20
Utah & Northern Railroad, xii, 199,
 225–26, **226**
Utah-Idaho Sugar Co., 42, **42**
Utica, 290, **290**
Utopia, 58

Valier, 68–70, **69**
Valier Land and Water Co., 69
Valley County, 26, 30
*Valley County News*, 29
Vanada, 382
Van Orsdale, (Lt.) John T., 85
Van Wyck, Henry, 154
Vaux, Augustus, 396
Verendyre, Gaultier de Varennes de la, 334
Vestal, Stanley, 13
Victor, Chief, 144
Vida, 306
Vietnam War, xiv, 148, 149–51, 325
*Vigilante Days and Ways*, 235

vigilantes, xii, 38, 145, 234–37, 297
*Vigilantes of Montana*, 235
Vigilante Trail, 234–35
Villa, Poncho, 69
Villard, Henry, 204–6, 321, 349
Vincent, Bruce, 193
Vine, Bob, 219
Virginia City, xi, 145, 225, 229, 234–40,
 **235**, 248, 323, 329
Von Herbulis, Albert O., 250

Waid, D. S., 374
Walking Coyote, Sam, 169
Walla Walla, Wash., xi, 5, 134–36, 145,
 175, 257
Wallop, Oliver, 378
Walsh, Thomas, xiii, 9
Warm Springs, 210
Warm Springs Creek, 217
Warner, Charles Dudley, 18
Warren, Conrad Kohrs, 207
Washington, Dennis, 217
Washoe, 353
Washoe Smelter, **218**, 219, **220**
Waterton Lake, 124
Waterton Lake Chalet, 97
Waterton Park, 116, 125
W Bar, 394
Weather Service. *See* National Weather
 Service
Weeksville, 171
Weeping Wall, 111–13
Weldy, Brown B., 59
Wells, John, 252
Wells, Fargo & Co., 225
Westby, 27
Western Energy Co., 382
Western Lumber Co., 176
West Glacier, 83, 85, 94, 104, 105
West Yellowstone, 241, 327, **329**, 330
W. E. Tierney Co., 254
Weyerhaeuser Lumber Co., 152
wheat, 11
Wheatland County, 273, 313
Wheeler, 34
Wheeler, Burton K., 9
White, Jack, 228
White Cliffs, 3, 16
Whitefish, 94, 95, 153, 155–57
Whitefish Lake, 155

Whitehall, 242, 244
Whitehead, Dora, 111
Whitehead, Joseph, 110–11, **110**
Whitehead, William, 110–11, **110**
White Motor Co., 115, 116
White Sulphur Springs, 284–87, **285**, 295
White Sulphur Springs & Yellowstone Park Railroad, 287
Whitfield, William, 346
Whitford, Bill, 112
Whoop-up Trail, 64–66
Wibaux, 383, 393–95
Wibaux, Pierre, 393–94, **393**
Wickes, 7
Wild Bunch, 26
Wilderness Act, xiv, 179
wilderness movement, 179–80
Wilderness Society, 179
Williams, Lewis, 387
Williams, Tom, 242
Williston Basin, 10, 305, 392, 397
Willow Creek, 76, 350
Willow Creek anticline, 78
Wilsall, 343, 344
Wilson, George R. "Two Dot," 315
Wilson, Louis B., 190
Wilson, Sam, 328
Wilson, Woodrow, 52
Windham, 290
wind power, 306, 344
Winnett, 300
Winnett, Walter, 300
winter of 1886–87, xii, 3, 7, 78, 270, 297, 358, 394
Wisdom, 231
Wolf Creek, 167
Wolf Point, 22, 23–24, 398; Wild Horse Stampede, 23
Wood, Maria, 53
Woody Mountain Trail, 27
Wooley's Ranch, 374

Worden, 368
Worden, Francis L., 141, 145
Works Progress Administration, 35, 324
World War I, 9, 125, 126, 148, 153, 176, 292, 294
World War II, 10, 30, 43, 87, 103, 106, 148, 149, 239, 251, 255–57, 280, 281, 354; conscientious objectors, 106
WPA. *See* Works Progress Administration
Wright, Alex, 59
Wright, Frank Lloyd, 186, 187
Wys, Peter, 246

XIT Ranch, 391

Yale Oil Co., 360, **360**
Yankee Jim Canyon, 340
Yanktoni Sioux tribe, 22
Yeager, Red, 236
Yegan Brothers Mercantile, 360
Yellow Bay, 164
Yellowstone City, 340
Yellowstone Land and Colonization Co., 391
Yellowstone National Park, 43, 240, 255, 287, 318, 326, 330, 333, 337, 338, 340, 342; forest fires in, xiv, 352–53
Yellowstone River, xi, xii, xiii, 3, 4, 16, 317, 323, 333–37, **333**, 339, 340, 343, 345, 355–58, 368, 369, 372, 373, 386–88, 391, 392, 395
Yellowstone Trail, 336–38, 383
Yellowstone Valley, 309, 313, 348
Yellowtail, Robert, 366
Yellowtail Dam, 366
Yellow Wolf, 230
Young, Christopher W. "Shorty," 46–48
Yucca Theater, 370, **370**

Zortman, 36
Zurich, 30

## ABOUT THE AUTHOR

Don Spritzer, a native of Colorado, has lived in Montana for thirty years. He earned his doctorate in history from the University of Montana. Currently working as a reference librarian at the Missoula Public Library, Mr. Spritzer has served on Hellgate Elementary School's board for the past twelve years. In addition to several articles on Montana history, he has published two previous books, *Waters of Wealth: The Story of the Kootenai River and Libby Dam* and *Senator James E. Murray and the Limits of Post-war Liberalism*. Mr. Spritzer enjoys fishing, hunting, and hiking in Montana, and his hobbies include building model airplanes. The father of two grown sons, he resides in Missoula with his wife, Kathy.

Check for our books at your local bookstore. Most stores will be happy to order any which they do not stock. We encourage you to patronize your local bookstore. Or order directly from us, either by mail, using the enclosed order form or our toll-free number, 1-800-234-5308, and putting your order on your MasterCard or VISA charge card. We will gladly send you a free catalog upon request.

Some other Roadside History titles of interest:

| | | |
|---|---|---|
| _____Roadside History of Arizona | paper/$18.00 | |
| _____Roadside History of Arkansas | paper/$18.00 | cloth/$30.00 |
| _____Roadside History of California | paper/$18.00 | cloth/$30.00 |
| _____Roadside History of Florida | paper/$18.00 | cloth/$30.00 |
| _____Roadside History of Idaho | paper/$18.00 | cloth/$30.00 |
| _____Roadside History of Montana | paper/$20.00 | cloth/$32.00 |
| _____Roadside History of Nebraska | paper/$18.00 | cloth/$30.00 |
| _____Roadside History of New Mexico | paper/$18.00 | |
| _____Roadside History of Oklahoma | paper/$20.00 | |
| _____Roadside History of Oregon | paper/$18.00 | |
| _____Roadside History of South Dakota | paper/$18.00 | cloth/$25.00 |
| _____Roadside History of Texas | paper/$18.00 | cloth/$30.00 |
| _____Roadside History of Utah | paper/$18.00 | cloth/$30.00 |
| _____Roadside History of Vermont | paper/$15.00 | |
| _____Roadside History of Wyoming | paper/$18.00 | cloth/$30.00 |
| _____Roadside History of Yellowstone Park | paper/$10.00 | |

Please include $3.00 per order to cover shipping and handling.

Send the books marked above. I enclose $ _____

Name_____

Address _____

City/State/Zip _____

☐ Payment enclosed (check or money order in U.S. funds)

Bill my:  ☐ VISA    ☐ MasterCard   Expiration Date: _____

Card No. _____

Signature _____

MOUNTAIN PRESS PUBLISHING COMPANY
P.O. Box 2399 • Missoula, MT 59806
Order Toll Free 1-800-234-5308
Have your Visa or MasterCard ready.
e-mail: mtnpress@montana.com • website: www.mtnpress.com